Instant Pot Duo Crisp Air Fryer Cookbook

550 Effortless Instant Pot Air Fryer Crisp Recipes For Beginners

Pamela Thibeault

Copyright © 2020 by Pamela Thibeault

All rights reserved worldwide.

ISBN: 979-8563418783

No part of this book may be reproduced or transmitted in any form or by any means, electronic or mechanical, including photocopying, recording or by any information storage and retrieval system, without written permission from the publisher, except for the inclusion of brief quotations in a review.

Warning-Disclaimer

The purpose of this book is to educate and entertain. The author or publisher does not guarantee that anyone following the techniques, suggestions, tips, ideas, or strategies will become successful. The author and publisher shall have neither liability or responsibility to anyone with respect to any loss or damage caused, or alleged to be caused, directly or indirectly by the information contained in this book.

CONTENTS

Introduction 9

Breakfast 11

1. Cheesy Prosciutto Egg Bake 11
2. Crispy Pancetta Hash with Baked Eggs 11
3. Shakshuka with Goat Cheese 11
4. Strawberry Bread French Toast 12
5. Raspberry-Cranberry Chia Oatmeal 12
6. Kale-Egg Frittata 12
7. Sausage Wrapped Scotch Eggs 13
8. Spicy Deviled Eggs 13
9. French Dip Sandwiches 13
10. Savory Custards with Ham & Cheese 14
11. Butternut Squash Cake Oatmeal 14
12. Barbecue Chicken Sandwiches 14
13. Egg Crumpet Sandwich 15
14. Herbed Homemade Ghee 15
15. Maple Giant Pancake 15
16. Orange Pepper and Artichoke Frittata 16
17. Plum Breakfast Clafoutis 16
18. Chai Latte Steel-Cut Oatmeal 16
19. Cheese & Bacon Grits 17
20. Feta & Poached Egg Tomato Topper 17
21. Ham and Cheese Sandwich 17
22. Sausage and Bacon Cheesecake 18
23. Veggie Salmon Balls 18
24. Prosciutto, Mozzarella & Egg in a Cup 18
25. Onion and Cheese Omelet 19
26. Quick Soft-Boiled Eggs 19
27. Cinnamon Pumpkin Oatmeal 19
28. Paprika Shirred Eggs 19
29. Creamy Zucchini Muffins 20
30. Toasted Herb and Garlic Bagel 20
31. Raspberry and Vanilla Pancake 20
32. Three Meat Cheesy Omelet 20
33. Very Berry Breakfast Puffs 21
34. Crustless Mediterranean Quiche 21
35. Sweet Bread Pudding with Raisins 21

Lunch Recipes 22

36. Egg Rolls 22
37. Tomato Soup with Cheese Croutons 22
38. Curry Egg Salad 22
39. Homemade Vegetables Soup 23
40. Ham & Mozzarella Eggplant Boats 23
41. Garlicky Chicken on Green Bed 23
42. Sweet Potato & Egg Salad 24
43. Cheat Hawaiian Pizza 24
44. Italian Sausage Patties 24
45. Chicken Noodle Soup 24
46. Pickle and Potato Salad with Feta 25
47. Warm Bacon & Potato Salad 25
48. Quick Chicken Noodle Soup 25
49. Homemade Chicken Soup 26
50. Cream of Pumpkin Chipotle Soup 26
51. Classic French Onion Soup 26
52. Broccoli & Potato Soup 27
53. Minestrone Soup 27
54. Vegetable Soup 27
55. Cream of Mushroom & Spinach Soup 28
56. Hearty Winter Vegetable Soup 28
57. Spicy Acorn Squash Soup 28
58. Cauliflower Cheese Soup 29
59. Mexican-Style Chicken Soup 29
60. Chicken & Farro Soup 29
61. Chicken Broth 30
62. Beef Neck Bone Stock 30
63. Ramen Spicy Soup with Collard Greens 30
64. Perfect Chicken Wings Broth 30
65. Basic Applesauce with Cinnamon 31
66. Leek and Potato Soup with Sour Cream 31
67. Ragu Bolognese 31
68. Red Lentil Soup with Tortilla Topping 32
69. Vegetarian Black Bean Soup 32
70. Spicy Borscht Soup 32
71. Two-Bean Zucchini Soup 32
72. Flavorful Vegetable Stock 33
73. Creamy Quinoa & Mushroom Pilaf 33
74. Spicy Beef Broth 33
75. Butternut Squash Curry 34
76. Fire-Roasted Tomato and Chorizo Soup 34
77. Acorn Squash Soup with Coconut Milk 34

Snacks, Appetizers & Sides 35

78. Tangy Cheesy Arancini 35
79. Sweet Paprika Hard-Boiled Eggs 35
80. Brazilian Cheese Balls 35
81. Kale-Artichoke Bites 36
82. Hot Chicken Wings 36
83. Hot Buttery Chicken Meatballs 36
84. Cheesy Smashed Sweet Potatoes 37
85. BBQ Chicken Drumsticks 37
86. Cheese bombs wrapped in Bacon 37
87. Fried Beef Dumplings 38
88. Buffalo Chicken Meatballs with Ranch Dip . 38
89. Asparagus Wrapped in Prosciutto with Dip . 38

90.	Holiday Egg Brulee 39	102.	Crispy Cheesy Straws 42
91.	Creamy Tomato & parsley Dip 39	103.	Chicken and Cheese Bake 42
92.	Bacon & Cheese Dip 39	104.	Melt-in-the-Middle Meatballs 43
93.	Scrumptious Honey-Mustard Hot Dogs 40	105.	Eggplant Chips with Honey 43
94.	Teriyaki Chicken Wings 40	106.	Air Fried Pin Wheels 43
95.	Wrapped Asparagus in Bacon 40	107.	Parmesan Cabbage Side Dish 44
96.	Green Vegan Dip 40	108.	Nutty & Zesty Brussels Sprouts with Raisins 44
97.	Homemade Spinach Hummus 41	109.	Cumin Baby Carrots 44
98.	Sweet-Heat Pickled Cucumbers 41	110.	Garlic and Rosemary Mushrooms 44
99.	Crispy Rosemary Potato Fries 41	111.	Tomato & Mozzarella Bruschetta 45
100.	New York Steak and Minty Cheese 42	112.	Turkey Scotch Eggs 45
101.	Cauliflower and Cheddar Tater Tots 42	113.	Herby Fish Skewers 45

Vegetables & Vegan 46

114.	Bok Choy & Zoodle Soup 46	152.	Vegetarian Minestrone Soup 59
115.	Rice Stuffed Zucchini Boats 46	153.	Fall Celeriac Pumpkin Soup 59
116.	Garganelli with Swiss Cheese and Mushrooms ... 46	154.	Green Beans with Feta & Nuts 60
117.	Swiss Cheese & Mushroom Tarts 47	155.	Pesto Quinoa Bowls with Veggies 60
118.	Rice & Olives Stuffed Mushrooms 47	156.	Carrot & Lentil Chili 60
119.	Squash Parmesan & Linguine 48	157.	Asparagus with Feta 60
120.	Pine nuts and Steamed Asparagus 48	158.	Steamed Artichokes with Lemon Aioli 61
121.	Mushroom Risotto with Swiss Chard 48	159.	Thai Vegetable Stew 61
122.	Sticky Noodles with Tofu & Peanuts 49	160.	Parsley Mashed Cauliflower 61
123.	Spinach & Butternut Squash Stew 49	161.	Mashed Parsnips & Cauliflower 62
124.	Easy Spanish Rice 49	162.	Spicy Cauliflower Rice with Peas 62
125.	Cream of Cauliflower & Butternut Squash 50	163.	Garlic Veggie Mash with Parmesan 62
126.	Tangy Risotto & Roasted Bell Peppers 50	164.	Honey-Glazed Acorn Squash 62
127.	Roasted Squash & Rice with Crispy Tofu 50	165.	Red Beans & Rice 63
128.	Cajun Baked Turnips 51	166.	Quick Crispy Kale Chips 63
129.	Zucchini & Quinoa Stuffed Red Peppers 51	167.	Artichoke with Garlic Mayo 63
130.	Creamy Cauliflower & Asparagus Farfalle 52	168.	Avocado Rolls 64
131.	Spinach Pesto Spaghetti Squash 52	169.	Spicy Pepper & Sweet Potato Skewers 64
132.	Crème de la Broc 52	170.	Pasta with Roasted Veggies 64
133.	Pilau Rice with Veggies 53	171.	Veggie Skewers 64
134.	Pesto Minestrone with Cheesy Bread 53	172.	Potato Filled Bread Rolls 65
135.	Cheesy Stuffed Mushrooms 54	173.	Quinoa & Veggie Stuffed Peppers 65
136.	Easy Green Squash Gruyere 54	174.	Vegetable Tortilla Pizza 65
137.	Mashed Broccoli with Cream Cheese 54	175.	Roasted Vegetable Salad 66
138.	Eggplant Lasagna 55	176.	Simple Air Fried Ravioli 66
139.	Chipotle Chili 55	177.	Poblano & Tomato Stuffed Squash 66
140.	Vegan Carrot Gazpacho 55	178.	Herby Millet with Cherry Tomatoes 66
141.	Buttered Leafy Greens 56	179.	Green Lasagna Soup 67
142.	Green Cream Soup 56	180.	Chipotle Vegetarian Chili 67
143.	Asian-Style Tofu Soup 56	181.	Crispy Nachos 67
144.	Indian Vegan Curry 57	182.	Colorful Vegetable Medley 68
145.	Aloo Gobi with Cilantro 57	183.	Grilled Tofu Sandwich 68
146.	Punjabi Palak Paneer 57	184.	Paneer Cheese Balls 68
147.	Green Minestrone 58	185.	Morning Burrito Bowls 68
148.	Mushroom Brown Rice Pilaf 58	186.	Paneer Cutlet 69
149.	Creamy Mashed Potatoes with Spinach 58	187.	Rosemary Sweet Potato Medallions 69
150.	Herby-Garlic Potatoes 58	188.	Quick Crispy Cheese Lings 69
151.	Tahini Sweet Potato Mash 59		

Fish & Seafood 70

189. Herb Salmon with Barley & Haricot Verts 70
190. Lemon Cod Goujons & Rosemary Chips 70
191. Crispy Cod on Lentils 70
192. Tuna Salad with Asparagus & Potatoes 71
193. Farfalle Tuna Casserole with Cheese 71
194. Autumn Succotash with Basil-Crusted Fish 72
195. Traditional Mahi Mahi 72
196. Salmon with Dill Chutney 72
197. Cajun Salmon with Creamy Grits 73
198. Mackerel en Papillote with Vegetables 73
199. Haddock with Sanfaina 74
200. Mediterranean-Style Steamed Cod 74
201. Pistachio Crusted Salmon 74
202. Italian-Style Flounder 75
203. Monk Fish with Greens 75
204. Steamed Sea Bass with Turnips 75
205. Parmesan Tilapia 76
206. Paprika & Garlic Salmon 76
207. Fish Finger Sandwich 76
208. Cajun Salmon with Lemon 76
209. Spicy Tangy Salmon with Wild Rice 77
210. Tuna Patties 77
211. Cod Cornflakes Nuggets 77
212. Alaskan Cod with Fennel & Beans 78
213. Quick & Easy Fried Salmon 78
214. Sausage & Shrimp Paella 78
215. Smoked Salmon Pilaf with Walnuts 79
216. Mushroom & Shrimp Egg Wrappers 79
217. White Wine Black Mussels 80
218. Crabmeat with Broccoli Risotto 80
219. Chorizo & Shrimp Boil 80
220. Scottish Seafood Curry 81
221. Spaghetti with Arugula & Scallops 81
222. Potato Chowder with Peppery Prawns 82
223. Seafood Gumbo 82
224. Prawn Toast 82
225. Mussel Chowder with Oyster Crackers 83
226. Creamy Crab Soup 83
227. Parsley Oyster Stew 84
228. White Wine Mussels 84
229. Crab Cakes 84
230. Paella Señorito 84
231. Penne all'Arrabbiata with Seafood & Chorizo 85
232. Seared Scallops with Butter-Caper Sauce 85
233. Delicious Coconut Shrimp 85

Poultry Recipes 86

234. Lemon Chicken Tenders with Broccoli 86
235. Crispy Chicken Thighs with Carrot Roast 86
236. Chicken with Crunchy Coconut Dumplings 86
237. Garlic Herb Roasted Chicken 87
238. Sweet Sesame Chicken Wings 87
239. Quick Chicken Fried Rice 88
240. Black Refried Beans & Chicken Fajitas 88
241. Chicken with Cilantro Rice 88
242. Chicken Cassoulet with Frijoles 89
243. Chicken Florentine 89
244. Chicken Potato Pot Pie 90
245. Herbed Chicken & Biscuit Chili 90
246. Herby Chicken Breasts 90
247. BBQ Chicken & Kale Quesadillas 91
248. Wine Chicken with Mushrooms & Brussel Sprouts 91
249. Italian Chicken with Herby Dumplings 92
250. Lemon and Paprika Chicken Thighs 92
251. Saucy Shredded Chicken 92
252. Mexican Chicken & Wild Rice Bowls 93
253. Chicken with Tomato Salsa 93
254. Chicken Shawarma Wrap 94
255. Tandoori Chicken Thighs 94
256. Hot Crispy Chicken with Potatoes 95
257. Chicken Meatballs Primavera 95
258. Cajun Roasted Chicken with Potato Mash 96
259. Chicken Chili with Cannellini Beans 96
260. Cheesy Buffalo Chicken 96
261. Chicken & Green Bean Coconut Curry 97
262. Mediterranean Stuffed Chicken Breasts 97
263. Coq au Vin 98
264. Traditional Chicken Cordon Bleu 98
265. Mexican Green Chili Chicken 99
266. White Wine Chicken 99
267. Chicken Caesar Salad with Salted Croutons 100
268. Pesto Chicken with Roasted Pepper Sauce 100
269. Chicken Noodle Soup with Crispy Bacon 100
270. Tandoori Chicken with Cilantro Sauce 101
271. Chicken & Veggie Tacos with Guacamole 101
272. Spinach & Mushroom Chicken Stew 102
273. Chicken with Beans & Bacon 102
274. Spicy Salsa Chicken with Feta 102
275. Sticky Orange Chicken 103
276. Chicken Cacciatore 103
277. Honey-Garlic Chicken 103
278. BBQ Chicken Drumettes 104
279. Sage Chicken Thighs 104
280. Paprika Buttered Chicken 104
281. Whole Chicken with Lemon & Onion Stuffing ... 105
282. Buffalo Chicken & Navy Bean Chili 105
283. Chicken Chickpea Chili 105
284. Indian Butter Chicken 106
285. Chicken in Tikka Masala Sauce 106
286. Chicken with BBQ Sauce 106
287. Pulled Chicken & Peach Salsa 107
288. Pesto Stuffed Chicken with Green Beans 107
289. Salsa Verde Chicken 107
290. Cajun Chicken with Rice & Peas 108
291. Spicy Chicken Wings with Lemon 108

292. Chicken Meatballs in Tomato Sauce 108	318. Tom Yum Wings 117
293. Chicken in Pineapple Gravy 109	319. Cordon Bleu Chicken 117
294. Za'atar Chicken with Lemony Couscous 109	320. Korean-Style Barbecued Satay 117
295. Juicy Orange Chicken 109	321. Herby Chicken with Asparagus Sauce 118
296. Hawaiian-Style Chicken Sliders with Salad .. 110	322. Greek-Style Chicken with Potatoes 118
297. Creamy Chicken and Quinoa Soup 110	323. Honey-Glazed Chicken Kabobs 118
298. Honey-Garlic Chicken & Okra 110	324. Chicken Stroganoff with Fetucini 119
299. Asian-Style Chicken 111	325. Rosemary Lemon Chicken 119
300. Crumbed Sage Chicken Scallopini 111	326. Turkey Stuffed Potatoes 119
301. Chicken with Prunes 111	327. Greek-Style Chicken 120
302. Creamy Chicken Pasta with Pesto Sauce 112	328. Buttermilk Chicken Thighs 120
303. Thyme Chicken with Veggies 112	329. Sticky Drumsticks 120
304. Cajun Shredded Chicken & Wild Rice 112	330. Sweet Garlicky Chicken Wings 120
305. Chicken & Zucchini Pilaf 113	331. Tuscany-Style Turkey Soup 121
306. Lettuce Chicken Carnitas Wraps 113	332. Chicken Tenders with Broccoli & Rice 121
307. Hot Chicken Wings 113	333. Asian Turkey Lettuce Cups 121
308. Sriracha Chicken with Black Beans 114	334. Spicy Buttered Turkey 122
309. Chicken & Sweet Potato Corn Chowder 114	335. Thyme Turkey Nuggets 122
310. Winter Chicken Thighs with Cabbage 114	336. Lemon Turkey Risotto 122
311. Saucy Chicken Breasts 115	337. Turkey Meatballs with Rigatoni 122
312. Chicken with Tomatoes & Capers 115	338. Turkey and Brown Rice Salad with Peanuts 123
313. Chicken Burgers with Avocado 115	339. Creamy Turkey Enchilada Casserole 123
314. Shredded Chicken with Lentils & Rice 116	340. Spicy Chicken Wings 124
315. Crunchy Chicken Schnitzels 116	341. Spicy Turkey Casserole 124
316. Chicken Fajitas with Avocado 116	342. Greek Turkey Meatballs 124
317. Basil & Cheddar Stuffed Chicken 116	

Rice, Grains & Pasta 125

343. Indian-Style Beef with Rice 125	362. Chorizo Mac and Cheese 130
344. Creamed Kale Parmesan Farro 125	363. Indian Yellow Lentils 131
345. Simple Brown Rice 125	364. South American Black Bean Chili 131
346. Veggie Quinoa Bowls with Pesto 126	365. Pomodoro Sauce with Rigatoni and Kale 131
347. Shrimp Risotto with Vegetables 126	366. Spicy Pinto Bean and Corn Stew 132
348. Red Lentil & Spinach Dhal 126	367. Simple Jasmine Rice 132
349. Spicy Lentils with Chorizo 127	368. Chili-Garlic Rice Noodles with Tofu 132
350. Baked Garbanzo Beans & Pancetta 127	369. Chicken Ragù Bolognese 132
351. Three-Bean Veggie Chili 127	370. Chicken and Chickpea Stew 133
352. Black Beans Tacos 128	371. Turkey Fajita Tortiglioni 133
353. Parsley-Lime Bulgur Bowl 128	372. Rigatoni with Sausage and Spinach 134
354. Creamy Grana Padano Risotto 128	373. Black-Eyed Peas with Kale 134
355. Lemony Wild Rice Pilaf 128	374. Shrimp Lo Mein 134
356. Spinach and Kidney Bean Stew 129	375. Cheese and Spinach Stuffed Shells 135
357. Tri-Color Quinoa and Pinto Bean Bowl 129	376. Chipotle Mac and Cheese 135
358. Easy Vegan Sloppy Joes 129	377. Pasta Caprese Ricotta-Basil Fusilli 135
359. Rice Pilaf with Mushrooms 130	378. Beef-Stuffed Pasta Shells 136
360. Quinoa with Carrots and Onion 130	379. Pork Spaghetti with Spinach and Tomatoes ... 136
361. Cherry Tomato-Basil Linguine 130	380. Baked Rigatoni with Beef Tomato Sauce 136

Beef, Pork & Lamb 137

381. Ground Beef Stuffed Empanadas 137	387. Sweet Gingery Beef & Broccoli 139
382. Winter Pot Roast with Biscuits 137	388. Beef & Broccoli Sauce 139
383. Smoky Horseradish Spare Ribs 138	389. Honey Short Ribs with Rosemary Potatoes 140
384. Steak with Chips 138	390. Sticky BBQ Baby Back Ribs 140
385. Thai Roasted Beef 138	391. Beef Congee (Chinese Rice Porridge) 140
386. Greek Beef Gyros 139	392. Pineapple Appetizer Ribs 141

#	Title	Page
393.	Beef Carnitas	141
394.	Classic Carbonnade Flamande	141
395.	Peanut Sauce Beef Satay	142
396.	Cheeseburgers in Hoagies	142
397.	Beef & Cabbage Stew	143
398.	Tasty Baby Porcupine Meatballs	143
399.	Pot Roast with Broccoli	143
400.	Beef & Green Bell Pepper Pot	144
401.	Beef Soup with Tortillas	144
402.	Beef and Bell Pepper with Onion Sauce	144
403.	Beef & Pepperoncini Peppers	145
404.	Short Ribs with Egg Noodles	145
405.	Asian Beef Curry	146
406.	Beef & Cheese Stuffed Mushrooms	146
407.	Beef Stew with Beer	146
408.	Meatballs with Spaghetti Sauce	147
409.	Spiced Beef Chili	147
410.	Spiced Beef Shapes	147
411.	Beef & Garbanzo Bean Chili	148
412.	Cheddar Cheeseburgers	148
413.	Beef & Vegetable Stew	148
414.	Beef Roast with Peanut Satay Sauce	149
415.	Chipotle Beef Brisket	149
416.	Brisket Chili con Carne	149
417.	Meatloaf with Cheesy Mashed Potatoes	150
418.	Beef & Pumpkin Stew	150
419.	Beef & Cherry Tagine	150
420.	Beef Pho with Swiss Chard	151
421.	Caribbean Ropa Vieja	151
422.	Short Ribs with Mushrooms & Asparagus Sauce	152
423.	Meatballs with Marinara Sauce	152
424.	Beef Stew with Veggies	152
425.	Beef & Bacon Chili	153
426.	Braised Short Ribs with Creamy Sauce	153
427.	Italian-Style Pot Roast	154
428.	Stewed Beef with Portobello Mushrooms	154
429.	BBQ Sticky Baby Back Ribs with	154
430.	Swedish Meatballs with Mashed Cauliflower	155
431.	Beer-Braised Short Ribs with Mushrooms	155
432.	Classic Beef Bourguignon	156
433.	Beef & Turnip Chili	156
434.	Mississippi Pot Roast with Potatoes	156
435.	Traditional Beef Stroganoff	157
436.	Peppercorn Meatloaf	157
437.	Italian Beef Sandwiches with Pesto	157
438.	Ranch Flavored Pork Roast with Gravy	158
439.	Hot Pork Carnitas Lettuce Cups	158
440.	Tomatillo & Sweet Potato pork Chili	158
441.	Sweet-Garlic Pork Tenderloin	159
442.	Pork Tenderloin with Garlic and Ginger	159
443.	Mediterranean Tender Pork Roast	160
444.	Pork Sandwiches with Slaw	160
445.	Cuban-Style Pork	160
446.	BBQ Pork Ribs	161
447.	Garlicky Braised Pork Neck Bones	161
448.	Sweet & Sour Pork	161
449.	Crispy Pork Fajitas	162
450.	Garlick & Ginger Pork with Coconut Sauce	162
451.	Pork Chops with Broccoli and Gravy	162
452.	Pork Chops with Squash Purée	163
453.	Pork Tenderloin with Sweet Pepper Sauce	163
454.	The Crispiest Roast Pork	164
455.	Pork Carnitas Wraps	164
456.	Savory Pork Loin with Celery Sauce	164
457.	Pulled Pork Tacos	165
458.	Spicy Pork Roast with Peanut Sauce	165
459.	Pork Chops with Plum Sauce	165
460.	Baby Back Ribs with BBQ Sauce	166
461.	Red Pork & Chickpea Stew	166
462.	Jamaican Pulled Pork with Mango Sauce	166
463.	Chunky Pork Meatloaf with Mashed Potatoes	167
464.	Italian Sausage with Potato Mash & Gravy	167
465.	Ragu with Pork & Rigatoni	168
466.	Ranch Pork with Mushroom Sauce	168
467.	Apple & Onion Topped Pork Chops	168
468.	Pork Chops with Cremini Mushroom Sauce	169
469.	Honey Barbecue Pork Ribs	169
470.	Philippine-Style Pork Chops	169
471.	Char Siew Pork Ribs	170
472.	Juicy Barbecue Pork Chops	170
473.	Bolognese-Style Pizza	170
474.	Teriyaki Pork Noodles	171
475.	Italian Sausage with Garlic Mash	171
476.	Potato & Ground Pork Chili	171
477.	Vietnamese Pork Soup	172
478.	Sweet Potato Gratin with Peas & Prosciutto	172
479.	Chorizo Stuffed Yellow Bell Peppers	172
480.	Sausage with Noodles and Braised Cabbage	173
481.	Italian Sausage & Cannellini Stew	173
482.	Calzones with Sausage and Mozzarella	174
483.	Beer-Braised Hot Dogs with Peppers	174
484.	Sweet Carrots with Crumbled Bacon	174
485.	Holiday Honey-Glazed Ham	175
486.	Sausage with Celeriac & Potato Mash	175
487.	Tasty Ham with Collard Greens	176
488.	Winter Minestrone with Pancetta	176
489.	Holiday Apricot-Lemon Ham	176
490.	Crunchy Cashew Lamb Rack	176
491.	Herbed Lamb Chops	177
492.	Lamb Chops & Creamy Potato Mash	177

Desserts & Beverages 178

#	Title	Page
493.	Wheat Flour Cinnamon Balls	178
494.	White Filling Coconut and Oat Cookies	178
495.	Apple Vanilla Hand Pies	178
496.	Raspberry Crumble	179
497.	Almond Banana Dessert	179
498.	Dark Chocolate Brownies	179
499.	Raspberry Cream Tart	180
500.	Vanilla Hot Lava Cake	180

501. Mixed Berry Cobbler 181
502. White Chocolate Chip Cookies 181
503. Tasty Créme Brulee 181
504. New York Cheesecake 182
505. Simple Vanilla Cheesecake 182
506. Chocolate and Banana Squares 182
507. Holiday Cranberry Cheesecake 183
508. Strawberry & Lemon Ricotta Cheesecake 183
509. Berry Vanilla Pudding 184
510. Chocolate Vanilla Swirl Cheesecake 184
511. Air Fried Doughnuts 184
512. Classic Caramel-Walnut Brownies 185
513. Cinnamon Apple Crisp 185
514. Blueberry Muffins 186
515. Molten Lava Cake 186
516. Cheat Apple Pie 186
517. Lemon Cheesecake with Strawberries 186
518. Pumpkin Cake 187
519. Homemade Apple Cider 187
520. No Flour Lime Muffins 188
521. The Most Chocolaty Fudge 188
522. Air Fried Snickerdoodle Poppers 188
523. Valencian Horchata 188
524. Pineapple Cake 189
525. Cinnamon Mulled Red Wine 189
526. Moon Milk 189
527. Raspberry Cheesecake 190
528. Chocolate Soufflé 190
529. Lemon & Blueberries Compote 190
530. Almond Milk 190
531. Tiramisu Cheesecake 191
532. Coconut Pear Delight 191
533. Pear Wedges 191
534. Delicious Pecan Stuffed Apples 192
535. Tasty Coconut Cake 192
536. Brown Sugar & Butter Bars 192
537. Cherry Pie 192
538. Milk Dumplings in Sweet Sauce 193
539. Poached Peaches 193
540. Savory Peaches with Chocolate Biscuits 193
541. Almond and Apple Delight 194
542. Gingery Chocolate Pudding 194
543. Fruity Sauce 194
544. Orange Banana Bread 194
545. Vanilla Chocolate Spread 195
546. Apricots with Honey Sauce 195
547. Coconut Milk Crème Caramel 195
548. Chocolate Fondue 196
549. Homemade Egg Custard 196
550. Cinnamon Butternut Squash Pie 196

Recipe Index **197**

INTRODUCTION

Hello…and welcome to my book about the Instant Pot Duo Crisp Pressure Cooker. Let me share all my favorite and amazing recipes with you, so you can make delicious and scrumptious meals for your family and friends. I'll also let you know what the Instant Pot is all about, so you can see how easy it is to use.

Let me start by saying that I love my Instant Pot! This is the one kitchen tool I can't live without. I used to make meals for my family just because I needed to put something on the table. Now I make great and stunning meals because I'm love in again with cooking for my family.

I've perfected the art of using the Instant Pot… and now I'm sharing it all with you in my recipe book. The Instant Pot is more than just a pressure cooker and air fryer combo. It elevates foods in ways you never imagined.

I've created recipes for every meal and occasion… all the way from breakfast to comforting weeknight dinners to elaborate Sunday dinners when you want to impress family and friends. I've got a recipe for you for all cuisines – fried chicken, stews, soups, and casseroles. And then there's those sweets and desserts that make the perfect finish to any meal. All here for you in one collection of my best recipes.

Just use the Instant Pot once, and you'll be hooked. You'll never go back to cooking food in the oven or on the stovetop ever again. Before you get ready to start cooking, let's find out what the Instant Pot is all about.

What is the Instant Pot Duo Crisp Air Fryer?

The buzz about the Instant Pot Duo Crisp is true. It uses cutting edge technology to let you air fry foods as well as get all the benefits of a pressure cooker…all in one! You're probably wondering how that can be possible - to have two very different kitchen appliances in one. It's easy. The Instant Pot is both because it has two lids.

Having this one amazing appliance means you can get rid of your pressure cooker, instant pot, dehydrator, roasting pan, air fryer, and slow cooker. Just think of all the kitchen space you'll have when you just have one appliance, the Instant Pot, doing all the cooking for you.

Let's look at a closer look at all the benefits of owning one.

Benefits of Using the Isntant Pot Pressure Cooker

It's both an Air Fryer and Pressure Cooker at the same time

I can't say it enough. The convenience of having an air fryer and pressure cooker in one appliance makes your life a breeze. And all those added features the Instant Pot has makes it even better. How many times have you tried to get the Instant Pot of the kitchen appliance cupboard, only to have to move the slow cooker and the pressure cooker out of the way? It's happened to me too many times to count! With the Instant Pot, you can retire those other appliances and free up valuable space in your kitchen.

Get rid of other cookbooks

Meal planning is so much easier with this appliance. You don't have to look through three different cookbooks to find the recipe you want to use – Instant Pot, or maybe it's the slow cooker this time? Now you can use just one set of recipes… my own recipes that let you use the Instant Pot for every meal.

Prepare budget-friendly and healthy meals

Eating meat every day can get expensive. When you have the Instant Pot, you can make delicious meals using lentil and beans. I use these ingredients in many of my recipes – and my meals are never dull or boring. The Instant Pot also lets you cook cheaper cuts of meat to perfection. When you pressure cook a beef shank, it comes out tender and juicy, cooked with sealed in moisture that you don't get when you cook it any other way.

Skip the fats and oils

It's all about frying with the Instant Pot – air frying that is. This means you can enjoy the taste and convenience of fried foods without using all that oil. This is perfect if you're watching what you eat – and trying to eat healthier. Foods are cooked in added liquid or in their own juices, staying moist and delicious.

Add a crispy finish to pressure cooked foods

One of the biggest benefits of the Instant Pot Duo Crisp, and one of my personal favorites, the finishing touches you can add to food before you serve it. When you cook some foods in the pressure cooker, it can be hard to get a nice crispy finish after it's been cooked. Now, with the Instant Pot, once you've pressure cooked a whole chicken, you can just remove the liquid and turn on the crisping function. The chicken skin is nicely crisped up, making for a great meal that's sure to impress your family.

Instant Pot DUO CRISP RECIPES

The recipes in this book are my absolute favorite… and they're a great introduction to the Instant Pot, highlighting just what this amazing kitchen tool can do for you.

Before you start cooking, here's some valuable information for using my recipes:

Brown and sear some food before putting into the Instant Pot

Follow my recipes… in some of them, I'll have you brown or sear some of the ingredients, particularly meats before you start the cooking process. This is so that the juices are sealed into the food, making it cook up that much more tender.

Check some foods to avoid over-cooking

Some foods are easy to over-cook, such as baked foods. In my recipes, I'll remind you if you need to check to avoid over-cooking.

Use hot water when pressure cooking

If you add a tablespoon or two of hot water when you're using a pressure cooker, the pressure will build up faster.

The Bake & Broil function is great for finishing off meals

Many of my recipes use the broil setting to finish off foods and give them a nice, lovely crispy topping. Remember to check during the cooking process to see how crisp the food is getting – you don't want to over-crisp!

Adjusting cooking time

If you're using fewer ingredients, then my recipe calls for remember to adjust the cooking time to a little less. The same goes if you're using more ingredients than my recipe calls for…adjust, so the Instant Pot cooks a little longer. Just be sure to check near the end of cooking time to see if needs to cook longer.

From Slow Cooker to Instant Pot

Foods cooked in a slow cooker for 4 hours on high can be quickly cooked in the Instant Pot for only 25 to 30 minutes! Follow my recipe… I might have you add a bit more liquid than if you were cooking in a slow cooker.

As you can see, the Instant Pot is just what you need in your life. You'll be cooking exceptional meals in no time! I hope you enjoy my favorite recipes… these are the ones I make over and over again for my family and friends. It's time to choose your first recipe… and get your Instant Pot Duo Crisp cooking great food!

BREAKFAST

Cheesy Prosciutto Egg Bake

Servings: 4 | Ready in about: 45 minutes

INGREDIENTS

- 4 eggs
- 1 cup whole milk
- 1 tsp salt
- 1 tsp freshly ground black pepper
- 1 cup shredded Monterey Jack cheese
- 1 orange bell pepper, chopped
- 8 oz prosciutto, chopped
- 1 cup water

DIRECTIONS

Break the eggs into a bowl, pour in the milk, salt, and black pepper and whisk until combined. Stir in the Monterey Jack Cheese. Put the bell pepper and prosciutto in a cake pan. Then, pour over the egg mixture, cover the pan with aluminum foil, and put on the trivet. Put the trivet in your Instant Pot and pour it into the water.

Seal the pressure lid, choose Pressure Cook, and set to High. Set the time to 20 minutes. When done cooking, do a quick pressure release and carefully remove the lid after the pressure has completely escaped. When baking is complete, take the pan out of the pot, and set it on a heatproof surface, and cool for 5 minutes.

Crispy Pancetta Hash with Baked Eggs

Servings: 4 | Ready in about: 50 minutes

INGREDIENTS

- 6 slices pancetta, chopped
- 1 white onion, diced
- 2 potatoes, peeled and diced
- 1 tsp sweet paprika
- Salt and black pepper to taste
- 4 eggs

DIRECTIONS

Choose Sauté on your Instant Pot. Lay the pancetta in the pot and cook, stirring occasionally, for 5 minutes, or until the pancetta is crispy. Stir in the onion, potatoes, sweet paprika, salt, and black pepper. Close the air fry lid.

Choose Bake, set the temperature to 350°F, and the time to 25 minutes. Cook until the turnips are soft and golden brown, stirring occasionally. Crack the eggs on top of the hash, close the air fry lid again, and choose Bake and the time to 10 minutes. Cook the eggs and check two or three times until your desired crispiness has been achieved.

Shakshuka with Goat Cheese

Servings: 4 | Ready in about: 50 minutes

INGREDIENTS

- 3 tbsp ghee
- 1 small red onion, chopped
- ½ red bell pepper, seeded and chopped
- 1 banana pepper, seeded and minced
- 2 garlic cloves, chopped
- Salt and ground black pepper to taste
- 29 oz canned tomatoes with their juice
- ½ tsp smoked paprika
- ½ tsp red chili flakes
- 4 eggs
- ⅓ cup crumbled goat cheese
- 2 tbsp fresh cilantro, chopped

DIRECTIONS

Choose Sauté on your Instant Pot. Melt the ghee and sauté the onion, bell pepper, banana pepper, and garlic. Season lightly with salt and cook for 2 minutes until the vegetables are fragrant. Stir in tomatoes, smoked paprika, red chili flakes, and pepper. Seal the pressure lid, choose Pressure Cook on High and adjust the timer to 4 minutes.

When done, perform a quick pressure release. Gently crack the eggs onto the tomato sauce in different areas. Seal the pressure lid again, choose Steam and adjust the cook time to 3 minutes. When ready, carefully open the pressure lid. Sprinkle with the shakshuka with goat cheese and cilantro. Dish into a serving platter and serve.

Strawberry Bread French Toast

Servings: 4 | Ready in about: 45 minutes

INGREDIENTS

- 3 eggs
- ¼ cup milk
- 1 tbsp sugar
- 1 tsp vanilla extract
- 1 tsp cinnamon powder
- 6 slices brioche, cubed
- 3 strawberries, sliced, divided
- 2 tbsp brown sugar, divided
- ¼ cup ricotta cheese
- 2 tbsp firm unsalted butter, sliced
- ¼ cup chopped almonds
- 2 tbsp maple syrup

DIRECTIONS

Crack the eggs into a bowl and whisk with the milk, sugar, vanilla, and cinnamon. Grease a baking dish with cooking spray and in a single layer, spread half of the brioche cubes in the pan. Layer half of the strawberries on the bread and dust with 1 tablespoon brown sugar. Spoon and spread the ricotta cheese on top of the strawberries.

Then, make another layer of bread, strawberries, brown sugar, and ricotta cheese. Pour the egg mixture all over the layered ingredients ensuring to give the bread a good coat. Pour 1 cup water into your Instant Pot. Fix the pan on the trivet, and put the trivet with the pan in the pot. Seal the pressure lid, choose Pressure Cook on High.

Set the timer to 20 minutes. Once the timer has read to the end, perform a quick pressure release to let all the pressure out, and carefully open the lid. Top the French toast with the sliced butter, almonds, and maple syrup. Close the air fry lid, choose Bake, and set the temperature to 390°F for 5 minutes. Check the toast's doneness for your desired crispiness, otherwise, cook for a few more minutes. Serve immediately.

Raspberry-Cranberry Chia Oatmeal

Servings: 4 | Ready in about: 30 minutes

INGREDIENTS

- 2 cups old fashioned oatmeal
- 3¾ cups water
- ¼ cup plain vinegar
- ½ tsp nutmeg powder
- 1 tbsp cinnamon powder
- ½ tsp vanilla extract
- ½ cup dried cranberries + for garnish
- 2 raspberries, sliced
- Honey, for topping

DIRECTIONS

Combine the oatmeal, water, vinegar, nutmeg, cinnamon, vanilla, cranberries, and raspberries in your Instant Pot. Seal the pressure lid, hit Pressure Cook on High, and set the timer to 11 minutes. When ready, perform a natural pressure release for 10 minutes, then a quick pressure release to let off any remaining pressure, and carefully open the lid. Stir the oatmeal, drizzle with honey and more dried cranberries, and serve immediately.

Kale-Egg Frittata

Servings: 6 | Ready in about: 20 minutes

INGREDIENTS

- 6 large eggs
- 2 tbsp heavy cream
- ½ tsp grated nutmeg
- Salt and black pepper to taste
- 1 ½ cups kale, chopped
- ¼ cup grated Parmesan cheese

DIRECTIONS

In a bowl, beat eggs, nutmeg, pepper, salt, and cream until smooth. Stir in Parmesan cheese and kale. Apply a cooking spray to a cake pan. Wrap aluminum foil around outside of the pan to cover completely. Place egg mixture into the prepared pan. Add 1 cup water into your Instant Pot and set in a trivet.

Gently lay the pan onto the trivet. Seal the pressure lid, choose Pressure Cook on High, and set the timer to 10 minutes. When ready, release the pressure quickly.

Sausage Wrapped Scotch Eggs

Servings: 4 | Ready in about: 55 minutes

INGREDIENTS

1 cup water
4 eggs
12 oz Italian sausage patties
1 cup panko bread crumbs
2 tbsp melted unsalted butter

DIRECTIONS

Pour 1 cup of water into the inner pot. Put a trivet in the pot and carefully place the eggs on top. Seal the pressure lid, choose Pressure Cook on High, and the cook time to 3 minutes. While cooking the eggs, fill half a bowl with cold water and about a cup full of ice cubes to make an ice bath. After cooking, perform a quick pressure release, and carefully open the lid. Pick up the eggs into the ice bath. Allow cooling for 3 to 4 minutes. Peel the eggs.

Pour the water out of the inner pot and return the pot to the base. Fix in a trivet. Place an egg on each sausage patty. Pull the sausage around the egg and seal the edges. In a small bowl, mix the breadcrumbs with the melted butter. One at a time, dredge the sausage-covered eggs in the crumbs, pressing into the breadcrumbs for a thorough coat.

Arrange on a baking dish. Place the eggs on the trivet. Close the air fry lid, choose Air Fry, adjust the temperature to 400°F, and the cook time to 15 minutes. When the timer has ended, the crumbs should be crisp and a deep golden brown color. Remove the eggs and allow cooling for several minutes. Slice the eggs in half and serve.

Spicy Deviled Eggs

Servings: 6 | Ready in about: 20 minutes

INGREDIENTS

1 cup water
10 large eggs
¼ cup cream cheese
¼ cup mayonnaise
Salt and ground black pepper to taste
¼ tsp chili powder

DIRECTIONS

Add water to your Instant Pot. Insert the eggs into the steamer basket and place into yhe pot. Seal the pressure lid, choose Pressure Cook on High, and set the timer to 5 minutes. When ready, release the pressure quickly. Drop eggs into an ice bath to cool. Peel eggs and halve them. Transfer yolks to a bowl and use a fork to mash. Stir in cream cheese, and mayonnaise. Season. Ladle yolk mixture into egg whites.

French Dip Sandwiches

Servings: 8 | Ready in about: 1 hour 35 minutes

INGREDIENTS

2 ½ lb beef roast
2 tbsp olive oil
1 onion, chopped
4 garlic cloves, sliced
½ cup dry red wine
2 cups beef broth stock
1 tsp dried oregano
16 slices Fontina cheese
8 split hoagie rolls

DIRECTIONS

Warm oil on Sauté in your Instant Pot and brown the beef for 2 to 3 minutes per side; reserve. Add onion and cook for 3 minutes. Mix in garlic and cook for one a minute until soft. Add red wine to deglaze. Mix in broth and take back the juices and beef to your pressure cooker. Over the meat, scatter some oregano. Seal the pressure lid.

Choose Pressure Cook on High, and set the timer to 50 minutes. Release pressure naturally for around 10 minutes. Transfer the beef to a cutting board and slice. Roll the sliced beef and add a topping of onions. Each sandwich should be topped with 2 slices fontina cheese. Place the sandwiches in the pot, close the air fry lid and select Air Fry. Adjust the temperature to 400°F and the time to 3 minutes. Serve.

Savory Custards with Ham & Cheese

Servings: 4 | Ready in about: 40 minutes

INGREDIENTS

2 serrano ham slices, halved widthwise
4 large eggs
1 oz cottage cheese, at room temperature
¼ cup half and half
¼ tsp salt
Ground black pepper to taste
¼ cup grated Emmental cheese
¼ cup caramelized white onions

DIRECTIONS

Preheat your Instant Pot by choosing Sauté and put in the serrano ham. Cook for 3 to 4 minutes or until browned. Remove to a paper towel-lined plate. Next, use a brush to coat the inside of four 1- cup ramekins with the ham fat. Set the cups aside, then, empty and wipe out the inner pot with a paper towel, and return the pot to the base.

Crack the eggs into a bowl and add the cottage cheese, half and half, salt, and several grinds of black pepper. Use a hand mixer to whisk the ingredients until co cheese lumps remain. Stir in the grated emmental cheese and mix again to incorporate the cheese. Lay a piece of ham in the bottom of each custard cup.

Evenly share the onions among the cups as well as the egg mixture. Cover each cup with aluminum foil. Pour 1 cup of water into the inner pot and fix in a trivet. Arrange the ramekins on top. Lock the pressure lid in Seal position. Choose Pressure Cook on High, and set the timer to 7 minutes. After cooking, perform a quick pressure release. Use tongs to remove the custard cups from the pressure cooker. Cool for 1 to 2 minutes before serving.

Butternut Squash Cake Oatmeal

Servings: 4 | Ready in about: 35 minutes

INGREDIENTS

3 ½ cups coconut milk
1 cup steel-cut oats
1 cup shredded Butternut Squash
½ cup sultanas
⅓ cup honey
1 tsp ground cinnamon
¾ tsp ground ginger
½ tsp salt
½ tsp fresh orange zest
¼ tsp ground nutmeg
¼ cup toasted walnuts, chopped
½ tsp vanilla extract

DIRECTIONS

In the pressure cooker, mix sultanas, orange zest, ginger, milk, honey, squash, salt, oats, and nutmeg. Seal the pressure lid, choose Pressure Cook on High, and set the timer to 12 minutes. When ready, do a natural pressure release for 10 minutes. Into the oatmeal, stir in the vanilla extract and sugar. Top with walnuts and serve.

Barbecue Chicken Sandwiches

Servings: 4 | Ready in about: 45 minutes

INGREDIENTS

4 chicken thighs, boneless and skinless
2 cups barbecue sauce
1 onion, minced
2 garlic cloves, minced
2 tbsp minced fresh parsley
1 tbsp lemon juice
1 tbsp mayonnaise
1 ½ cups iceberg lettuce, shredded
4 burger buns

DIRECTIONS

Season the chicken with salt, and transfer into the inner pot. Add in garlic, onion and barbeque sauce. Coat the chicken by turning in the sauce. Seal the pressure lid, choose Pressure Cook on High, and set the timer to 15 minutes. When ready, do a natural pressure release for 10 minutes. Shred the chicken and mix into the sauce.

Press Sauté and let the mixture to simmer for 15 minutes to thicken the sauce, until desired consistency. In a large bowl, mix the lemon juice, mayonnaise, salt, and parsley. Toss lettuce into the mixture to coat. Separate the chicken in equal parts to match the sandwich buns. Apply lettuce for topping and complete the sandwiches.

Egg Crumpet Sandwich

Servings: 2 | Ready in about: 25 minutes

INGREDIENTS

2 tbsp butter
2 tbsp chopped bacon
2 eggs, large
Salt and ground black pepper to taste
2 tbsp Monterey Jack cheese, grated
2 crumpets, split

DIRECTIONS

Brush two cups with 1 tbsp of butter. Share the bacon into the cups, crack an egg into each one, and prick the egg yolks with a toothpick in different places. Sprinkle the top with salt and black pepper and divide the cheese on top to cover the eggs. Cover the cups with aluminium foil and crimp the sides down.

Pour 1 cup of water into your Instant Pot, fix a trivet at the bottom the pot, and arrange the cups on top. Seal the pressure lid, select Pressure. Adjust the pressure to High, and the cook time to 1 minute. When done cooking, perform a quick pressure release and carefully open the lid. Remove the trivet and cups without taking off the foil.

Empty the water from the inner pot and return the pot to the base. Use tongs to lift the cups into the bottom of the pot and fix a trivet in the upper position of the pot. Cover the air fry lid, choose Broil, and adjust the time to 2 minutes. While heating, spread the remaining butter over the crumpet halves. Open the air fry lid.

Arrange the crumpet halves on the trivet with the buttered-side up, and close the lid. Choose Broil again and adjust the time to 4 minutes. When ready, transfer to a cutting board and remove the cups. Run a butter knife in and around the cups and turn out each egg onto the lower half of each crumpet. Top with the other half and serve.

Herbed Homemade Ghee

Servings: 10 | Ready in about: 17 minutes

INGREDIENTS

8 oz unsalted butter, softened
2 tbsp parsley, minced
1tbsp fresh chives, chopped
Sea salt to taste

DIRECTIONS

Set your Instant Pot to Sauté. Melt butter and cook for 7-9 minutes as you stir in cycles of 3 minutes until browning. Allow the butter to slightly cool. Use cheesecloth to strain the butter into a sealable container. Add in parsley, chives, and salt and stir thoroughly. Let cool before closing the lid. Keep in the fridge until ready to use.

Maple Giant Pancake

Servings: 6 | Ready in about: 30 minutes

INGREDIENTS

3 cups flour
¾ cup sugar
5 eggs
⅓ cup olive oil
⅓ cup sparkling water
⅓ tsp salt
1 ½ tsp baking soda
2 tbsp maple syrup
A dollop of whipped cream to serve

DIRECTIONS

Start by pouring the flour, sugar, eggs, olive oil, sparkling water, salt, and baking soda into a food processor and blend until smooth. Pour the batter into your Instant Pot and let it sit in there for 15 minutes. Close the lid and secure the pressure valve. Select the Pressure Cook on Low pressure for 10 minutes.

Once the timer goes off, quick-release the pressure valve to let out any steam and open the lid. Gently run a spatula around the pancake to let loose any sticking. Once ready, slide the pancake onto a serving plate and drizzle with maple syrup. Top with the whipped cream to serve.

Orange Pepper and Artichoke Frittata

Servings: 4 | Ready in about: 60 minutes

INGREDIENTS

- 2 tbsp unsalted butter
- ½ small red onion, chopped
- ¼ large orange bell pepper, chopped
- 1 cup coarsely chopped artichoke hearts
- 8 large eggs
- Salt and ground black pepper to taste
- ¼ cup full cream milk
- ¾ cup shredded Colby cheese, divided
- ¼ cup grated Pecorino Romano

DIRECTIONS

On your Instant Pot, press Sauté. Melt the butter and sauté the onion, bell pepper, and artichoke hearts for 5 minutes or until the onion and pepper are soft. While the vegetables soften, whisk the eggs with salt and allow sitting for 1 minute. Pour the milk into the eggs and whisk again then stir ½ cup of colby cheese into the mixture.

When the vegetables are cooked, pour the egg mixture into the pot. Gently stir to distribute the vegetables. Cook the eggs, undisturbed, until the edges are set, 7 to 9 minutes. Run a silicone spatula around the edges of the frittata to loosen from the side of the pot. Close the air fry lid. Choose Bake and set to 390°F and the time to 3 minutes.

After 1 minute, open the lid and sprinkle the remaining Colby and the Pecorino Romano cheese over the frittata. Close the lid and cook for 2 minutes. Open the lid by which time the cheese should have melted and the top not browned, but set. Sprinkle the frittata with black pepper, let rest for 2 minutes, and slice into wedges, to serve.

Plum Breakfast Clafoutis

Servings: 4 | Ready in about: 60 minutes

INGREDIENTS

- 2 tsp butter, softened
- 1 cup plums, chopped
- ⅔ cup whole milk
- ⅓ cup half and half
- ⅓ cup sugar
- ½ cup flour
- 2 large eggs
- ¼ tsp cinnamon
- ½ tsp vanilla extract
- A pinch of salt
- 2 tbsp confectioners' sugar

DIRECTIONS

Grease four ramekins with the butter and divide the plums into each cup. Pour the milk, half and half, sugar, flour, eggs, cinnamon, vanilla, and salt in a bowl and use a hand mixer to whisk the ingredients on medium speed until the batter is smooth, about 2 minutes. Pour the batter over the plums two-third way up.

Pour 1 cup of water into the inner pot. Fix a trivet at the bottom of the pot and put the ramekins on the trivet. Lay a square of aluminium foil on the ramekins but don't crimp. Put the pressure lid together and lock in Seal position. Choose Pressure Cook on High and set the time to 11 minutes.

When ready, perform a quick pressure release. Use tongs to remove the foil. Close the air fry lid and choose Bake. Adjust the temperature to 400°F and the time to 6 minutes. Press Start to brown the top of the clafoutis. Check after about 4 minutes to ensure the clafoutis are lightly browned. Bake for a few more minutes. Remove the ramekins onto a flat surface. Cool for 5 minutes, and then dust with the confectioners' sugar. Serve warm.

Chai Latte Steel-Cut Oatmeal

Servings: 4 | Ready in about: 20 minutes

INGREDIENTS

- 3 ½ cups milk
- ½ cup raw peanuts
- 1 cup steel-cut oats
- ¼ cup agave syrup
- 1 tsp coffee
- 1 ½ tsp ground ginger
- 1 ¼ tsp ground cinnamon
- ½ tsp salt
- ¼ tsp ground allspice
- ¼ tsp ground cardamom
- 1 tsp vanilla extract

DIRECTIONS

Using an immersion blender, puree peanuts and milk to obtain smooth consistency. Transfer into the cooker pot. To the peanuts-milk mixture, add agave syrup, oats, ginger, allspice, cinnamon, salt, cardamom, tea leaves, and cloves to mix well. Seal the pressure lid, choose Pressure Cook on High, and set the timer to 12 minutes. Let pressure to release naturally on completing the cooking cycle. Add vanilla to the oatmeal and stir before serving.

Cheese & Bacon Grits

Servings: 4 | Ready in about: 20 minutes

INGREDIENTS

3 slices smoked bacon, diced
1 ½ cups grated Cheddar cheese
1 cup ground Grits
2 tsp butter
Salt and black pepper to taste
½ cup milk

DIRECTIONS

To preheat your Instant Pot, select Sauté. Cook bacon until crispy, about 5 minutes. Set aside. Add the grits, butter, milk, ½ cup water, salt, and pepper to the pot and stir using a spoon. Seal the pressure lid. Choose Pressure Cook and cook for 3 minutes on High. Once the timer has ended, do a quick pressure release.

Add in cheddar cheese and give the pudding a good stir with the same spoon. Close crisping lid, press Bake button and cook for 8 minutes on 370°F. When ready, dish the cheesy grits into serving bowls and spoon over the crisped bacon. Serve right away with toasted bread.

Feta & Poached Egg Tomato Topper

Servings: 4 | Ready in about: 10 minutes

INGREDIENTS

4 large eggs
4 small slices feta cheese
2 Heirloom tomatoes, halved crosswise
Salt and black pepper to taste
1 tsp chopped fresh herbs, of your choice
2 tbsp grated Parmesan cheese

DIRECTIONS

Pour 1 cup water into your Instant Pot and fit in a trivet. Grease the ramekins with the cooking spray and crack each egg into them. Season with salt and pepper. Cover the ramekins with aluminum foil. Place the cups on the trivet. Seal the lid. Select Steam mode for 3 minutes on High pressure. Do a quick pressure release.

Remove the ramekins onto a flat surface. On serving plates, share the halved tomatoes and feta and toss the eggs in the ramekin over on each tomato half. Sprinkle with salt and pepper, Parmesan, and garnish with herbs.

Ham and Cheese Sandwich

Servings: 1 | Ready in about: 10 minutes

INGREDIENTS

2 tsp butter
2 slices of bread
2 slices of American cheese
1 slice of ham

DIRECTIONS

Spread one teaspoon of butter on the outside of each of the bread slices. Place one cheese slice on the inside of one bread slice, top with ham slice and another cheese slice. Cover with the second bread slice to create the sandwich.

Place into the air fry basket, close the air fry lid, and cook for 4 minutes on Air Fry at 390°F. Flip the sandwich and cook for 4 minutes. Cut diagonally the sandwich and serve immediately with ketchup or chutney.

Sausage and Bacon Cheesecake

Servings: 6 | Ready in about: 25 minutes

INGREDIENTS

- 8 eggs, cracked into a bowl
- 8 oz breakfast sau sage, chopped
- 3 bacon slices, chopped
- 1 large green bell pepper, chopped
- 1 large red bell pepper, chopped
- 1 cup chopped green onion
- 1 cup grated Cheddar cheese
- 1 tsp red chili flakes
- Salt and black pepper to taste
- ½ cup milk
- 4 slices bread, cut into ½ -inch cubes
- 2 cups water

DIRECTIONS

Add the eggs, sausage chorizo, bacon slices, green and red bell peppers, green onion, chili flakes, cheddar cheese, salt, pepper, and milk to a bowl and use a whisk to beat them together. Grease a bundt pan with cooking spray and pour the egg mixture into it. After, drop the bread slices in the egg mixture all around while using a spoon to push them into the mixture. Open your Instant Pot, pour in water, and fit a trivet at the center of the pot.

Place bundt pan on the trivet and seal the pressure lid. Select Pressure Cook on High for 6 minutes. Once the timer goes off, do a quick pressure release. Run a knife around the egg in the bundt pan, close the air fry lid and cook for another 4 minutes on Bake on 380°F. When ready, place a serving plate on the bundt pan, and then, turn the egg bundt over. Use a knife to cut the egg into slices. Serve with a sauce of your choice.

Veggie Salmon Balls

Servings: 4 | Ready in about: 40 minutes

INGREDIENTS

- 2 (5 oz) packs steamed salmon flakes
- 1 Red onion, chopped
- 1 tsp garlic powder
- 2 tbsp olive oil
- 1 red bell pepper, seeded and chopped
- 4 tbsp butter, divided
- 3 eggs, cracked into a bowl
- 1 cup breadcrumbs
- 4 tbsp mayonnaise
- 2 tsp Worcestershire sauce
- ¼ cup chopped parsley
- 3 large potatoes, cut into chips

DIRECTIONS

Turn on your Instant Pot and select Sauté. Heat the oil and add half of the butter. Once it has melted, add the onions and the chopped red bell peppers. Cook for 6 minutes while stirring occasionally. In a mixing bowl, add salmon flakes, sautéed red bell pepper and onion, breadcrumbs, eggs, mayonnaise, Worcestershire sauce, garlic powder, salt, pepper, and parsley. Use a spoon to mix well while breaking the salmon into the tiny pieces.

Mold 4 patties out of the mixture. Add the remaining butter to melt, and when melted, add the patties. Fry for 4 minutes, flipping once. Then, close the air fry lid, select Bake mode and bake for 4 minutes on 390°F. Remove them onto a wire rack to rest. Serve the cakes with a side of lettuce and potato salad with a mild drizzle of vinaigrette.

Prosciutto, Mozzarella & Egg in a Cup

Servings: 2 | Ready in about: 20 minutes

INGREDIENTS

- 2 slices bread
- 2 prosciutto slices, chopped
- 2 eggs
- 4 tomato slices
- 2 tbsp grated mozzarella
- 2 tbsp mayonnaise

DIRECTIONS

Grease two large ramekins with cooking spray. Place one bread slice in the bottom of each ramekin. Arrange 1 prosciutto slice and 2 tomato slices on top of each bread slice. Divide the mozzarella between the ramekins. Crack the eggs over the mozzarella. Season with salt and pepper. Place in your Instant Pot and set it to 390°F. Close the air fry lid and cook for 10 minutes on Air Fry mode. Top with mayonnaise to serve.

Onion and Cheese Omelet

Servings: 1 | Ready in about: 10 minutes

INGREDIENTS

2 eggs
2 tbsp grated cheddar cheese
1 tsp soy sauce
½ onion, sliced
¼ tsp pepper
1 tbsp olive oil

DIRECTIONS

Whisk the eggs with pepper, onion, and soy sauce in a bowl until combined. Grease a baking tray with olive oil and pour in the eggs. Close the air fry lid and cook for 6 minutes on Air Fry mode at 350°F. Once the timer beeps, top with the grated cheddar cheese. Fold the omelet in half and serve with a green salad.

Quick Soft-Boiled Eggs

Servings: 4 | Ready in about: 15 minutes

INGREDIENTS

4 large eggs
1 cups water
Salt and ground black pepper, to taste

DIRECTIONS

To the pressure cooker pot, add water and place a trivet. Carefully place eggs on it. Seal the pressure lid, choose Pressure Cook on High, and set the timer to 3 minutes. When cooking is complete, do a quick pressure release. Allow cooling completely in an ice bath. Peel the eggs and season with salt and pepper before serving.

Cinnamon Pumpkin Oatmeal

Servings: 4 | Ready in about: 25 minutes

INGREDIENTS

1 tbsp butter
2 cups steel cut oats
¼ tsp cinnamon
1 cup pumpkin puree
3 tbsp maple syrup
½ cup pumpkin seeds, toasted

DIRECTIONS

Melt butter on Sauté in your Instant Pot. Add in cinnamon, oats, salt, pumpkin puree and 3 cups water. Seal the pressure lid, choose Pressure Cook on High, and set the timer to 10 minutes. When cooking is complete, do a quick release. Open the lid and stir in maple syrup and top with toasted pumpkin seeds to serve.

Paprika Shirred Eggs

Servings: 2 | Ready in about: 20 minutes

INGREDIENTS

2 tsp butter, for greasing
4 eggs, divided
2 tbsp heavy cream
4 slices of ham
3 tbsp Parmesan cheese, grated
¼ tsp paprika
¼ tsp pepper
2 tsp chopped chives

DIRECTIONS

Grease a pie pan with the butter. Arrange the ham slices on the bottom of the pan to cover it completely. Use more slices if needed. Whisk one egg along with the heavy cream, salt, and pepper, in a small bowl. Pour the mixture over the ham slices. Crack the other eggs over the ham. Scatter Parmesan cheese over, close the air fry lid and cook for 14 minutes on Air Fry mode at 390°F. Sprinkle with paprika and garnish with chives.

Creamy Zucchini Muffins

Servings: 4 | Ready in about: 20 minutes

INGREDIENTS

1 ½ cups flour
1 tsp cinnamon
3 eggs

2 tsp baking powder
1 cup milk
2 tbsp butter, melted

1 tbsp yogurt
½ cup shredded zucchini
2 tbsp cream cheese

DIRECTIONS

In a bowl, whisk the eggs along with a pinch of salt, cinnamon, cream cheese, sifted flour, and baking powder. In another bowl, combine all liquid ingredients. Gently mix the dry and liquid mixtures. Stir in zucchini. Line the muffin tins and pour in the batter. Close the air fry lid and cook for 12 minutes on Air Fry mode at 350°F.

Once the timer beeps, check to ensure the muffins are set. If necessary, return them to your Instant Pot, and cook for 2-3 more minutes. Transfer to a cooling rack before serving. Serve with a scraping of butter.

Toasted Herb and Garlic Bagel

Servings: 1 | Ready in about: 6 minutes

INGREDIENTS

2 tbsp butter, softened
1 tsp dried basil

1 tsp dried parsley
1 tsp garlic powder

1 tbsp Parmesan cheese
1 bagel, halved

DIRECTIONS

Place the bagel halves in your Instant Pot, close the air fry lid and cook for 3 minutes on Air Fry mode at 390°F. Combine the butter, Parmesan, garlic, basil, and parsley, in a small bowl. Season with salt and pepper, to taste. Spread the mixture onto the toasted bagel. Return the bagel to the and cook for an additional 3 minutes on Roast mode. Serve with tangy tomato relish on the side.

Raspberry and Vanilla Pancake

Servings: 4 | Ready in about: 15 minutes

INGREDIENTS

2 cups all-purpose flour
1 cup milk
3 eggs, beaten

1 tsp baking powder
1 cup brown sugar
1 ½ tsp vanilla extract

½ cup frozen raspberries, thawed
2 tbsp maple syrup
A pinch of salt

DIRECTIONS

In a bowl, mix the sifted flour, baking powder, salt, milk, eggs, vanilla extract, sugar, and maple syrup, until smooth. Gently stir in the raspberries. Grease the air fry basket with cooking spray. Drop the batter into the basket. Close the air fry lid and cook for 10 minutes on Air Fry mode at 390°F. Serve the pancake right away.

Three Meat Cheesy Omelet

Servings: 2 | Ready in about: 20 minutes

INGREDIENTS

1 beef sausage, chopped
4 slices prosciutto, chopped
3 oz salami, chopped

1 cup grated mozzarella cheese
4 eggs
1 tbsp chopped onion

1 tbsp ketchup
A pinch of salt

DIRECTIONS

Preheat your Instant Pot to 350°F on Air Fry mode. Whisk the eggs with the ketchup in a bowl. Stir in the onion. Spritz the inside of the air fry basket with a cooking spray. Add and brown the sausage for about 2 minutes. Combine the egg mixture, mozzarella cheese, salami and prosciutto. Pour the egg mixture over the sausage and stir it. Close the air fry lid and cook for 10 minutes. Once the timer beeps, ensure the omelet is just set. Serve.

Very Berry Breakfast Puffs

Servings: 3 | Ready in about: 20 minutes

INGREDIENTS

3 pastry dough sheets
2 tbsp mashed strawberries
2 tbsp mashed raspberries
¼ tsp vanilla extract
2 cups cream cheese
1 tbsp honey

DIRECTIONS

Divide the cream cheese between the dough sheets and spread it evenly. In a small bowl, combine the berries, honey, and vanilla. Divide the mixture between the pastry sheets. Pinch the ends of the sheets, to form puff.

You can seal them by brushing some water onto the edges, or even better, use egg wash. Lay the puffs into a lined baking dish. Place the dish into your Instant Pot, close the air fry lid and cook for 15 minutes on Air Fry mode at 390°F. Once the timer beeps, check the puffs to ensure they're puffed and golden. Serve warm.

Crustless Mediterranean Quiche

Servings: 2 | Ready in about: 40 minutes

INGREDIENTS

4 eggs
½ cup chopped tomatoes
1 cup crumbled feta cheese
1 tbsp chopped basil
1 tbsp chopped oregano
¼ cup chopped kalamata olives
¼ cup chopped onion
2 tbsp olive oil
½ cup milk

DIRECTIONS

Brush a pie pan with the olive oil. Beat the eggs along with the milk, salt, and pepper. Stir in all of the remaining ingredients. Pour the egg mixture into the pan. Close the air fry lid and cook for 30 minutes on Air Fry mode at 340°F. Leave to cool before serving.

Sweet Bread Pudding with Raisins

Servings: 3 | Ready in about: 45 minutes

INGREDIENTS

8 slices of bread
½ cup buttermilk
¼ cup honey
1 cup milk
2 eggs
½ tsp vanilla extract
2 tbsp butter, softened
¼ cup sugar
4 tbsp raisins
2 tbsp chopped hazelnuts
Cinnamon for garnish

DIRECTIONS

Beat the eggs along with the buttermilk, honey, milk, vanilla, sugar, and butter. Stir in raisins and hazelnuts. Cut the bread into cubes and place it in a bowl. Pour the milk mixture over the bread. Let soak for about 10 minutes.

Close the air fry lid and cook the bread pudding for 25 minutes on Roast mode. Leave the dessert to cool for 5 minutes, then invert onto a plate and sprinkle with cinnamon to serve.

LUNCH RECIPES

Egg Rolls

Servings: 3 | Ready in about: 18 minutes

INGREDIENTS

12 egg roll wrappers
1 cup ground beef
2 garlic cloves, minced

½ onion, chopped
1 large grated carrot
1 cup grated mozzarella cheese

2 tsp olive oil
¼ tsp salt
¼ tsp pepper

DIRECTIONS

Place the onion, garlic, carrot, and beef in a saucepan over medium heat, and cook for 6-7 minutes. Take the pan off the heat. Leave to cool for a few minutes, then mix in the mozzarella. Season to taste with salt, and pepper. Grease your Instant Pot cooking basket with 1 tsp of the olive oil and set aside. Lay the egg roll sheets onto a dry and clean surface. Divide the mixture between them.

Roll the egg rolls and tuck the corners and edges in to create secure rolls. Lower the rolls into the cooking basket and brush them with the remaining olive oil. Close the air fry lid and cook for 13 minutes on Air Fry mode at 390°F. Once ready, check if the rolls are golden and crispy. Serve with green salad.

Tomato Soup with Cheese Croutons

Servings: 6 | Ready in about: 1 hour

INGREDIENTS

2 tbsp olive oil
1 onion, chopped
1 carrot, peeled and chopped
1 garlic clove, minced

1 cup vegetable stock
28 oz canned tomatoes
1 cup heavy cream
4 Monterey Jack cheese, sliced

4 slices of bread
2 Gouda cheese, sliced
4 tbsp butter, at room temperature
2 tbsp parsley, finely chopped

DIRECTIONS

Warm oil on Sauté in your Instant Pot. Add in garlic, onion, carrot, pepper and salt and sauté for 6 minutes until soft. To your Instant Pot, add vegetable stock to deglaze. Scrape any brown bits from the pot. Mix the stock with tomatoes. Seal the pressure lid, choose Pressure Cook on High, and set the timer to 30 minutes.

When the cooking is over, let naturally release pressure, for about 10 minutes. Transfer soup to a blender and process to get a smooth consistency. Add in heavy cream and stir. Add pepper and salt for seasoning. Place 2 slices Monterey Jack cheese onto 1 bread slice and cover with 1 Gouda cheese slice, and the second slice of bread. Spread a tbsp of butter and parsley over the top. Do the same with the rest of the cheese, bread, parsley, and butter.

Place the sandwiches on the air fry basket. Spread 1 tbsp butter on top of each sandwich. Close the air fry lid, choose Air Fry, set the temperature to 390°F, and set the time to 5 minutes. After 3 minutes, flip the sandwiches and cook for 2 minutes. Transfer sandwiches to a cutting board and chop into bite-sized cubes. Divide the soup into serving plates and apply a topping of parsley cheese croutons before serving.

Curry Egg Salad

Servings: 6 | Ready in about: 10 minutes

INGREDIENTS

2 cups water
Cooking spray
6 eggs

¼ cup crème frâiche
2 spring onions, minced
1 tbsp dill, minced

1 tbsp curry paste
2 tsp mustard
Salt and black pepper to taste

DIRECTIONS

Grease a cake pan with cooking spray. Carefully crack in the eggs. To the inner pot, add water. Set the pan with the eggs on the trivet. Seal the pressure lid, choose Pressure Cook on High, and the timer to 5 minutes.

Once ready, do a quick release. Drain any water from the eggs in the pan. Loosen the eggs on the edges with a knife. Transfer to a cutting board and chop into smaller sizes. Transfer the chopped eggs to a bowl. Add in onion, mustard, salt, dill, crème fraîche, curry powder, and black pepper.

Homemade Vegetables Soup

Servings: 5 | Ready in about: 40 minutes

INGREDIENTS

2 tbsp olive oil
1 leek, sliced
2 cloves garlic, minced
2 carrots, diced
1 celery stalk, chopped
4 potatoes, quartered
1 red bell pepper, diced
¼ tsp red pepper flakes
Salt and black pepper to taste
1 ½ cups vegetable stock
2 tbsp parsley

DIRECTIONS

Heat olive oil on Sauté in your Instant Pot. Add garlic and leek and cook for 5 minutes. Add in red bell pepper, carrots, salt, potatoes, red pepper flakes, and pepper. Mix in vegetable stock. Seal the pressure lid, choose Pressure Cook on High, and set the timer to 15 minutes. When ready, allow the pressure to release naturally for 10 minutes. Add cilantro and coconut milk to the soup. Use an immersion blender to blend the soup until smooth.

Ham & Mozzarella Eggplant Boats

Servings: 2 | Ready in about: 17 minutes

INGREDIENTS

2 eggplants
6 ham slices, chopped
1 cup mozzarella cheese, shredded
1 tsp dried parsley
Salt and black pepper to taste
Cooking spray

DIRECTIONS

Grease the air fry basket with cooking spray. Cut the eggplants lengthwise in half and scoop some of the flesh out, leaving the skin intact. Season with salt and pepper. Chop the scooped flesh and mix with mozzarella, salt, and pepper. Divide the cheese mixture between the eggplant halves. Cover with ham slices, and sprinkle with parsley. Put the eggplant in the greased basket, close the air fry lid and cook for 12 minutes on Air Fry mode at 350°F.

Garlicky Chicken on Green Bed

Servings: 1 | Ready in about: 20 minutes

INGREDIENTS

½ cup baby spinach leaves
½ cup shredded romaine lettuce
3 large kale leaves, chopped
4 oz chicken breasts, cubed
3 tbsp olive oil, divided
1 tsp balsamic vinegar
1 garlic clove, minced
Salt and black pepper to taste

DIRECTIONS

Place the chicken in a bowl along with 1 tbsp olive oil and garlic. Season with salt and pepper; toss to combine. Place on a lined baking dish and cook for 14 minutes on Roast mode in your Instant Pot at 390°F. Add the greens in a large bowl. Pour the remaining olive oil, balsamic vinegar, salt, and pepper, and toss to combine. When the timer rings out, remove the chicken. Arrange the greens on a serving platter and top with the chicken to serve.

Sweet Potato & Egg Salad

Servings: 8 | Ready in about: 20 minutes

INGREDIENTS

1 ½ cups water
6 sweet potatoes, peeled and diced
4 large eggs
2 ½ cups mayonnaise
¼ cup dill, chopped
⅓ cup Greek yogurt
Salt and ground black pepper to taste
½ cup Arugula

DIRECTIONS

To your Instant Pot, add water. Place eggs and potatoes into a steamer basket, transfer to the pot, and seal the pressure lid. Choose Pressure Cook and set timer to 4 minutes. After cooking has completed, release pressure quickly. Open the lid. Take out the eggs and place in a bowl of ice-cold water for purposes of cooling.

In a large bowl, combine yogurt, mayonnaise, and dill. In a separate bowl, mash potatoes using a potato masher. Mix with mayonnaise mixture to coat. Skin and dice the eggs and transfer to the potato salad and mix. Add pepper and salt to the salad before serving.

Cheat Hawaiian Pizza

Servings: 2 | Ready in about: 15 minutes

INGREDIENTS

2 tortillas
8 ham slices
8 mozzarella slices
8 thin pineapple slices
2 tbsp tomato sauce
Fresh basil leaves, chopped

DIRECTIONS

Spread each tortilla with tomato sauce. Scatter over the ham, pineapple, and mozzarella. Place the pizza into the air fry basket, close the air fry lid and cook for 10 minutes on Air Fry mode. When the timer beeps, remove and allow to sit for 2 minutes before slicing. Sprinkle the basil over and serve with napkins.

Italian Sausage Patties

Servings: 4 | Ready in about: 20 minutes

INGREDIENTS

1 lb ground Italian sausage
¼ cup breadcrumbs
1 tsp dried parsley
1 tsp red pepper Flakes
¼ tsp garlic powder
1 egg, beaten

DIRECTIONS

Line the basket with parchment paper. Combine all ingredients in a large bowl. Use your hands (clean!) to combine the mixture thoroughly. Make patties out of the sausage mixture and arrange them on the basket. Close the air fry lid and cook for 14 minutes on Air Fry at 350°F. After 7 minutes, flip each patty. Serve with tzatziki sauce.

Chicken Noodle Soup

Servings: 6 | Ready in about: 40 minutes

INGREDIENTS

1 tbsp olive oil
1 onion, minced
3 cloves garlic, minced
1 turnip, chopped
1 cup celery rib, chopped
1 tbsp dry basil
1 bay leaf
6 cups chicken broth
1 lb chicken breasts, bone-in, skin-on
8 oz extra-wide dry egg noodles
Salt and ground black pepper to taste

DIRECTIONS

Set your Instant Pot to Sauté. Warm olive oil stir in garlic and onion, and cook for 3 minutes until soft. Mix in celery, bay leaf, basil, and turnip. Add 3 cups chicken broth to the pot and deglaze. Scrape any brown bits from the pan's bottom and add chicken. Seal the pressure lid, choose Pressure Cook, and set the timer to 10 minutes.

When ready, naturally release the pressure for 10 minutes. Transfer chicken breasts to another bowl. Do away with the skin and bones. Shred the meat. Set the pot to Sauté. Add the chicken back to the pot. Add the noodles and the remaining stock. Simmer the stock for 10 minutes until noodles are done. Add pepper and salt for seasoning.

Pickle and Potato Salad with Feta

Serves: 12 | Ready in about about: 30 minutes

INGREDIENTS

3 lb potatoes, peeled and chopped
3 cups water
1 tsp salt

1 cup mayonnaise
¼ cup mustard
¼ cup pickle

¼ cup diced white onion, chopped
1 cup feta cheese, crumbled
Salt to taste

DIRECTIONS

In your Instant Pot, mix salt, water, and potatoes. Seal the pressure lid, select Pressure Cookand cook for 6 minutes on High. Once ready, do a natural release for 10 minutes. Drain the potatoes and chop into small pieces. In a bowl, mix salt, pickles, mayonnaise, potatoes, mustard, and onion to get the desired consistency. Chill for one hour while covered. Top with feta cheese to serve.

Warm Bacon & Potato Salad

Servings: 6 | Ready in about: 19 minutes

INGREDIENTS

6 slices smoked bacon, chopped
½ cup apple cider vinegar
½ cup water

3 tbsp honey
2 tsp mustard
1 tsp fresh flat-leaf parsley, chopped

Salt and black pepper to taste
6 red potatoes, peeled and quartered
2 red onions, sliced

DIRECTIONS

Set to Sauté your Instant Pot and brown the bacon for 2 minutes per side. Set aside. In a bowl, mix honey, salt, mustard, vinegar, water, and black pepper. In the inner pot, add potatoes, chopped bacon, and onions and top with vinegar mixture. Seal the pressure lid, choose Pressure Cook on High, and set the timer to 6 minutes. When ready, allow the pressure to release naturally for 10 minutes. Sprinkle with parsley and serve.

Quick Chicken Noodle Soup

Servings: 6 | Ready in about: 15 minutes

INGREDIENTS

1 tbsp canola oil
6 spring onions, chopped
2 garlic cloves, finely diced

1 carrot, chopped
2 celery stalks, chopped finely
2 chicken breasts, cut into chunks

6 cups chicken broth
8 oz dry egg noodles
2 tbsp chopped fresh parsley leaves

DIRECTIONS

Heat oil on Sauté in your Instant Pot. Add in celery, spring onion, garlic, and carrots. Cook for 5 minutes until tender. Add in chicken, egg noodles, and broth. Seal the pressure lid, choose Pressure Cook, and set the timer to 15 minutes. When ready, do a quick release. Add in parsley. Taste and adjust the seasoning before serving.

Homemade Chicken Soup

Servings: 8 | Ready in about: 1 hour 10 minutes

INGREDIENTS

1 ½ lb chicken drumsticks, boneless
4 celery stalks
1 cup fennel bulb, chopped
2 onions, diced

2 carrots, diced
2 garlic cloves
3 parsley, chopped
2 bay leaves

½ cup matzo meal
2 eggs, beaten
2 tbsp canola oil
1 tsp baking powder

DIRECTIONS

In your pressure cooker, add chicken drumsticks, bay leaves, onion, carrots, pepper, garlic, parsley, salt, and fennel. Add enough water such that ingredients are covered by 2 inches. Seal the pressure lid, choose Pressure Cook on High, and set the timer to 30 minutes. Release natural pressure for 10 minutes.

Mix baking powder, eggs, oil, pepper, salt and matzo meal in a small bowl. Use a plastic wrap to close the bowl and place in a refrigerator for 10 minutes. Get rid of celery stalks from the pressure cooker. Transfer chicken to a cutting board and strip and shred it from the bones. Take back to the pot. Select Sauté and boil the soup. Roll matzo mixture into 1-inch balls and place in the boiling soup. Cook for 3 mins to heat through as you gently stir.

Cream of Pumpkin Chipotle Soup

Servings: 4 | Ready in about: 25 minutes

INGREDIENTS

1 tbsp olive oil
1 onion, chopped
2 chipotle peppers, finely minced

¼ tsp grated nutmeg
¼ tsp ground cloves
1 pinch ground cinnamon

1 butternut pumpkin, cut into pieces
4 cups vegetable broth
1 cup half-and-half

DIRECTIONS

Warm oil on Sauté in your Instant Pot and sauté nutmeg, pepper, clove, cinnamon, and onion for 3 minutes. Add pumpkin and cook for 5 minutes as you stir infrequently. Pour in broth. Add chipotle peppers and remaining pumpkin. Seal the pressure lid, choose Pressure Cook, and set the timer to 10 minutes. When ready, release pressure quickly. Stir in half-and-half and transfer to a blender to purée until you obtain a smooth consistency.

Classic French Onion Soup

Servings: 8 | Ready in about: 45 minutes

INGREDIENTS

2 tbsp butter
8 cups thinly sliced onions
½ cup water
2 tsp sugar

1 tsp salt
½ tsp ground black pepper
½ cup dry white wine
4 cups beef stock

2 sprigs fresh thyme
2 bay leaves
4 baguette slices
1 cup Swiss cheese, shredded

DIRECTIONS

Melt butter on Sauté in your Instant Pot. Add in onions and cook for 3 to 5 minutes until soft. To the onions, add water, pepper, sugar, and salt, and pepper as you stir. Seal the pressure lid, press Pressure Cook on High, and set the timer to 15 minutes. Once ready, do a quick release. Add beef stock, bay leaves and thyme sprigs into the pot.

Seal the pressure lid again, choose Pressure Cook, and set the timer to 4 minutes. Quick-release pressure. Remove the bay leaves and thyme and discard. Divide into bowls. Top with ¼ cup swiss cheese and 1 baguette slice. Transfer the bowls to the air fryer basket and cook for 2 to 4 minutes on Roast at 400°F.

Broccoli & Potato Soup

Servings: 4 | Ready in about: 35 minutes

INGREDIENTS

⅓ cup butter
1 head broccoli, cut into florets
2 cloves garlic, minced

1 onion, chopped
2 ½ lb potatoes, peeled and chopped
4 cups vegetable broth

½ cup heavy cream
Cheddar cheese, grated for garnish
½ cup fresh chopped scallions

DIRECTIONS

Melt the butter on Sauté in your Instant Pot. Add onion and garlic and cook for 5 minutes. Add in broth, potatoes, and broccoli, and mix well. Seal the pressure lid, choose Pressure Cook on High, and set the timer to 5 minutes.

When ready, allow the pressure to release naturally for 10 minutes. Transfer the mixture in an immersion blender and puree until smooth. Add in heavy cream and season with pepper and salt. Top with cheese and scallions.

Minestrone Soup

Servings: 6 | Ready in about: 25 minutes

INGREDIENTS

2 tbsp olive oil
1 yellow onion, diced
1 cup celery, chopped
1 carrot, peeled and diced
1 green bell pepper, chopped
2 cloves garlic, minced

3 cups chicken broth
½ tsp dried parsley
½ tsp dried thyme
½ tsp dried oregano
Salt and ground black pepper to taste
2 bay leaves

1 (28 oz) can diced tomatoes
1 (6 oz) can tomato paste
2 cups kale
1 (14 oz) can Navy beans, rinsed
½ cup white rice
¼ cup Parmesan cheese

DIRECTIONS

Warm olive oil on Sauté in your Instant Pot. Stir in carrot, celery and onion and cook for 5 to 6 minutes until soft. Add garlic and bell pepper and cook for 2 minutes as you stir until aromatic. Stir in pepper, thyme, stock, salt, parsley, oregano, tomatoes, bay leaves, and tomato paste to dissolve. Mix in rice. Seal the pressure lid.

Choose Pressure Cook on High, and set the timer to 15 minutes. Once ready, do a quick pressure release. Add kale to the liquid and stir. Use residual heat in slightly wilting the greens. Get rid of bay leaves. Stir in navy beans. Serve topped with parmesan cheese.

Vegetable Soup

Servings: 8 | Ready in about: 42 minutes

INGREDIENTS

2 tbsp olive oil
1 cup leeks, chopped
2 garlic cloves, minced
4 cups vegetable stock
1 carrot, diced
1 parsnip, diced

1 celery stalk, diced
1 cup sliced mushrooms
1 cup broccoli florets
1 cup cauliflower florets
½ red bell pepper, diced
¼ head green cabbage, chopped

½ cup green beans
2 tbsp nutritional yeast
½ tsp dried thyme
½ salt, or more to taste
½ tsp ground black pepper
½ cup fresh parsley, chopped

DIRECTIONS

Heat oil on Sauté in your Instant Pot. Add in garlic and onion and cook for 6 minutes until slightly browned. Add in vegetable stock, carrot, celery, broccoli, bell pepper, green beans, salt, nutritional yeast, cabbage, cauliflower, mushrooms, potato, thyme, and pepper. Seal the pressure lid, choose Pressure Cook on High, and set the timer to 25 minutes. When ready, release natural pressure 10 minutes. Stir in parsley and serve.

Cream of Mushroom & Spinach Soup

Servings: 4 | Ready in about: 25 minutes

INGREDIENTS

1 tbsp olive oil
8 Button Mushrooms, sliced
1 cup spinach, chopped
1 red onion, chopped

4 cups vegetable stock
2 sweet potatoes, peeled and chopped
2 tbsp white wine
1 tbsp dry Porcini mushrooms, soaked

½ tsp sea salt
1 cup creme fraiche
½ tsp black pepper

DIRECTIONS

Set your Instant Pot to Sauté. Add in olive oil and sliced mushrooms and cook for 3 to 5 minutes until browning on both sides; reserve. Add onion and spinach, and cook for 3 to 5 minutes until onion is translucent. Stir in chopped mushrooms, and cook for a further 5 minutes as you stir occasionally until golden brown.

Pour in wine to deglaze the bottom of the pot. Cook for 5 minutes until all the wine evaporates. Mix in the remaining chopped fresh mushrooms, potatoes, soaked mushrooms, wine, vegetable stock, and salt.

Seal the pressure lid, choose Pressure Cook on High, and set the timer to 5 minutes. Once cooking is complete, do a quick release. Add in pepper and creme fraiche to mix. Using an immersion blender, whizz the mixture until smooth. Stir in the sautéed mushrooms. Add reserved mushrooms for garnish before serving.

Hearty Winter Vegetable Soup

Servings: 5 | Ready in about: 30 minutes

INGREDIENTS

2 tbsp olive oil
1 onion, chopped
2 carrots, peeled and chopped
1 cup celery, chopped
2 cloves garlic, minced

5 cups chicken broth
2 turnips, peeled and chopped
28 oz canned tomatoes
15 oz canned garbanzo beans, rinsed
1 cup frozen green peas

2 bay leaves
1 sprig fresh sage
Salt and ground black pepper to taste
¼ cup parmesan cheese, grated

DIRECTIONS

Set your Instant Pot to Sauté. Warm oil, stir in celery, carrots, and onion, and cook for 4 minutes until soft. Add in garlic and cook for 30 seconds until crispy. To the pot, add vegetable broth, parsnip, garbanzo beans, bay leaves, tomatoes, pepper, salt, peas, and sage. Seal the pressure lid, press Pressure Cook on High, and set the timer to 12 minutes. Once done, release remaining pressure quickly. Serve topped with parmesan cheese.

Spicy Acorn Squash Soup

Servings: 4 | Ready in about: 25 minutes

INGREDIENTS

4 cups vegetable broth
2 tbsp butter
1 onion, diced

1 (2 lb) acorn squash, chopped
2 carrots, peeled and diced
½ tsp ground cinnamon

¼ tsp chili pepper
½ cup coconut milk
1/3 cup sour cream

DIRECTIONS

Set your Instant Pot to Sauté. Melt butter. Add onion and cook for 3 minutes until soft. Add in carrots, cinnamon, squash, salt, and chili pepper and stir-fry for 2 minutes until fragrant. Add the stock to the vegetable mixture. Seal the pressure lid, choose Pressure Cook on High, and set the timer to 12 minutes. Quick-release the pressure.

Add soup to a food processor and puree to obtain a smooth consistency. Take the soup back to the pot, stir in coconut milk until you get a consistent color. Divide into serving bowls. Serve hot with a dollop of sour cream.

Cauliflower Cheese Soup

Servings: 5 | Ready in about: 20 minutes

INGREDIENTS

2 tbsp butter
½ tbsp olive oil
1 onion, chopped
2 stalks celery, chopped
1 large head cauliflower, cut into florets
1 potato, peeled and finely diced
3 cups vegetable broth
2 cups milk
4 oz blue cheese

DIRECTIONS

Set your Instant Pot to Sauté. Warm oil and butter. Add celery and onion and sauté for 3 to 5 minutes until onion becomes fragrant. Stir in half the cauliflower and cook for 5 minutes. Add in stock, bay leaf and the remaining cauliflower. Seal the pressure lid, choose Pressure Cook on High, and set the timer to 5 minutes.

When ready, release the pressure quickly. Remove the bay leaf and discard. Place the soup in an immersion blender, add in the milk and puree until smooth. Spoon the soup into bowls and top with blue cheese before.

Mexican-Style Chicken Soup

Servings: 5 | Ready in about: 35 minutes

INGREDIENTS

5 boneless, skinless chicken thighs
5 cups chicken broth
14 oz canned whole tomatoes, chopped
2 jalapeno peppers, chopped
2 tbsp tomato puree
3 cloves garlic, minced
1 tbsp chili powder
1 tbsp ground cumin
½ tsp dried oregano
1 (14.5 oz) can black beans, rinsed
2 cups frozen corn kernels, thawed
Crushed tortilla chips for garnish
¼ cup Cheddar cheese, shredded
Fresh cilantro, chopped for garnish

DIRECTIONS

Place the chicken in your pressure cooker. Add oregano, garlic, tomato puree, chicken stock, cumin, tomatoes, chili powder, and jalapeno peppers. Seal the pressure lid, choose Pressure Cook on High, and set the timer to 10 minutes. When ready, release pressure quickly. Transfer the chicken to a large plate.

On Sauté cook corn and black beans. Shred the chicken with a pair of forks, and return to the pot, stirring well. Simmer the soup for 5 minutes until heated through. Divide in serving plates. Add a topping of cilantro, shredded cheese and crushed tortilla chips.

Chicken & Farro Soup

Servings: 6 | Ready in about: 1 hour

INGREDIENTS

1 tbsp olive oil
4 boneless, skinless chicken thighs
¼ cup white wine
1 cup farro
1 large onion, sliced
2 celery stalks, cut into squares
3 large carrots, sliced
1 tsp garlic powder
1 tsp ground cumin
1 bay leaf
6 cups chicken broth
2 tsp fresh parsley leaves to garnish

DIRECTIONS

Warm oil on Sauté in your Instant Pot. Brown the chicken on all sides, approximately 6 minutes. Transfer the chicken to a bowl. To your Instant Pot, add wine to deglaze, scraping any brown bits present at the bottom of the cooker. Mix the wine with farro, cumin, stock, onion, carrots, celery, garlic powder, and bay leaf.

Close the lid and turn steam vent to sealing. Seal the pressure lid, choose Pressure Cook on High, and set the timer to 20 minutes. When cooking is done, naturally release the pressure for about 10 minutes. Divide between serving bowls and add parsley for garnish.

Chicken Broth

Servings: 16 | Ready in about: 50 minutes

INGREDIENTS

2 lb chicken carcasses
4 carrots, cut into chunks
1 cup leeks, chopped
1 onion, quartered

1 cup celery, chopped
2 large garlic cloves
1 sprig fresh thyme
1 bunch fresh parsley

Salt to taste
10 peppercorns
2 bay leaves

DIRECTIONS

To your Instant Pot, add chicken carcasses, onion, pepper, thyme, celery, carrots, garlic, parsley, and bay leaves. Top with enough water. Seal the pressure lid, press Pressure Cook, and set the timer to 30 minutes. When ready, release the pressure quickly. Use a colander to drain the broth and do away with solids. Allow the broth to cool.

Beef Neck Bone Stock

Servings: 8 | Ready in about: 2 hour 10 minutes

INGREDIENTS

1 carrot, chopped
2 onions, chopped
2 cups celery, chopped

2 lb Beef Neck Bones
12 cups water, or more
1 tsp cider vinegar

2 bay leaves
10 peppercorns
Salt to taste

DIRECTIONS

To your Instant Pot, add carrot, ginger, vinegar, onion, and beef bones. Add enough water to cover ingredients. Seal the pressure lid, press Pressure Cook on High, and set the timer to 120 minutes. Release pressure naturally for about 20 minutes. Remove the bones and bay leaves, and discard. Use a fine-mesh strainer to strain the liquid. Allow the broth to cool. From the surface, skim fat and throw away. Refrigerate for a maximum of 7 days.

Ramen Spicy Soup with Collard Greens

Servings: 4 | Ready in about: 20 minutes

INGREDIENTS

1 tbsp olive oil
½ tsp ground ginger
2 tbsp garlic, minced
6 cups chicken broth stock

2 tbsp soy sauce
1 tbsp chili powder
1 cup mushrooms, sliced
10 oz ramen noodles

1 lb fresh collard greens, trimmed
A bunch of fresh cilantro, chopped
1 red chilli, sliced to serve

DIRECTIONS

Set your Instant Pot to Sauté. Warm oil, stir in garlic and ginger, and cook for 2 minutes until soft. Add vegetable stock to the pot. Mix in chili powder, ramen noodles and soy sauce. Seal the pressure lid, press Pressure Cook on High, and set the timer to 10 minutes. When ready, release pressure quickly. Stir in collard greens until wilted. Ladle the soup into serving bowls and add red chili and cilantro to serve.

Perfect Chicken Wings Broth

Servings: 8 | Ready in about: 1 hour 30 minutes

INGREDIENTS

2 lb chicken wings
4 spring onions, diced

2 large carrots, diced
4 cloves garlic

1 small handful fresh parsley
1 bay leaf

DIRECTIONS

To your Instant Pot, add chicken, carrots, parsley, onions, garlic, and bay leaf. Pour in 6 cups water. Seal the pressure lid, choose Pressure Cook on High, and set the timer to 45 minutes. Release pressure naturally for about 10 minutes. Use a fine-mesh strainer to strain the broth and Allow cooling to room temperature. Transfer the broth to containers and seal. Place in the refrigerator for a maximum of one week.

Basic Applesauce with Cinnamon

Servings: 4 | Ready in about: 45 minutes

INGREDIENTS

4 apples, cored, sliced
1 tsp ground cinnamon
1 tsp honey

DIRECTIONS

Add apples, cinnamon, ½ cup water, and honey to your Instant Pot. Seal the pressure lid, choose Pressure Cook on High, and set the timer to 4 minutes. Once ready, release pressure naturally for 10 minutes. For smooth applesauce, puree the mixture in a blender. Allow cooling before transferring in containers for storage.

Leek and Potato Soup with Sour Cream

Servings: 5 | Ready in about: 30 minutes

INGREDIENTS

2 tbsp butter
3 leeks, white part only, thinly sliced
2 cloves garlic, minced
4 cups vegetable broth
3 potatoes, peeled and cubed
½ cup sour cream
2 tbsp rosemary
2 bay leaves
2 tbsp fresh chives, to garnish

DIRECTIONS

Melt butter on Sauté in your Instant Pot. Stir in garlic and leeks and cook for 3 to 4 minutes until soft. Stir in bay leaves, potatoes, and broth. Seal the pressure lid, press Pressure Cook on High, and set the timer to 15 minutes. When ready, release pressure quickly. Remove the bay leaves and cobs and discard. Transfer soup to a blender and puree soup to obtain a smooth consistency. Season. Top with chives. Serve with sour cream.

Ragu Bolognese

Servings: 10 | Ready in about: 45 minutes

INGREDIENTS

4 oz bacon, chopped
1 tbsp butter
1 large onion, minced
2 celery stalks, minced
2 large carrots, minced
2 lb ground beef
3 tbsp dry white wine
2 (28 oz) cans crushed tomatoes
3 bay leaves
Sea salt and black pepper to taste
½ cup yogurt
¼ cup chopped fresh basil

DIRECTIONS

Set your Instant Pot to Sauté. Place in bacon and cook until crispy for 4 to 5 minutes. Mix in celery, butter, carrots, and onion, and continue cooking for about 5 minutes until vegetables are softened. Mix in ¼ tsp pepper, ½ tsp salt, and beef, and cook for 4 minutes until golden brown. Stir in the wine and allow to soak, approximately 4 more minutes. Add in bay leaves, tomatoes, and remaining pepper and salt.

Seal the pressure lid, choose Pressure Cook on High, and set the timer to 15 minutes. Once ready, release pressure naturally for 10 minutes. Add yogurt and stir. Serve alongside noodles and use basil to garnish.

Red Lentil Soup with Tortilla Topping

Servings: 6 | Ready in about: 50 minutes

INGREDIENTS

2 ½ cups vegetable broth
1 ½ cups tomato sauce
1 onion, chopped
1 cup dry red lentils

½ cup prepared salsa verde
2 garlic cloves, minced
1 tbsp smoked paprika
2 tsp ground cumin

1 tsp chili powder
¼ tsp cayenne pepper
Salt and ground black pepper to taste
Crushed tortilla chips for garnish

DIRECTIONS

To your Instant Pot , add in tomato sauce and vegetable broth. Stir in onion, salsa verde, cumin, cayenne pepper, chili powder, garlic, red lentils, and paprika. Season with salt and pepper. Seal the pressure lid, press Pressure Cook on High, and set the timer to 20 minutes. Release pressure quicky. Add crushed tortilla topping.

Vegetarian Black Bean Soup

Servings: 6 | Ready in about: 30 minutes

INGREDIENTS

1 tsp olive oil
1 onion, chopped
2 celery stalks, chopped

3 carrots, chopped
2 serrano peppers, chopped
5 cups vegetable broth

30 oz canned diced tomatoes
1 (14 oz) can black beans, rinsed
¼ cup chopped fresh cilantro

DIRECTIONS

Set your Instant Pot to Sauté. Warm oil. Add in carrots, onion, jalapeño peppers and celery and cook for 6 to 7 minutes until soft. Mix in broth, sea salt, black beans, tomatoes, and cilantro. Seal the pressure lid, press Pressure Cook on High, and set the timer to 8 minutes. Once ready, release pressure naturally for 10 minutes.

Spicy Borscht Soup

Servings: 4 | Ready in about: 30 minutes

INGREDIENTS

2 tbsp olive oil
1 cup leeks, chopped
1 tsp garlic, smashed
2 beets, peeled and diced

1 tbsp cayenne pepper, finely minced
1 dried habanero pepper, crushed
4 cups beef stock
3 cups white cabbage, shredded

Salt and black pepper to taste
2 tsp red wine apple cider vinegar
¼ tsp paprika
Greek yogurt for garnish

DIRECTIONS

Set your Instant Pot to Sauté. Warm the oil, stir in garlic and leeks, and cook for 5 minutes until soft. Mix in the remaining ingredients. Seal the lid, choose Pressure Cook on High, and set the timer to 20 minutes. When ready, do a quick pressure release. Place in serving bowls and apply a topping of Greek yogurt before serving.

Two-Bean Zucchini Soup

Servings: 5 | Ready in about: 35 minutes

INGREDIENTS

1 tbsp olive oil
1 onion, chopped
2 cloves garlic, minced
5 cups vegetable broth

1 cup dried chickpeas
½ cup pinto beans, soaked overnight
½ cup navy beans, soaked overnight
3 carrots, chopped

1 large celery stalk, chopped
1 tsp dried thyme
16 oz zucchini noodles
Sea salt and black pepper to taste

DIRECTIONS

Set your Instant Pot to Sauté. Warm oil, stir in garlic and onion and cook for 5 minutes until golden brown. Mix in pepper, vegetable broth, carrots, salt, celery, beans, and thyme. Seal the pressure lid, choose Pressure Cook on High, and set the timer to 15 minutes. Once ready, naturally pressure release for about 10 minutes. Mix zucchini noodles into the soup and stir until wilted. Adjust the seasoning.

Flavorful Vegetable Stock

Servings: 10 | Ready in about: 55 minutes

INGREDIENTS

2 onions, chopped
2 cups celery, chopped
2 carrots, chopped
4 garlic cloves
1 cup kale
1 cup bell pepper, chopped
A handful of rosemary
A handful of parsley
10 peppercorns
2 bay leaves
Salt to taste
8 cups cold water, filtered

DIRECTIONS

To your Instant Pot, add onions, carrots, parsley, bay leaves, garlic, kale, celery, rosemary, and peppercorns. Top with cold water. Seal the pressure lid, press Pressure Cook, and set the timer to 15 minutes. Release pressure naturally for 15 minutes. Use a wide and shallow bowl to hold the stock you strain through a fine-mesh strainer. Allow cool to room temperature. Seal into jars and place in the refrigerator.

Creamy Quinoa & Mushroom Pilaf

Servings: 4 | Ready in about: 20 minutes

INGREDIENTS

4 cups vegetable broth
1 carrot, peeled and chopped
1 stalk celery, diced
2 cups quinoa, rinsed
1 cup mushrooms, sliced
1 onion, chopped
2 garlic cloves, smashed
1 tsp salt
½ tsp dried thyme
3 tbsp butter
½ cup heavy cream

DIRECTIONS

Melt the butter on Sauté in your Instant Pot. Add onion, garlic, celery, and carrot, and cook for 8 minutes. Mix in broth, thyme, quinoa, mushrooms, and salt. Seal the pressure lid, choose Pressure Cook, and set the timer to 10 minutes. Release pressure quickly. Stir in heavy cream. Cook for 2 minutes to obtain a creamy consistency. Serve.

Spicy Beef Broth

Servings: 8 | Ready in about: 1 hour 10 minutes

INGREDIENTS

2 lb beef stew meat
2 leeks, chopped
1 onion, chopped
2 cups celery, chopped
2 red chilies, deseeded and chopped
2 carrots, chopped
1 tsp fresh ginger, grated
4 garlic cloves
8 cups water
1 tsp cider vinegar
Salt to taste

DIRECTIONS

In your Instant Pot, mix meat, celery, garlic carrots, leeks, onion, red chilies, and ginger. Top with vinegar and water. Seal the pressure lid, choose Pressure Cook, and set the timer to 45 minutes. Release pressure naturally for 10 minutes. Strain the broth into a bowl. Add salt for seasoning. Serve or refrigerate using sealable containers.

Butternut Squash Curry

Servings: 5 | Ready in about: 30 minutes

INGREDIENTS

1½ lb butternut squash, chopped
4 cups chicken stock
½ cup buttermilk
4 spring onions, chopped into lengths

2 tbsp curry powder
1½ tsp ground turmeric
1½ tsp ground cumin
¼ tsp cayenne pepper, or more to taste

2 bay leaves
Salt and black pepper to taste
A bunch of cilantro leaves, chopped

DIRECTIONS

In your pressure cooker's pot, stir in squash, buttermilk, curry powder, turmeric, spring onions, stock, cumin, and cayenne pepper. Apply pepper and salt for seasoning. Add bay leaves to the liquid and ensure they are submerged.Seal the pressure lid, choose Pressure Cook on High, and set the timer to 10 minutes.

When ready, naturally release the pressure for 10 minutes. Discard bay leaves. Transfer the soup to a blender and process until smooth. Use a fine-mesh strainer to strain the soup. Garnish with cilantro before serving.

Fire-Roasted Tomato and Chorizo Soup

Servings: 6 | Ready in about: 30 minutes

INGREDIENTS

1 tbsp olive oil
2 shallots, sliced
3 cloves garlic, minced
1 tsp salt

4 cups beef broth
28 oz fire-roasted diced tomatoes
½ cup fresh ripe tomatoes
½ cup raw cashews

1 tbsp red wine vinegar
3 chorizo sausage, chopped
½ tsp ground black pepper
½ cup thinly sliced fresh basil

DIRECTIONS

Warn oil on Sauté in your Instant Pot and cook chorizo until crispy. Remove to a to a plate lined with paper towel. To the pot, add in garlic and onion and cook for 5 minutes until soft. Season with salt. Stir in red wine vinegar, broth, diced tomatoes, cashews, tomatoes, and black pepper. Seal the pressure lid, choose Pressure Cook on High.

Set the timer to 8 minutes. When ready, release pressure quickly. Pour the soup into an immersion blender and process to obtain a smooth consistency. Divide into deep bowls, top with crispy chorizo and decorate with basil.

Acorn Squash Soup with Coconut Milk

Servings: 6 | Ready in about: 1 hour PREP TIME: 25 minutes COOK TIME: 25 minutes

INGREDIENTS

1 tbsp olive oil
1 onion, diced
1 stalk celery, diced
1 large carrot, diced

2 garlic cloves, minced
1 lb acorn squash, peeled diced
6 cups chicken stock
Juice from 1 lemon

1 cup coconut milk
Salt and freshly ground black pepper
2 tbsp cilantro leaves, chopped

DIRECTIONS

Heat oil on Sauté in your Instant Pot and stir-fry carrot, celery, garlic, salt and onion, for 4 to 5 minutes until soft. Mix acorn squash with the vegetables and cook for 1 more minute until tender. Pour in chicken broth.

Seal the pressure lid, press Pressure Cook on High, and set the timer to 20 minutes. Release pressure naturally for 10 minutes. Add in lemon juice and coconut milk and stir. Transfer the soup to an a blender and process to obtain a smooth consistency. You may add pepper and salt if desired. Garnish with cilantro and black pepper to serve.

SNACKS, APPETIZERS & SIDES

Tangy Cheesy Arancini

Servings: 6 | Ready in about: 105 minutes

INGREDIENTS

½ cup olive oil, plus 1 tbsp
1 small white onion, diced
2 garlic cloves, minced
5 cups chicken stock

½ cup apple cider vinegar
2 cups short-grain rice
1½ cups grated Parmesan cheese, plus more for garnish

1 cup chopped green beans
Salt and black pepper to taste
2 cups fresh panko bread crumbs
2 large eggs

DIRECTIONS

Choose Sauté on your Instant Pot. Add 1 tablespoon of oil and the onion, cook the onion until translucent, add the garlic and cook further for 2 minutes or until the garlic starts getting fragrant. Stir in the stock, vinegar, and rice. Seal the pressure lid, choose Pressure Cook on High, and set the time to 7 minutes.

After cooking, perform a natural pressure release for 10 minutes, then a quick pressure release and carefully open the pressure lid. Stir in the Parmesan cheese, green beans, salt, and pepper to mash the rice until a risotto forms. Spoon the mixture into a bowl and set aside to cool completely. Clean the pot.

In a bowl, combine the breadcrumbs and the remaining olive oil. In another bowl, lightly beat the eggs. Form 12 balls out of the risotto or as many as you can get. Dip each into the beaten eggs, and coat in the breadcrumb mixture. Put half of the rice balls in the air fry basket in a single layer. Close the air fry lid, hit Air Fry, set the temperature to 400°F, and set the time to 10 minutes. Leave to cool before serving.

Sweet Paprika Hard-Boiled Eggs

Servings: 3 | Ready in about: 25 minutes

INGREDIENTS

6 eggs

Salt and ground black pepper, to taste

1 tsp sweet paprika

DIRECTIONS

To your Instant Pot, add 1 cup water and place a trivet on top. Lay eggs on the trivet. Seal the lid, choose Pressure Cook on High, and set the timer to 5 minutes. Once ready, do a natural release for 10 minutes. Transfer the eggs to ice-cold water to cool completely. When cooled, peel and slice; season. Sprinkle with sweet paprika to serve.

Brazilian Cheese Balls

Servings: 4 | Ready in about: 35 minutes

INGREDIENTS

2 cups flour
1 cup milk

A pinch of salt
2 eggs, cracked into a bowl

2 cups grated mozzarella cheese
½ cup olive oil

DIRECTIONS

Select Sauté on your Instant Pot. Add the milk, oil, and salt, and let boil. Add the flour and mix it vigorously with a spoon. Let the mixture cool. Once cooled, use a hand mixer to mix the dough well, and add the eggs and cheese while still mixing. The dough should be thick and sticky.

Use your hands to make 14 balls out of the mixture, and put them in the greased basket. Put the air fry basket the pot and close the air fry lid. Select Air Fry, set the temperature to 380°F and set the timer to 15 minutes. At the 7-minute mark, shake the balls. Serve with lemon aioli, garlic mayo or ketchup.

Kale-Artichoke Bites

Servings: 8 | Ready in about: 70 minutes

INGREDIENTS

¼ cup frozen chopped kale
¼ cup finely chopped artichoke hearts
¼ cup ricotta cheese
2 tbsp grated Parmesan cheese

¼ cup goat cheese
1 large egg white
1 tsp dried basil
1 lemon, zested

½ tsp salt
½ tsp freshly ground black pepper
4 sheets frozen phyllo dough, thawed
1 tbsp olive oil

DIRECTIONS

In a bowl, mix kale, artichoke hearts, ricotta cheese, Parmesan, goat cheese, egg white, basil, lemon zest, salt, and pepper. Place a phyllo sheet on a clean flat surface. Brush with olive oil, place a second phyllo sheet on top, and brush with oil. Continue layering to form a pile of 4 oiled sheets. Working from the short side, cut the phyllo sheets into 8 strips. Cut the strips in half to form 16 strips. Spoon 1 tbsp of filling onto 1 short side of every strip.

Fold a corner to cover the filling to make a triangle. Continue repeatedly folding to the end of the strip, creating a triangle-shaped phyllo packet. Repeat the process with the other phyllo bites. Place half of the pastry in the air fry basket in a single layer. Close the lid, choose Air Fry, set the temperature to 350°F, and the timer to 12 minutes.

After 6 minutes, open the lid, and flip the bites. Return the basket to the pot and close the lid to continue baking. When ready, take out the bites into a plate. Serve warm.

Hot Chicken Wings

Servings: 4 | Ready in about: 60 minutes

INGREDIENTS

½ cup sriracha sauce
2 tbsp butter, melted

1 tbsp lemon juice
2 lb chicken wings, frozen

½ (1-oz) ranch salad mix
½ tsp paprika

DIRECTIONS

Mix ½ cup water, sriracha, butter and lemon juice or vinegar in your Instant Pot. In the air fry basket, put the wings, and then the basket into the pot. Seal the pressure lid, choose Pressure Cook on High, set the timer at 5 minutes. When the timer is done reading, perform a quick pressure release, and carefully open the lid.

Pour the paprika and ranch dressing all over the chicken and oil with cooking spray. Cover the air fry lid. Choose Air Fry, set the temperature to 390°F, and the timer to 15 minutes. Choose Start to commence frying.

After half the cooking time, open the lid, remove the basket and shake the wings. Oil the chicken again with cooking spray and return the basket to the pot. Close the lid and continue cooking until the wings are crispy.

Hot Buttery Chicken Meatballs

Servings: 6 | Ready in about: 90 minutes

INGREDIENTS

1 lb ground chicken
1 green bell pepper, minced
2 celery stalks, minced

¼ cup crumbled queso fresco
¼ cup hot sauce
¼ cup panko bread crumbs

1 egg
2 tbsp melted butter
½ cup water

DIRECTIONS

Choose Sauté on your Instant Pot. In a bowl, evenly combine the chicken, bell pepper, celery, queso fresco, hot sauce, breadcrumbs, and egg. Form meatballs out of the mixture. Then, pour the melted butter into the pot and fry the meatballs in batches until lightly browned on all sides. Remove the meatballs to a plate.

Put the air fry basket in the pot. Pour in the water and put all the meatballs in the basket. Seal the pressure lid, choose Pressure Cook on High, and set the timer to 5 minutes. When done, perform a quick pressure release.

Remove the water. Close the air fry lid. Choose Air Fry, set the temperature to 400°F, and set the time to 10 minutes. After 5 minutes, open the lid, lift the basket and shake the meatballs. Return the basket to the pot and close the lid to continue cooking until the meatballs are crispy.

Cheesy Smashed Sweet Potatoes

Servings: 4 | Ready in about: 70 minutes

INGREDIENTS

12 oz baby sweet potatoes
1 tsp melted butter
¼ cup shredded Monterey Jack cheese
¼ cup sour cream
2 slices bacon, cooked and crumbled
1 tbsp chopped scallions

DIRECTIONS

Toss the sweet potatoes with the melted butter until evenly coated. Add the sweet potatoes to the air fry basket. Close the air fry lid, choose Air Fry, set the temperature to 350°F. Cook for 30 minutes. After 15 minutes, open the lid, pull out the basket and shake the potatoes. Return the basket to the pot and close the lid to continue cooking.

When ended, check the sweet potatoes for your desired crispiness, which should also be fork tender. Take out the sweet potatoes from the basket and use a large spoon to crush the soft potatoes just to split lightly. Top with the cheese, sour cream, bacon, and scallions, and season with salt.

BBQ Chicken Drumsticks

Servings: 6 | Ready in about: 30 minutes

INGREDIENTS

3 lb chicken drumsticks
3 tbsp garlic powder
Salt to taste
1 cup Barbecue sauce
¼ cup butter, melted
½ cup water

DIRECTIONS

Season drumsticks with garlic powder and salt. Pour the water in your Instant Pot and fit in a trivet. Arrange the drumsticks on top, seal the pressure lid, and select Pressure Cook for 5 minutes. Once the timer has ended, do a natural pressure release for 10 minutes, and then a quick pressure release to let out any more steam. Remove the drumsticks to a air fry basket and add the butter and half of the barbecue sauce.

Stir the chicken until well coated in the sauce. Insert the air fry basket in your Instant Pot and close the air fry lid. Select Air Fry, set to 380°F, and cook for 10 minutes. Select Start. Once nice and crispy, remove drumsticks to a bowl, and top with the remaining barbecue sauces. Stir and serve the chicken with a cheese dip.

Cheese bombs wrapped in Bacon

Servings: 8 | Ready in about: 20 minutes

INGREDIENTS

16 oz Mozzarella, cut into 8 pieces
8 bacon slices, cut in half
3 tbsp butter, melted

DIRECTIONS

Wrap each cheese string with a slice of bacon and secure the ends with toothpicks. Set aside. Grease the air fry basket with the melted butter and add in the bombs. Close the air fry lid, select Air Fry mode, and set the temperature to 370°F and set the time to 10 minutes. At the 5-minute mark, turn the bombs. When ready, remove to a paper-lined plate to drain the excess oil. Serve on a platter with toothpicks and tomato dip.

Fried Beef Dumplings

Servings: 8 | Ready in about: 45 minutes

INGREDIENTS

- 8 oz ground beef
- ½ cup grated cabbage
- 1 carrot, grated
- 1 large egg, beaten
- 1 garlic clove, minced
- 2 tbsp coconut aminos
- ½ tbsp melted ghee
- ½ tbsp ginger powder
- ½ tsp salt
- ½ tsp freshly ground black pepper
- 20 wonton wrappers
- 2 tbsp olive oil

DIRECTIONS

In a large bowl, mix the beef, cabbage, carrot, egg, garlic, coconut aminos, ghee, ginger, salt, and black pepper. Put the wonton wrappers on a clean flat surface and spoon 1 tablespoon of the beef mixture into the middle of each wrapper. Run the edges of the wrapper with a little water. Fold the wrapper to cover the filling into a semi-circle shape and pinch the edges to seal. Brush the dumplings with olive oil.

Lay the dumplings in the preheated basket, choose Air Fry, set the temperature to 400°F, and set the time to 12 minutes. frying. After 6 minutes, open the lid, pull out the basket and shake the dumplings. Return the basket to the pot and close the lid to continue frying until the dumplings are crispy to your desire.

Buffalo Chicken Meatballs with Ranch Dip

Servings: 4 | Ready in about: 34 minutes

INGREDIENTS

- 5 tbsp Hot sauce
- 2 tbsp Buffalo wing sauce
- 1 lb ground chicken

For the dip
- ½ cup Roquefort cheese, crumbled
- ¼ tbsp heavy cream

- 1 egg, beaten
- 2 tbsp minced garlic
- 2 tbsp olive oil

- 2 tbsp mayonnaise
- Juice from ½ lemon

- 2 tbsp chopped green onions
- Green onions for garnish
- Salt and black pepper to taste

- 2 tbsp olive oil

DIRECTIONS

Mix all salsa ingredients in a bowl until uniform and creamy, and refrigerate. Add the ground chicken, salt, garlic, and two tablespoons of green onions. Mix well with your hands. Rub your hands with some oil and form bite-size balls out of the mixture. Lay onto air fry basket. Spray with cooking spray.

Select Air Fry, set the temperature to 385°F and the time to 14 minutes. At the 7-minute mark, turn the meatballs. Add the hot sauce and butter to a bowl and microwave them until the butter melts. Mix the sauce with a spoon. Pour the hot sauce mixture and a half cup of water over the meatballs.

Seal the pressure lid and select Pressure Cook on High for 10 minutes. Once the timer has ended, do a quick pressure release. Dish the meatballs. Garnish with green onions, and serve with Roquefort sauce.

Asparagus Wrapped in Prosciutto with Dip

Servings: 6 | Ready in about: 15 minutes

INGREDIENTS

- 1 lb asparagus, stalks trimmed

For the Dip:
- 1 cup canned garbanzo beans
- 1 medium onion, diced
- 2 cloves of garlic, minced

- 10 oz Prosciutto, thinly sliced

- 2 medium jalapeños, chopped
- 1 cup crushed tomatoes
- 1 cup vegetable broth

- Cooking spray

- 1 ½ tbsp olive oil
- 1 tsp paprika
- ½ tsp chili powder

SNACKS, APPETIZERS & SIDES

DIRECTIONS

Add the garbanzo beans, onion, jalapeños, garlic, tomatoes, broth, oil, paprika, chili powder, and salt to your Instant Pot. Seal the pressure lid and select Pressure Cook on High for 8 minutes. Once the timer has ended, do a quick pressure release, and open the pot. Transfer the ingredients to a food processor, and blend until creamy and smooth. Set aside. Wrap each asparagus with a slice of prosciutto from top to bottom.

Grease the air fry basket with cooking spray, and add in the wrapped asparagus. Close the air fry lid, select Air Fry mode at 370°F and set the time to 8 minutes. At the 4-minute mark, turn the bombs. Remove the wrapped asparagus onto a plate and serve with bean dip.

Holiday Egg Brulee

Servings: 8 | Ready in about: 12 minutes

INGREDIENTS

8 large eggs

Salt to taste

1 cup water

DIRECTIONS

Pour the water in your Instant Pot and fit in a trivet. Put the eggs on the trivet in a single layer, seal the pressure lid, and select Pressure on High Pressure for 5 minutes. Once the timer has ended, do a quick pressure release, and open the pot. Remove the eggs into the ice bath and peel the eggs.

Put the peeled eggs in a plate and slice them in half. Sprinkle a bit of salt on them and then followed by the sugar. Lay onto air fry basket. Select Air Fry mode, set the temperature to 390°F and the time to 3 minutes.

Creamy Tomato & parsley Dip

Servings: 6 | Ready in about: 18 minutes

INGREDIENTS

1 cup chopped tomatoes
10 oz shredded Parmesan cheese

¼ cup chopped parsley
10 oz cream cheese

½ cup heavy cream
1 cup water

DIRECTIONS

Pour the tomatoes, parsley, heavy cream, cream cheese, and water in your Instant Pot. Seal the pressure lid and select Pressure for 3 minutes at High. Once the timer has ended, do a natural pressure release for 10 minutes. Stir the mixture with a spoon while mashing the tomatoes with the back of the spoon.

Add the parmesan cheese and Close the air fry lid. Select Bake mode, set the temperature to 370°F and the time to 3 minutes. Dish the dip into a bowl and serve with chips or veggie bites.

Bacon & Cheese Dip

Servings: 10 | Ready in about: 10 minutes

INGREDIENTS

4 chopped tomatoes
1¼ cup shredded Monterey Jack cheese

1 ¼ cups cream cheese
10 bacon slices, chopped roughly

1 cup water

DIRECTIONS

On your Instant Pot and select Air Fry. Set the temperature to 370°F and the time to 8 minutes. Add the bacon and close the air fry lid. When ready, add the water, cream cheese, and tomatoes. Do Not Stir. Seal the pressure lid and select Pressure Cook for 5 minutes. Do a quick pressure release. Stir in the cheddar cheese. Serve.

Scrumptious Honey-Mustard Hot Dogs

Servings: 4 | Ready in about: 22 minutes

INGREDIENTS

20 Hot Dogs, cut into 4 pieces
1 tsp Dijon mustard
1½ tsp soy sauce
¼ cup honey
¼ cup red wine vinegar
Salt and black pepper to taste
½ cup tomato puree
¼ cup water

DIRECTIONS

Add the tomato puree, red wine vinegar, honey, soy sauce, Dijon mustard, salt, and black pepper in a medium bowl. Mix them with a spoon. Put sausage weenies in the air fry basket, and close the air fry lid.

Select Air Fry. Set the temperature to 370°F and the timer to 4 minutes. At the 2-minute mark, turn the sausages. Once ready, open the lid and pour the sweet sauce over the sausage weenies. Seal the pressure lid and select Pressure Cook on High for 3 minutes. Once the timer has ended, do a quick pressure release. Serve and enjoy.

Teriyaki Chicken Wings

Servings: 6 | Ready in about: 30 minutes

INGREDIENTS

1 tbsp honey
1 cup teriyaki sauce
1 tsp finely ground black pepper
2 lb chicken wings
2 tbsp cornstarch
1 tsp sesame seeds

DIRECTIONS

In your Instant Pot, combine honey, teriyaki sauce and black pepper until the honey dissolves completely. Toss in chicken to coat. Seal the pressure lid, choose Pressure Cook on High, and set the timer to 10 minutes.

When ready, release the pressure quickly. Transfer chicken wings to a platter. Mix 2 tbsp cold water with the cornstarch. Press Sauté and stir in cornstarch slurry into the sauce and cook for 3 to 5 minutes until thickened. Top the chicken with thickened sauce. Add a garnish of sesame seeds, and serve.

Wrapped Asparagus in Bacon

Servings: 6 | Ready in about: 30 minutes

INGREDIENTS

1 lb asparagus spears, trimmed
1 lb bacon, sliced
½ cup Parmesan cheese, grated

DIRECTIONS

Place the bacon slices out on a work surface, top each one with one asparagus spear and half of the cheese. Wrap the bacon around the asparagus. Line the air fry basket with parchment paper. Arrange the wraps into the basket. Scatter over the remaining cheese, season with salt and black pepper, and spray with cooking spray. Close the air fry lid and cook for 8 to 10 minutes on Roast mode at 390°F. If necessary work in batches. Serve hot.

Green Vegan Dip

Servings: 4 | Ready in about: 20 minutes

INGREDIENTS

10 oz canned green chiles
2 cups broccoli florets
1 cup water
¾ cup green bell pepper, chopped
¼ cup raw cashews
¼ cup soy sauce
½ tsp sea salt
¼ tsp chili powder
¼ tsp garlic powder

DIRECTIONS

In the cooker, add cashews, broccoli, green bell pepper, and water. Seal the pressure lid, choose Pressure Cook on High, and set the timer to 5 minutes. When ready, release the pressure quickly. Drain water from the pot. Add the liquid from canned green chilies, salt, garlic powder, chili powder, soy sauce, and cumin. Use an immersion blender to blend the mixture until smooth. Set aside. Stir green chilies through the dip. Serve.

Homemade Spinach Hummus

Servings: 12 | Ready in about: 1 hour 10 minutes

INGREDIENTS

8 cups water
2 cups dried chickpeas
5 tbsp grapeseed oil

Salt to taste
½ cup tahini
5 tbsp lemon juice

2 cups spinach, chopped
5 garlic cloves, crushed

DIRECTIONS

In your Instant Pot, mix 2 tbsp oil, water, salt, and chickpeas. Seal the pressure lid, choose Pressure Cook on High, and set the timer to 35 minutes. When ready, release the pressure quickly. In a small bowl, reserve ½ cup of the cooking liquid and drain chickpeas. Mix half the reserved cooking liquid and chickpeas in a food processor.

Puree until no large chickpeas remain. Add remaining cooking liquid, spinach, lemon juice, salt, garlic, and tahini. Process hummus for 8 minutes until smooth. Stir in the remaining 3 tbsp of olive oil before serving.

Sweet-Heat Pickled Cucumbers

Servings: 6 | Ready in about: 5 minutes

INGREDIENTS

1 lb small cucumbers, sliced into rings
2 cups white vinegar
1 cup water

1 cup sugar
¼ cup green garlic, minced
2 tbsp Dill Pickle Seasoning

2 tsp salt
1 tsp cumin

DIRECTIONS

To your Instant Pot, add sliced cucumber, vinegar and pour water on top. Sprinkle sugar over cucumbers. Add cumin, dill pickle seasoning, and salt. Stir well to dissolve the sugar. Seal the pressure lid, choose Pressure Cook on High, and set the timer to 4 minutes. When ready, release the pressure quickly. Ladle cucumbers into a large storage container and pour cooking liquid over the top. Chill for 1 hour.

Crispy Rosemary Potato Fries

Servings: 4 | Ready in about: 30 minutes

INGREDIENTS

4 russet potatoes, cut into sticks
2 tbsp butter, melted

2 garlic cloves, crushed
1 tsp fresh rosemary, chopped

Salt and black pepper to taste

DIRECTIONS

Add butter, garlic, salt, and pepper to a bowl. Toss until the sticks are well-coated. Lay the potato sticks into the air fry basket. Close the air fry lid and cook for 15 minutes at 390°F. Shake the potatoes every 5 minutes.

Once ready, check to ensure the fries are golden and crispy all over if not, return them to cook for a few minutes. Divide standing up between metal cups lined with nonstick baking paper, and serve sprinkled with rosemary.

New York Steak and Minty Cheese

Servings: 4 | Ready in about: 15 minutes

INGREDIENTS

2 New York strip steaks
12 kalamata olives
8 oz halloumi cheese
2 tbsp chopped parsley
2 tbsp chopped mint
Juice and zest of 1 lemon

DIRECTIONS

Season the steaks with salt and pepper, and gently brush with olive oil. Place into your Instant Pot, close the air fry lid and cook for 6 minutes (for medium rare) on Air Fry mode at 350°F. When ready, remove to a plate and set aside. Drizzle the cheese with olive oil and place it in the pot. Cook for 4 minutes. Remove to a serving platter and serve with sliced steaks and olives, sprinkled with herbs, and lemon zest and juice.

Cauliflower and Cheddar Tater Tots

Servings: 10 | Ready in about: 35 minutes

INGREDIENTS

2 lb cauliflower florets, steamed
5 oz cheddar cheese
1 onion, diced
1 cup breadcrumbs
1 egg, beaten
1 tsp chopped parsley
1 tsp chopped oregano
1 tsp chopped chives
1 tsp garlic powder

DIRECTIONS

Mash the cauliflower and place it in a large bowl. Add the onion, parsley, oregano, chives, garlic powder, salt, and pepper, and cheddar cheese. Mix with hands until thoroughly combined. Form 12 balls out of the mixture.

Line a baking sheet with wax paper. Dip half of the tater tots into the egg and then coat with breadcrumbs. Arrange them on the baking sheet, close the air fry lid, and cook in your Instant Pot at 350°F for 15 minutes on Air Fry mode. Repeat with the other half.

Crispy Cheesy Straws

Servings: 8 | Ready in about: 45 minutes

INGREDIENTS

2 cups cauliflower florets, steamed
1 egg
3 ½ oz oats
1 red onion, diced
1 tsp mustard
5 oz cheddar cheese

DIRECTIONS

Add the oats to a food processor and process until they resemble breadcrumbs. Place the steamed florets in a cheesecloth and squeeze out the excess liquid. Put the florets in a bowl and add in the rest of the ingredient. Mix to combine the ingredients thoroughly. Take a little bit of the mixture and twist it into a straw.

Place in the lined air fry basket. Repeat with the rest of the mixture. Close the air fry lid and cook for 10 minutes on Air Fry mode at 350°F. After 5 minutes, turn them over and cook for an additional 10 minutes.

Chicken and Cheese Bake

Servings: 6 | Ready in about: 1 hour 18 minutes

INGREDIENTS

1 lb chicken breast
½ cup breadcrumbs
10 oz Cheddar cheese
½ cup sour cream
10 oz cream cheese
½ cup water

DIRECTIONS

Open your Instant Pot and add the chicken, water, and cream cheese. Seal the pressure lid and select Pressure Cook on High for 10 minutes. Once the timer has ended, do a quick pressure release, and open the pot. Shred the chicken with two forks and add the cheddar cheese. Sprinkle with breadcrumbs, and close the air fry lid. Select Bake set the temperature to 380°F and the timer to 3 minutes. Serve warm with veggie bites.

Melt-in-the-Middle Meatballs

Servings: 6 | Ready in about: 30 minutes

INGREDIENTS

2 lb ground beef
1 potato, shredded
2 eggs, beaten

2 tbsp chopped chives
½ tsp garlic powder
Salt and black pepper to taste

½ cup Parmesan cheese, grated
1 package cooked spaghetti to serve
2 cups tomato sauce to serve

DIRECTIONS

In a large bowl, combine the potato, salt, pepper, garlic powder, eggs, and chives. Form 12 balls out of the mixture. Spray with cooking spray. Arrange half of the balls onto a lined air fry basket. Close the air fry lid and cook for 14 minutes on Air Fry mode at 330°F. After 7 minutes, turn the meatballs. Repeat with the other half. Serve over cooked spaghetti mixed with tomato sauce, sprinkled with Parmesan cheese.

Eggplant Chips with Honey

Servings: 4 | Ready in about: 20 minutes

INGREDIENTS

2 eggplants
2 tsp honey

⅓ cup olive oil
⅓ cup cornstarch

1 tsp dry thyme
A pinch of salt

DIRECTIONS

Cut the eggplants in slices of ½ -inch each.

In a big bowl, mix the cornstarch, ½ cup water , olive oil, and eggplant slices, until evenly coated. Line the air fry basket with baking paper and spray with olive oil. Place the eggplants in the basket, scatter with thyme and cook for 15 minutes on Air Fry mode, shaking every 5 minutes at 390°F. When ready, transfer the eggplants to a serving platter and drizzle with honey. Serve with yogurt dip.

Air Fried Pin Wheels

Servings: 6 | Ready in about: 50 minutes

INGREDIENTS

1 sheet puff pastry
8 ham slices

1 ½ cups Gruyere cheese, grated
4 tsp Dijon mustard

DIRECTIONS

Place the pastry on a lightly floured flat surface. Brush the mustard over and arrange the ham slices. Top with cheese. Start at the shorter edge and roll up the pastry. Wrap it in a plastic foil and place in the freezer for about half an hour, until it becomes firm and comfortable to cut. Slice the pastry into 6 rounds.

Line the air fry basket with parchment paper, and arrange the pinwheels on top. Close the air fry lid and cook for 10 minutes on Air Fry mode at 390°F. Leave to cool on a wire rack before serving.

Parmesan Cabbage Side Dish

Servings: 4 | Ready in about: 30 minutes

INGREDIENTS

½ head of cabbage, cut into 4 wedges
4 tbsp butter, melted

2 cup Parmesan cheese
Salt and black pepper to taste

1 tsp smoked paprika

DIRECTIONS

Line the basket with parchment paper. Brush the butter over the cabbage wedges. Season with salt and pepper. Coat the cabbage with the Parmesan cheese. Arrange in the basket and sprinkle with paprika. Close the air fry lid and cook for 15 minutes on Air Fry mode, flip over and cook for an additional 10 minutes at 330°F.

Nutty & Zesty Brussels Sprouts with Raisins

Servings: 4 | Ready in about: 45 minutes

INGREDIENTS

14 oz Brussels sprouts, steamed
2 oz raisins

1 tbsp olive oil
Juice and zest of 1 orange

2 oz toasted pine nuts

DIRECTIONS

Soak the raisins in the orange juice and let sit for about 20 minutes. Drizzle the Brussels sprouts with the olive oil, and place them in the air fry basket. Close the air fry lid and cook for 15 minutes on Air Fry mode at 390°F. Remove to a bowl and top with pine nuts, raisins, and orange zest.

Cumin Baby Carrots

Servings: 4 | Ready in about: 25 minutes

INGREDIENTS

1 ¼ lb baby carrots
2 tbsp olive oil

1 tsp cumin seeds
½ tsp cumin powder

½ tsp garlic powder
1 handful cilantro, chopped

DIRECTIONS

Place the baby carrots in a large bowl. Add cumin seeds, cumin, olive oil, salt, garlic powder, and pepper, and stir to coat them well. Put the carrots in the air fry basket, close the air fry lid and cook for 20 minutes on Roast at 390°F. Remove to a platter and sprinkle with chopped cilantro, to serve.

Garlic and Rosemary Mushrooms

Servings: 4 | Ready in about: 20 minutes

INGREDIENTS

2 rosemary sprigs
12 oz button mushrooms

¼ cup melted butter
Salt and black pepper to taste

3 garlic cloves, minced

DIRECTIONS

Wash and pat dry the mushrooms and cut them in half. Place in a large bowl. Add the remaining ingredients to the bowl and toss well to combine. Transfer the mushrooms to the basket of your Instant Pot. Close the air fry lid and cook for 12 minutes on Air Fry mode, shaking once halfway through at 350°F.

Tomato & Mozzarella Bruschetta

Servings: 2 | Ready in about: 15 minutes

INGREDIENTS

1 Italian Ciabatta Sandwich Bread
Olive oil to brush
2 tomatoes, chopped
2 garlic cloves, minced
1 cup grated mozzarella cheese
Basil leaves, chopped
Salt and pepper to taste

DIRECTIONS

Cut the bread in half, lengthways, then each piece again in half. Drizzle each bit with olive oil and sprinkle with garlic. Top with the grated cheese, salt, and pepper. Place the bruschetta pieces into the air fry basket, close the air fry lid and cook for 12 minutes on Air Fry mode at 380°F. At 6 minutes, check for doneness. Once your Instant Pot beeps, remove the bruschetta to a serving platter, spoon over the tomatoes and chopped basil to serve.

Turkey Scotch Eggs

Servings: 6 | Ready in about: 20 minutes

INGREDIENTS

10 oz ground turkey
4 eggs, soft boiled, peeled
1 white onion, chopped
½ cup flour
2 garlic cloves, minced
2 eggs, lightly beaten
Salt and pepper to taste
½ cup breadcrumbs
1 tsp dried mixed herbs

DIRECTIONS

Mix the ground turkey, onion, garlic, salt, and pepper. Shape into 4 balls. Wrap the turkey mixture around each egg, and ensure the eggs are well covered. Dust each egg ball in flour, then dip in the beaten eggs and finally roll in the crumbs, until coated. Spray with cooking spray.

Lay the eggs into the air fry basket. Set the temperature to 390°F, close the air fry lid and cook for 15 minutes. After 8 minutes, turn the eggs. Slice in half and serve warm.

Herby Fish Skewers

Servings: 4 | Ready in about: 75 minutes

INGREDIENTS

3 tbsp olive oil
2 garlic cloves, grated
1 tsp dill, chopped
1 tsp parsley, chopped
Salt to taste
1 lemon, juiced and zested
1 lemon, cut in wedges to serve
1 lb cod loin, boneless, skinless, cubed

DIRECTIONS

In a bowl, combine the olive oil, garlic, dill, parsley, salt, and lemon juice. Stir in the cod and place in the fridge to marinate for 1 hour. Thread the cod pieces onto halved skewers. Arrange into the greased air fry basket, close the air fry lid, and cook for 10 minutes at 390°F. Flip them over halfway through cooking. When ready, remove to a serving platter, scatter lemon zest and serve with wedges.

VEGETABLES & VEGAN

Bok Choy & Zoodle Soup

Servings: 6 | Ready in about: 35 minutes

INGREDIENTS

6 oz Shitake mushrooms, stems removed and sliced to a 2-inch thickness

1 lb baby bok choy, stems removed
3 carrots, peeled and sliced diagonally
2 zucchinis, spiralized
2 sweet onion, chopped

2-inch ginger, chopped
2 cloves garlic, peeled
2 tbsp sesame oil
2 tbsp soy sauce

2 tbsp chili paste
Salt to taste
Chopped green onion to garnish
Sesame seeds to garnish

DIRECTIONS

In a food processor, add the chili paste, ginger, onion, and garlic. And process them until they are pureed. Turn on your Instant Pot and select Sauté. Pour in the sesame oil. Once it has heated, add the onion puree and cook for 3 minutes while stirring constantly to prevent burning. Add 6 cups water, mushrooms, soy sauce, and carrots.

Close the lid, secure the pressure valve, and select Pressure Cook on High for 5 minutes. Once the timer has ended, do a quick pressure release and open the lid. Add the zucchini noodles and bok choy, and stir to ensure that they are well submerged in the liquid. Adjust the taste with salt, cover the pot with the air fry lid.

Let the vegetables cook for 10 minutes on Broil mode. Use a soup spoon to dish the soup with veggies into soup bowls. Sprinkle with green onions and sesame seeds. Serve as a complete meal.

Rice Stuffed Zucchini Boats

Servings: 4 | Ready in about: 55 minutes

INGREDIENTS

2 small zucchini
½ cup cooked white short-grain rice
½ cup canned white beans, drained

½ cup chopped tomatoes
½ cup chopped toasted cashew nuts
½ cup grated Parmesan cheese, divided

2 tbsp melted butter, divided
Salt and black pepper to taste

DIRECTIONS

Cut each zucchini in half and then cut in half lengthwise and scoop out the pulp. Chop the pulp roughly and place in a medium bowl. In the bowl, add the rice, beans, tomatoes, cashew nuts, ¼ cup of Parmesan cheese, 1 tablespoon of melted butter, salt, and black pepper. Combine the mixture well but not to break the beans.

Spoon the mixed ingredients into the zucchini boats and arrange them on the basket. Close the air fry lid. Choose Air Fry, set the temperature to 400°F, and the time to 15 minutes. After 15 minutes, sprinkle the zucchini boats with the remaining Parmesan and butter. Close the air fry lid.

Choose Broil, set the time to 5 minutes, and choose Start to broil. When done cooking, ensure it is as crisp as you desire; otherwise broil for a few more minutes. Remove the zucchinis and serve.

Garganelli with Swiss Cheese and Mushrooms

Servings: 4 | Ready in about: 60 minutes

INGREDIENTS

8 oz garganelli
1 (12–fluid oz) can evaporated milk
1 ½ tsp salt
1 large egg

1 ½ tsp arrowroot starch
8 oz Swiss cheese, shredded
1 recipe sautéed mushrooms
2 tbsp chopped fresh cilantro

3 tbsp sour cream
1½ cups panko breadcrumbs
3 tbsp melted unsalted butter
3 tbsp grated Cheddar cheese

DIRECTIONS

Pour the garganelli into the inner pot, add half of the evaporated milk, 1 ¼ cups water, and salt. Seal the pressure lid, choose Pressure Cook on High, and the time to 4 minutes. In a bowl, whisk the remaining milk with the egg. In another bowl, combine the arrowroot starch with the Swiss cheese.

When the pasta has cooked, perform a natural pressure release for 10 minutes. Open the lid. Pour in the milk-egg mixture and a large handful of the starch mixture. Stir to melt the cheese and then add the remaining cheese in 3 or 4 batches while stirring to melt. Mix in the mushrooms, cilantro, and sour cream.

In a bowl, mix the breadcrumbs, melted butter, and cheddar cheese. Then, sprinkle the mixture evenly over the pasta. Close the air fry lid. Choose Broil and adjust the time to 5 minutes. Press Start to begin crisping. When done, the top should be brown and crispy, otherwise broil further for 3 minutes, and serve immediately.

Swiss Cheese & Mushroom Tarts

Servings: 4 | Ready in about: 75 minutes

INGREDIENTS

2 tbsp melted butter, divided
1 small white onion, sliced
5 oz oyster mushrooms, sliced
¼ tsp salt
¼ tsp freshly ground black pepper
¼ cup dry white wine
1 sheet puff pastry, thawed
1 cup shredded Swiss cheese
1 tbsp thinly sliced fresh green onions

DIRECTIONS

Choose Sauté on your Instant Pot. Add 1 tablespoon of butter, the onion, and mushrooms to the pot. Sauté for 5 minutes or until the vegetables are tender and browned. Season with salt and black pepper.

Pour in the white wine, and cook until evaporated, about 2 minutes. Spoon the vegetables into a bowl and set aside. Unwrap the puff pastry and cut into 4 squares. Pierce the dough with a fork and brush both sides with the remaining oil. Share half of the cheese over the puff pastry squares, leaving a ½- inch border around the edges.

Also, share the mushroom mixture over the pastry squares and top with the remaining cheese. Put 1 tart in the air fry basket. Close the air fry lid, choose Air Fry, set the temperature to 400°F, and set the time to 6 minutes.

After 6 minutes, check the tart for your preferred brownness. Take the tart out of the basket and transfer to a plate. Repeat the process with the remaining tarts. Garnish with the green onions and serve.

Rice & Olives Stuffed Mushrooms

Servings: 4 | Ready in about: 70 minutes

INGREDIENTS

4 Portobello mushrooms, stems and gills removed
2 tbsp melted butter
½ cup brown rice, cooked
1 tomato, seed removed and chopped
¼ cup black olives, pitted and chopped
1 green bell pepper, seeded and diced
½ cup feta cheese, crumbled
1 lemon, juiced
Salt and black pepper to taste
Minced fresh cilantro for garnish

DIRECTIONS

Brush the mushrooms with the melted butter. Open the air fry lid and arrange the mushrooms open-side up and in a single layer in the air fry basket. Close the air fry lid. Choose Air Fry, set the temperature to 375°F, and the time to 20 minutes. In a bowl, combine the rice, tomato, olives, bell pepper, feta, lemon juice, salt, and pepper.

Open the air fry lid and spoon the rice mixture equally into the 4 mushrooms. Close the lid. Choose Air Fry, set the temperature to 350°F, and set the time to 8 minutes. Press Start to commence cooking. When the mushrooms are ready, remove to a plate, garnish with fresh cilantro and serve immediately.

Squash Parmesan & Linguine

Servings: 4 | Ready in about: 75 minutes

INGREDIENTS

1 lb linguine
2 tsp salt
4 cups water + 2 tbsp
1 cup flour

2 eggs
1 cup seasoned panko breadcrumbs
½ cup grated Parmesan + for garnish
1 yellow squash, peeled and sliced

1 (24-oz) tomato sauce
2 tbsp olive oil
1 cup shredded mozzarella cheese
Minced fresh cilantro for garnish

DIRECTIONS

Break the spaghetti in half and place in your Instant Pot. Pour 4 cups of water and 1 teaspoon of salt. Seal the pressure lid, choose Pressure Cook on High, and set the time to 2 minutes. In a bowl, combine the flour and the remaining salt evenly. In another bowl, whisk the eggs and 2 tablespoons of water.

In a third bowl, mix the breadcrumbs and Parmesan cheese. Coat each squash slice in the flour. Shake off the excess flour, dip the slice in the egg wash, and then dredge in the breadcrumbs. Place on a plate and set aside. When ready, perform a quick pressure release. Drain the pasta through a colander and transfer to the pot.

Pour all but ¼ cup of the tomato sauce over the linguine. Mix gently. Fix a trivet inside the pot over the linguine. Place the breaded squash on the trivet and lightly brush with oil. Close the air fry lid. Choose Air Fry, set the temperature to 350°F, and set the time to 15 minutes. Press Start to cook.

When done cooking, spread the remaining tomato sauce on top of the squash and sprinkle with the mozzarella cheese. Close the air fry lid again, choose Broil, and set the time to 3 minutes. When ready, spoon the pasta into plates, place the breaded squash to the side, and garnish with fresh cilantro.

Pine nuts and Steamed Asparagus

Servings: 4 | Ready in about: 15 minutes

INGREDIENTS

1 ½ lb asparagus, ends trimmed
Salt and pepper, to taste

1 cup water
1 tbsp butter

½ cup chopped Pine Nuts
1 tbsp olive oil to garnish

DIRECTIONS

Open your Instant Pot, pour the water, and fit in a trivet. Place the asparagus on the trivet, close the air fry lid, select Air Fry, and set the time to 8 minutes at 380°F. At the 4-minute mark, turn the asparagus over. When ready, remove to a plate, sprinkle with salt and pepper, and set aside. Select Sauté on your Instant Pot and melt the butter. Add the pine nuts and cook for 3 minutes until golden. Pour over the asparagus and drizzle olive oil.

Mushroom Risotto with Swiss Chard

Servings: 4 | Ready in about: 60 minutes

INGREDIENTS

3 tbsp ghee, divided
1 small bunch Swiss chard, chopped
1 cup short-grain rice

⅓ cup white wine
2 cups vegetable stock
½ tsp salt

½ cup sautéed mushrooms
½ cup caramelized onions
⅓ cup grated Pecorino Romano cheese

DIRECTIONS

Press Sauté on your Instant Pot. Melt 2 tbsp of ghee and sauté the Swiss chard for 5 minutes until wilted. Set aside. Use a paper towel to wipe out any remaining liquid in the pot and melt the remaining ghee. Stir in rice and cook for 1 minute. Add the wine and cook for 3 minutes with occasional stirring until the wine has evaporated.

Add in stock and salt. Stir to combine. Seal the pressure lid, choose Pressure Cook on High, and the time to 8 minutes. When the timer is done reading, perform a quick pressure release. Stir in the mushrooms, swiss chard, and onions and let the risotto heat for 1 minute. Mix in the cheese to melt. Serve immediately.

Sticky Noodles with Tofu & Peanuts

Servings: 4 | Ready in about: 20 minutes

INGREDIENTS

1 package tofu, cubed
8 oz egg noodles
2 bell peppers, sliced
¼ cup soy sauce
¼ cup orange juice
1 tbsp fresh ginger, peeled and minced
2 tbsp vinegar
1 tbsp sesame oil
1 tbsp sriracha
¼ cup roasted peanuts
3 scallions, thinly sliced

DIRECTIONS

In your Instant Pot, mix tofu, bell peppers, orange juice, sesame oil, ginger, egg noodles, soy sauce, vinegar, and sriracha. Cover with enough water. Seal the pressure lid, choose Pressure Cook, and set the timer to 2 minutes. When ready, release the pressure quickly. Apply a topping of scallions and peanuts before serving.

Spinach & Butternut Squash Stew

Servings: 6 | Ready in about: 65 minutes

INGREDIENTS

1 tbsp butter
1 white onion, diced
4 garlic cloves, minced
2 lb butternut squash, peeled and cubed
4 cups vegetable broth
1 (15-oz) can sundried tomatoes,
2 (15-oz) cans chickpeas, drained
1½ tsp cumin powder
½ tsp smoked paprika
1 tsp coriander powder
Salt and black pepper to taste
4 cups baby spinach

DIRECTIONS

Chose Sauté on your Instant Pot. Melt the butter and add in the onion and garlic. Cook, stirring occasionally, for 5 minutes or until soft and fragrant. Add the butternut squash, vegetable broth, tomatoes, chickpeas, cumin, paprika, coriander, salt, and black pepper to the pot. Put the pressure lid together and lock in the Seal position.

Choose Pressure Cook on High and set the time to 8 minutes. When the timer is done reading, perform a quick pressure release. Stir in the spinach to wilt, adjust the taste with salt and black pepper, and serve warm.

Easy Spanish Rice

Servings: 4 | Ready in about: 50 minutes

INGREDIENTS

3 tbsp ghee
1 small onion, chopped
2 garlic cloves, minced
1 banana pepper, seeded and chopped
1 cup jasmine rice
⅓ cup red salsa
¼ cup stewed tomatoes
½ cup vegetable stock
1 tsp Mexican Seasoning Mix
1 (16-oz) can pinto beans, drained
1 tsp salt
1 tbsp chopped fresh parsley

DIRECTIONS

On your Instant Pot, choose Sauté. Add the ghee to melt and cook the onion, garlic, and banana pepper in the ghee. Cook for 2 minutes or until fragrant. Stir in the rice, salsa, tomato sauce, vegetable stock, Mexican seasoning, pinto beans, and salt. Seal the pressure lid, choose Pressure Cook on High and adjust the cook time to 6 minutes. After cooking, do a natural pressure release for 10 minutes. Stir in the parsley, dish the rice, and serve.

Cream of Cauliflower & Butternut Squash

Servings: 4 | Ready in about: 32 minutes

INGREDIENTS

2 tsp olive oil
1 large white onion, chopped
4 cloves garlic, minced
1 (2 lb) butternut squash, cubed
2 heads cauliflower, cut in florets
3 cups vegetable broth
3 tsp paprika
Salt and black pepper to taste
1 cup milk, full fat

Topping: Grated Cheddar cheese, crumbled bacon, chopped chives, pumpkin seeds

DIRECTIONS

Select Sauté on your Instant Pot. Heat olive oil, add the white onion and garlic and sauté for 3 minutes. Pour in the butternut squash, cauliflower florets, broth, paprika, pepper, and salt. Stir the ingredients with a spoon. Close the lid, secure the pressure valve, select Pressure Cook on High pressure and adjust the time for 8 minutes.

Once the timer has ended, do a quick pressure release, and open the lid. Stir in the milk and use a stick blender to puree the soup. Adjust the seasoning. Stir in cheese, close the air fry lid and cook for 2 minutes on Broil mode. Dish the soup into serving bowls. Add the remaining toppings to the soup and serve warm.

Tangy Risotto & Roasted Bell Peppers

Servings: 4 | Ready in about: 80 minutes

INGREDIENTS

2 tbsp ghee
1 garlic clove, minced
5 cups vegetable stock
¼ cup freshly squeezed lemon juice
1 tsp grated lemon zest
2 cups carnaroli rice
4 mixed bell peppers, cut diagonally
2 tbsp unsalted butter
1 ½ cups grated Parmesan + for garnish

DIRECTIONS

On your Instant Pot, choose Sauté. Melt the ghee and cook the garlic until fragrant, about 1 minute. Then, pour the stock, lemon juice, lemon zest, and rice into your Instant Pot. Sprinkle with 1 teaspoon of salt and stir to combine well. Seal the pressure lid, hit Pressure Cook, set to High, and the timer to 7 minutes. While the rice cooks in a bowl, toss the peppers with the remaining ghee, salt, and black pepper.

When the timer has ended, do a natural pressure release for 10 minutes. Stir the butter into the rice until properly mixed. Then, put a trivet inside the pot in the higher position, which will be over the risotto. Arrange the bell peppers on the trivet. Close the air fry lid. Choose Broil and set the time to 8 minutes.

When done cooking, take out the trivet from the pot. Stir the Parmesan cheese into the risotto. To serve, spoon the risotto into serving plates, top with the bell peppers and garnish with extra Parmesan. Serve immediately.

Roasted Squash & Rice with Crispy Tofu

Servings: 4 | Ready in about: 70 minutes

INGREDIENTS

¾ cup water
1 small butternut squash, diced
2 tbsp melted butter, divided
Salt and black pepper to taste
1 tbsp coconut aminos
1 (15-oz) block extra-firm tofu, cubed
2 tsp arrowroot starch
1 cup jasmine rice, cooked

DIRECTIONS

Pour the rice and water into your Instant Pot. Seal the pressure lid, choose Pressure Cook and set the time to 2 minutes. In a bowl, toss the butternut squash with 1 tbsp of melted butter and season with salt and pepper. Set aside. In another bowl, mix the remaining butter with the coconut aminos, and toss the tofu in the mixture.

Pour the arrowroot starch over the tofu and toss again to combine well. When done cooking the rice, perform a quick pressure release, and carefully open the pressure lid. Put a trivet in your Instant Pot in the higher position and line with aluminum foil. Arrange the tofu and butternut squash on the trivet.

Close the air fry lid. Choose Air Fry, set the temperature to 400°F, and set the time to 20 minutes. After 10 minutes, use tongs to turn the butternut squash and tofu. When done cooking, check for your desired crispiness and serve the tofu and squash with the rice.

Cajun Baked Turnips

Servings: 4 | Ready in about: 85 minutes

INGREDIENTS

- 4 small turnips, scrubbed clean
- ¼ cup whipping cream
- ¼ cup sour cream
- ½ cup chopped roasted red bell pepper
- 1 tsp Cajun seasoning mix
- 1½ cups shredded Monterey Jack cheese
- 4 green onions, chopped, divided
- ⅓ cup grated Parmesan cheese

DIRECTIONS

Pour 1 cup of water into your Instant Pot. Put in a trivet and place the turnips on top. Seal the pressure lid, choose Pressure Cook on High, and the cooking time to 10 minutes. After cooking, perform a natural pressure release for 5 minutes. Remove the turnips to a cutting board and allow cooling.

Slice off a ½-inch piece from the top and the longer side of each turnip. Scoop the pulp into a bowl, including the flesh from the sliced tops making sure not to rip the skin of the turnip apart. In the bowl with the pulp, add the whipping cream and sour cream and use a potato mash to break the pulp and mix the ingredients until smooth.

Stir in the roasted bell pepper, Cajun seasoning, and Monterey Jack cheese. Fetch out 2 tablespoons of green onions and stir the remaining into the mashed turnips. Fill the turnip skins with the mashed mixture and sprinkle with the Parmesan. Pour the water into the inner pot and return the pot to the base.

Put the air fry basket into your Instant Pot. Close the air fry lid, choose Air Fry, adjust the temperature to 375°F, and the time to 2 minutes. When the timer is done, put the turnips in the basket. Close the air fry lid, choose Air Fry, adjust the temperature to 375°F, and the cook time to 15 minutes. Garnish with the reserved onions.

Zucchini & Quinoa Stuffed Red Peppers

Servings: 4 | Ready in about: 40 minutes

INGREDIENTS

- 4 red bell peppers
- 2 large tomatoes, chopped
- 1 small onion, chopped
- 2 cloves garlic, minced
- 1 tbsp olive oil
- 1 cup quinoa, rinsed
- 2 cups vegetable broth
- 1 small zucchini, chopped
- ½ tsp smoked paprika
- ½ cup chopped mushrooms
- Salt and black pepper to taste
- 1 cup grated Gouda cheese

DIRECTIONS

Select Sauté on your Instant Pot. Heat the olive oil and then add the onion and garlic. Sauté for 3 minutes to soften, stirring occasionally. Include the tomatoes, cook for 3 minutes and then add the quinoa, zucchinis, and mushrooms. Season with paprika, salt, and black pepper and stir with a spoon. Cook for 5-7 minutes.

Use a knife to cut the bell peppers in halves (lengthwise) and remove their seeds and stems. Spoon the quinoa mixture into the bell peppers. Put the peppers in a greased baking dish and pour the broth over. Wipe the pot clean with some paper towels, and pour the 1 cup water into it. After, fit the steamer rack at the bottom of the pot.

Place the baking dish on the rack, cover with aluminum foil, seal the lid, and select Pressure Cook for 15 minutes. Do a quick pressure release. Remove the aluminum foil and sprinkle with the gouda cheese. Close the air fry lid, select Bake and cook for 10 minutes at 375°F. Serve the peppers right away.

VEGETABLES & VEGAN

Creamy Cauliflower & Asparagus Farfalle

Servings: 4 | Ready in about: 60 minutes

INGREDIENTS

- 1 bunch asparagus, chopped
- 2 cups cauliflower florets
- 3 tbsp melted butter, divided
- Salt to taste
- 10 oz farfalle
- 3 garlic cloves, minced
- 2 ½ cups vegetable stock
- ½ cup heavy cream
- 1 cup cherry tomatoes, halved
- ¼ cup chopped basil
- ½ cup grated Parmesan cheese

DIRECTIONS

Put the air fry basket in your Instant Pot. Close the air fry lid, choose Air Fry, adjust the temperature to 375°F, and the time to 2 minutes. Pour the asparagus and cauliflower into a large bowl and drizzle with 1 tablespoon of melted butter. Season with ½ teaspoon of salt and toss. Open the cooker and transfer the vegetables to the basket.

Close the air fry lid, choose Air Fry, adjust the temperature to 375°F, and set the timer to 10 minutes. Press Start to begin roasting. After 5 minutes, carefully open the lid and mix the vegetables. Close the lid and continue cooking. When done roasting, take out the basket, and cover the top with aluminum foil. Set aside.

Place the farfalle into the inner pot and add the remaining butter. Using tongs, toss the farfalle to coat, and add the remaining salt, garlic, and water. Stir to combine. Seal the pressure lid, choose Pressure Cook on High, and the cooking time to 5 minutes. After cooking, do a quick pressure release and carefully open the lid.

Stir the heavy cream and tomatoes into the pasta, tossing well. Choose Sauté. Press Start to simmer the cream until the sauce has your desired consistency. Gently mix in the asparagus and cauliflower. Allow warming to soften the vegetables, then stir in the basil and Parmesan cheese. Dish the creamy farfalle and serve warm.

Spinach Pesto Spaghetti Squash

Servings: 4 | Ready in about: 11 minutes

INGREDIENTS

- 4 lb spaghetti squash
- 1 cup water

For the Pesto

- ½ cup spinach, chopped
- 2 tbsp walnuts
- 2 garlic cloves, minced
- Zest and juice from ½ lemon
- Salt and ground pepper, to taste
- ⅓ cup extra virgin olive oil

DIRECTIONS

In a food processor, put all the pesto ingredients and blend until everything is well incorporated. Season to taste and set aside. Put the squash on a flat surface and use a knife to slice in half lengthwise. Scoop out all seeds and discard them. Open your Instant Pot, pour the water into it and fit a trivet at the bottom.

Place the squash halves on the trivet, seal the lid, and select Steam for 5 minutes. Once ready, do a quick pressure release. Remove the squash halves onto a cutting board and use a fork to separate the pulp strands into spaghetti-like pieces. Return to the pot and close the air fry lid. Cook for 2 minutes on Broil. Top with the spinach pesto.

Crème de la Broc

Servings: 6 | Ready in about: 25 minutes

INGREDIENTS

- 1 ½ cups grated yellow and white Cheddar + extra for topping
- 3 cups heavy cream
- 3 cups vegetable broth
- 4 tbsp butter
- 4 tbsp flour
- 4 cups chopped broccoli florets
- 1 medium Red onion, chopped
- 3 cloves garlic, minced
- 1 tsp Italian Seasoning
- 1 ½ oz cream cheese

DIRECTIONS

Select Sauté on your Instant Pot and melt the butter once the pot is ready. Add the flour and use a spoon to stir until it clumps up. Gradually pour in the heavy cream while stirring until white sauce forms. Fetch out the butter sauce into a bowl and set aside. Add the onions, garlic, broth, broccoli, Italian seasoning, and cream cheese.

Use a wooden spoon to stir the mixture. Seal the lid, and select Pressure Cook on High for 12 minutes. Once the timer has ended, do a quick pressure release. Add in butter sauce and cheddar cheese, salt, and pepper. Close the air fry lid and cook on Broil mode for 3 minutes. Dish the soup, top with extra cheese, and serve.

Pilau Rice with Veggies

Servings: 4 | Ready in about: 30 minutes

INGREDIENTS

3 tbsp olive oil
1 tbsp ginger, minced
1 cup onion, chopped
1 cup green peas
1 cup carrot, chopped

1 cup mushroom, chopped
1 cup broccoli, chopped
1 tbsp chili powder
½ tbsp ground cumin
1 tsp garam masala

½ tsp turmeric powder
1 cup basmati rice, rinsed and drained
2 cups vegetable broth
1 tbsp lemon juice
2 tbsp chopped fresh cilantro

DIRECTIONS

Warm 1 tbsp olive oil on Sauté in your Instant Pot. Add in onion and ginger and cook for 3 minutes until soft. Stir in broccoli, green peas, mushrooms, and carrots. Cook for 1 more minute. Add turmeric powder, chili powder, garam masala, and cumin for seasoning. Cook for 1 minute until soft. Add ¼ cup water into the pot to deglaze.

Scrape the bottom to get rid of any browned bits. To the vegetables, add the remaining water and rice. Seal the pressure lid, choose Pressure Cook on High, and set the timer to 1 minute. Release pressure naturally. Use a fork to fluff rice, sprinkle with lemon juice. Divide onto plates and garnish with cilantro.

Pesto Minestrone with Cheesy Bread

Servings: 4 | Ready in about: 60 minutes

INGREDIENTS

3 tbsp ghee
1 medium red onion, diced
1 celery stalk, diced
1 large carrot, peeled and diced
1 small yellow squash, diced
1 (14-oz) can chopped tomatoes

1 (27-oz) can cannellini beans, rinsed
3 cups water
1 cup chopped zucchini
1 bay leaf
1 tsp mixed herbs
¼ tsp cayenne pepper

1 Pecorino Romano rind
3 tbsp butter, at room temperature
¼ cup grated Pecorino Romano cheese
1 garlic clove, minced
4 slices white bread
⅓ cup pesto

DIRECTIONS

On your Instant Pot, choose Sauté. Melt the ghee and sauté the onion, celery, and carrot for 3 minutes or until the vegetables start to soften. Stir in the yellow squash, tomatoes, beans, water, zucchini, bay leaf, mixed herbs, cayenne pepper, salt, and Pecorino Romano rind. Seal the pressure lid, choose Pressure Cook on High, and set the time to 4 minutes. In a bowl, mix the butter, shredded cheese, and garlic. Spread the mixture on the bread slices.

After cooking the soup, perform a natural pressure release for 10 minutes. Carefully open the lid. Adjust the taste of the soup with salt and black pepper, and remove the bay leaf. Put a trivet in the upper position of the pot and lay the bread slices on the trivet with the buttered-side up. Close the air fry lid.

Choose Broil, adjust the cook time to 5 minutes, and press Start to begin broiling. When the bread is crispy, remove the trivet and set aside. Ladle the soup into bowls and drizzle the pesto over. Serve with the garlic toasts.

Cheesy Stuffed Mushrooms

Servings: 4 | Ready in about: 40 minutes

INGREDIENTS

10 white mushrooms, stems removed
¼ cup roasted red bell peppers, chopped
1 red bell pepper, seeded and chopped
1 green onion, chopped
1 small onion, chopped
¼ cup grated Parmesan cheese
1 tbsp butter
½ tsp dried oregano
Salt and black pepper to taste

DIRECTIONS

Turn on your Instant Pot and select Sauté. Melt the butter and add the roasted and fresh peppers, green onion, onion, oregano, salt, and pepper. Use a spoon to mix and cook for 2 minutes. Spoon the bell pepper mixture into the mushrooms and place the stuffed mushrooms in the pot. Pour in ½ cup water. Seal the lid.

Select Pressure Cook on High for 5 minutes. Once the timer has ended, do a quick pressure release and open the lid. Sprinkle with parmesan cheese and close the air fry lid. Select Bake adjust the temperature to 380°F, and the time to 2 minutes and press Start button. Remove the stuffed mushrooms onto a plate and repeat the cooking process for the remaining mushrooms. Serve hot with a side of steamed green veggies and a sauce.

Easy Green Squash Gruyere

Servings: 4 | Ready in about: 70 minutes

INGREDIENTS

1 large green squash, sliced
3 tbsp melted unsalted butter
1½ cups panko breadcrumbs
⅓ cup grated Gruyere cheese
2 cups tomato sauce
1 cup shredded mozzarella cheese

DIRECTIONS

Season the squash with salt and place it on a wire rack to drain liquid for 10 minutes. In a bowl, combine melted butter, breadcrumbs, and Gruyere cheese. Rinse the squash slices with water and blot dry with paper towels. Arrange the squash in the inner pot in a single layer as much as possible and pour the tomato sauce over the slices.

Seal the pressure lid, choose Pressure Cook on High, and the time to 5 minutes. When the timer has read to the end, perform a quick pressure release. Sprinkle the squash slices with the mozzarella cheese. Close the air fry lid. Choose Bake, adjust the temperature to 375°F, and the cooking time to 2 minutes. Press Start to broil.

After, carefully open the lid and sprinkle the squash with the breadcrumb mixture. Close the air fry lid again, choose Bake, adjust the temperature to 375°F, and the cooking time to 8 minutes. Press Start to continue broiling.

Mashed Broccoli with Cream Cheese

Servings: 4 | Ready in about: 12 minutes

INGREDIENTS

3 heads broccoli, chopped
6 oz cream cheese
2 cloves garlic, crushed
2 tbsp butter, unsalted
Salt and black pepper to taste
2 cups water

DIRECTIONS

Turn on your Instant Pot and select Sauté. Drop in the butter; once it melts, add the garlic and cook for 30 seconds while stirring frequently to prevent the garlic from burning. Then, add the broccoli, water, salt, and pepper. Close the lid, secure the pressure valve, and select Pressure Cook on High for 5 minutes.

Once the timer has ended, do a quick pressure release and use a stick blender to mash the ingredients until smooth to your desired consistency and well combined. Stir in Cream cheese. Adjust the taste with salt and pepper. Close the air fry lid and cook for 2 minutes on Broil mode. Serve warm.

Eggplant Lasagna

Servings: 4 | Ready in about: 25 minutes

INGREDIENTS

3 large eggplants, sliced in ¼ inches
4 ¼ cups Marinara sauce
1 ½ cups shredded Mozzarella cheese
Cooking spray
Chopped fresh basil to garnish
¼ cup Parmesan cheese, grated

DIRECTIONS

Open the pot and grease it with cooking spray. Arrange the eggplant slices in a single layer on the bottom of the pot and sprinkle some cheese all over it. Arrange another layer of eggplant slices on the cheese, sprinkle this layer with cheese also, and repeat the layering of eggplant and cheese until both ingredients are exhausted.

Lightly spray the eggplant with cooking spray and pour the marinara sauce all over it. Close the lid and pressure valve, and select Pressure Cook on High for 8 minutes. Once the timer has stopped, do a quick pressure release, and open the lid. Sprinkle with Parmesan cheese, close the air fry lid and cook for 10 minutes on Bake at 380°F.

With two napkins in hand, gently remove the inner pot. Allow cooling for 10 minutes before serving. Garnish the lasagna with basil and serve warm as a side dish.

Chipotle Chili

Servings: 4 | Ready in about: 35 minutes

INGREDIENTS

4 celery stalks, chopped
2 (15-oz) cans diced tomatoes
1 tbsp olive oil
3 carrots, chopped
2 cloves garlic, minced
2 tsp smoked paprika
2 green bell pepper, diced
1 tbsp cinnamon powder
1 tbsp cumin powder
1 sweet onion, chopped
2 cups tomato sauce
1.5 oz dark chocolate, chopped
1 small chipotle, minced
1 ½ cups walnuts, chopped + to garnish
Chopped cilantro to garnish

DIRECTIONS

On your Instant Pot and select Sauté. Heat the oil and add the onion, celery, and carrots. Sauté for 4 minutes. Add the garlic, cumin, cinnamon, and paprika. Stir and cook for 2 minutes. Include bell peppers, tomatoes, tomato sauce, chipotle, ½ cup water, and walnuts stir. Seal the lid and select Pressure Cook for 15 minutes.

Once the timer has ended, do a quick pressure release, and open the lid. Pour the chopped chocolate in and stir it until it melts and is well incorporated into the chili. Adjust the taste with salt and pepper. Close the air fry lid and cook for 5 minutes on Broil. Garnish it with the remaining walnuts and cilantro. Serve with some noodles.

Vegan Carrot Gazpacho

Servings: 4 | Ready in about: 2 hour 30 minutes

INGREDIENTS

1 lb trimmed carrots
1 pinch salt
1 lb tomatoes, chopped
1 cucumber, peeled and chopped
¼ cup extra-virgin olive oil
2 tbsp lemon juice
1 red onion, chopped
2 cloves garlic
2 tbsp white wine vinegar

DIRECTIONS

To your Instant Pot, add carrots, salt, and water. Seal the pressure lid, choose Pressure Cook on High, and set the timer to 20 minutes. Once ready, do a quick release. Set the beets in a bowl and place in the refrigerator to cool.

In a blender, add carrots, cucumber, red onion, pepper, garlic, olive oil, tomatoes, lemon juice, vinegar, and salt. Blend until very smooth. Place gazpacho in a serving bowl, chill while covered for 2 hours.

VEGETABLES & VEGAN

Buttered Leafy Greens

Servings: 4 | Ready in about: 10 minutes

INGREDIENTS

2 lb baby spinach
1 lb kale leaves
½ lb Swiss chard
1 tbsp dried basil
Salt and black pepper to season
½ tbsp butter

DIRECTIONS

Turn on your Instant Pot, add the ½ cup water and fit a trivet at the bottom of the pot. Put the spinach, swiss chard, and kale on the trivet. Close the lid, secure the pressure valve, and select Steam mode on High pressure for 3 minutes. Once the timer has ended, do a quick pressure release and open the lid.

Remove the trivet with the wilted greens onto a plate and discard the water from the pot. Select Sauté and add the butter. Add the spinach and kale back to the pot and the dried basil. Season with salt and pepper and stir. Close the air fry lid and cook for 4 minutes on Bake at 380°F. Dish the greens into serving plates and serve as a side dish.

Green Cream Soup

Servings: 4 | Ready in about: 22 minutes

INGREDIENTS

½ lb kale leaves, chopped
½ lb spinach leaves, chopped
½ lb Swiss chard leaves, chopped
1 tbsp olive oil
1 onion, chopped
4 cloves garlic, minced
4 cups vegetable broth
1 ¼ cup heavy cream
Salt and pepper, to taste
1 ½ tbsp white wine vinegar
Chopped Peanuts to garnish

DIRECTIONS

Turn on your Instant Pot and select Sauté. Add the olive oil; once it has heated, add the onion and garlic and sauté for 2-3 minutes until soft. Add greens and vegetable broth. Close the lid, secure the pressure valve, and select Pressure Cook on High for 10 minutes. Once the timer has ended, do a quick pressure release.

Add the white wine vinegar, salt, and pepper. Use a stick blender to puree the ingredients in the pot. Close the air fry lid and cook for 3 minutes on Broil. Stir in heavy cream. Sprinkle with peanuts and serve.

Asian-Style Tofu Soup

Servings: 4 | Ready in about: 25 minutes

INGREDIENTS

2 tbsp Korean red pepper flakes (gochugaru)
16 oz firm Tofu
7 cloves garlic, minced
1 tbsp sugar
1 tbsp olive oil
2 tbsp ginger paste
¼ cup soy sauce
3 cup sliced bok choy
6 oz dry egg noodles
4 cups vegetable broth
1 cup sliced Shitake mushrooms
½ cup chopped cilantro

DIRECTIONS

Drain the liquid out of the tofu, pat the tofu dry with paper towels, and use a knife to cut them into 1-inch cubes. Turn your Instant Pot on and select Sauté. Pour the oil to heat, add the garlic and ginger, and sauté for 2 minutes. Add the sugar, broth, and soy sauce. Stir and cook for 30 seconds. Include the tofu and bok choy.

Seal the lid and select Pressure Cook on High for 10 minutes. Once the timer has ended, do a quick pressure release and open the lid. Add the zucchini noodles, give it a good stir, and close the air fry lid. Let the soup cook for 4 minutes on Broil mode. Use a soup spoon to fetch the soup into soup bowls, top with cilantro and enjoy.

Indian Vegan Curry

Servings: 3 | Ready in about: 25 minutes

INGREDIENTS

- 1 tbsp butter
- 1 onion, chopped
- 2 cloves garlic, minced
- 1 tsp ginger, grated
- 1 tsp ground cumin
- 1 tsp red chili powder
- 1 tsp salt
- ½ tsp ground turmeric
- 1 (15 oz) can chickpeas, drained
- 1 tomato, diced
- ⅓ cup water
- 5 cups collard greens, chopped
- ½ tsp garam masala
- 1 tsp lemon juice

DIRECTIONS

Melt butter on Sauté in your Instant Pot. Toss in the onion and cook for 2 minutes until soft. Mix in ginger, cumin powder, turmeric, red chili powder, garlic, and salt and cook for 30 seconds until crispy. Stir in tomatoes. In the pot, mix ⅓ water, tomato and chickpeas. Seal the pressure lid, choose Pressure Cook on High for 4 minutes.

When ready, release the pressure quickly. Into the chickpea mixture, stir in lemon juice, collard greens and garam masala until well coated. Cook for 2 to 3 minutes until collard greens wilt. Serve over rice or naan.

Aloo Gobi with Cilantro

Servings: 4 | Ready in about: 40 minutes

INGREDIENTS

- 1 tbsp vegetable oil
- 1 head cauliflower, cut into florets
- 1 potato, peeled and diced
- 1 tbsp ghee
- 2 tsp cumin seeds
- 1 onion, minced
- 4 garlic cloves, minced
- 1 tomato, cored and chopped
- 1 jalapeño pepper, deseeded and minced
- 1 tbsp curry paste
- 1 tsp ground turmeric
- ½ tsp chili pepper
- 1 cup water
- Salt to taste
- A handful of cilantro leaves, chopped

DIRECTIONS

Warm oil on Sauté in your Instant Pot. Add in potato and cauliflower and cook for 8 to 10 minutes until lightly browned. Add salt for seasoning. Set the vegetables to a bowl. Add ghee to the pot. Mix in cumin seeds and cook for 10 seconds until they start to pop. Add onion and garlic and cook for 3 minutes until softened.

Add in tomato, curry paste, chili pepper, jalapeño, curry, and turmeric and cook for 5 minutes until the tomato starts to break down. Return potato and cauliflower to the pot. Add water and salt and stir. Seal the pressure lid, choose Pressure Cook, and set the timer to 4 minutes. Release pressure naturally. Top with cilantro and serve.

Punjabi Palak Paneer

Servings: 4 | Ready in about: 20 minutes

INGREDIENTS

- ¼ cup milk
- 2 tbsp butter
- 1 tsp cumin seeds
- 1 tsp coriander seeds
- 1 tomato, chopped
- 1 tsp minced fresh ginger
- 1 tsp minced fresh garlic
- 1 red onion, chopped
- 1 lb spinach, chopped
- 1 tsp salt, or to taste
- 2 cups paneer, cubed
- 1 tsp chili powder

DIRECTIONS

Warm butter on Sauté in your Instant Pot. Add in garlic, cumin seeds, coriander seeds, chili powder, ginger, and garlic and fry for 1 minute until fragrant. Add onion and cook for 2 more minutes until crispy. Add in 1 cup water and spinach. Seal the pressure lid, choose Pressure Cook, and set the timer to 1 minute. When ready, release the pressure quickly. Pulse in a blender to obtain a smooth paste. Mix paneer and tomato with spinach mixture.

Green Minestrone

Servings: 4 | Ready in about: 30 minutes

INGREDIENTS

2 tbsp olive oil
1 head broccoli, cut into florets
4 celery stalks, sliced thinly

1 leek, sliced thinly
1 zucchini, chopped
1 cup green beans

2 cups vegetable broth
3 whole black peppercorns
2 cups chopped kale

DIRECTIONS

To your Instant Pot, add broccoli, leek, green beans, salt, peppercorns, zucchini, and celery. Mix in vegetable broth, oil, and cover with water. Seal the pressure lid, choose Pressure Cook on High, and set the timer to 4 minutes. Release pressure naturally for 5 minutes, then release the remaining pressure quickly. Add kale into the soup and stir. Set to Keep Warm and cook until tender.

Mushroom Brown Rice Pilaf

Servings: 4 | Ready in about: 15 minutes

INGREDIENTS

2 cups brown rice, rinsed
4 cups vegetable broth

3 tsp olive oil
1 cup Portobello mushrooms, sliced

¼ cup Romano cheese, grated
2 sprigs parsley, to garnish

DIRECTIONS

Heat the oil on Sauté in your Instant Pot and stir-fry the mushrooms for 3 minutes until golden. Season with salt, and add rice and broth. Close the lid, secure the pressure valve, and select Pressure Cook on High for 5 minutes. Once the timer has ended, do a quick pressure release and open the lid. Spread the cheese over and close the air fry lid. Select Bake, adjust to 375°F and the timer to 2 minutes. To serve, top with freshly chopped parsley.

Creamy Mashed Potatoes with Spinach

Servings: 6 | Ready in about: 30 minutes

INGREDIENTS

3 lb potatoes, peeled and quartered
1½ cups water

½ cup milk
⅓ cup butter

2 tbsp chopped fresh chives
2 cups spinach, chopped

DIRECTIONS

In your Instant Pot, mix water, salt and potatoes. Seal the pressure lid, choose Pressure Cook on High, and set the timer to 8 minutes. When ready, release the pressure quickly. Drain potatoes, and reserve the liquid in a bowl.

In a large bowl, mash the potatoes. Mix with butter and milk. Season with pepper and salt. With reserved cooking liquid, thin the potatoes to attain the desired consistency. Put the spinach in the remaining potato liquid and stir until wilted. Season with salt and pepper. Drain and serve with potato mash. Garnish with pepper and chives.

Herby-Garlic Potatoes

Servings: 4 | Ready in about: 30 minutes

INGREDIENTS

1 ½ lb potatoes
3 tbsp butter
3 cloves garlic, thinly sliced

2 tbsp fresh rosemary, chopped
½ tsp fresh thyme, chopped
½ tsp fresh parsley, chopped

¼ tsp ground black pepper
½ cup vegetable broth

DIRECTIONS

Pierce each potato to ensure there are no blowouts when placed under pressure. Melt butter on Sauté in your Instant Pot. Add in potatoes, rosemary, parsley, pepper, thyme, and garlic, and cook for 10 minutes until potatoes are browned. In a bowl, mix miso paste and vegetable stock. Stir into the mixture in the pressure cooker. Seal the pressure lid, choose Pressure Cook on High, and set the timer to 5 minutes. Do pressure quickly.

Tahini Sweet Potato Mash

Servings: 4 | Ready in about: 25 minutes

INGREDIENTS

2 lb sweet potatoes, peeled and cubed
2 tbsp tahini
1 tbsp sugar
¼ tsp ground nutmeg
Chopped fresh chives, for garnish
sea salt to taste

DIRECTIONS

To your Instant Pot, add 1 cup cold water and set a steamer basket into it. Add in sweet potato cubes. Seal the pressure lid, choose Pressure Cook, and set the timer to 8 minutes. When ready, release the pressure quickly. In a bowl, add cooked sweet potatoes and slightly mash. Using a hand mixer, whip in nutmeg, sugar, and tahini until the sweet potatoes attain the consistency you desire. Add salt for seasoning. Top with chives and serve.

Vegetarian Minestrone Soup

Servings: 4 | Ready in about: 40 minutes

INGREDIENTS

1 (15.5 oz) can Cannellini beans
1 Potato, peeled and diced
1 carrot, peeled and chopped
1 cup chopped butternut squash
2 small Red onions, cut into wedges
1 cup chopped celery
1 tbsp chopped fresh rosemary
8 sage leaves, chopped finely
1 bay leaf
4 cups vegetable broth
2 tsp olive oil
2 tbsp chopped fresh parsley

DIRECTIONS

Add the potato, carrot, squash, onion, celery, rosemary, sage, bay leaf, vegetable broth, salt, pepper, and olive oil to the pot of your Instant Pot. Close the lid, secure the pressure valve, and select Pressure Cook for 7 minutes.

Once done, do a quick pressure release. Add the cannellini beans and stir. Close the air fry lid and cook for 5 minutes on Broil. Garnish with fresh parsley and serve with a side of crusted bread.

Fall Celeriac Pumpkin Soup

Servings: 4 | Ready in about: 30 minutes

INGREDIENTS

1 celeriac, peeled and cubed
16 oz pumpkin puree
5 stalks celery, chopped
1 white onion, chopped
1 lb green beans, cut in 5 strips each
2 cups vegetable broth
3 cups spinach leaves
1 tbsp chopped basil leaves
¼ tsp dried thyme
⅛ tsp rubbed sage
Salt to taste

DIRECTIONS

Open your Instant Pot and pour in the celeriac, pumpkin puree, celery, onion, green beans, vegetable broth, basil leaves, thyme, sage, and salt. Seal the lid and select Steam for 5 minutes. Once ready, do a quick pressure release. Add in the spinach and stir. Close the air fry lid and cook for 3 minutes on Broil. Serve the soup into bowls.

Green Beans with Feta & Nuts

Servings: 6 | Ready in about: 15 minutes

INGREDIENTS

Juice from 1 lemon
1½ cups water

2 lb green beans, trimmed
1 cup chopped toasted pine nuts

1 cup feta cheese, crumbled
6 tbsp olive oil

DIRECTIONS

Add water to your Instant Pot. Set a trivet over the water. Loosely heap green beans on the trivet. Seal lid and cook on High Pressure for 5 minutes. When the cooking cycle is complete, release pressure quickly. Drop green beans into a salad bowl. Top with olive oil, feta cheese, pepper, and pine nuts.

Pesto Quinoa Bowls with Veggies

Servings: 2 | Ready in about: 30 minutes

INGREDIENTS

1 cup quinoa, rinsed
2 cups water
Salt and ground black pepper to taste
1 small beet, peeled and cubed

1 cup broccoli florets
1 carrot, peeled and chopped
½ lb Brussels sprouts
2 eggs

1 avocado, thinly sliced
¼ cup pesto sauce
Lemon wedges, for serving

DIRECTIONS

In your Instant Pot, mix water, salt, quinoa and pepper. Set a trivet to the pot over quinoa. On the trivet, place eggs, Brussels sprouts, broccoli, beet cubes, carrots, pepper, and salt. Seal the pressure lid, choose Pressure Cook on High, and set the timer to 1 minute. Release pressure naturally for 10 minutes. Remove the trivet from the pot.

Set the eggs in a bowl of ice water. Peel and halve the eggs. Use a fork to fluff the quinoa. Separate quinoa, broccoli, avocado, carrots, beet, Brussels sprouts, eggs, and a dollop of pesto into two bowls. Serve alongside a lemon.

Carrot & Lentil Chili

Servings: 4 | Ready in about: 30 minutes

INGREDIENTS

1 tbsp olive oil
1 onion, chopped
1 cup celery, chopped
2 garlic cloves, sliced

1 onion, chopped
3 cups vegetable stock
1 cup dried lentils, rinsed
4 carrots, halved lengthwise

1 tbsp harissa, or more to taste
½ tsp sea salt
A handful of fresh parsley, chopped

DIRECTIONS

Warm olive oil on Sauté in your Instant Pot. Add in onion, garlic, and celery, and cook for 5 minutes until onion is soft. Mix in lentils, carrots, and vegetable stock. Seal the pressure lid, choose Pressure Cook on High, and set the timer to 10 minutes. Release pressure naturally. Mix lentils with salt and harissa and serve topped with parsley.

Asparagus with Feta

Servings: 4 | Ready in about: 15 minutes

INGREDIENTS

1 cup water
1 lb asparagus spears, ends trimmed

1 tbsp olive oil
Salt and black pepper to taste

1 lemon, cut into wedges
1 cup feta cheese, cubed

DIRECTIONS

Into your Instant Pot, add water and set trivet over the water. Place steamer basket on the trivet. Place the asparagus into the steamer basket. Seal the pressure lid, choose Pressure Cook on High, and set the timer to 1 minute. When ready, release the pressure quickly. Add olive oil in a bowl and toss in asparagus until well coated. Season with pepper and salt. Serve alongside feta cheese and lemon wedges.

Steamed Artichokes with Lemon Aioli

Servings: 4 | Ready in about: 20 minutes

INGREDIENTS

4 artichokes, trimmed
1 lemon, halved
1 tsp lemon zest

1 tbsp lemon juice
3 cloves garlic, crushed
½ cup mayonnaise

1 cup water
Salt
1 small handful parsley, chopped

DIRECTIONS

On the artichokes cut ends, rub with lemon. Add water into your Instant Pot. Set a trivet over the water. Place the artichokes into the steamer basket with the points upwards. Sprinkle each with salt. Seal lid and cook on High pressure for 10 minutes. When ready, release the pressure quickly. In a bowl, combine mayonnaise, garlic, lemon juice, and lemon zest. Season to taste with salt. Serve with warm steamed artichokes sprinkled with parsley.

Thai Vegetable Stew

Servings: 4 | Ready in about: 30 minutes

INGREDIENTS

1 tbsp coconut oil
1 cup onion, chopped
1 tbsp fresh ginger, minced
2 garlic cloves, minced

3 carrots, peeled and chopped
1 red bell pepper, sliced
1 orange bell pepper, sliced
1 (14 oz) can coconut milk

1 cup bok choy, chopped
½ cup water
2 tbsp red curry paste

DIRECTIONS

Melt coconut oil on Sauté in your Instant Pot. Add in onion and cook for 3 to 4 minutes until soft. Add garlic and ginger and cook for 30 more seconds until soft. Mix in orange bell pepper, red bell pepper and carrots.

Cook for 3 to 4 minutes until the peppers become soft and tender. Add curry paste, bok choy, coconut milk, and water and stir well to obtain a consistent color of the sauce. Seal lid and cook for 1 minute on High Pressure. When ready, release the pressure quickly. Serve hot!

Parsley Mashed Cauliflower

Servings: 4 | Ready in about: 15 minutes

INGREDIENTS

1 head cauliflower
1 tbsp butter

¼ tsp celery salt
¼ cup heavy cream

1 tbsp fresh parsley, finely chopped
⅛ tsp freshly ground black pepper

DIRECTIONS

Into your Instant Pot, add 2 cups water and set trivet on top and lay cauliflower head onto the trivet. Seal the pressure lid, choose Pressure Cook on High, and set the timer to 8 minutes. Release the pressure quickly. Remove the trivet and drain liquid from the pot before returning to the base. Take back the cauliflower to the pot with pepper, heavy cream, salt, and butter. Use an immersion blender to blend until smooth. Top with parsley.

Mashed Parsnips & Cauliflower

Servings: 8 | Ready in about: 15 minutes

INGREDIENTS

1 ½ lb parsnips, peeled and cubed
1 head cauliflower, cut into small florets
2 garlic cloves
Salt and black pepper to taste
2 cups water
¼ cup sour cream
¼ cup grated Parmesan cheese
1 tbsp butter
2 tbsp minced chives

DIRECTIONS

In your Instant Pot, mix parsnips, garlic, water, salt, cauliflower, and pepper. Seal the pressure lid, choose Pressure Cook, and set the timer to 4 minutes. When ready, release the pressure quickly. Drain parsnips and cauliflower and return to pot. Add Parmesan, butter, and sour cream. Use a potato masher to mash until the desired consistency is attained. Into the mashed parsnip, add 1 tbsp chives. Place on a serving plate and garnish with remaining chives.

Spicy Cauliflower Rice with Peas

Servings: 2 | Ready in about: 15 minutes

INGREDIENTS

1 head cauliflower, cut into florets
1 cup water
2 tbsp olive oil
1 tsp chili powder
¼ cup green peas
1 tbsp chopped fresh parsley

DIRECTIONS

Into your Instant Pot, add water. Set a trivet over water. Add cauliflower into the steamer basket. Seal the pressure lid, choose Pressure Cook on High, and set the timer to 1 minute. When ready, release the pressure quickly. Remove the trivet. Drain water from the pot, pat dry, and return to pressure cooker base.

Set to Sauté the pot. Warm oil. Add in cauliflower and stir to break into smaller pieces like rice. Stir in chili powder, peas and salt. Place the cauliflower rice into plates and add parsley for garnishing.

Garlic Veggie Mash with Parmesan

Servings: 6 | Ready in about: 15 minutes

INGREDIENTS

3 lb Yukon Gold potatoes, chopped
1 ½ cups cauliflower, broken into florets
1 carrot, chopped
1 cup Parmesan cheese, shredded
¼ cup butter, melted
¼ cup milk
1 tsp salt
1 garlic clove, minced
Fresh parsley for garnish

DIRECTIONS

To your Instant Pot, add veggies, salt and cover with enough water. Seal the pressure lid, choose Pressure Cook on High, and set the timer to 10 minutes. When ready, release the pressure quickly. Drain the vegetables and mash them with a potato masher. Add garlic, butter and milk, and whisk until everything is well incorporated. Serve topped with parmesan cheese and chopped parsley.

Honey-Glazed Acorn Squash

Servings: 4 | Ready in about: 30 minutes

INGREDIENTS

½ cup water
3 tbsp honey, divided
1 lb acorn squash, cut into chunks
2 tbsp butter
1 tbsp dark brown sugar
1 tbsp cinnamon

DIRECTIONS

In a small bowl, mix 1 tbsp honey and water. Pour into your Instant Pot. Add in squash. Seal the and cook on Pressure Cook for 4 minutes. When ready, release the pressure quickly. Transfer the squash to a serving dish.

Turn your Instant Pot to Sauté. Mix brown sugar, cinnamon, the remaining 2 tbsp honey and the liquid in the pot Cook as you stir for 4 minutes to obtain a thick consistency and starts to turn caramelized and golden. Spread honey glaze over squash. Add pepper and salt for seasoning.

Red Beans & Rice

Servings: 4 | Ready in about: 1 hour

INGREDIENTS

1 cup red beans, rinsed
½ cup rice, rinsed
2 tbsp olive oil

½ tsp cayenne pepper
1 ½ cups vegetable broth
1 onion, diced

1 red bell pepper, diced
1 stalk celery, diced
1 tbsp fresh thyme leaves, or to taste

DIRECTIONS

Into your Instant Pot, add beans and water to cover about 1-inch. Seal the pressure lid, choose Pressure Cook on High, and set the timer to 1 minute. When ready, release the pressure quickly. Drain the beans and set aside. Rinse and pat dry the inner pot. Return inner pot to pressure cooker, add oil to the pot and press Sauté.

Add onion to the oil and cook for 3 minutes until soft. Add celery and pepper and cook for 1 to 2 minutes until fragrant. Add garlic and cook for 30 seconds until soft. Add rice. Transfer the beans back into inner pot and top with broth. Stir black pepper, thyme, cayenne pepper, and salt into the mixture.

Seal the pressure lid, choose Pressure Cook on High, and set the timer to 15 minutes. When ready, release pressure quickly. Add more thyme, black pepper and salt as desired.

Quick Crispy Kale Chips

Servings: 2 | Ready in about: 9 minutes

INGREDIENTS

4 cups kale, stemmed and packed
2 tbsp of olive oil

1 tbsp of yeast flakes
1 tsp of vegan seasoning

Salt to taste

DIRECTIONS

In a bowl, add the oil, kale, vegan seasoning, and yeast and mix well. Dump the kale in the air fry basket. Set the heat to 370°F, close the air fry lid and fry for a total of 6 minutes on Air Fry mode. Shake it from time to time.

Artichoke with Garlic Mayo

Servings: 4 | Ready in about: 20 minutes

INGREDIENTS

2 large artichokes
2 cups water

2 garlic cloves, smashed
½ cup mayonnaise

Salt and black pepper to taste
Juice of 1 lime

DIRECTIONS

Using a serrated knife, trim about 1 inch from the artichokes' top. Into your Instant Pot, add water and set trivet over. Lay the artichokes on the trivet. Seal lid and cook for 14 minutes. When ready, release the pressure quickly. Mix the mayonnaise with garlic and lime juice. Season with salt and pepper. Serve.

Avocado Rolls

Servings: 5 | Ready in about: 15 minutes | Servings: 5

INGREDIENTS

3 avocados, pitted and peeled
10 egg roll wrappers
1 tomato, diced
¼ tsp pepper
½ tsp salt

DIRECTIONS

Place all filling ingredients in a bowl. Mash with a fork until somewhat smooth. Divide the feeling between the egg wrappers. Wet your finger and brush along the edges so the wrappers can seal well. Roll and seal the wrappers. Arrange them on the lined air fry basket, and place it into your Instant Pot. Close the air fry lid and cook at 350°F for 5 minutes on Air Fry mode. Serve with chili dipping.

Spicy Pepper & Sweet Potato Skewers

Servings: 1 | Ready in about: 20 minutes

INGREDIENTS

1 large sweet potato
1 beetroot
1 green bell pepper
1 tsp chili flakes
¼ tsp black pepper
½ tsp turmeric
¼ tsp garlic powder
¼ tsp paprika
1 tbsp olive oil

DIRECTIONS

Soak 3 to 4 skewers until ready to use. Peel the veggies and cut them into bite-sized chunks. Place the chunks in a bowl along with the remaining ingredients. Mix until fully coated. Thread the veggies in this order: potato, pepper, beetroot. Place in your Instant Pot, close the air fry lid and cook for 15 minutes on Air Fry mode at 350°F. Flip skewers halfway through.

Pasta with Roasted Veggies

Servings: 6 | Ready in about: 25 minutes

INGREDIENTS

1 lb penne, cooked
1 zucchini, sliced
1 pepper, sliced
1 acorn squash, sliced
4 oz mushrooms, sliced
½ cup kalamata olives, pitted, halved
¼ cup olive oil
1 tsp Italian seasoning
1 cup grape tomatoes, halved
3 tbsp balsamic vinegar
2 tbsp chopped basil
Salt and pepper, to taste

DIRECTIONS

Combine the pepper, zucchini, squash, mushrooms, and olive oil, in a large bowl. Season with salt and pepper. Close the air fry lid and cook the veggies for 15 minutes on Air Fry mode at 380°F. In a large bowl, combine the penne, roasted vegetables, olives, tomatoes, Italian seasoning, and vinegar. Sprinkle basil and serve.

Veggie Skewers

Servings: 4 | Ready in about: 20 minutes

INGREDIENTS

2 tbsp cornflour
⅔ cup canned beans
⅓ cup grated carrots
2 boiled and mashed potatoes
¼ cup chopped fresh mint leaves
½ tsp garam masala powder
½ cup paneer
1 green chili
1-inch piece of fresh ginger
3 garlic cloves
Salt to taste

DIRECTIONS

Soak 12 skewers until ready to use. Place the beans, carrots, garlic, ginger, chili, paneer, and mint, in a food processor and process until smooth. Transfer to a bowl. Add the mashed potatoes, cornflour, salt, and garam masala powder to the bowl. Mix until fully incorporated. Divide the mixture into 12 equal pieces. Shape each of the pieces around a skewer. Close the air fry lid and cook the skewers for 10 minutes on Air Fry mode at 390°F.

Potato Filled Bread Rolls

Servings: 4 | Ready in about: 25 minutes

INGREDIENTS

8 slices of bread
5 large potatoes, boiled, mashed
½ tsp turmeric

2 green chilies, deseeded, chopped
1 medium onion, chopped
½ tsp mustard seeds

1 tbsp olive oil
2 sprigs curry leaf
Salt to taste

DIRECTIONS

Combine the olive oil, onion, curry leaves, and mustard seeds in the air fry basket. Cook for 5 minutes. Mix the onion mixture with the mashed potatoes, chilies, turmeric, and some salt. Divide the dough into 8 equal pieces.

Trim the sides of the bread, and wet it with some water. Make sure to get rid of the excess water. Take one wet bread slice in your palm and place one of the potato pieces in the center. Roll the bread over the filling, sealing the edges. Place the rolls onto a prepared baking dish, close the air fry lid and cook for 12 minutes on Air Fry at 350°F.

Quinoa & Veggie Stuffed Peppers

Servings: 1 | Ready in about: 16 minutes

INGREDIENTS

¼ cup cooked quinoa
1 bell pepper
½ tbsp diced onion

½ diced tomato, plus one tomato slice
¼ tsp smoked paprika
Salt and pepper, to taste

1 tsp olive oil
¼ tsp dried basil

DIRECTIONS

Core and clean the bell pepper to prepare it for stuffing. Brush the pepper with half of the olive oil on the outside. In a small bowl, combine all of the other ingredients, except the tomato slice and reserved half-teaspoon olive oil.

Stuff the pepper with the filling. Top with the tomato slice. Brush the tomato slice with the remaining half-teaspoon of oil and sprinkle with basil. Close the air fry lid and cook for 10 minutes on Air Fry mode at 350°F.

Vegetable Tortilla Pizza

Servings: 1 | Ready in about: 15 minutes

INGREDIENTS

1 ½ tbsp tomato paste
¼ cup grated cheddar cheese
¼ cup grated mozzarella cheese
1 tbsp cooked sweet corn

4 zucchini slices
4 eggplant slices
4 red onion Rings
½ green bell pepper, chopped

3 cherry tomatoes, quartered
1 tortilla
¼ tsp basil
¼ tsp oregano

DIRECTIONS

Spread the tomato paste on the tortilla. Arrange the zucchini and eggplant slices first, then green peppers, and onion rings. Lay the cherry tomatoes and sprinkle the sweet corn over. Sprinkle with oregano and basil. Top with cheddar and mozzarella. Place in the pot close the air fry lid and cook for 10 minutes on Air Fry mode at 350°F.

Roasted Vegetable Salad

Servings: 1 | Ready in about: 25 minutes

INGREDIENTS

1 potato, peeled and chopped
¼ onion, sliced
1 carrot, sliced diagonally
½ small beetroot, sliced
1 cup cherry tomatoes
Juice of 1 lemon
A handful of rocket salad
A handful of baby spinach
3 tbsp canned chickpeas
½ tsp cumin
½ tsp turmeric
¼ tsp sea salt
2 tbsp olive oil
Parmesan shavings

DIRECTIONS

Combine the onion, potato, cherry tomatoes, carrot, beetroot, cumin, seas salt, turmeric, and 1 tbsp olive oil in a bowl. Place in your Instant Pot, close the air fry lid and cook for 20 minutes on Air Fry mode at 390°F. Let cool for 2 minutes. Place the rocket, salad, spinach, lemon juice, and 1 tbsp olive oil, into a serving bowl. Mix to combine. Stir in the roasted veggies. Top with chickpeas and Parmesan shavings.

Simple Air Fried Ravioli

Servings: 6 | Ready in about: 15 minutes

INGREDIENTS

1 package cheese ravioli
2 cup Italian breadcrumbs
¼ cup Parmesan cheese
1 cup buttermilk
1 tsp olive oil
¼ tsp garlic powder

DIRECTIONS

In a bowl, combine the crumbs, Parmesan, garlic powder, and olive oil. Dip the ravioli in the buttermilk and then coat them with the breadcrumb mixture. Line a baking sheet with parchment paper and arrange the ravioli on it. Place in your Instant Pot and cook for 5 minutes on Air Fry at 390°F. Serve the ravioli with marinara jar sauce.

Poblano & Tomato Stuffed Squash

Servings: 3 | Ready in about: 50 minutes

INGREDIENTS

½ butternut squash
6 grape tomatoes, halved
1 poblano pepper, cut into strips
¼ cup grated mozzarella, optional
2 tsp olive oil divided
Salt and pepper, to taste

DIRECTIONS

Cut trim the ends and cut the squash lengthwise. Scoop the flash out, so you make room for the filling. Brush 1 tsp oil over the squash. Place in your Instant Pot and roast for 30 minutes.

Combine the other teaspoon of olive oil with the tomatoes and poblanos. Season with salt and pepper. Place the peppers and tomatoes into the squash. Close the air fry lid and cook for 15 minutes on Air Fry mode at 350°F.

Herby Millet with Cherry Tomatoes

Servings: 8 | Ready in about: 1 hour 15 minutes

INGREDIENTS

2 cups millet, rinsed and drained
4 cups vegetable stock
½ sweet onion, chopped
1 cup cherry tomatoes, cut into halves
1 tbsp fresh sage, chopped
1 tsp fresh thyme, chopped
1 tsp fresh parsley, chopped
Salt and ground black pepper to taste

DIRECTIONS

Add millet, onion, and vegetable stock the inner pot of your Instant Pot. Seal the pressure lid, choose Pressure Cook on High, and set the timer to 10 minutes. When ready, release pressure quickly. Fluff the millet with a fork, add in herbs and tomatoes and apply a seasoning of pepper and salt.

Green Lasagna Soup

Servings: 4 | Ready in about: 30 minutes

INGREDIENTS

1 tsp olive oil
1 cup leeks, chopped
2 garlic cloves minced
1 cup tomato paste

1 cup tomatoes, chopped
1 carrot, chopped
½ lb broccoli, chopped
¼ cup dried green lentils

2 tsp Italian seasoning
Salt to taste
2 cups vegetable broth
3 lasagna noodles

DIRECTIONS

Warm oil on Sauté in your Instant Pot. Add garlic and leeks and cook for 2 minutes until soft. Add tomato paste, carrot, Italian seasoning, broccoli, tomatoes, lentils, and salt. Stir in vegetable broth and lasagna pieces.

Seal the pressure lid, choose Pressure Cook on High, and set the timer to 3 minutes. Release pressure naturally for 10 minutes, then release the remaining pressure quickly. Divide soup into serving bowls and serve.

Chipotle Vegetarian Chili

Servings: 12 | Ready in about: 45 minutes

INGREDIENTS

1 (28 oz) can diced tomatoes
2 cups cashews, chopped
1 cup onion, chopped
1 cup red lentils

1 cup red quinoa
3 chipotle peppers, chopped
3 garlic cloves, minced
2 tbsp chili powder

1 tsp salt
2 cups carrots, chopped
1 (15 oz) can black beans, rinsed
¼ cup fresh parsley, chopped

DIRECTIONS

In your Instant Pot, mix tomatoes, onion, chipotle peppers, chili powder, lentils, walnuts, carrots, quinoa, garlic, and salt. Stir 4 cups water. Seal the pressure lid, choose Pressure Cook on High, and set the timer to 30 minutes. When ready, release the pressure quickly. Into the chili, add black beans. Simmer on Keep Warm until heated through. Add ¼ cup to 1 cup water if you want a thinner consistency. Top with a garnish of parsley.

Crispy Nachos

Servings: 2 | Ready in about: 20 minutes

INGREDIENTS

1 cup sweet corn
1 cup all-purpose flour

1 tbsp butter
½ tsp chili powder

2-3 tbsp water
Salt to taste

DIRECTIONS

Add a small amount of water to the sweet corn and grind until you obtain an excellent paste. In a bowl, add the flour, the salt, the chili powder, the butter and mix very well. Add the corn and stir well.

Start to knead with your palm until you obtain a stiff dough. Dust a little bit of flour and spread the batter with a rolling pin. Make it around ½ inch thick. Cut it in any shape you want and cook in your Instant Pot for 10 minutes on Air Fry mode at 350°F. Serve with guacamole salsa.

Colorful Vegetable Medley

Servings: 4 | Ready in about: 15 minutes

INGREDIENTS

1 small head broccoli, broken into florets
16 asparagus, trimmed
1 head cauliflower, broken into florets
5 oz green beans
2 carrots, cut into ¼-inch rounds
Salt to taste

DIRECTIONS

Into your Instant Pot, add 1 cup water and set trivet on top of water and place steamer basket on top of the trivet. In an even layer, spread green beans, broccoli, cauliflower, asparagus, and carrots in the steamer basket. Seal the pressure lid, choose Pressure Cook on High, and set the timer to 3 minutes on High. When ready, release the pressure quickly. Remove steamer basket from cooker and add salt to vegetables for seasoning. Serve immediately.

Grilled Tofu Sandwich

Servings: 1 | Ready in about: 20 minutes

INGREDIENTS

2 slices of bread
1-inch thick Tofu slice
¼ cup red cabbage, shredded
2 tsp olive oil divided
¼ tsp vinegar
Salt and pepper, to taste

DIRECTIONS

Place the bread slices and toast for 3 minutes on Roast mode at 350°F. Set aside. Brush the tofu with 1 tsp of oil, and place in the basket of your Instant Pot. Bake for 5 minutes on each side on Roast mode at 350°F. Combine the cabbage, remaining oil, and vinegar, and season with salt and pepper. Place the tofu on top of one bread slice, place the cabbage over, and top with the other bread slice.

Paneer Cheese Balls

Servings: 2 | Ready in about: 12 minutes

INGREDIENTS

2 oz paneer cheese
2 tbsp flour
2 medium onions, chopped
1 tbsp corn flour
1 green chili, chopped
A 1-inch ginger piece, chopped
1 tsp red chili powder
a few leaves of coriander, chopped
1 tbsp olive oil

DIRECTIONS

Mix all ingredients, except the oil and the cheese. Take a small part of the mixture, roll it up and slowly press to flatten it. Stuff in 1 cube of cheese and seal the edges. Repeat with the rest of the mixture. Close the air fry lid and fry the balls in your Instant Pot for 12 minutes on Air Fry mode and at 390°F. Serve hot, with ketchup.

Morning Burrito Bowls

Servings: 4 | Ready in about: 30 minutes

INGREDIENTS

2 tbsp olive oil
1 onion
2 garlic cloves, minced
1 tbsp chili powder
2 tsp ground cumin
2 tsp paprika
1 tsp salt
½ tsp black pepper
¼ tsp cayenne pepper
1 cup quinoa, rinsed
1 (14.5 oz) can diced tomatoes
1 (14.5 oz) can black beans, drained
1 ½ cups vegetable stock
1 cup frozen corn kernels
2 tbsp chopped cilantro
1 tbsp roughly chopped fresh coriander
Cheddar cheese, grated for garnish
1 avocado, sliced

DIRECTIONS

Warm oil on Sauté in your Instant Pot. Add in onion and cook for 3 to 5 minutes until fragrant. Add garlic and cook for 2 more minutes until soft and golden brown. Add in chili powder, paprika, cayenne pepper, salt, cumin, and black pepper and cook for 1 minute until spices are soft. Pour quinoa into onion and spice mixture.

Stir to coat quinoa completely in spices. Add diced tomatoes, black beans, vegetable stock, and corn. Stir to combine. Seal the pressure lid, choose Pressure Cook for 7 minutes. When ready, release the pressure quickly. Fluff quinoa and season with pepper and salt. Stir in cilantro and top with cheese and avocado slices.

Paneer Cutlet

Servings: 1 | Ready in about: 15 minutes

INGREDIENTS

2 cup grated paneer
1 cup grated cheese
½ tsp chai masala
1 tsp butter
½ tsp garlic powder
1 small onion, finely chopped

DIRECTIONS

Mix all ingredients in a bowl. Make cutlets out of the mixture and place them on the greased baking dish. Place the baking dish in your Instant Pot and cook the cutlets on Air Fry for 10 minutes at 350°F.

Rosemary Sweet Potato Medallions

Servings: 4 | Ready in about: 25 minutes

INGREDIENTS

1 cup water
1 tbsp fresh rosemary
1 tsp garlic powder
4 sweet potatoes, scrubbed clean
2 tbsp butter
Salt to taste

DIRECTIONS

Into your Instant Pot, add water and place a trivet over the water. Use a fork to prick sweet potatoes all over and set onto the trivet. Seal the pressure lid, choose Pressure Cook on High, and set the timer to 12 minutes.

When ready, release the pressure quickly. Transfer sweet potatoes to a cutting board and slice into 1/2-inch medallions and ensure they are peeled. Melt butter on Sauté. Add in the medallions and cook each side for 2 to 3 minutes until browned. Apply salt and garlic powder to season. Serve topped with fresh rosemary.

Quick Crispy Cheese Lings

Servings: 4 | Ready in about: 15 minutes

INGREDIENTS

4 cups grated cheddar cheese
1 cup all-purpose flour
1 tbsp butter
1 tbsp baking powder
¼ tsp chili powder
¼ tsp salt

DIRECTIONS

Mix the flour and the baking powder. Add the chili powder, salt, butter, cheese and 1-2 tbsp of water to the mixture. Make a stiff dough. Knead the dough for a while. Sprinkle a tbsp or so of flour on the table.

Take a rolling pin and roll the dough into ½-inch thickness. Cut the dough in any shape you want. Close the air fry lid and fry the cheese lings for 6 minutes at 370°F on Air Fry mode.

FISH & SEAFOOD

Herb Salmon with Barley & Haricot Verts

Servings: 4 | Ready in about: 50 minutes

INGREDIENTS

- 1 cup pearl barley
- 2 cups water
- 4 salmon fillets
- 8 oz green beans haricot verts, trimmed
- 1 tbsp olive oil
- Salt and black pepper to taste
- 4 tbsp melted butter
- ½ tbsp brown sugar
- ½ tbsp freshly squeezed lemon juice
- ½ tsp dried rosemary
- 2 garlic cloves, minced
- ½ tsp dried thyme

DIRECTIONS

Pour the barley and water into your Instant Pot and mix to combine. Place in a trivet. Lay the salmon fillets on the trivet. Seal the pressure lid, choose Pressure Cook on High and set the time to 2 minutes. In a bowl, toss the green beans with olive oil, pepper, and salt. In another bowl, mix pepper, salt, butter, brown sugar, lemon juice, rosemary, garlic, and rosemary. When done cooking the rice and salmon, perform a quick pressure release.

Gently pat the salmon dry with a paper towel, then coat with the buttery herb sauce. Position the haricots vert around the salmon. Close the air fry lid, choose Broil and set the time to 7 minutes. When ready, remove the salmon from the trivet, and serve with the barley and haricots vert.

Lemon Cod Goujons & Rosemary Chips

Servings: 4 | Ready in about: 100 minutes

INGREDIENTS

- 2 eggs
- 1 cup arrowroot starch
- 1 cup flour
- ½ tbsp cayenne powder
- 1 tbsp cumin powder
- Salt and black pepper to taste
- 4 cod fillets, cut into strips
- Zest and juice from 1 lemon
- 2 potatoes, cut into chips
- 2 tbsp olive oil
- 3 tbsp fresh rosemary, chopped
- 4 lemon wedges to serve

DIRECTIONS

In a bowl, whisk the eggs, lemon zest, and lemon juice. In another bowl, combine the arrowroot starch, flour, cayenne powder, cumin, black pepper, and salt. Coat each cod strip in the egg mixture, and then dredge in the flour mixture, coating well on all sides. Place the coated fish in the greased basket and oil with cooking spray.

Close the air fry lid. Choose Air Fry, set the temperature to 375°F, and the time to 15 minutes. Toss the potatoes with oil and season with salt and pepper. After 15 minutes, check the fish making sure the pieces are as crispy as desired. Remove the fish from the basket. Pour the potatoes into the basket.

Close the air fry lid, choose Air Fry, set the temperature to 400°F, and the time to 24 minutes. After 12 minutes, open the lid, and shake the fries. Return the basket to the pot and close the lid to continue cooking until crispy. When ready, sprinkle with fresh rosemary. Serve the fish with the potatoes and lemon wedges.

Crispy Cod on Lentils

Servings: 4 | Ready in about: 65 minutes

INGREDIENTS

- 1 tbsp olive oil
- 2 cups lentils, soaked
- 1 yellow bell pepper, diced
- 1 red bell pepper, diced
- 4 cups vegetable broth
- 1 cup panko breadcrumbs
- 4 tbsp melted butter
- ¼ cup minced fresh cilantro
- 1 tsp lemon zest
- 1 lemon, juiced
- 1 tsp salt
- 4 cod fillets

DIRECTIONS

Choose Sauté on your Instant Pot. Combine the oil, lentils, bell peppers in the pot and cook for 1 minute. Mix in the broth. Seal the pressure lid, choose Pressure Cook, and set the time to 6 minutes. In a bowl, combine the breadcrumbs, butter, cilantro, lemon zest, lemon juice, and salt. Spoon the breadcrumb mixture on the cod fillet.

When cooking ended, perform a quick pressure release. Fix a trivet in the pot, which will be over the lentils. Lay the cod fillets on the trivet. Close the air fry lid. Choose Air Fry, set the temperature to 350°F, and set the time to 12 minutes. When ready, share the lentils into four serving plates, and top with salmon.

Tuna Salad with Asparagus & Potatoes

Servings: 4 | Ready in about: 60 MinutesUTES

INGREDIENTS

1½ lb potatoes, quartered
3 tbsp olive oil
Salt and black pepper to taste

8 oz asparagus, cut into three
2 tbsp red wine vinegar, divided
½ cup pimento stuffed green olives

½ cup chopped roasted red peppers
2 tbsp chopped fresh parsley
2 cans tuna, drained

DIRECTIONS

Pour 1 cup water into your Instant Pot and set in a trivet. Place the potatoes on the trivet. Seal the pressure lid. Choose Pressure Cook on High and the cook time to 4 minutes. After pressure cooking, perform a quick pressure release and carefully open the pressure lid. Take out a trivet, empty the water, and return the pot to the base. Arrange the potatoes and asparagus on the air fry basket. Drizzle some olive oil on them and season with salt.

Place the basket in the pot. Close the air fry lid, choose Air Fry, adjust the temperature to 375°F, and the cook time to 12 minutes. After 8 minutes, open the lid, and check the veggies. The asparagus will have started browning and crisping. Gently toss with the potatoes and close the lid. Continue cooking for the remaining 4 minutes.

Pour the asparagus and potatoes into a salad bowl. Sprinkle with some red wine vinegar and mix to coat. In a bowl, pour the remaining oil, remaining vinegar, salt, and pepper. Whisk to combine. Add in the roasted red peppers, olives, parsley, and tuna. Drizzle the dressing over the salad and mix to coat. Serve.

Farfalle Tuna Casserole with Cheese

Servings: 4 | Ready in about: 60 minutes

INGREDIENTS

1 tbsp olive oil
1 medium onion, chopped
1 large carrot, chopped
6 oz farfalle

1 (12-oz) can full cream milk
1 cup vegetable broth
2 cups shredded Monterey Jack cheese
2 tsp cornstarch

2 (5- to 6-oz) cans tuna, drained
1 cup chopped green beans
2 ½ cups panko breadcrumbs
3 tbsp butter, melted

DIRECTIONS

On your Instant Pot, choose Sauté. Heat the oil until shimmering and sauté the onion and carrots for 3 minutes, stirring, until softened. Add the farfalle, ¾ cup of milk, broth, and salt to the pot. Stir to combine and submerge the farfalle in the liquid with a spoon. Seal the pressure lid, choose Pressure Cook, and the cook time to 5 minutes. After cooking, do a quick pressure release and carefully open the pressure lid.

Choose Sauté and adjust to Less for low heat. Pour the remaining milk on the farfalle. In a medium bowl, mix the cheese and cornstarch evenly and add the cheese mixture by large handfuls to the sauce while stirring until the cheese melts and the sauce thickens. Add the tuna and green beans, gently stir. Heat for 2 minutes.

In another bowl, mix the crumbs and melted butter. Spread the crumbs over the casserole. Close the air fry lid and press Broil. Adjust the time to 5 minutes. When ready, the topping should be crisp and brown. Serve immediately.

Autumn Succotash with Basil-Crusted Fish

Servings: 4 | Ready in about: 65 minutes

INGREDIENTS

- 1 tbsp olive oil
- ½ small onion, chopped
- 1 garlic clove, minced
- 1 medium red chili, seeded and chopped
- 1 cup frozen corn
- 1 cup frozen mixed beans
- 1 cup butternut squash, cubed
- 1 bay leaf
- ¼ tsp cayenne pepper
- ¼ cup chicken stock
- ½ tsp Worcestershire sauce
- 1 tsp salt, divided
- 4 white fish fillets, at least 1 inch thick
- ¼ cup mayonnaise
- 1 tbsp Dijon-style mustard
- 1 ½ cups breadcrumbs
- 1 large tomato, seeded and chopped
- ¼ cup chopped fresh basil

DIRECTIONS

Press Sauté on your Instant Pot. Heat the oil and sauté the onion, garlic, and red chili pepper in the oil for 4 minutes or until the vegetables are soft. Stir in the corn, squash, mixed beans, bay leaf, cayenne, stock, Worcestershire sauce, and ½ teaspoon salt. Seal the pressure lid, choose Pressure Cook and the cook time to 5 minutes.

Season the fish fillets with the remaining salt. In a small bowl, mix the mayonnaise and mustard. Pour the breadcrumbs and basil into another bowl. Use a brush to spread the mayonnaise mixture on all sides of the fish and dredge each piece in the basil breadcrumbs to be properly coated.

Once the succotash is ready, perform a quick pressure release and carefully open the pressure lid. Stir in the tomato and remove the bay leaf. Set a trivet in the upper position of the pot, line with aluminum foil, and carefully lay the fish in a trivet. Oil the top of the fish with cooking spray. Close the air fry lid and choose Bake.

Adjust the temperature to 375°F and the time to 8 minutes. After 4 minutes, open the lid. Turn them over and oil the other side with cooking spray. Close the lid and continue cooking. Serve the fillets with the succotash.

Traditional Mahi Mahi

Servings: 4 | Ready in about: 10 minutes

INGREDIENTS

- 4 Mahi Mahi fillets, fresh
- 4 cloves garlic, minced
- 1 ¼ -inch ginger, grated
- Salt and black pepper
- 2 tbsp chili powder
- 1 tbsp Sriracha sauce
- 1 ½ tbsp maple syrup
- 1 lime, juiced
- 1 cup water

DIRECTIONS

Place mahi mahi on a plate and season with salt and pepper on both sides. In a bowl, add garlic, ginger, chili powder, sriracha sauce, maple syrup, and lime juice. Use a spoon to mix it. Brush the mixture on the fillet.

Then, open your Instant Pot, pour in the water and fit a trivet at the bottom of the pot. Put the fillets on the trivet. Close the lid, secure the pressure valve, and select Steam mode on High pressure for 5 minutes. Once ready, do a quick pressure release, and open the lid. Remove the mahi mahi onto serving plates. Serve with steamed or braised asparagus. For a crispier taste, cook them for 2 minutes on Air Fry mode, at 300°F.

Salmon with Dill Chutney

Servings: 2 | Ready in about: 15 minutes

INGREDIENTS

- 2 salmon fillets

For Chutney
- ¼ cup fresh dill
- Juice from ½ lemon
- Juice from ½ lemon
- Sea salt to taste
- ¼ cup extra virgin olive oil
- ¼ tsp paprika

DIRECTIONS

In a food processor, blend all the chutney ingredients until creamy. To your Instant Pot, add 1 cup water and place a trivet. Arrange salmon fillets skin-side down on the trivet. Drizzle lemon juice over salmon and apply a seasoning of paprika. Seal the lid, choose Pressure Cook, and set the timer to 3 minutes. When ready, release the pressure quickly. Season the fillets with pepper and salt, transfer to a serving plate and top with the dill chutney.

Cajun Salmon with Creamy Grits

Servings: 4 | Ready in about: 100 minutes

INGREDIENTS

¾ cup corn grits
1 ½ cups coconut milk
1 ½ cups vegetable stock

3 tbsp butter, divided
Salt to taste
½ tbsp Cajun seasoning

1 tbsp packed brown sugar
4 salmon fillets, skin removed
Cooking spray

DIRECTIONS

Pour the grits into a heatproof bowl. Add the coconut milk, stock, 1 tablespoon of butter, and salt. Stir and cover the bowl with foil. Pour the water into your Instant Pot. Put in a trivet and place the bowl on top. Seal the pressure lid, choose Pressure Cook and the cook time to 15 minutes. In a bowl combine Cajun, brown sugar, and salt.

Oil the fillets on one side with cooking spray and place one or two at a time with sprayed-side down into the spice mixture. Oil the other sides and turn over to coat that side in the seasoning. Repeat the process with the remaining fillets. Once the grits are ready, perform a natural pressure release for 10 minutes.

Remove the trivet and bowl from the pot. Add the remaining butter to the grits and stir to combine well. Cover again with aluminum foil and return the bowl to the pot (without a trivet). Fix a trivet in the upper position of the pot and put the salmon fillets on the trivet. Close the air fry lid and choose Bake.

Adjust the temperature to 400°F and the cook time to 12 minutes. After 6 minutes, open the lid and use tongs to turn the fillets over. Close the lid and continue cooking. When the salmon is ready, take out a trivet. Remove the bowl of grits and take off the foil. Stir and serve immediately with the salmon.

Mackerel en Papillote with Vegetables

Servings: 6 | Ready in about: 25 minutes + marinating time

INGREDIENTS

3 large whole mackerel, cut into 2 pieces
1 lb asparagus, trimmed
1 carrot, cut into sticks
1 celery stalk, cut into sticks

½ cup butter, at room temperature
6 medium tomatoes, quartered
1 large brown onion, sliced thinly
1 Orange Bell pepper, cut into sticks

Salt and black pepper to taste
2 ½ tbsp Pernod
3 cloves garlic, minced
2 lemons, cut into wedges

DIRECTIONS

Cut out 6 pieces of parchment paper a little longer and wider than a piece of fish with kitchen scissors. Then, cut out 6 pieces of foil slightly longer than the parchment papers. Lay the foil wraps on a flat surface and place each parchment paper on each aluminium foil. In a bowl, add tomatoes, onions, garlic, bell pepper, pernod, butter, asparagus, carrot, celery, salt, and pepper. Use a spoon to mix them.

Place each fish piece on the layer of parchment and foil wraps. Spoon the vegetable mixture on each fish. Wrap the fish and place the packets in the refrigerator for 2 hours. Remove the fish to a flat surface. Pour in your Instant Pot 1 cup water and fit a trivet. Put the packets on the trivet. Seal the lid and select Steam for 3 minutes.

Once the timer has ended, do a quick pressure release, and open the lid. Remove the trivet with the fish packets onto a flat surface. Carefully open the foil and using a spatula. Return the packets to the pot, on top of the trivet. Close the air fry lid and cook on Air Fry for 3 minutes at 300°F. Then, remove to serving plates. Serve with lemon.

Haddock with Sanfaina

Servings: 4 | Ready in about: 40 minutes

INGREDIENTS

4 haddock fillets
¼ tsp salt
3 tbsp olive oil
½ small onion, sliced
1 jalapeño pepper, seeded and minced

2 large garlic cloves, minced
1 eggplant, cubed
1 bell pepper, chopped
1 (14.5-oz) can diced tomatoes, drained
1 bay leaf

½ tsp dried basil
⅓ cup sliced green olives
¼ cup chopped fresh chervil, divided
3 tbsp capers, divided

DIRECTIONS

Season the fish on both sides with salt, place in the refrigerator, and make the sauce. Press Sauté on your Instant Pot. Melt the butter until no longer foaming. Add onion, eggplant, bell pepper, jalapeño, and garlic. Sauté for 5 minutes. Stir in the tomatoes, bay leaf, basil, olives, half of the chervil, and half of the capers. Remove the fish from the refrigerator and lay on the vegetables in the pot.

Seal the pressure lid, choose Pressure Cook, adjust the pressure to Low and the cook time to 3 minutes. After cooking, do a quick pressure release and carefully open the lid. Remove and discard the bay leaf. Transfer the fish to a serving platter and spoon the sauce over. Sprinkle with the remaining chervil and capers. Serve.

Mediterranean-Style Steamed Cod

Servings: 4 | Ready in about: 20 minutes

INGREDIENTS

1 lb cherry tomatoes, halved
1 bunch fresh thyme sprigs
4 fillets cod

1 tsp olive oil
1 clove garlic, pressed
1 cup white rice

1 cup Kalamata olives
2 tbsp pickled capers
1 tbsp olive oil, divided

DIRECTIONS

Line a parchment paper to the steamer basket of your Instant Pot. Place about half the tomatoes in a single layer on the paper. Sprinkle with thyme, reserving some for garnish. Arrange cod fillets on the top of tomatoes. Sprinkle with a little bit of olive oil. Spread the garlic, pepper, salt, and remaining tomatoes over the fish. In the pot, mix rice and water. Lay a trivet over the rice and 2 cups water. Lower steamer basket onto the trivet.

Seal the pressure lid, choose Pressure Cook on High, and set the timer to 7 minutes. When ready, release the pressure quickly. Remove the steamer basket and trivet from the pot. Use a fork to fluff rice. Plate the fish fillets and apply a garnish of olives, reserved thyme, pepper, remaining olive oil, and capers. Serve with rice.

Pistachio Crusted Salmon

Servings: 1 | Ready in about: 15 minutes

INGREDIENTS

1 salmon fillet
1 tsp mustard
3 tbsp pistachios

Pinch of sea salt
Pinch of garlic powder
Pinch of black pepper

1 tsp lemon juice
1 tsp grated Parmesan cheese
1 tsp olive oil

DIRECTIONS

Whisk the mustard and lemon juice together. Season the salmon with salt, pepper, and garlic powder. Brush the olive oil on all sides. Brush the mustard-lemon mixture on top of the salmon. Chop the pistachios finely, and combine them with the Parmesan cheese. Sprinkle them on top of the salmon. Place the salmon in the air fry basket with the skin side down. Close the air fry lid and cook for 10 minutes on Air Fry mode at 350°F.

Italian-Style Flounder

Servings: 4 | Ready in about: 70 minutes

INGREDIENTS

3 slices prosciutto, chopped
½ small red onion, chopped
Salt and black pepper to taste
2 (6-oz) bags baby kale
½ cup whipping cream
4 flounder fillets
3 tbsp unsalted butter, melted
2 tbsp chopped fresh parsley
1 cup panko breadcrumbs

DIRECTIONS

On your Instant Pot, choose Sauté. Add the prosciutto and cook until crispy, about 6 minutes. Stir in the red onions and cook for about 2 minutes or until the onions start to soften. Sprinkle with salt. Fetch the kale into your Instant Pot and cook, stirring frequently until wilted and most of the liquid has evaporated, about 4-5 minutes.

Mix in the whipping cream. Lay the flounder fillets over the kale in a single layer. Brush 1 tablespoon of the melted butter over the fillets and sprinkle with the remaining salt and black pepper. Close the air fry lid and choose Bake. Adjust the temperature to 300°F and the cook time to 3 minutes.

Combine the remaining butter, parsley and breadcrumbs in a bowl. When done, open the air fry lid. Spoon the breadcrumbs mixture on the fillets. Close the air fry lid and choose Bake. Adjust the temperature to 400°F and the cook time to 6 minutes. After about 4 minutes, open the lid and check the fish. The breadcrumbs should be golden brown and crisp. If not, close the lid and continue to cook for an additional two minutes.

Monk Fish with Greens

Servings: 4 | Ready in about: 22 minutes

INGREDIENTS

2 tbsp olive oil
4 monk fish fillets, cut in 2 pieces each
½ cup chopped green beans
2 cloves garlic, sliced
1 cup kale leaves
½ lb baby bok choy, chopped largely
1 lemon, zested and juiced
Lemon wedges to serve
Salt and white pepper to taste

DIRECTIONS

Pour the coconut oil, garlic, red chili, and green beans in your Instant Pot. Stir fry for 5 minutes on Sauté. Add the kale leaves, and cook them to wilt, about 3 minutes. Place the fish on a plate and season with salt, white pepper, and lemon zest. After, remove the green beans and kale into a plate and set aside.

Back to the pot, add the olive oil and fish. Brown the fillets on each side for about 2 minutes and then add the bok choy in. Pour the lemon juice over the fish and gently stir. Cook for 2 minutes. Spoon the fish with bok choy over the green beans and kale. Serve with a side of lemon wedges and there, you have a complete meal.

Steamed Sea Bass with Turnips

Servings: 4 | Ready in about: 15 minutes

INGREDIENTS

1 lemon, sliced
4 sea bass fillets
4 sprigs thyme
1 white onion, sliced into thin rings
2 turnips, sliced
2 tsp olive oil

DIRECTIONS

Add 1 cup water to your Instant Pot. Set in a trivet. Line a parchment paper to the bottom of steamer basket. Place lemon slices in a single layer on the trivet. Arrange fillets on the top, cover with onion and thyme sprigs and top with turnip slices. Drizzle olive oil over the mixture. Put steamer basket onto the trivet. Seal lid and cook on Low for 8 minutes. When ready, release pressure quickly. Serve over the delicate onion rings and thinly sliced turnips.

Parmesan Tilapia

Servings: 4 | Ready in about: 15 minutes

INGREDIENTS

¾ cup grated Parmesan cheese
1 tbsp olive oil

2 tsp paprika
1 tbsp chopped parsley

¼ tsp garlic powder
4 tilapia fillets

DIRECTIONS

Mix parsley, Parmesan, garlic, salt, and paprika, in a shallow bowl. Brush the olive oil over the fillets, and then coat them with the Parmesan mixture. Place the tilapia onto a lined baking sheet, and then into your Instant Pot. Close the air fry lid and cook for about 4 to 5 minutes on all sides on Air Fry mode at 350°F. Serve.

Paprika & Garlic Salmon

Servings: 4 | Ready in about: 10 minutes

INGREDIENTS

4 (5 oz) salmon fillets
2 tsp cumin powder
1 ½ tsp paprika

2 tbsp chopped parsley
2 tbsp olive oil
2 tbsp hot water

1 tbsp maple syrup
2 cloves garlic, minced
1 lime, juiced

DIRECTIONS

In a bowl, add cumin, paprika, parsley, olive oil, hot water, maple syrup, garlic, and lime juice. Mix with a whisk. Set aside. Open your Instant Pot and pour in 1 cup water. Fit in a trivet. Place salmon on the trivet. Seal the lid and select Steam for 3 minutes. Once the timer has ended, do a quick pressure release and open the pot.

Close the air fry lid and cook on Air Fry mode for 3 minutes at 300°F. Use a set of tongs to transfer the salmon to a serving plate and drizzle the lime sauce all over it. Serve with steamed swiss chard.

Fish Finger Sandwich

Servings: 4 | Ready in about: 20 minutes

INGREDIENTS

4 cod fillets
2 tbsp flour
10 capers

4 bread rolls
2 oz breadcrumbs
4 tbsp pesto sauce

4 lettuce leaves
Salt and black pepper to taste

DIRECTIONS

Season the fillets with some salt and pepper, and coat them with the flour, and then dip in the breadcrumbs. You should get at the layer of breadcrumbs, that's why we don't use eggs for this recipe. Arrange the fillets onto a baking mat. Close the air fry lid and cook for about 10 to 15 minutes on Air Fry mode at 390°F.

Cut the bread rolls in half. Place a lettuce leaf on top of the bottom halves. Place the fillets over. Spread a tsp of pesto sauce on top of each fillet. Top with the remaining halves.

Cajun Salmon with Lemon

Servings: 1 | Ready in about: 10 minutes

INGREDIENTS

1 salmon fillet
¼ tsp brown sugar

Juice of ½ lemon
1 tbsp Cajun seasoning

2 lemon wedges
1 tbsp chopped parsley, for garnishing

DIRECTIONS

Meanwhile, combine the sugar and lemon and coat the salmon with this mixture thoroughly. Coat the salmon with the Cajun seasoning as well. Place a parchment paper into your Instant Pot, close the air fry lid and cook the salmon for 7 minutes on Air Fry mode at 350°F. Serve with lemon wedges and chopped parsley.

Spicy Tangy Salmon with Wild Rice

Servings: 4 | Ready in about: 50 minutes

INGREDIENTS

1 cup wild rice
1 cup vegetable stock
4 skinless salmon fillets
A bunch of asparagus, cut diagonally

3 tbsp olive oil, divided
Salt and black pepper to taste
2 limes, juiced
2 tbsp honey

1 tsp sweet paprika
2 jalapeño peppers, seeded and diced
4 garlic cloves, minced
2 tbsp chopped fresh parsley

DIRECTIONS

Pour the brown rice and vegetable stock in your Instant Pot. Stir to combine. Put a trivet in the pot and lay the salmon fillets on the trivet. Seal the pressure lid, choose Pressure Cook on High, and set the time to 2 minutes. In a bowl, toss the broccoli with 1 tablespoon of olive oil and season with the salt and black pepper.

In another bowl, evenly combine the remaining oil, the lime juice, honey, paprika, jalapeño, garlic, and parsley. When done cooking, do a quick pressure release, and carefully open the pressure lid. Pat the salmon dry with a paper towel and coat the fish with the honey sauce while reserving a little for garnishing.

Arrange the asparagus around the salmon. Close the air fry lid, choose Broil and set the time to 7 minutes. When ready, remove the salmon. Dish the salmon with asparagus and rice. Garnish with parsley and remaining sauce.

Tuna Patties

Servings: 2 | Ready in about: 50 minutes

INGREDIENTS

5 oz of canned tuna
1 tsp lime juice
1 tsp paprika

¼ cup flour
½ cup milk
1 small onion, diced

2 eggs
1 tsp chili powder, optional
½ tsp salt

DIRECTIONS

Place all ingredients in a bowl, and mix to combine. Make two large patties, or a few smaller ones, out of the mixture. Place them on a lined sheet and refrigerate for 30 minutes. Close the air fry lid and cook the patties for about 6 minutes on each side on Roast mode at 350°F.

Cod Cornflakes Nuggets

Servings: 4 | Ready in about: 25 minutes

INGREDIENTS

1 ¼ lb cod fillets, cut into chunks
½ cup flour

1 egg
1 tbsp water

1 cup cornflakes
1 tbsp olive oil

DIRECTIONS

Add the oil and cornflakes in a food processor, and process until crumbed. Season the fish chunks with salt and pepper. Beat the egg along with 1 tbsp water. Dredge the chunks in flour first, then dip in the egg, and coat with cornflakes. Arrange on a lined sheet. Close the air fry lid and cook at 350°F for 15 minutes on Air Fry mode.

Alaskan Cod with Fennel & Beans

Servings: 4 | Ready in about: 25 minutes

INGREDIENTS

2 Alaskan cod fillets, cut into 4 pieces each
4 tbsp olive oil
2 cloves garlic, minced
2 small onions, chopped
½ cup olive brine
3 cups chicken broth
½ cup tomato puree
1 head fennel, quartered
1 cup pinto beans, soaked, drained
1 cup green olives, pitted and crushed
½ cup basil leaves
Lemon slices to garnish

DIRECTIONS

Heat the olive oil on Sauté in your Instant Pot and add the garlic and onion. Stir-fry until the onion softens. Pour in chicken broth and tomato puree. Let simmer for about 3 minutes. Add fennel, olives, beans, salt, and pepper. Seal the lid and select Steam mode on High pressure for 10 minutes. Once ready, do a quick pressure release.

Transfer the beans to a plate with a slotted spoon. Add the cod pieces to the cooker. Close the lid again, secure the pressure valve, and select Steam mode on Low pressure for 3 minutes. Once the timer has ended, do a quick pressure release. Remove the cod to soup plate, top with beans and basil, and spoon the broth over. Serve.

Quick & Easy Fried Salmon

Servings: 1 | Ready in about: 13 minutes

INGREDIENTS

1 salmon fillet
1 tbsp soy sauce
¼ tsp garlic powder

DIRECTIONS

Combine the soy sauce with the garlic powder. Brush the mixture over the salmon. Place the salmon onto a sheet of parchment paper and inside your Instant Pot. Close the air fry lid and cook for 10 minutes on Air Fry at 350°F, until crispy on the outside and tender on the inside.

Sausage & Shrimp Paella

Servings: 4 | Ready in about: 70 minutes

INGREDIENTS

1 tbsp melted butter
1 lb andouille sausage, sliced
1 white onion, chopped
4 garlic cloves, minced
½ cup dry white wine
1 cup Spanish rice
2 cup chicken stock
1½ tsp sweet paprika
1 tsp turmeric powder
1 lb baby squid, cut into ¼-inch rings
1 lb jumbo shrimp, peeled and deveined
1 red bell pepper, diced

DIRECTIONS

Choose Sauté on your Instant Pot. Melt the butter and add the sausage. Cook until browned on both sides, about 3 minutes while stirring frequently. Remove the sausage to a plate and set aside. Sauté the onion and garlic in the same fat for 3 minutes until fragrant and pour in the wine. Use a wooden spoon to scrape the bottom of the pot of any brown bits and cook for 2 minutes or until the wine reduces by half. Stir in the rice and chicken stock.

Season with paprika, turmeric, black pepper, and salt. Seal the pressure lid, choose Pressure Cook and set to High. Set the time to 5 minutes, then When done cooking, do a quick pressure release and carefully open the lid. Choose Sauté. Add the squid and shrimp to the pot and stir gently without mashing the rice.

Seal the pressure lid again and cook for 6 minutes, until the shrimp are pink and opaque. Return the sausage to the pot and mix in the bell pepper. Warm through for 2 minutes. Dish the paella and serve immediately.

Smoked Salmon Pilaf with Walnuts

Servings: 4 | Ready in about: 60 minutes

INGREDIENTS

½ cup walnut pieces
1 tbsp ghee
4 green onions, chopped
1 cup basmati rice
1 cup frozen corn, thawed
1 tsp salt
1 smoked salmon fillet, flaked
2 tsp prepared horseradish
1 medium tomato, seeded and diced

DIRECTIONS

Pour the walnuts into a heatproof bowl. Put the air fry basket in the inner pot and the bowl in the basket. Close the air fry lid and choose Air Fry. Adjust the temperature to 375°F and the time to 5 minutes. Press Start to begin toasting the walnuts. After the cooking time is over, carefully take the bowl and basket out of the pot and set aside.

On the pot, choose Sauté. Add the ghee to melt and sauté the white part of the green onions for about a minute, or until starting to soften. Stir in rice and corn, stirring occasionally for 2 minutes or until starting to be fragrant. Add 2 cups water and salt. Seal the pressure lid, choose Pressure Cook on High and the time to 3 minutes.

After cooking, perform a natural pressure release for 10 minutes, and carefully open the lid. Fluff the rice gently with a fork. Stir in the flaked salmon, green parts of the green onions, and the horseradish. Add the tomato and allow sitting a few minutes to warm through. Spoon the pilaf into bowls and top with walnuts. Serve.

Mushroom & Shrimp Egg Wrappers

Servings: 4 AS AN APPETIZER | Ready in about: 70 minutes

INGREDIENTS

2 tbsp coconut aminos
1 tbsp dry white wine
2 tsp plain vinegar
3 cups shredded cabbage
3 green onions, chopped
1 large carrot, peeled and grated
1 tsp ginger puree
2 garlic cloves, minced
1 tsp sugar
2 tsp peanut oil
¼ tsp freshly ground black pepper
½ cup sautéed mushrooms, chopped
8 oz shrimp, peeled and chopped
1 tsp arrowroot starch
10 egg roll wrappers

DIRECTIONS

Mix the coconut aminos, white wine, and vinegar in your Instant Pot. Stir in the cabbage, green onions, carrot, ginger, garlic, sugar, and peanut oil. Seal the pressure lid, choose Pressure Cook, and the cook time to 2 minutes. After cooking, do a quick pressure release. Stir in the pepper, mushrooms, and shrimp.

Choose Sauté and simmer the shrimp and mushrooms for about 5 minutes until almost all of the liquid has dried up. Spoon the filling into a bowl and set aside to cool. Wipe out the inner pot with a paper towel and return the pot to the base. In a bowl, combine the arrowroot and 1 tbsp water. Lay an egg roll wrapper on a clean flat surface with a corner side facing you. Dip your index finger in the starch mixture and lightly moisten the edges of the wrapper.

With a slotted spoon, fetch a ¼ cup of filling onto the wrapper, just below the center. Fold the bottom corner of the wrapper over the filling, tuck under the filling, roll once and fold both sides in. Continue rolling up tightly and repeat the process with the remaining wrappers. Close the air fry lid and choose Air Fry.

Adjust the temperature to 390°F and the time to 5 minutes. Lay 5 egg rolls in the air fry basket and oil with the cooking spray. Flip and oil the other sides. When the pot is ready, fix the basket in the inner pot. Close the air fry lid and choose Air Fry. Adjust the temperature to 390°F and the cook time to 15 minutes.

After 6 minutes, open the lid and check the egg rolls, which should be golden brown and crisp on top. Otherwise, close the lid and cook for 2 minutes more. Flip the rolls with tongs and cook further for 5 to 6 minutes or until crisp on the other side too. Repeat the frying process for the remaining egg rolls. When ready, use tongs to remove the egg rolls into a plate. Allow cooling for a few minutes before serving.

White Wine Black Mussels

Servings: 4 | Ready in about: 45 minutes

INGREDIENTS

1 ½ lb black mussels, cleaned and de-bearded
3 tbsp olive oil
3 large chilies, seeded and chopped
3 cloves garlic, peeled and crushed
1 white onion, chopped finely
10 tomatoes, skin removed and chopped
4 tbsp tomato paste
1 cup dry white wine
3 cups vegetable broth
⅓ cup fresh basil leaves

DIRECTIONS

Heat the olive oil on Sauté and stir-fry the onion, chilies, and garlic, and cook for 2 minutes, stirring frequently. Stir in the tomatoes and tomato paste, and cook for 2 more minutes. Pour in the wine and vegetable broth. Let simmer for 5 minutes. Add the mussels, close the lid, secure the pressure valve, and press Steam for 3 minutes.

Once the timer has ended, do a natural pressure release for 15 minutes. Remove and discard any unopened mussels. Add half of the basil and stir. Close the air fry lid and cook on Broil for 5 minutes. Dish the mussels with sauce and garnish it with the remaining basil. Serve with crusted bread.

Crabmeat with Broccoli Risotto

Servings: 4 | Ready in about: 80 minutes

INGREDIENTS

1 lb broccoli, chopped into 1-inch pieces
1 tbsp olive oil
2 tbsp ghee
1 small onion, chopped (about ½ cup)
1 cup short grain rice
⅓ cup white wine
2 cups vegetable stock
8 oz lump crabmeat
⅓ cup grated Pecorino Romano cheese

DIRECTIONS

Choose Air Fry your Instant Pot. Adjust the temperature to 375°F and the time to 2 minutes. Add the broccoli in the air fry basket and drizzle with the olive oil. Season with ½ teaspoon of salt and toss. Put the basket in the inner pot. Close the air fry lid, choose Air Fry, adjust the temperature to 375°F and the cook time to 10 minutes.

After 5 minutes, open the lid and stir the broccoli, then resume cooking. When done, take out the basket and set aside. Choose Sauté. Melt the ghee. Add and sauté the onion for 5 minutes until softened. Stir in the rice for 1 minute. Add in wine and cook for 3 minutes, stirring often, until the liquid has almost completely evaporated.

Pour in vegetable stock and the remaining salt. Stir to combine. Seal the pressure lid, choose Pressure Cook on High, and the cook time to 8 minutes. After cooking, perform a quick pressure release and carefully open the pressure lid. Gently stir in the crabmeat, and cheese. Taste and adjust the seasoning. Serve immediately.

Chorizo & Shrimp Boil

Servings: 4 | Ready in about: 30 minutes

INGREDIENTS

3 red potatoes
3 ears corn, cut into 1½-inch rounds
1 cup white wine
4 chorizo sausages, sliced
1 lb shrimp, peeled and deveined
2 tbsp of seafood seasoning
Salt to taste
1 lemon, cut into wedges
¼ cup butter, melted

DIRECTIONS

To your Instant Pot, add all ingredients except butter and lemon wedges. Do not stir. Pour in 2 cups water. Seal the pressure lid, choose Pressure Cook, and set the timer to 2 minutes. When ready, release the pressure quickly. Drain the mixture through a colander. Transfer to a serving platter. Serve with melted butter and lemon wedges.

Scottish Seafood Curry

Servings: 8 | Ready in about: 45 minutes

INGREDIENTS

Seafood

½ lb squid, cut into 1-inch rings
½ lb langoustine tall meat
½ lb Sscallop meat
½ lb mussels

Curry

4 tbsp olive oil
2 cups shellfish stock
2 curry leaves
2 tbsp Shallot puree
3 tbsp yellow curry paste
2 tbsp ginger paste
2 tbsp garlic paste
1 ½ tbsp chili powder
1 ½ tbsp chili paste
2 tbsp lemongrass paste
½ tsp turmeric powder
2 tsp shrimp powder
1 tsp shrimp paste
1 ½ cups coconut milk
1 cup milk
1 tbsp Grants Scotch Whiskey
2 tbsp fish curry powder
Salt to taste

Vegetables

¼ cup diced tomatoes
¼ cup chopped onion
¼ cup chopped okra
¼ cup chopped eggplants

DIRECTIONS

Add olive oil, shallot paste, yellow curry paste, ginger puree, garlic paste, lemongrass paste, chili paste, shrimp paste, and curry leaves. Stir-fry for 10 minutes on Sauté mode, until well combined and aromatic. Next, add turmeric powder, fish curry powder, and shrimp powder. Stir-fry for another minute.

Pour in the shellfish stock and close the air fry lid. Cook on Broil mode for 15 minutes. Open the lid, and add the scallops, squid, chopped onion, okra, tomatoes, and aubergine. Stir lightly. Close the pressure lid, secure the pressure valve, and select Steam mode on High pressure for 5 minutes.

Once ready, do a quick pressure release. Add in milk, coconut milk, whiskey, and salt. Stir carefully not to mash the aubergine. Select Sauté and add mussels and langoustine. Stir carefully. Simmer the sauce for 3 minutes. Dish the seafood with sauce and veggies into serving bowls. Serve with a side of broccoli mash.

Spaghetti with Arugula & Scallops

Servings: 4 | Ready in about: 50 minutes

INGREDIENTS

1¼ lb scallops, peeled and deveined
1½ tsp salt, divided
1 tbsp melted butter
2 large garlic cloves, minced, divided
¼ cup white wine
10 oz spaghetti
2½ cups water
⅓ cup tomato puree
½ tsp red chili flakes or to taste
1 tsp grated lemon zest
1 tbsp lemon juice
6 cups arugula

DIRECTIONS

Arrange the scallops in the air fry basket. Season with ½ teaspoon salt, melted butter, and 1 minced garlic clove. Toss to coat and put the basket in the inner pot. Close the air fry lid, choose Air Fry, adjust the temperature to 400°F and the cook time to 6 minutes. After 3 minutes, open the lid and use tongs to turn the scallops. Close the lid and resume cooking. Remove onto a plate and set aside.

On your Instant Pot, choose Sauté. Pour in the white wine and simmer for 1 to 2 minutes until reduced by half. Add the spaghetti, water, remaining salt, garlic, puréed tomato, and chili flakes. Stir to combine. Lock the pressure lid into place and set to Seal. Choose Pressure Cook on High and the cook time to 5 minutes.

After cooking, perform a quick pressure release and carefully open the lid. Stir in the lemon zest, juice, and arugula until wilted and soft. Add the scallops and heat through for a few minutes. Serve immediately.

Potato Chowder with Peppery Prawns

Servings: 4 | Ready in about: 80 minutes

INGREDIENTS

4 slices serrano ham, chopped
4 tbsp minced garlic, divided
1 onion, chopped
2 Yukon Gold potatoes, chopped

16 oz frozen corn
2 cups vegetable broth
1 tsp dried rosemary
Salt and black pepper to taste

16 prawns, peeled and deveined
2 tbsp olive oil
½ tsp red chili flakes
¾ cup heavy cream

DIRECTIONS

Choose Sauté on your Instant Pot. Add 1 tbsp the olive oil and cook serrano ham, 2 tbsp garlic, and onion, stirring occasionally, for 5 minutes. Fetch out one-third of the serrano ham into a bowl for garnishing. Add the potatoes, corn, broth, rosemary, salt, and pepper to the pot. Seal the lid, hit Pressure Cook and cook for 10 minutes.

In a bowl, toss the prawns in the remaining garlic, salt, black pepper, the remaining olive oil, and the red chili flakes. When done cooking, do a quick pressure release and carefully open the pressure lid. Stir in the heavy cream and fix a trivet the pot over the chowder. Spread the prawn in a trivet. Close the air fry lid.

Choose Broil and set the time to 8 minutes. When the timer has ended, remove the trivet from the pot. Ladle the corn chowder into serving bowls and top with the prawns. Garnish with the reserved ham and serve immediately.

Seafood Gumbo

Servings: 4 | Ready in about: 90 minutes

INGREDIENTS

1 lb jumbo shrimp
8 oz lump crabmeat
1½ tsp salt divided
¼ cup olive oil, plus 2 tsp
⅓ cup all-purpose flour

1½ tsp Cajun seasoning
1 medium onion, chopped
1 small red bell pepper, chopped
2 celery stalks, chopped
2 garlic cloves, minced

1 small banana pepper, minced
3 cups chicken broth
1 cup jasmine rice
¾ cup water
2 green onions, finely sliced

DIRECTIONS

Lay the shrimp in the air fry basket. Season with salt and some olive oil. Toss to coat and fix the basket in the inner pot. Close the air fry lid and choose Air Fry. Adjust the temperature to 400°F and the cook time to 6 minutes. After 3 minutes, open the lid and toss the shrimp. Close the lid and resume cooking. When ready, the shrimp should be opaque and pink. Remove the basket and set aside.

Choose Sauté. Heat the remaining olive oil. Whisk in the flour with and cook the roux that forms for 5 minutes, stirring constantly, until the roux has the color of peanut butter. Stir in the Cajun, onion, bell pepper, celery, garlic, and banana pepper for about 5 minutes until the mixture slightly cools. Add the chicken broth and crabmeat, stir.

Put the rice into a heatproof bowl. Add water and salt. Cover the bowl with foil. Put a trivet in the pot and set the bowl on the trivet. Seal the lid, choose Pressure Cook, and the time to 6 minutes. After cooking, perform a natural pressure for 10 minutes. Take out the trivet and bowl. Stir the shrimp into the gumbo to heat it up for 3 minutes. Fluff the rice and divide into bowls. Spoon the gumbo around the rice and garnish with the green onions.

Prawn Toast

Servings: 2 | Ready in about: 12 minutes

INGREDIENTS

6 prawns, shells removed, chopped
1 large spring onion, finely sliced

3 white slices of bread
½ cup sweet corn

1 egg white, whisked
1 tbsp black sesame seeds

DIRECTIONS

In a bowl, place the prawns, corn, spring onion and the black sesame seeds. Add the whisked egg white, and mix the ingredients. Spread the mixture over the bread slices. Place the prawns in the air fry basket and sprinkle with oil. Close the air fry lid and fry the prawns until golden, for 8-10 minutes at 390°F on Air Fry mode. Serve.

Mussel Chowder with Oyster Crackers

Servings: 4 | Ready in about: 75 minutes

INGREDIENTS

3 (6-oz) cans chopped mussels, drained, liquid reserved
2 cups oyster crackers
2 tbsp melted ghee
¼ cup grated Pecorino Romano cheese
½ tsp garlic powder
1 tsp salt, divided

2 thick pancetta slices, cut into thirds
2 celery stalks, chopped
1 medium onion, chopped
1 tbsp flour
¼ cup white wine

1 cup clam juice
1 lb parsnips, peeled and cut into chunks
1 bay leaf
1 ½ cups heavy cream
2 tbsp chopped fresh chervil

DIRECTIONS

In a bowl, pour the oyster crackers. Drizzle with melted ghee, add the cheese, garlic powder, and salt. Toss to coat the crackers. Transfer to the air fry basket. Once the pot is ready, open the pressure lid and fix the basket in your Instant Pot. Close the lid and choose Air Fry. Adjust the temperature to 375°F and the cook time to 6 minutes.

After 3 minutes, open the lid and mix the crackers with a spoon. Close the lid and resume cooking until crisp and lightly browned. Take out the basket and let it cool. On the pot, choose Sauté. Add the pancetta and cook for 5 minutes, turning once or twice, until crispy. Remove the pancetta to a paper towel-lined plate. Set aside.

Sauté the celery and onion in the pancetta grease for 1 minute or until the vegetables start softening. Mix the flour into the vegetables to coat evenly and pour the wine over the veggies. Cook for about 1 minute or until reduced by about one-third. Pour in the clam juice, the reserved mussel liquid, parsnips, remaining salt, and bay leaf.

Seal the pressure lid, choose Pressure Cook and the cook time to 4 minutes. After cooking, perform a natural pressure release for 10 minutes. Stir in mussels and heavy cream. Choose Sauté. Simmer the chowder and heat the mussels. Remove and discard the bay leaf after. Spoon the soup into bowls and crumble the pancetta over the top. Garnish with the chervil and a handful of oyster crackers, serving the remaining crackers on the side.

Creamy Crab Soup

Servings: 4 | Ready in about: 45 minutes

INGREDIENTS

2 lb Crabmeat Lumps
6 tbsp butter
6 tbsp flour
1 white onion, chopped
3 tsp minced garlic

2 celery stalk, diced
1 ½ cup chicken broth
¾ cup heavy cream
½ cup Half and Half cream
2 tsp hot sauce

3 tsp Worcestershire sauce
3 tsp old bay Seasoning
¾ cup Muscadet
Lemon juice to serve
Chopped dill to serve

DIRECTIONS

Melt the butter on Sauté in your Instant Pot and mix in the all-purpose flour, in a fast motion to make a rue. Add celery, onion, and garlic. Stir and cook until soft and crispy, for 3 minutes. While stirring, gradually add the half and half cream, heavy cream, and broth. Let simmer for 2 minutes. Add Worcestershire sauce, old bay seasoning, Muscadet, and hot sauce. Stir and let simmer for 15 minutes. Add the crabmeat and mix it well into the sauce.

Close the air fry lid and cook on Broil mode for 10 minutes to soften the meat. Dish into serving bowls, garnish with dill and drizzle squirts of lemon juice over. Serve with a side of garlic crusted bread.

Parsley Oyster Stew

Servings: 4 | Ready in about: 12 minutes

INGREDIENTS

- 2 cups heavy cream
- 2 cups chopped celery
- 2 cups bone broth
- 3 (10 oz) jars shucked oysters in liqueur
- 3 Shallots, minced
- 3 tbsp olive oil
- Salt and white pepper to taste
- 3 cloves garlic, minced
- 3 tbsp chopped parsley

DIRECTIONS

To your Instant Pot, add oil, garlic, shallot, and celery. Stir-fry them for 2 minutes on Sauté and add the heavy cream, broth, and oysters. Stir once or twice. Close the lid, secure the pressure valve, and select Steam mode on High pressure for 3 minutes. Once the timer has stopped, do a quick pressure release, and open the lid.

Season with salt and white pepper. Close the air fry lid and cook for 5 minutes on Broil mode. Stir and dish the oyster stew into serving bowls. Garnish with parsley and top with some croutons.

White Wine Mussels

Servings: 5 | Ready in about: 15 minutes

INGREDIENTS

- 1 cup white wine
- 2 lb mussels, cleaned and debearded
- Juice from 1 lemon

DIRECTIONS

In your Instant Pot, mix ½ cup water and wine. Put the mussels into a steamer basket. Insert a trivet in the pot and lower steamer basket onto the trivet. Seal lid and cook on Pressure Cook for 1 minute. When ready, release the pressure quickly. Remove unopened mussels. Coat the mussels with the wine mixture. Serve with French fries.

Crab Cakes

Servings: 4 | Ready in about: 55 minutes

INGREDIENTS

- ½ cup cooked crab meat
- ¼ cup chopped red onion
- 1 tbsp chopped basil
- ¼ cup chopped celery
- ¼ cup chopped red pepper
- 3 tbsp mayonnaise
- Zest of ½ lemon
- ¼ cup breadcrumbs
- 2 tbsp chopped parsley
- Old Bay seasoning, as desired
- Cooking spray

DIRECTIONS

Place all ingredients in a large bowl and mix well until thoroughly incorporated. Make 4 large crab cakes from the mixture and place on a lined sheet. Refrigerate for 30 minutes. Spay the air basket with cooking spray and arrange the crab cakes in it. Close the air fry lid and cook for 7 minutes on each side on Air Fry at 390°F.

Paella Señorito

Servings: 5 | Ready in about: 25 minutes

INGREDIENTS

- ¼ cup olive oil
- 1 onion, chopped
- 1 red bell pepper, diced
- 2 garlic cloves, minced
- 1 tsp paprika
- 1 tsp turmeric
- Salt and ground white pepper to taste
- 1 cup bomba rice
- ¼ cup frozen green peas
- 2 cups fish broth
- 1 lb frozen shrimp, peeled and deveined
- 1 lemon, cut into wedges

DIRECTIONS

Warm oil on Sauté in your Instant Pot. Add in bell pepper and onion and garlic and cook for 3 minutes until soft. Add paprika, white pepper, salt, and turmeric and cook for 1 minute. Stir in fish broth and rice. Add shrimp in the rice mixture. Seal the lid, choose Pressure Cook, and set timer to 5 minutes. When ready, release the pressure quickly. Stir in green peas and let sit for 5 minutes until green peas are heated through. Garnish with lemon.

Penne all'Arrabbiata with Seafood & Chorizo

Servings: 4 | Ready in about: 50 minutes

INGREDIENTS

1 tbsp olive oil
1 onion, diced
16 oz penne
1 (24-oz) jar Arrabbiata sauce
3 cups fish broth
1 chorizo, sliced
8 oz shrimp, peeled and deveined
8 oz scallops
12 clams, cleaned and debearded

DIRECTIONS

Choose Sauté on your Instant Pot. Heat the oil and add the chorizo, onion, and garlic. Sauté them for about 5 minutes. Stir in the penne, Arrabbiata sauce, and broth. Season with the black pepper and salt and mix. Seal the pressure lid, choose Pressure Cook on High and set the time to 2 minutes. Do a quick pressure release.

Choose Sauté. Stir in the shrimp, scallops, and clams. Put the pressure lid together and set to the Vent position. Cover and cook for 5 minutes, until the clams have opened and the shrimp and scallops are opaque and cooked through. Discard any unopened clams. Spoon the seafood and chorizo pasta into serving bowls and serve warm.

Seared Scallops with Butter-Caper Sauce

Servings: 6 | Ready in about: 18 minutes

INGREDIENTS

2 lb sea scallops, foot removed
10 tbsp butter, unsalted
4 tbsp capers, drained
4 tbsp olive oil
1 cup dry white wine
3 tsp lemon zest

DIRECTIONS

Melt the butter to caramel brown on Sauté in your Instant Pot. Fetch the butter out into a bowl. Heat the oil in the pot, add the scallops and sear them until golden brown, about 5 minutes; reserve. Pour the white wine in the pot to deglaze the bottom while using a spoon to scrape the bottom of the pot of any scallop bits. Add the capers, butter, and lemon zest. Stir the mixture once gently. Spoon the sauce with capers over the scallops. Serve.

Delicious Coconut Shrimp

Servings: 2 | Ready in about: 30 minutes

INGREDIENTS

8 large shrimp
½ cup breadcrumbs
8 oz coconut milk
½ cup shredded coconut
¼ tsp salt
¼ tsp pepper
½ cup orange jam
1 tsp mustard
1 tbsp honey
½ tsp cayenne pepper
¼ tsp hot sauce

DIRECTIONS

Combine breadcrumbs, cayenne, shredded coconut, salt, and pepper in a bowl. Dip the shrimp in the coconut milk, then in the coconut crumbs. Arrange in the lined air fry basket, close the air fry lid and cook for 20 minutes on Air Fry at 350°F. Whisk the jam, honey, hot sauce, and mustard. Serve the shrimp with the sauce.

POULTRY RECIPES

Lemon Chicken Tenders with Broccoli

Servings: 2 | Ready in about: 70 minutes

INGREDIENTS

1 cup basmati rice
1 cup plus 2 tbsp water
1 head broccoli, cut into florets
2 tbsp melted butter, divided
¼ tsp salt
¼ tsp freshly ground black pepper
4 boneless, skinless chicken tenders
¼ cup barbecue sauce
¼ cup lemon marmalade
½ tbsp soy sauce
1 tbsp sesame seeds, for garnish
2 tbsp sliced green onions, for garnish

DIRECTIONS

Pour the rice and water into your Instant Pot and stir to combine. Seal the pressure lid, choose Pressure Cook on High, and the timer to 2 minutes. In a bowl, toss the broccoli with 1 tablespoon of melted butter, and season with salt and black pepper. When done cooking, perform a quick pressure release, and carefully open the lid.

Place a trivet inside the pot, which will be over the rice. Then, spray a trivet with cooking spray. Lay the chicken tenders on the trivet and brush with the remaining melted butter. Arrange the broccoli around the chicken. Close the air fry lid. Choose Air Fry, set the temperature to 400°F, and set the time to 10 minutes. Press Start to begin.

In a bowl, mix the barbecue sauce, lemon marmalade, and soy sauce. When done crisping, coat the chicken with the lemon sauce. Turn the chicken over and apply the lemon sauce on the other side. Close the air fry lid, select Broil for 5 minutes. After cooking is complete, check for your desired crispiness and remove the trivet from the pot. Spoon the rice into plates with chicken and broccoli. Top with sesame seeds and green onions and serve.

Crispy Chicken Thighs with Carrot Roast

Servings: 4 | Ready in about: 50 minutes

INGREDIENTS

1 ½ cups chicken broth
1 cup basmati rice
4 bone-in, skin-on chicken thighs
2 carrots, chopped
2 tbsp melted butter
2 tsp chicken seasoning
Salt to taste
2 tsp chopped fresh thyme

DIRECTIONS

Pour the chicken broth and rice into your Instant Pot. Then, put in a trivet. Arrange the chicken thighs on the trivet, skin side up, and arrange the carrots around the chicken. Put the pressure lid together and lock in the Seal position. Choose Pressure Cook on High and the time to 2 minutes.

When done, perform a quick pressure release. Brush the carrots and chicken with the melted butter. Season the chicken with the chicken seasoning and salt. Also, season the carrots with the thyme and salt. Close the air fry lid, choose Broil and set the time to 10 minutes. When done cooking, check for your desired crispiness, and turn the pot off. Spoon the rice into serving plates, and serve the chicken and carrots over the rice.

Chicken with Crunchy Coconut Dumplings

Servings: 6 | Ready in about: 70 minutes

INGREDIENTS

1 package refrigerated biscuits, at room temperature
1 tbsp ghee
1 white onion, chopped
2 carrots, diced
2 celery stalks, diced
1 lb chicken breasts, cubed
2 cups chicken stock
1 tsp fresh rosemary
½ tsp salt
½ cup heavy cream

DIRECTIONS

Choose Sauté on your Instant Pot. Melt the ghee and sauté the onion until softened, about 3 minutes. Pour the carrots, celery, chicken, and stock into the pot. Season with rosemary and salt. Put the pressure lid together and lock in the Seal position. Choose Pressure Cook on High, and set the time to 2 minutes.

When done cooking, perform a quick pressure release, and carefully open the lid. Stir the heavy cream into the soup. Place a trivet in the higher position inside the pot, over the soup, and arrange the biscuits in a single layer on the trivet. Close the air fry lid. Choose Broil and set the time to 15 minutes. When ready, allow the biscuit and soup to rest for a few minutes and then serve.

Garlic Herb Roasted Chicken

Servings: 4 | Ready in about: 70 minutes

INGREDIENTS

1 (3½-lb) whole chicken
½ cup white wine
Juice of 1 lemon
2 limes, juiced
3 tbsp olive oil
¼ cup coconut aminos
2 tbsp Italian herb mix
1 ½ tbsp ground cumin
6 cloves garlic, grated

DIRECTIONS

Remove the neck from inside the chicken's cavity, trim off the excess fat and any remaining feathers. Rinse the chicken thoroughly with water and tie the legs with butcher's twine. Pour the wine and lemon juice into your Instant Pot. Place the chicken in the air fry basket and fix the basket in the higher position of the pot.

Put the pressure lid together and lock in the Seal position. Choose Pressure Cook and set to High. Set the time to 20 minutes. When the timer is done, perform a quick pressure release, and carefully open the pressure lid. In a bowl, combine the lime juice, the olive oil, coconut aminos, Italian herb mix, cumin, garlic and salt.

Mix until thoroughly combined. Brush the mixture over the chicken. Close the air fry lid. Choose Air Fry, set the temperature to 400°F, and set the time to 15 minutes. After about 10 minutes, lift the air fry lid and sprinkle the chicken with the fresh rosemary. Close the air fry lid and continue cooking. Carefully open the lid and transfer the chicken to a plate. Let the chicken rest for 10 minutes before cutting and serving.

Sweet Sesame Chicken Wings

Servings: 4 | Ready in about: 65 minutes

INGREDIENTS

24 chicken wings
2 tbsp sesame oil
2 tbsp hot garlic sauce
2 tbsp honey
2 garlic cloves, minced
1 tbsp toasted sesame seeds

DIRECTIONS

Pour 1 cup of water into your Instant Pot and place a trivet in the pot. Place the chicken wings on the trivet. Seal the pressure lid, choose Pressure Cook on High, and the cooking time to 10 minutes. While the wings cook, prepare the glaze. In a large bowl, whisk the sesame oil, hot garlic sauce, honey, and garlic.

After cooking, perform a quick pressure release, and carefully open the lid. Remove the trivet from the pot and empty the water in the pot. Return the pot to the base. Close the air fry lid and choose Air Fry. Adjust the temperature to 375°F and the time to 3 minutes to preheat the inner pot. Toss the wings in the sauce to coat.

Put the wings in the air fry basket, leaving any excess sauce in the bowl. Place the basket in the pot and close the air fry lid. Choose Air Fry and adjust the cooking time to 15 minutes. Press Start to commence crisping. After 8 minutes, open the lid and use tongs to turn the wings. Close the lid to resume browning until the wings are crisp and the glaze set. Before serving, drizzle with any remaining sauce and sprinkle with the sesame seeds.

Quick Chicken Fried Rice

Servings: 4 | Ready in about: 60 minutes

INGREDIENTS

1 tbsp ghee
1 onion, diced
4 garlic cloves, minced
1 lb chicken breasts, diced
Salt black pepper to taste
2 cups chicken broth
¼ cup coconut aminos
1 cup long grain rice
1 (16-oz) bag frozen mixed vegetables

DIRECTIONS

Press Sauté on your Instant Pot.

Melt the ghee and sauté the onion for 3 minutes. Add and sauté the garlic until fragrant, about 1 minute. Put the chicken in the pot and season with the and black pepper. Cook for 5 minutes to brown the chicken.

Pour the chicken broth, coconut aminos, and rice into the pot. Put the pressure lid together and lock the pressure release valve in the Seal position. Choose Pressure Cook on High, and set the time to 3 minutes. When done, perform a quick pressure and carefully open the lid. Pour the frozen vegetables into your Instant Pot. Choose Sauté to heat the vegetables through. Cook for 5 minutes while stirring occasionally. Serve.

Black Refried Beans & Chicken Fajitas

Servings: 4 | Ready in about: 40 minutes

INGREDIENTS

1 large (27-oz) can black beans
1 garlic clove, crushed
1 bacon slice, halved widthwise
¼ cup water
4 tbsp olive oil, divided
1 lb chicken breasts, sliced
1 yellow bell pepper, sliced
1 red bell pepper, sliced
1 small onion, cut into 8 wedges
1 jalapeño pepper, sliced
1 tsp salt
1 tbsp Mexican seasoning mix
Corn tortillas to serve
Avocado slices to serve
Salsa to serve

DIRECTIONS

Pour the beans with liquid into your Instant Pot. Stir in the garlic, bacon, water, and 2 tablespoons of olive oil. Seal the pressure lid, choose Pressure Cook on High and the cooking time to 5 minutes. In a large bowl, mix the chicken, yellow and red bell peppers, jalapeño, and onion. Drizzle with the remaining oil, sprinkle with salt and Mexican seasoning and toss to coat. Set aside. When the beans are ready, do a quick pressure release.

Pour out the beans with liquid into a bowl. Remove and discard the bacon pieces and garlic clove. Fetch out about ¼ cup of the liquid and reserve it. Then, use a potato masher to break the beans into the remaining liquid until smooth while adding more liquid if needed. Cover the bowl with aluminum foil.

Add the vegetables and chicken to the air fry basket. Close the air fry lid. Choose Air Fry. Adjust the temperature to 375°F and the cooking time to 10 minutes. Press Start to begin browning. After 5 minutes, open the lid and use tongs to turn the vegetables and chicken. Continue cooking until the vegetables are slightly browned and the chicken tender. Wrap the chicken and beans in warm tortillas and garnish with the avocado and salsa to serve.

Chicken with Cilantro Rice

Servings: 4 | Ready in about: 70 minutes

INGREDIENTS

2 tbsp ghee
1 red onion, diced
1 yellow bell pepper, diced
1 tbsp cayenne powder
1 tsp ground cumin
1 tsp Italian herb mix
1 cup basmati rice
¾ cup chicken broth
½ cup tomato sauce
1 lb bone-in, skin-on chicken thighs
Chopped fresh cilantro for garnish
Lime wedges, for serving

DIRECTIONS

Choose Sauté on your Instant Pot. Melt half of the ghee and cook the onion for 3 minutes, stirring occasionally, until softened. Include the yellow bell pepper, cayenne pepper, cumin, and herb mix and cook for 2 minutes more with frequent stirring. Pour the rice, broth, and tomato sauce into the pot. Place a trivet in the higher position of the pot, which is over the rice. Put the chicken on the trivet. Seal the pressure lid, choose Pressure Cook

Set the time to 30 minutes. When the time is over, perform a quick pressure release and carefully open the lid. Brush the chicken thighs with the remaining ghee. Close the air fry lid. Choose Broil and set the time to 5 minutes. Plate the chicken, garnish with cilantro, and serve with lime wedges.

Chicken Cassoulet with Frijoles

Servings: 4 | Ready in about: 60 minutes

INGREDIENTS

4 small chicken thighs, bone-in skin-on
Salt and black pepper to taste
2 pancetta slices, cut into thirds
1 medium carrot, diced
½ small onion, diced
½ cup dry red wine
1 cup Pinto Beans Frijoles, soaked
3 cups chicken stock
1 cup panko breadcrumbs

DIRECTIONS

Season the chicken on both sides with salt and black pepper and set aside on a wire rack. On your Instant Pot, choose Sauté. Add the pancetta slices in a single layer and cook for 3 to 4 minutes or until browned on one side. Turn and brown the other side. Remove the pancetta to a paper towel-lined plate. Put the chicken thighs in the pot, and fry for 6-7 minutes or until it is golden brown on both sides. Use tongs to pick the chicken into a plate.

Carefully pour out all the fat from the pot, leaving about 1 tablespoon to coat the bottom of the pot. Reserve the remaining fat in a small bowl. Sauté the carrots and onion in the pot for 3 minutes with frequent stirring, until the onion begins to brown. Stir in the wine while scraping off the brown bits at the bottom. Allow boiling until the wine reduces by one-third and stir in the beans and chicken stock.

Seal the pressure lid, choose Pressure Cook on High and the cooking time to 25 minutes. When done cooking, perform a quick pressure release and carefully open the lid. Return the chicken to the pot and cook for 10 minutes. Combine the breadcrumbs with the reserved fat until evenly mixed.

When done cooking, perform a natural pressure release for 5 minutes, then a quick pressure release to let out any remaining steam, and carefully open the lid. Crumble the pancetta over the cassoulet. Spoon the breadcrumbs mixture on top of the beans while avoiding the chicken as much as possible. Close the air fry lid, choose Broil, adjust the time to 7 minutes, and When the cassoulet is ready, allow resting for a few minutes before serving.

Chicken Florentine

Servings: 4 | Ready in about: 30 minutes

INGREDIENTS

4 chicken thighs, cut into 1-inch pieces
1 tbsp olive oil
1 ½ cups chicken broth
Salt to taste
1 cup chopped sun dried tomatoes with herbs
2 tbsp Italian Seasoning
2 cups baby spinach
¼ tsp red pepper flakes
6 oz softened cream cheese, cut into small cubes
1 cup shredded Pecorino cheese

DIRECTIONS

Pour the chicken broth into the pressure cooker, and add the Italian seasoning, chicken, tomatoes, salt, and red pepper flakes. Stir them with a spoon. Seal the lid and select Pressure Cook on High for 12 minutes. Once the timer has ended, do a quick pressure release. Stir in spinach, Parmesan, and cream cheese until the cheese melt and is fully incorporated. Close the air fry lid and cook on Broil for 5 minutes. Serve.

Chicken Potato Pot Pie

Servings: 6 | Ready in about: 70 minutes

INGREDIENTS

4 tbsp butter
1 onion, diced
2 garlic cloves, minced
2 lb boneless chicken breasts, cubed
2 potatoes, diced
1 cup chicken broth
½ tsp salt
½ tsp freshly ground black pepper
8 oz frozen sweetcorn
½ cup whipping cream
1 piecrust, at room temperature

DIRECTIONS

Choose Sauté on your Instant Pot. Melt the ghee and sauté garlic and onion until softened, about 3 minutes. Add the chicken, potatoes, and broth to the pot. Season with salt and black pepper. Seal the pressure lid.

Choose Pressure Cook on High, and the time to 10 minutes. When done cooking, do a quick pressure release. Select Sauté. Pour the frozen sweetcorn and whipping cream into the pot. Stir until the sauce thickens, about 3 minutes. Place the piecrust on top of vegetables and cream mixture, folding over the edges if necessary.

Cut out a small dent in the center of the pie to allow steam to escape when baking. Close the air fry lid. Choose Broil and set the time to 10 minutes. When ready, remove the inner pot from the pot and place it on a heat-resistant surface. Let the potpie rest for 10 to 15 minutes before serving.

Herbed Chicken & Biscuit Chili

Servings: 6 | Ready in about: 90 minutes

INGREDIENTS

1 package refrigerated biscuits, at room temperature
1 tbsp olive oil
1 onion, chopped
2 garlic cloves, minced
1½ lb ground chicken
1 tbsp ground cilantro
1 tbsp dried oregano
4 cups chicken broth
⅛ tsp salt
⅛ tsp black pepper

DIRECTIONS

Choose Sauté on your Instant Pot. Pour the oil, chicken, onion, and garlic into the inner pot and sauté until the onion is softened, about 3 minutes. Add the cilantro, oregano, broth, salt, and black pepper to the pot. Put the pressure lid together and lock in the Seal position. Choose Pressure Cook on High. Set the time to 10 minutes

When the time is over, perform a quick pressure release. Spread the biscuits in a single layer over the chili. Close the air fry lid. Choose Broil and set the time to 15 minutes. Choose Start. When ready, remove the pot from the pot and place it on a heat-resistant surface. Let the chili and biscuits rest for 10 to 15 minutes before serving.

Herby Chicken Breasts

Servings: 4 | Ready in about: 15 minutes

INGREDIENTS

4 boneless, skinless chicken breasts
½ tsp salt
1 cup water
¼ cup dry white wine
½ tsp rosemary
½ tsp mint
½ tsp marjoram
½ tsp sage

DIRECTIONS

Sprinkle salt over the chicken and set it in your Instant Pot. Mix in mint, rosemary, marjoram, and sage. Pour wine and water around the chicken. Seal the pressure lid, choose Pressure Cook on High, and set the timer to 6 minutes. Release the pressure naturally for 10 minutes.

BBQ Chicken & Kale Quesadillas

Servings: 4 | Ready in about: 40 minutes

INGREDIENTS

¼ cup butter, divided
1 (10-to 12-oz) bag fresh baby kale
1 jalapeño pepper, minced
¼ cup minced onion
3 oz cottage cheese, at room temperature
2 tsp Mexican seasoning mix
1 cup shredded cooked chicken
6 oz shredded Cheddar cheese
Cooking spray
4 medium flour tortillas
⅓ cup grated Pecorino Romano cheese

DIRECTIONS

On your Instant Pot, choose Sauté. Melt 1 tbsp butter until foaming. Add the kale and cook for 1 to 2 minutes or until wilted while stirring occasionally. Mix in the jalapeño and onion, continue cooking for 3 minutes, stirring occasionally, until the vegetables have softened and most of the liquid from the kale has evaporated. Mix in the cottage cheese to melt and add the Mexican seasoning and the chicken. Stir to combine.

Spoon the filling into a bowl and stir in the shredded cheddar cheese. Set aside. Use a paper towel to wipe out the inner pot and return the pot to the base. Oil a trivet with cooking spray and fix in the upper position of the pot. Close the air fry lid and choose Air Fry. Adjust the temperature to 375°F and the time to 5 minutes. Press Start.

To assemble the quesadillas, place a tortilla on a clean flat surface. Brush the top with olive oil and sprinkle 1 teaspoon of Pecorino Romano cheese on top. Press the cheese down with the palm of your hand to stick to the tortilla. Spread about a ⅓ cup of filling over half the tortilla, leaving a ¼-inch border. Fold the other half over the filling and press gently. Repeat the process with the remaining tortillas, filling, and Pecorino Romano cheese.

Carefully transfer two quesadillas to the prepared rack. Close the air fry lid and choose Air Fry. Adjust the temperature to 375°F and the cooking time to 6 minutes. After 3 minutes, or when they are browned on top, use a spatula to flip the quesadillas. Continue cooking until browned on both sides.

Once ready, remove the trivet from the pot and use the spatula to transfer the quesadillas to the bottom of the pot to keep warm while you work on the other quesadillas. Return the empty rack to the pot and place the two remaining uncooked quesadillas on the trivet. Repeat the cooking process. Serve the quesadillas with guacamole.

Wine Chicken with Mushrooms & Brussel Sprouts

Servings: 4 | Ready in about: 40 minutes

INGREDIENTS

4 chicken thighs, bone-in skin-on
Salt and black pepper to taste
1 tbsp olive oil
½ small onion, sliced
½ cup dry white wine
⅓ cup chicken stock
1 cup halved Brussel sprouts
1 bay leaf
¼ tsp dried rosemary
1 cup sautéed Mushrooms
¼ cup heavy cream

DIRECTIONS

Season the chicken on both sides with salt. On your Instant Pot, choose Sauté. Heat olive oil and add the chicken thighs. Fry for 4 to 5 minutes or until browned. Turn and lightly sear the other side, about 1 minute. Use tongs to remove the chicken into a plate and spoon out any thick coating of oil in your Instant Pot.

Sauté the onion in the pot and season with salt. Cook for about 2 minutes to soften and just beginning to brown for 2 minutes. Stir in the white wine and bring to a boil for 3 minutes or until reduced by about half. Mix in the chicken stock, brussel sprouts, bay leaf, rosemary, and several grinds of black pepper. Arrange the chicken thighs on top with skin-side up. Seal the pressure lid, choose Pressure Cook on High and the time to 5 minutes.

When the timer is over, perform a quick pressure release. Remove the bay leaf. Remove the chicken onto the trivet and stir the mushrooms into the sauce. Set a trivet in the pot. Close the air fry lid and choose Bake. Adjust the temperature to 375°F for 12 minutes. When ready, transfer the chicken to a platter. Stir the heavy cream into the sauce. Spoon the sauce and vegetables over the chicken to serve.

Italian Chicken with Herby Dumplings

Servings: 4 | Ready in about: 40 minutes

INGREDIENTS

For the Dumplings
1 large egg
¾ cup heavy cream
6 oz self-rising flour
1 tsp dried mixed herbs

For the Chicken
3 tbsp butter
3 tbsp flour
1 tsp Italian seasoning mix
3 cups chicken stock
1 ¼ lb skinless, chicken thighs, cubed
2 large celery stalks, chopped
3 large carrots, cut into coins
⅔ cup peas, frozen
1 cup frozen pearl onions

DIRECTIONS

To make the dumplings, whisk the egg and heavy cream in a bowl until evenly combined and stir in the flour and mixed herbs until a stiff but soft dough forms. Refrigerate the dough while you make the chicken.

On your Instant Pot, choose Sauté. Melt the butter, stir in the flour and Italian seasoning. Cook for 3 to 4 minutes, stirring occasionally, until the roux is golden brown. Pour in stock, whisking until combined. Cook until the sauce has slightly thickened. Add the chicken, celery, and carrots to the inner pot. Seal the pressure lid, choose Pressure Cook on High, and the cooking time to 6 minutes. Once ready, perform a quick pressure release.

Remove and discard the bay leaf. Stir in the peas and onion. Take out the dumpling from the fridge and drop in small spoonfuls into the chicken and vegetables. Seal the pressure lid, choose Pressure Cook on High and the cooking time to 2 minutes. After cooking, perform a quick pressure release and carefully open the lid. Close the air fry lid and choose Broil. Adjust the cooking time to 7 minutes. Ladle into bowls and serve.

Lemon and Paprika Chicken Thighs

Servings: 4 | Ready in about: 26 minutes

INGREDIENTS

4 chicken thighs
1 ½ tbsp olive oil
½ tsp garlic powder
Salt and black pepper to taste
½ tsp red pepper flakes
½ tsp smoked paprika
1 small onion, chopped
2 cloves garlic, sliced
½ cup chicken broth
1 tsp Italian Seasoning
1 lemon, zested and juiced
1 ½ tbsp heavy cream
Lemon slices to garnish
Chopped parsley to garnish

DIRECTIONS

Preheat your Instant Pot by selecting Sauté. Warm the olive oil and add the chicken thighs. Cook to brown e for about 3 minutes. Remove the chicken to a plate. Melt the butter and add garlic, onion, and lemon juice. Deglaze the bottom of the pot and cook for 1 minute. Add the Italian seasoning, broth, lemon zest, and the chicken.

Close the pressure lid, secure the pressure valve, select Pressure on High for 10 minutes. When ready, do a quick pressure release. Open the lid. Stir in the heavy cream. Close the air fry lid and select Broil mode. Set the time to 5 minutes. Serve with the steamed kale and spinach mix. Garnish with the lemons slices and parsley.

Saucy Shredded Chicken

Servings: 4 | Ready in about: 35 minutes

INGREDIENTS

4 chicken breasts, skinless
¼ cup Sriracha sauce
2 tbsp butter
1 tsp grated ginger
2 cloves garlic, minced
½ tsp Cayenne pepper

½ tsp red chili flakes
½ cup honey
½ cup chicken broth
Salt and black pepper to taste
Chopped scallion to garnish

DIRECTIONS

In a bowl, pour the chicken broth. Mix in honey, ginger, sriracha sauce, red pepper flakes, cayenne pepper, and garlic. Put the chicken on a plate and season with salt and pepper. Select Sauté on your Instant Pot. Melt the butter and add the chicken. Brown on both sides for about 3 minutes. Add the chicken back, and pour the pepper sauce over. Close the pressure lid, secure the pressure valve, and select Pressure Cook on High for 20 minutes.

When ready, do a natural pressure release for 5 minutes and open the lid. Remove the chicken onto a cutting board and shred using two forks. Return the shredded chicken to the pot, close the air fry lid and select Air Fry mode. Adjust the time to 4 minutes at 385°F. When ready, transfer the chicken to a serving bowl, pour the sauce over, and garnish with the scallions. Serve with a side of sauteéd mushrooms.

Mexican Chicken & Wild Rice Bowls

Servings: 4 | Ready in about: 30 minutes

INGREDIENTS

4 chicken breasts
2 cups chicken broth
2 ¼ packets Taco Seasoning

1 cup wild rice, rinsed
1 green bell pepper, seeded and diced
1 red bell pepper, seeded and diced

1 cup salsa
Salt and black pepper to taste
1 cup sour cream

To Serve:
Grated cheese, of your choice

Chopped cilantro

Avocado slices

DIRECTIONS

Pour the chicken broth into the inner pot, add the chicken. Pour the taco seasoning over. Add the salsa and stir lightly with a spoon. Close the pressure lid, secure the pressure valve, and select Pressure on High for 15 minutes. Once the timer has ended, do a quick pressure release, and open the lid. Add the wild rice and peppers.

Use a spoon to push them into the sauce. Close the pressure lid, secure the pressure valve, and select Pressure Cook on High for 8 minutes. Once the timer has ended, do a quick pressure release, and open the lid. Gently stir the mixture, adjust the taste with salt and pepper. Stir in sour cream, close the air fry lid and select Broil. Cook for 2 minutes. Spoon the chicken into serving bowls. Top it with avocado slices, cilantro and some cheese. Serve.

Chicken with Tomato Salsa

Servings: 4 | Ready in about: 30 minutes

INGREDIENTS

4 chicken thighs, skinless but with bone
4 tbsp olive oil
1 cup crushed tomatoes
1 large red bell pepper, seeded and diced

1 green bell pepper, seeded and diced
1 Red onion, diced
Salt and black pepper to taste
1 tbsp chopped basil

½ cup chicken broth
1 bay leaf
½ tsp dried oregano

DIRECTIONS

Place the chicken on a clean flat surface and season with salt and pepper. On your Instant Pot, choose Sauté and heat the oil. Once heated, add the chicken to brown on both sides for 6 minutes. Then, add the onions and peppers. Cook for 5 minutes until nice and soft. Add bay leaf, salt, broth, pepper, and oregano. Stir using a spoon. Close the pressure lid, secure the pressure valve, and select Pressure Cook on High for 15 minutes.

Once the timer has ended, do a natural pressure release for 5 minutes. Discard the bay leaf. Stir in tomatoes, close the air fry lid, select Broil mode and cook for 25 minutes. Dish the chicken with the sauce into a serving bowl and garnish with the chopped basil. Serve over a bed of steamed squash spaghetti.

Chicken Shawarma Wrap

Servings: 4 | Ready in about: 35 minutes

INGREDIENTS

1 ½ lb boneless skinless chicken breasts
Salt and black pepper to taste
2 tbsp olive oil
2 tbsp yogurt

2 tbsp freshly squeezed lemon juice
3 garlic cloves, minced
1 tsp ground cumin
¼ tsp cinnamon powder

1 tsp smoked paprika
¼ tsp turmeric
¼ tsp cayenne pepper
4 flat breads, halved

For the Sauce
½ cup yogurt
½ tsp salt

1 tsp olive oil
1 small garlic clove, minced

2 tbsp Italian herb mix
1 tbsp chopped fresh cilantro

To Assemble
2 large tomatoes, sliced

½ medium cucumber, sliced

DIRECTIONS

Season the chicken with salt on both sides, put in a plastic zipper bag, and set aside. In a bowl, evenly mix the olive oil, yogurt, lemon juice, garlic, cumin, cinnamon, paprika, turmeric, black pepper, and cayenne pepper. Pour the marinade over the chicken, zip up the bag, and massage the bag to coat the chicken well with the marinade. Refrigerate the chicken for 1 hour or more to marinate.

Cover the flatbread with foil and place it at the bottom of the pot. Grease a trivet with cooking spray and fix it in the pot. Close the air fry lid and choose Air Fry. Adjust the temperature to 390°F and the time to 4 minutes. Press Start to preheat the pot. Take the chicken out of the refrigerator and remove from the bag while holding each piece to allow excess liquid drip into the bag. Lay the chicken on the trivet in a single layer.

Close the air fry lid and choose Air Fry. Adjust the temperature to 390°F and the time to 16 minutes. Press Start. After 8 minutes, flip the chicken and close the lid. Cook to crisp and brown the other side for 8 minutes. When the breasts are ready, transfer to a cutting board, and cut into thin slices. Take out the bread from the pot.

Prepare the sauce: pour the yogurt into a small bowl. Add the salt, olive oil, garlic, and Italian herb mix. Whisk the ingredients to combine and stir in the parsley. Spread 1 to 2 tablespoons of yogurt sauce into half a side of flatbread. Spoon in some chicken and add the tomato and cucumber slices. Repeat the process for the remaining bread. Wrap the bread over the filling, repeat the assembling process for the remaining bread and serve.

Tandoori Chicken Thighs

Servings: 4 | Ready in about: 45 minutes

INGREDIENTS

1½ lb chicken thighs, boneless skinless
1 cup plain Greek yogurt
1½ tsp garlic puree
1 tbsp ginger puree
1 tsp sweet paprika

½ tsp chili pepper
½ tsp garam masala
½ tsp ground cumin
1 tsp turmeric powder
Salt and black pepper to taste

1 cup long grain white rice, rinsed
¾ cup coconut milk
¼ cup water
½ cup cooked lima beans
1 tbsp chopped fresh parsley

DIRECTIONS

Season the chicken with salt and place it in a plastic zipper bag. Set aside and make the marinade. In a medium bowl, mix the yogurt, salt, garlic, ginger, paprika, chili pepper, garam masala, cumin, turmeric, and black pepper. Pour the marinade over the chicken. Zip the bag and rub the marinade on the chicken to coat properly. Set aside.

Pour the rice into your Instant Pot and mix in the coconut milk, water, and some salt to taste. Seal the pressure lid, choose Pressure Cook on High and the cooking time to 3 minutes. After cooking, perform a natural pressure release for 6 minutes and then a quick pressure release to let out the remaining pressure.

Carefully open the lid. Stir in the lima beans and cover the rice with aluminum foil to prevent the rice from drying out. Oil a trivet with cooking spray. Place in the pot and slide the legs on the trivet under the foil. Remove the chicken from the marinade, hold for a while to allow the excess liquid drip back into the bag.

Arrange the chicken on the greased rack in a single layer. Close the air fry lid and choose Broil. Adjust the cooking time to 16 minutes. After 8 minutes, open the lid and flip the chicken and close the lid. Cook until the second side is crisp and browned on the edges. Serve the chicken with rice and garnish with the parsley.

Hot Crispy Chicken with Potatoes

Servings: 4 | Ready in about: 35 minutes

INGREDIENTS

4 bone-in skin-on chicken thighs
½ tsp salt
2 tbsp melted butter
2 tsp Worcestershire sauce
2 tsp turmeric powder

1 tsp dried oregano
½ tsp dry mustard
½ tsp garlic powder
¼ tsp sweet paprika
2 dashes hot sauce

¼ cup chicken stock
1 tbsp olive oil
1 lb potatoes, quartered
2 carrots, sliced into rounds

DIRECTIONS

Season the chicken on both sides with salt. In a small bowl, mix the melted butter, Worcestershire sauce, turmeric, oregano, dry mustard, garlic powder, sweet paprika, and hot sauce to be properly combined and stir in the chicken stock. On your Instant Pot, choose Sauté. Heat olive oil and add the chicken thighs and fry for 4 to 5 minutes or until browned. Turn and briefly sear the other side, about 1 minute. Remove from the pot.

Add the potatoes and carrots to the pot and stir to coat with the fat. Pour in about half of the spicy sauce and mix to coat. Put the chicken thighs on top and drizzle with the remaining sauce. Seal the pressure lid, choose Pressure Cook and the cooking time to 3 minutes. After cooking, do a quick pressure release, and carefully open the lid.

Transfer the chicken to a trivet. Gently move the potatoes and carrots aside and fetch some of the sauce over the chicken. Mix the potatoes and carrots back into the sauce and carefully set a trivet in the pot. Close the air fry lid and choose Bake. Adjust the temperature to 375°F and the cooking time to 16 minutes. Press Start. When done, open the lid and transfer the potatoes, carrots, and chicken to a platter, drizzling with any remaining sauce.

Chicken Meatballs Primavera

Servings: 4 | Ready in about: 30 minutes

INGREDIENTS

1 lb ground chicken
1 egg, cracked into a bowl
6 tsp flour
Salt and black pepper to taste

2 tbsp chopped basil + extra to garnish
1 tbsp olive oil + ½ tbsp olive oil
1 ½ tsp Italian Seasoning
1 red bell pepper, seeded and sliced

2 cups chopped green beans
½ lb chopped asparagus
1 cup chopped tomatoes
1 cup chicken broth

DIRECTIONS

In a mixing bowl, add the chicken, egg, flour, salt, pepper, 2 tablespoons of basil, 1 tablespoon of olive oil, and Italian seasoning. Mix them well with hands and make 16 large balls out of the mixture. Set the meatballs aside. Select Sauté. Heat half teaspoon of olive oil, and add peppers, green beans, and asparagus. Cook for 3 minutes, stirring frequently. After 3 minutes, use a spoon the veggies onto a plate and set aside.

Pour the remaining oil ithe pot to heat. Fry the meatballs for 2 minutes on each side until brown lightly. Put the vegetables into the pot. Pour the chicken broth over it. Seal the lid and select Pressure Cook for 10 minutes. Do a quick pressure release. Close the air fry lid and select Air Fry. Cook for 5 minutes at 400°F until nice and crispy. Dish the meatballs with sauce into a serving bowl and garnish it with basil. Serve with over cooked pasta.

Cajun Roasted Chicken with Potato Mash

Servings: 4 | Ready in about: 70 minutes

INGREDIENTS

2 bone-in chicken breasts
4 tsp Cajun seasoning
¾ cup chicken stock
3 Yukon Gold potatoes, scrubbed
3 tbsp melted butter
2 tbsp warm heavy cream

DIRECTIONS

Pat the chicken dry with a paper towel and carefully slide your hands underneath the skin to slightly separate the meat from the skin. Then in a small bowl, combine salt and Cajun seasoning, and rub half of the mixture under the skin and cavity of the chicken. Pour the chicken stock into the inner pot of the pot. Fix a trivet in the pot and lay the chicken on the side in the center of a trivet. Also, arrange the potatoes around the chicken.

Seal the pressure lid, choose Pressure Cook on High and the cooking time to 13 minutes. Mix the remaining spice mixture with 2 tablespoons of the melted butter, and set aside. When done pressure cooking, perform a natural pressure release for 10 minutes. Remove the potatoes and chicken onto a cutting board.

Pour the cooking juices into a bowl and return the trivet with chicken only to the pot. Baste the outer side of the chicken with half of the spice- butter mixture. Close the air fry lid and choose Air Fry. Adjust the temperature to 400°F and the cooking time to 16 minutes. After 8 minutes, open the lid and flip the chicken over.

Baste this side with the remaining butter mixture and close the lid to continue cooking. With a potato masher, smoothly puree the potatoes, and add the remaining salt, melted butter, heavy cream, and 2 tablespoons of the reserved cooking juice. Stir to combine. Taste and adjust the seasoning with salt and pepper and cover the bowl with aluminum foil. After cooking, transfer the chicken to a cutting board, leaving a trivet in the pot.

Pour the remaining cooking sauce into your Instant Pot and choose Sauté. Place the bowl of potatoes on the trivet to keep warm as the sauce reduces. Press Start and boil the sauce for 2 to 3 minutes or until reduced by about half. Meanwhile, slice the chicken and lay the pieces on a platter. Remove the mashed potato from the pot and remove the trivet. Spoon the sauce over the chicken slices and serve with the creamy potatoes.

Chicken Chili with Cannellini Beans

Servings: 4 | Ready in about: 40 minutes

INGREDIENTS

3 chicken breasts, cubed
3 cups chicken broth
1 tbsp butter
1 white onion, chopped
29 oz canned Cannellini beans, drained
1 tsp cumin powder
1 tsp dried oregano
½ cup heavy whipping cream
1 cup sour cream

DIRECTIONS

On your Instant Pot, choose Sauté. Stir and let cook the chicken for 6 minutes. Stir in the cannellini beans, cumin powder, and oregano. Pour in the broth, stir, close the pressure lid, and secure the pressure valve. Select Pressure Cook on High for 10 minutes. Once the timer has ended, let the pot sit uncovered for 10 minutes, then do a quick pressure release. Stir in the whipping and sour cream. Close the air fry lid and select Broil mode. Cook for 2 minutes. Serve warm with a mix of steamed bell peppers and broccoli.

Cheesy Buffalo Chicken

Servings: 4 | Ready in about: 37 minutes

INGREDIENTS

4 chicken breasts, boneless and skinless
½ cup Hot sauce
2 large white onion, finely chopped
2 cups finely chopped celery
1 tbsp olive oil
1 tsp dried thyme

3 cups chicken broth
1 tsp garlic powder

½ cup Blue cheese + extra for serving
4 oz cream cheese, cubed in small pieces

Salt and pepper, to taste

DIRECTIONS

Put the chicken on a clean flat surface and season with pepper and salt. Set aside. Select Sauté. Heat in olive oil, add onion and celery. Sauté them, constant stirring, until they are nice and soft, for about 5 minutes. Add garlic powder and thyme. Stir and cook for about a minute, and add the chicken, hot sauce, and chicken broth.

Seal the pressure lid and select Pressure Cook on High for 15 minutes. Put the blue cheese and cream cheese in a bowl, and use a fork to mash them together. Set the resulting mixture aside. Once the timer has ended, do a quick pressure release. Take out the chicken onto a flat surface and use two forks to shred them.

Return shredded chicken to the pot, close the air fry lid, select Broil mode and cook for 5 minutes. Add the cheese to the pot and stir until is slightly incorporated into the sauce. Dish the buffalo chicken soup into bowls. Sprinkle the remaining cheese over the soup and serve with sliced baguette.

Chicken & Green Bean Coconut Curry

Servings: 8 | Ready in about: 32 minutes

INGREDIENTS

4 chicken breasts
4 tbsp red curry paste
½ cup chicken broth

2 cups coconut milk
4 tbsp sugar
2 red bell pepper, sliced

2 yellow bell peppers, sliced
2 cup green beans, cut in half
2 tbsp lime juice

DIRECTIONS

Add the chicken, red curry paste, salt, pepper, coconut milk, broth, and sugar in your Instant Pot. Close the pressure lid, secure the pressure valve, and select Pressure Cook on High for 15 minutes.

Once the timer has ended, do a quick pressure release, and open the lid. Remove the chicken onto a cutting board and close the air fry lid. Select Broil mode. Add the bell peppers, green beans, and lime juice. Stir the sauce with a spoon and cook for 4 minutes. Slice the chicken with a knife, pour the sauce and vegetables over and serve warm.

Mediterranean Stuffed Chicken Breasts

Servings: 4 | Ready in about: 30 minutes

INGREDIENTS

4 chicken breasts, skinless
Salt and black pepper to taste
1 cup baby spinach, frozen

½ cup crumbled Feta cheese
½ tsp dried oregano
½ tsp garlic powder

2 tbsp olive oil
2 tsp dried parsley
1 cup water

DIRECTIONS

Wrap the chicken in plastic and put on a cutting board. Use a rolling pin to pound flat to a quarter-inch thickness. Remove the plastic wrap. In a bowl, mix spinach, salt, and feta cheese and scoop the mixture onto the chicken breasts. Wrap the chicken to secure the spinach filling in it. Use toothpicks to secure the wrap firmly from opening.

Gently season the chicken pieces with oregano, parsley, garlic powder, and pepper. Select Sauté on your Instant Pot. Heat the oil, add the chicken, and sear to golden brown on each side. Work in 2 batches. Remove the chicken onto a plate and set aside. Pour the water into the pot and scrape the bottom of the pot to let loose any chicken pieces or seasoning that is stuck to the bottom of the pot. Fit in a trivet.

Transfer the chicken onto the trivet. Seal the lid and select Pressure Cook on High for 10 minutes. Once the timer has ended, do a quick pressure release. Close the air fry lid and cook on Bake mode for 5 minutes at 390°F. Plate the chicken and serve with a side of sautéed asparagus and some slices of tomatoes.

Coq au Vin

Servings: 4 | Ready in about: 60 minutes

INGREDIENTS

4 chicken leg quarters, skin on
1½ tsp salt
1 tbsp olive oil
4 serrano ham slices, cut into thirds

¼ cup brown onion slices
1¼ cups dry red wine
⅓ cup chicken stock
1 ½ tsp tomato puree

½ tsp brown sugar
Black pepper to taste
½ cup sautéed mushrooms
¾ cup shallots, sliced

DIRECTIONS

Season the chicken on both sides with 1 teaspoon of salt and set aside on a wire rack. On your Instant Pot, choose Sauté. Heat the olive oil, place the ham in the pot in a single layer and cook for 3 to 4 minutes or until browned. Remove the ham to a plate and set aside. Add the chicken quarters to the pot. Cook for 5 minutes or until the skin is golden brown. Turn the chicken over and cook further for 2 minutes. Remove to a plate.

Carefully pour out almost all the fat leaving about a tablespoon to cover the bottom of the pot. Then, stir in the sliced onion and cook until the onion begins to brown. Add ½ cup of red wine, stir, and scrape the bottom of the pan to let off any browned bits. Then, boil the mixture until the wine reduces by about 1/3, about 2 minutes.

Pour the remaining red wine, chicken stock, tomato puree, brown sugar, and a few grinds of black pepper into your Instant Pot. Boil the sauce for 1 minute, stirring to make sure the tomato paste is properly mixed. Add the chicken pieces with skin- side up, to the pot. Put the pressure lid in place and lock to seal. Choose Pressure Cook on High and the cooking time to 12 minutes. After cooking, perform a natural pressure release for 10 minutes.

Remove the chicken from the pot. Pour the sauce into a bowl and allow sitting until the fat rises to the top and starts firming up. Use a spoon to fetch off the fat on top of the sauce. Pour the sauce back to the pot and stir in the mushrooms and pearl onions. Place the chicken on the sauce with skin side up. Close the air fry lid and select Broil. Adjust the time to 7 minutes. When done, open the lid and transfer the chicken to a serving platter. Spoon the sauce with mushrooms and pearl onions all around the chicken and crumble the reserved ham on top.

Traditional Chicken Cordon Bleu

Servings: 4 | Ready in about: 35 minutes

INGREDIENTS

2 large boneless skinless chicken breasts
¾ tsp salt
12 oz broccoli, cut into florets

3 tbsp melted butter
4 tsp Dijon mustard
4 thin ham slices

4 thin slices Emmental cheese
⅔ cup panko bread crumbs
¼ cup grated Pecorino Romano cheese

DIRECTIONS

Put the chicken breasts on a cutting board and slice through the breasts to form two thinner pieces from each breast to make 4 pieces in total. Season the chicken on both sides with ½ teaspoon of salt. Pour a cup of water into the inner pot. Put a trivet in the lower position of the pot and lay the broccoli florets on the trivet. After, put the chicken on the broccoli. Seal the pressure lid, choose Pressure Cook on High and the time to 1 minute.

After cooking, perform a quick pressure release. Take out the trivet and set aside. Pour the water out of the pot. Place the chicken on the cutting board and the broccoli into your Instant Pot. Put 1 tablespoon of melted butter on the broccoli florets and sprinkle with the remaining salt. Stir to coat the broccoli with the butter.

Smear 1 teaspoon of mustard on each chicken piece. Lay each ham slice on each chicken and each Emmental cheese slice on each ham. In a small bowl, combine the breadcrumbs, remaining butter, and the Pecorino Romano cheese. Sprinkle the breadcrumb mixture equally over the chicken. Open the air fry lid and carefully transfer the chicken pieces to a trivet. Close the air fry lid and choose Air Fry. Adjust the temperature to 400°F and the cooking time to 10 minutes. When done cooking, the crumbs should be crisp and have obtained a deep golden brown. Transfer the chicken pieces to a platter and serve with the broccoli.

Mexican Green Chili Chicken

Servings: 4 | Ready in about: 40 minutes

INGREDIENTS

1 tbsp olive oil
12 oz, baby plum tomatoes, halved
¾ cup chicken stock
½ tsp salt
½ tsp ground cumin
1 tsp Mexican seasoning mix
1 ½ lb boneless skinless chicken breasts
2 jalapeño peppers, seeded and chopped
2 serrano peppers, cut into chunks
2 large garlic cloves, minced
1 small onion, sliced
¼ cup minced fresh cilantro
Tortilla chips
½ cup shredded Cheddar Cheese
½ lime, juiced

DIRECTIONS

On your Instant Pot, choose Sauté. Heat the olive oil add the plum tomatoes. Cook without turning, for 3 to 4 minutes. Add the chicken stock while scraping the bottom of the pot to dissolve any browned bits. Stir in the cumin, Mexican seasoning, and salt. Add the chicken, jalapeños, serrano pepper, garlic, onion, and half the cilantro. Seal the pressure lid, choose Pressure Cook on High and the cooking time to 10 minutes.

Grease a trivet with cooking spray and fix it in the upper position of the pot. Cut out a circle of aluminum foil and place on the trivet. Lay on a single layer of tortilla chips, sprinkle with half of the Cheddar cheese and repeat with another layer of chips and cheese. Set aside. After cooking, perform a natural pressure release for 5 minutes. Take out the chicken from the pot and set aside. Then, with an immersion blender, purée the vegetables into the sauce.

Shred the chicken with two forks and return the pieces to the sauce. Add the remaining cilantro and the lime juice. Taste and adjust the seasoning and carefully transfer chips to the pot. Close the air fry lid and choose Air Fry. Adjust the temperature to 375°F and the time to 5 minutes. When done cooking, open the lid. Carefully take out the trivet and pour the chips into a platter. Serve the chili in bowls with the chips on the side.

White Wine Chicken

Servings: 4 | Ready in about: 9 hours

INGREDIENTS

3 chicken legs, cut into drumsticks and thighs
8 oz Shiitake mushrooms, stems removed and cut into 4 pieces
3 skinny carrots, cut into 4 crosswise pieces each
2 bacon slices, chopped
1 ½ cups dry white wine
Salt and black pepper to taste
½ bunch thyme, divided
3 Shallots, peeled
3 tbsp butter, divided
2 cloves garlic, crushed
1 tbsp flour
3 tbsp chopped parsley for garnishing

DIRECTIONS

Put the chicken on a clean flat surface and season on both sides with salt and pepper. In a plastic zipper bag, pour the wine. Add half of the thyme and chicken. Zip the bag and shake to coat the chicken well with the wine. Place it in the refrigerator for 6 to 8 hours. After 8 hours, turn on your Instant Pot on High and fry the bacon on Sauté mode for about 8 minutes. Remove the bacon without the fat onto a plate using a slotted spoon. Set aside.

Pour the mushroom into the pot, season with salt and cook for 5 minutes. Then, remove at the side of the bacon. Remove the chicken from the refrigerator onto a clean flat surface. Take out and discard the thyme but reserve the marinade. Pat the chicken dry with paper towels. Melt half of the butter in the pot on Sauté. Place the chicken in the butter in batches and fry until dark golden brown on each side, about 12 minutes.

Addin bacon, mushrooms, shallots, garlic, carrots, and salt. Cook for 4 minutes and top with the wine and remaining thyme. Seal the pressure lid and select Pressure Cook for 15 minutes. Add the flour and the remaining butter in a bowl, and smash them together with a fork. Once the timer has ended, do a quick pressure release.

Discard the thyme. Add the flour mixture to the sauce in the pot, stir until well incorporated. Adjust the seasoning with salt and black pepper. Close the air fry lid and select Broil. Cook for 4 minutes. Top with parsley and serve.

Chicken Caesar Salad with Salted Croutons

Servings: 4 | Ready in about: 45 minutes

INGREDIENTS

2 chicken breasts, skinless boneless
1 garlic clove, minced
1 tbsp unsalted butter
2 tbsp olive oil
½ small Italian bread loaf, cubed
⅓ cup Caesar dressing, divided
1 romaine lettuce heart, torn
1 oz grated Parmigiano Reggiano cheese
2 tbsp grated Parmigiano Reggiano

DIRECTIONS

Pour 1 cup of water into your Instant Pot. Put in a trivet in and place the chicken on the trivet. Seal the pressure lid, choose Pressure Cook, adjust the pressure to Low and the cooking time to 5 minutes. Once done cooking, perform a natural pressure release for 10 minutes. Carefully open the lid. Set aside. In a heatproof bowl, combine garlic, butter, and olive oil. Put the bowl in the air fry basket and place the basket in the pot.

Close the air fry lid and choose Air Fry. Adjust the temperature to 375°F and the cooking time to 2 minutes. Press Start to preheat the pot and melt the butter. When done preheating, take out the basket from the pot and the bowl from the basket. Pour the bread cubes into the bowl and toss to be well-coated in the butter and oil. Transfer the bread to the air fry basket and the basket into your Instant Pot.

Close the air fry lid and choose Air Fry. Adjust the temperature to 375°F and the cooking time to 10 minutes. After 5 minutes, open the lid and toss the bread. Close the lid and continue cooking until the croutons are golden brown. Remove the basket from the pot and lightly season the croutons with salt. Allow cooling.

Cut the chicken into bite-size chunks. In a small bowl, toss the chicken with 3 tablespoons of Caesar dressing and set aside. Place the lettuce on a salad bowl, pour the remaining dressing over nad toss to coat well. Mix with chesse. Share the salad into bowls, top with chicken, then croutons, and sprinkle with extra cheese.

Pesto Chicken with Roasted Pepper Sauce

Servings: 4 | Ready in about: 23 minutes

INGREDIENTS

4 chicken breasts, skinless and boneless
½ cup heavy cream
½ cup chicken broth
⅓ tsp minced garlic
Salt and black pepper to taste
⅓ tsp Italian Seasoning
¼ cup roasted red peppers, chopped
1 tbsp basil pesto
1 tbsp cornstarch

DIRECTIONS

To your Instant Pot, add the chicken at the bottom. Pour the chicken broth and add Italian seasoning, garlic, salt, and pepper. Close the pressure lid, secure the pressure valve, and select Pressure Cook on High for 15 minutes. Once the timer has ended, do a natural pressure release for 5 minutes and open the lid.

Use a spoon to remove the chicken onto a plate. Scoop out any fat or unwanted chunks from the sauce. In a bowl, add the cream, cornstarch, red peppers, and pesto. Mix them with a spoon. Pour the creamy mixture into the pot and close the air fry lid. Select Broil and cook for 4 minutes. Serve the chicken with sauce.

Chicken Noodle Soup with Crispy Bacon

Servings: 8 | Ready in about: 33 minutes

INGREDIENTS

5 oz dry egg noodles
4 chicken breasts, skinless and boneless
1 large white onion, chopped
8 bacon slices, chopped
4 cloves garlic, minced
Salt and black pepper to taste
2 medium carrots, sliced
2 cups sliced celery
½ cup chopped parsley
1 ½ tsp dried thyme
8 cups chicken broth

DIRECTIONS

Turn on your Instant Pot and select Sauté. Add the chopped bacon and fry for 5 minutes until nicely brown and crispy. Remove to a paper towel to soak up excess oil and set aside. Add the onion and garlic to the pot and cook for 3 minutes until tender. Add the chicken breasts, noodles, carrots, celery, chicken broth, thyme, salt, and pepper. Seal the pressure lid and select Pressure Cook on High pressure. Adjust the time to 5 minutes.

Once the timer has ended, do a quick pressure release, and open the lid. Use a wooden spoon to remove the chicken onto a plate. Shred the chicken with two forks and add it back to the soup. Stir in the bacon. Close the air fry lid and cook on Broil for 5 minutes. Ladle the soup into serving bowls and serve with a side of bread.

Tandoori Chicken with Cilantro Sauce

Servings: 4 | Ready in about: 9 hour

INGREDIENTS

- 4 chicken thighs, skinless
- ½ cup Greek yogurt
- 1 tbsp olive oil
- 1 tbsp lemon juice
- 1 tbsp red chili powder
- 2 tsp salt
- 1 tsp garam masala
- ½ tsp ground turmeric
- ½ tbsp grated fresh ginger
- ½ tbsp minced garlic
- 1 cup water
- Cooking spray

Cilantro Sauce:
- A handful of fresh cilantro leaves
- 1 tsp cumin seeds
- ½ jalapeno pepper
- 2-3 garlic cloves
- 2 tsp honey
- 2 tsp lemon juice
- ¾ cup olive oil
- salt to taste

DIRECTIONS

In a large bowl, mix yogurt, lemon juice, garam masala, garlic, turmeric, red chili powder, vegetable oil, salt, and ginger. Use a paper towel to pat thighs. Place the thighs into a resealable plastic bag. Add in yogurt mixture and seal. Massage bag to ensure the marinade coats the chicken completely and place in the refrigerator for 12 hours. Take the chicken out of the refrigerator and set aside for 30 minutes before cooking.

Add water into your Instant Pot. Apply a cooking spray to your steamer and set in the pot over the water. Remove chicken from marinade and arrange on the trivet. Seal the pressure lid, choose Pressure Cook on High, and set the timer to 15 minutes. When ready, release the pressure quickly. In a blender, blend cilantro, water, garlic, honey, cumin, jalapeno pepper, salt and lemon juice until smooth. Over the chicken, drizzle sauce before serving.

Chicken & Veggie Tacos with Guacamole

Servings: 4 | Ready in about: 30 minutes

INGREDIENTS

- 2 lb chicken breasts, sliced
- ½ cup chicken broth
- 1 yellow onion, sliced
- 1 green bell pepper, seeded and sliced
- 1 yellow bell pepper, seeded and sliced
- 1 red bell pepper, seeded and sliced
- 2 tbsp cumin powder
- 2 tbsp chili powder
- Salt to taste
- ½ Lime
- Fresh cilantro, to garnish

Tacos, Guacamole, sour cream, Salsa, cheese for assembling

DIRECTIONS

Grease the inner pot with cooking spray and line the bottom with the peppers and onion. Lay the chicken on the bed of peppers. Sprinkle with salt, chili powder, and cumin powder. Squeeze some lime juice and pour in chicken broth. Seal the lid and select Pressure Cook on High for 15 minutes. Once ready, do a quick pressure release.

Close the air fry lid and cook for 5 minutes on Bake at 390°F. Dish the chicken with the vegetables and juice onto a large serving platter. Add sour cream, cheese, guacamole, salsa, and tacos in one layer on the side of the chicken.

Spinach & Mushroom Chicken Stew

Servings: 4 | Ready in about: 56 minutes

INGREDIENTS

4 chicken breasts, diced
1 ¼ lb white Button mushrooms, halved
3 tbsp olive oil
1 large onion, sliced
5 cloves garlic, minced
Salt and black pepper to taste
1 ¼ tsp cornstarch
½ cup spinach, chopped
1 ½ cups chicken stock
1 tsp Dijon mustard
1 ½ cup sour cream
3 tbsp chopped parsley

DIRECTIONS

On your Instant Pot, choose Sauté. Once the pot is ready, heat the olive oil then include the onion and sauté for 3 minutes until soft. Add the mushrooms, chicken, garlic, salt, pepper, Dijon mustard, and chicken broth. Stir well. Seal the lid and press Pressure Cooker for 15 minutes. Once done, do a natural pressure release for 5 minutes

Carefully open the lid. Stir the stew, remove the bay leaf, and scoop some of the liquid into a bowl. Add the cornstarch to the liquid and mix them until completely lump free. Pour the liquid into the sauce, stir it, and let the sauce thicken to your desired consistency. Top it with the sour cream, close the air fry lid and select Broil mode. Cook for 2 minutes. Garnish with the chopped parsley and serve with steamed green peas.

Chicken with Beans & Bacon

Servings: 4 | Ready in about: 45 minutes

INGREDIENTS

1 tbsp olive oil
4 slices bacon, crumbled
4 boneless, skinless chicken thighs
1 onion, diced
4 garlic cloves, minced
1 tbsp tomato paste
1 tbsp oregano
1 tbsp ground cumin
1 tsp chili powder
½ tsp cayenne pepper
1 (14.5 oz) can whole tomatoes
1 cup chicken broth
1 cup cooked corn
1 red bell pepper, chopped
15 oz red kidney beans, drained
1 cup shredded Monterey Jack cheese
1 cup sliced red onion
¼ cup chopped cilantro

DIRECTIONS

Warm oil on Sauté in your Instant Pot. Sear the chicken for 3 minutes for each side until browned. Set the chicken on a plate. In the same oil, fry bacon until crispy, about 5 minutes and set aside. Add in onions and cook for 2 to 3 minutes until fragrant. Stir in garlic, oregano, cayenne pepper, cumin, tomato paste, bell pepper, and chili powder and cook for 30 more seconds. Pour the chicken broth, salt, and tomatoes and bring to a boil.

Take back the chicken and bacon to the pot and ensure it is submerged in the liquid. Seal the pressure lid, choose Pressure Cook, and set the timer to 15 minutes. When ready, release the pressure quickly. Pour in the kidney beans. Press Sauté and bring the liquid to a boil. Cook for 10 minutes. Serve topped with cheese and cilantro.

Spicy Salsa Chicken with Feta

Servings: 6 | Ready in about: 30 minutes

INGREDIENTS

2 lb boneless skinless chicken drumsticks
¼ tsp salt
1 ½ cups hot tomato salsa
1 onion, chopped
1 cup feta cheese, crumbled

DIRECTIONS

Sprinkle salt over the chicken. Set in your Instant Pot. Stir in salsa to coat the chicken. Seal the pressure lid, choose Pressure Cook on High, and set the timer to 15 minutes. When ready, do a quick pressure release. Press Sauté and cook for 5 to 10 minutes as you stir until excess liquid has evaporated. Top with feta cheese and serve.

Sticky Orange Chicken

Servings: 4 | Ready in about: 30 minutes

INGREDIENTS

- 2 chicken breasts, cubed
- ½ cup honey
- ½ cup orange juice
- ⅓ cup soy sauce
- ⅓ cup chicken stock
- ⅓ cup hoisin sauce
- 1 garlic clove, minced
- 2 tsp cornstarch
- 2 tsp water
- 1 cup diced orange
- 3 cups hot cooked quinoa

DIRECTIONS

Arrange the chicken to the bottom of your Instant Pot. In a bowl, mix honey, soy sauce, garlic, hoisin sauce, chicken stock, and orange juice, until the honey is dissolved. Pour the mixture over the chicken. Seal the pressure lid, choose Pressure Cook on High, and set the timer to 7 minutes. When ready, release the pressure quickly.

Take the chicken from the pot and set in a bowl. Press Sauté. In a bowl, mix water with cornstarch, pour into the liquid in the pot and cook for 3 minutes until thick. Stir orange and chicken into the sauce until coated. Serve.

Chicken Cacciatore

Servings: 4 | Ready in about: 40 minutes

INGREDIENTS

- 2 tsp olive oil
- 1 lb chicken drumsticks, boneless, skinless
- 2 tsp salt
- 1½ tsp freshly ground black pepper
- 1 carrot, chopped
- 1 red bell pepper, chopped
- 1 yellow bell pepper, chopped
- 1 onion, chopped
- 4 garlic cloves, thinly sliced
- 2 tsp dried oregano
- 1 tsp dried basil
- 1 tsp dried parsley
- 1 pinch red pepper flakes
- 1 (28 oz) can diced tomatoes
- ½ cup dry red wine
- ¾ cup chicken stock
- 1 cup black olives, pitted and sliced
- 2 bay leaves

DIRECTIONS

Warm oil on Sauté in your Instant Pot. Add pepper and salt to the chicken drumsticks. In batches, sear the chicken for 5-6 minutes until golden brown. Set aside on a plate. Drain the cooker and remain with 1 tbsp of fat. In the hot oil, sauté onion, garlic, and bell peppers for 4 minutes until softened. Add red pepper flakes, basil, parsley, and oregano, and cook for 30 more seconds. Season with salt and pepper.

Stir in tomatoes, olives, chicken stock, red wine and bay leaves. Return chicken to the pot. Seal the pressure lid, choose Pressure Cook on High, and set the timer to 15 minutes. When ready, release the pressure quickly. Divide chicken between four serving bowls. Top with tomato mixture before serving.

Honey-Garlic Chicken

Servings: 4 | Ready in about: 30 minutes

INGREDIENTS

- 4 chicken breasts, cut into chunks
- 1 onion, diced
- 4 garlic cloves, smashed
- ½ cup honey
- 3 tbsp soy sauce
- 2 tbsp lime juice
- 2 tsp sesame oil
- 1 tsp rice vinegar
- 1 tbsp cornstarch

DIRECTIONS

Mix garlic, onion and chicken in your Instant Pot. In a bowl, combine honey, sesame oil, lime juice, soy sauce, 1 cup water, and rice vinegar. Pour over the chicken mixture. Seal the pressure lid, choose Pressure Cook on High, and set the timer to 15 minutes. When ready, release the pressure quickly. Mix 1 tbsp water and cornstarch until well dissolved. Stir into the sauce. Press Sauté. Simmer the sauce for 2 to 3 minutes as you stir until thickened.

BBQ Chicken Drumettes

Servings: 4 | Ready in about: 30 minutes

INGREDIENTS

2 lb chicken drumettes, bone-in, skin in
½ cup chicken broth
½ tsp dry mustard
½ tsp sweet paprika
½ tbsp cumin powder
½ tsp onion powder
¼ tsp Cayenne powder
1 stick butter, sliced in 5 pieces
BBQ sauce to taste

DIRECTIONS

Pour the chicken broth into the inner pot of your Instant Pot and insert a trivet. In a zipper bag, pour in dry mustard, cumin powder, onion powder, cayenne powder, salt, and pepper. Add the chicken, close the bag and shake to coat the chicken well with the spices. You can toss the chicken in the spices in batches too.

Then, remove the chicken from the bag and place on the trivet. Spread the butter slices on the drumsticks. Seal the lid and select Pressure Cook on High for 10 minutes. Once the timer has ended, do a quick pressure release, and open the lid. Remove the chicken onto a clean flat surface like a cutting board and brush them with the barbecue sauce using the brush. Return to a trivet and close the air fry lid. Cook for 10 minutes at 400°F on Air Fry mode.

Sage Chicken Thighs

Servings: 4 | Ready in about: 35 minutes

INGREDIENTS

2 lb chicken thighs, bone-in and skin on
2 tbsp olive oil
1 ½ cups diced tomatoes
¾ cup yellow onions
2 tsp minced garlic
½ cup balsamic vinegar
3 tsp chopped fresh sage
1 cup chicken broth
2 tbsp chopped parsley

DIRECTIONS

With paper towels, pat dry the chicken and season with salt and pepper. Select Sauté mode. Warm the olive and add the chicken with the skin side down. Cook to golden brown on each side, for about 9 minutes. Remove onto a clean plate. Add garlic, onions, and tomatoes to the pot and sauté for 3 minutes, stirring occasionally.

Pour the chicken broth, sage, and balsamic vinegar. Stir them using a spoon. Add the chicken back to the pot. Seal the lid and select Pressure Cook for 15 minutes. When ready, do a quick pressure release. Close the air fry lid and cook on Air Fry for 5 minutes at 400°F. Garnish with parsley and serve with roasted tomatoes and potatoes.

Paprika Buttered Chicken

Servings: 6 | Ready in about: 45 minutes

INGREDIENTS

1 cup chicken stock
½ cup white wine
½ onion, thinly sliced
2 cloves garlic, minced
3.5-lb whole chicken
Salt and black pepper to taste
½ tsp dried thyme
3 tbsp butter, melted
½ tsp paprika

DIRECTIONS

Into the pot, add onion, chicken stock, white wine, and garlic. Over the mixture, place a trivet. Apply pepper, salt, and thyme to the chicken. Lay onto trivet breast-side up. Seal the pressure lid, choose Pressure Cook on High, and set the timer to 26 minutes. When ready, release the pressure quickly. In a bowl, mix paprika and butter.

Remove the trivet with chicken from your pot. Get rid of onion and stock. Onto the chicken, brush butter mixture. Place it on the air fry basket and insert in the pot. Close the air fry lid, select Air Fry, and cook for 5 minutes at 400°F until the skin is crispy and browned. Let the chicken to cool for 5 minutes, then carve it to serve.

Whole Chicken with Lemon & Onion Stuffing

Servings: 6 | Ready in about: 55 minutes

INGREDIENTS

4 lb whole chicken
1 tbsp herbes de Provence Seasoning
1 tbsp olive oil
Salt and black pepper to taste
2 cloves garlic, peeled
1 tsp garlic powder
1 yellow onion, peeled and quartered
1 lemon, quartered
1 ¼ cups chicken broth

DIRECTIONS

Put the chicken on a clean flat surface and pat dry using paper towels. Sprinkle the top and cavity of the chicken with salt, pepper, Herbes de Provence, and garlic powder. Stuff the onion, lemon quarters, and garlic cloves into the cavity. In your Instant Pot, fit a trivet. Pour broth into the pot and place the chicken on the trivet. Seal the lid, and select Pressure Cook on High for 25 minutes. Once ready, do a natural pressure release for about 10 minutes.

Close the air fry lid and broil the chicken for 5 minutes on Broil mode to ensure that it attains a golden brown color on each side. Dish the chicken on a bed of steamed mixed veggies. Right here, the choice is yours to whip up some good veggies together as your appetite tells you.

Buffalo Chicken & Navy Bean Chili

Servings: 6 | Ready in about: 45 minutes

INGREDIENTS

1 tbsp olive oil
1 shallot, diced
½ cup fennel, chopped
¼ cup minced garlic
1 tbsp smoked paprika
2 tsp chili powder
2 tsp ground cumin
1 (28 oz) can crushed tomatoes
1 ½ lb chicken sausage, sliced
1 (14 oz) can tomatoes with green chilies
¾ cup Buffalo wing sauce
2 (14 oz) cans navy beans, drained

DIRECTIONS

Warm oil on Sauté in your Instant Pot. Add the sausages and brown for 5 minutes, turning frequently. Set aside on a plate. In the same fat, sauté onion, roasted red peppers, fennel, and garlic for 4 minutes until soft. Season with paprika, cumin, pepper, salt, and chili powder. Stir in crushed tomatoes, diced tomatoes with green chilies, buffalo sauce, and navy beans. Return the sausages to the pot. Seal the pressure lid, choose Pressure Cook on High, and set the timer to 30 minutes. When ready, do a quick pressure release. Spoon chili into bowls and serve.

Chicken Chickpea Chili

Servings: 4 | Ready in about: 25 minutes

INGREDIENTS

1 tbsp olive oil
3 large serrano peppers, diced
1 onion, diced
1 jalapeño pepper, diced
1 lb chicken breasts, cubed
1 tsp ground cumin
1 tsp minced fresh garlic
1 tsp salt
2 (14.5 oz) cans chickpeas, drained
2 ½ cups water, divided
2 tbsp chili powder
½ cup chopped fresh cilantro
½ cup shredded Monterey Jack cheese
1 lime, cut into six wedges

DIRECTIONS

Warm oil on Sauté in your Instant Pot. Add in onion, serrano peppers, and jalapeno pepper and cook for 5 minutes until tender. Add salt, cumin and garlic for seasoning. Stir chicken with vegetable mixture. Cook for 3 to 6 minutes until no longer pink. Add 2 cups water and chickpeas. Seal the pressure lid, choose Pressure Cook.

Set the timer to 5 minutes. Release pressure quickly. Stir chili powder with remaining ½ cup water. Press Sauté. Cook the chili until slightly thickened. Garnish with cheese and cilantro. Over the chili, squeeze a lime wedge.

Indian Butter Chicken

Servings: 6 | Ready in about: 30 minutes

INGREDIENTS

2 tbsp butter
1 large onion, minced
1 tbsp grated fresh ginger
1 tbsp minced fresh garlic
½ tsp ground turmeric

1 tbsp Kashmiri red chili powder
1 (14.5 oz) can coconut milk, refrigerated
2 lb boneless, skinless chicken legs
3 Roma tomatoes, pureed in a blender
½ cup chopped fresh cilantro, divided

2 tbsp Indian curry paste
2 tbsp dried fenugreek
2 tsp sugar
1 tsp garam masala
Salt to taste

DIRECTIONS

Set your Instant Pot to Sauté and melt butter. Add in salt and onion. Cook for 2 to 3 minutes until fragrant. Stir in ginger, turmeric, garlic, and red chili powder to coat. Cook for 2 more minutes. Place water and coconut cream into separate bowls. Stir the water from the coconut milk can, pureed tomatoes, and chicken with the onion mixture. Seal the pressure lid, choose Pressure Cook on High, and set the timer to 8 minutes.

When ready, release the pressure quickly. Stir sugar, coconut cream, fenugreek, curry paste, half the cilantro, and garam masala through the chicken mixture. Apply salt for seasoning. Simmer the mixture and cook for 10 minutes until the sauce thickens on Sauté. Garnish with the rest of the cilantro before serving.

Chicken in Tikka Masala Sauce

Servings: 4 | Ready in about: 40 minutes

INGREDIENTS

2 lb boneless, skinless chicken thighs,
2 tbsp olive oil
½ onion, chopped
2 garlic cloves, minced
3 tbsp tomato puree
1 tsp fresh ginger, minced

1 tbsp garam masala
2 tsp curry powder
1 tsp ground coriander
½ tsp ground cumin
⅛ tsp jalapeño pepper, chopped
29 oz canned tomato sauce

3 tomatoes, chopped
½ cup natural yogurt
1 lemon, juiced
3 cups cooked basmati rice
¼ cup fresh chopped cilantro leaves
4 lemon wedges

DIRECTIONS

Set your Instant Pot to Sauté. Warm oil. Add garlic and onion and cook for 3 minutes until soft. Stir in tomato puree, garam masala, cumin, curry powder, ginger, coriander, and jalapeño. Cook for 30 seconds until fragrant. Stir in tomato sauce and tomatoes. Simmer the mixture as you scrape the bottom to get rid of any browned bits.

Stir in chicken to coat. Seal the pressure lid, choose Pressure Cook on High, and set the timer to 10 minutes. When ready, release the pressure quickly. Press Sauté and simmer the sauce and cook for 3 to 5 minutes until thickened. Stir lemon juice and yogurt through the sauce. Serve garnished with lemon wedges and cilantro.

Chicken with BBQ Sauce

Servings: 6 | Ready in about: 20 minutes

INGREDIENTS

2 lb boneless skinless chicken breasts
1 tsp salt

1½ cups barbecue sauce
1 small onion, minced

1 cup carrots, thinly sliced
4 garlic cloves

DIRECTIONS

Apply a seasoning of salt to the chicken and place in the inner pot of the pot. Add onion, carrots, garlic and barbeque sauce. Toss the chicken to coat. Seal the pressure lid, choose Pressure Cook on High, and set the timer to 15 minutes. Once ready, do a quick release. Use two forks to shred chicken and stir into the sauce.

Pulled Chicken & Peach Salsa

Servings: 4 | Ready in about: 40 minutes

INGREDIENTS

15 oz canned peach chunks
4 boneless, skinless chicken thighs
14 oz canned diced tomatoes
2 cloves garlic, minced
½ tsp cumin
½ tsp salt
Cheddar shredded cheese
Fresh chopped mint leaves

DIRECTIONS

Strain canned peach chunks. Reserve the juice and set aside. To your Instant Pot, add chicken, tomatoes, cumin, garlic, peach juice, and salt. Seal the pressure lid, choose Pressure Cook on High, and set the timer to 15 minutes. When ready, do a quick pressure release. Shred chicken. Transfer to a serving plate. Add peach chunks to the cooking juices and mix until well combined. Pour the peach salsa over the chicken. Top with mint and cheese.

Pesto Stuffed Chicken with Green Beans

Servings: 4 | Ready in about: 20 minutes

INGREDIENTS

4 chicken breasts
1 tbsp butter
1 tbsp olive oil
¼ cup dry white wine
¾ cup chicken stock
1 tsp salt
1 cup green beans, trimmed and cut into 1-inch pieces

For pesto:
1 cup fresh basil
1 garlic clove, smashed
2 tbsp pine nuts
¼ cup Parmesan cheese
¼ cup extra virgin olive oil

DIRECTIONS

In a bowl, mix fresh basil, pine nuts, garlic, salt, pepper and Parmesan and place in food processor. Add in oil and process until the desired consistency is attained. Adjust seasoning. Apply a thin layer of pesto to one side of each chicken breast. Tightly roll into a cylinder and fasten closed with small skewers. Press Sauté. Add oil and butter.

Cook chicken rolls for 1 to 2 minutes per side until browned. Add in wine cook until the wine has evaporated, about 3-4 minutes. Add stock and salt into your Instant Pot. Top the chicken with green beans. Seal the pressure lid, choose Pressure Cook on High, and set the timer to 5 minutes. When ready, release the pressure quickly. Serve chicken rolls with cooking liquid and green beans.

Salsa Verde Chicken

Servings: 4 | Ready in about: 50 minutes

INGREDIENTS

1 jalapeño pepper, deveined and sliced
½ cup capers
¼ cup parsley
1 lime, juiced
1 tsp salt
¼ cup extra virgin olive oil
4 boneless skinless chicken breasts
2 cups water
1 cup quinoa, rinsed

DIRECTIONS

In a blender, mix olive oil, salt, lime juice, jalapeño pepper, capers, and parsley and blend until smooth. Arrange chicken breasts in the bottom of the pot pot. Over the chicken, add salsa verde mixture. In a bowl that can fit in the cooker, mix quinoa and water. Set a trivet onto chicken and sauce. Set the bowl onto the trivet. Seal the pressure lid, choose Pressure Cook on High, and set the timer to 20 minutes.

When ready, release the pressure quickly. Remove the quinoa bowl and trivet. Using two forks, shred chicken into the sauce. Stir to coat. Divide the quinoa, between plates. Top with chicken and salsa verde before serving.

Cajun Chicken with Rice & Peas

Servings: 4 | Ready in about: 30 minutes

INGREDIENTS

4 chicken breasts, sliced
1 garlic clove, minced
½ tsp paprika
¼ tsp dried oregano
¼ tsp dried thyme

⅛ tsp cayenne pepper
⅛ tsp ground white pepper
Salt to taste
1 tbsp oil olive
1 onion, chopped

1 tbsp tomato puree
2 cups chicken broth, divided
1 cup long grain rice
1 celery stalk, diced
1 cup frozen green peas

DIRECTIONS

Season chicken with garlic powder, oregano, white pepper, thyme, paprika, cayenne pepper, and salt. Warm the oil on Sauté in your Instant Pot. Add in onion and cook for 4 minutes until fragrant. Mix in tomato puree. Add ¼ cup chicken stock into the pot to deglaze the pan, scrape the pan's bottom to get rid of browned bits of food.

Mix in celery, rice, and the seasoned chicken. Add in the remaining broth to the chicken mixture. Seal the pressure lid, choose Pressure Cook on High, and set the timer to 8 minutes. Once ready, do a quick release. Mix in green peas, cover with the lid and let sit for 5 minutes. Serve warm.

Spicy Chicken Wings with Lemon

Servings: 4 | Ready in about: 40 minutes

INGREDIENTS

2 tbsp olive oil
8 chicken wings
½ tsp chili powder

½ tsp garlic powder
½ tsp onion powder
½ dried oregano

½ tsp cayenne pepper
½ cup chicken broth
2 lemons, juiced

DIRECTIONS

Coat the chicken wings with olive oil. Season with chili powder, onion powder, oregano, garlic powder, and cayenne pepper. In the steel pot of your Instant Pot, add your wings and chicken broth. Seal the pressure lid, choose Pressure Cook on High, and set the timer to 4 minutes. When ready, do a quick pressure release.

Onto a greased baking sheet, place the wings in a single layer and drizzle over the lemon juice. Place in the pot and close the air fry lid. Select Bake for 5 minutes at 400 F until the skin is crispy. Serve.

Chicken Meatballs in Tomato Sauce

Servings: 5 | Ready in about: 35 minutes

INGREDIENTS

1 lb ground chicken
3 tbsp red hot sauce
1 egg
⅓ cup crumbled blue cheese

¼ cup bread crumbs
¼ cup Pecorino cheese
1 tbsp ranch dressing
1 tsp dried basil

15 oz canned tomato sauce
1 cup chicken broth
2 tbsp olive oil
A handful of parsley, chopped

DIRECTIONS

In a bowl, mix ground chicken, egg, pecorino, basil, pepper, salt, ranch dressing, blue cheese, 3 tbsp hot sauce, and bread crumbs. Shape the mixture into meatballs. Warm oil on Sauté in your Instant Pot. Add in the meatballs and cook for 2 to 3 minutes until browned on all sides. Add in tomato sauce and broth. Seal the pressure lid.

Choose Pressure Cook on High, and set the timer to 7 minutes. When ready, release the pressure quickly. Remove meatballs carefully and place to a serving plate. Top with parsley and serve.

Chicken in Pineapple Gravy

Servings: 4 | Ready in about: 25 minutes

INGREDIENTS

1 tbsp olive oil
4 boneless, skinless chicken thighs,
¼ cup pineapple juice

2 tbsp ketchup
2 tbsp Worcestershire sauce
1 garlic clove, minced

1 tsp cornstarch
2 tsp water
A handful of fresh cilantro, chopped

DIRECTIONS

Warm oil on Sauté in your Instant Pot. In batches, sear chicken in oil for 3 minutes until golden brown. Set aside on a plate. Mix, pineapple juice, Worcestershire sauce, garlic, and ketchup. Add to the pot to deglaze, scrape the bottom to get rid of any browned bits of food. Place the chicken into the sauce and stir well to coat.

Seal the pressure lid, choose Pressure Cook, and set the timer to cook for 5 minutes. When ready, release the pressure quickly. In a bowl, mix water and cornstarch until well dissolved. Set to Sauté. Stir the cornstarch slurry into the sauce. Cook for 2 minutes until the sauce is well thickened. Set in serving bowls and cilantro to serve.

Za'atar Chicken with Lemony Couscous

Servings: 4 | Ready in about: 40 minutes

INGREDIENTS

4 chicken thighs
2 tbsp za'atar mix
1 tbsp ground sumac
sea Salt and black pepper to taste

2 tbsp butter
2 ½ cups chicken stock, divided
1 onion, thinly sliced
1 garlic clove, minced

1½ cups couscous
Juice from 1 lemon
Fresh parsley, chopped

DIRECTIONS

Season the chicken with salt, sumac, za'atar, and pepper. On your Instant Pot, choose Sauté. Melt butter and sear the chicken in batches for 5 minutes per batch until lightly browned. Set aside. In the pot, add ¼ cup chicken stock to deglaze, scrape the bottom to get rid of any browned bits of food. Add garlic and onion to the stock.

Cook for 3 minutes until soft. Add the remaining chicken stock into the pan. Add lemon juice and couscous. Add in chicken. Seal the pressure lid, choose Pressure Cook on High, and set the timer to 5 minutes. Naturally release the pressure for 5 minutes. Transfer the couscous and chicken to a serving plate. Add parsley to garnish.

Juicy Orange Chicken

Servings: 6 | Ready in about: 50 minutes

INGREDIENTS

2 tbsp olive oil
6 chicken breasts, cubed
⅓ cup chicken stock
¼ cup soy sauce

2 tbsp brown sugar
1 tbsp lemon juice
1 tbsp garlic powder
1 tsp chili sauce

1 cup orange juice
Salt and black pepper to taste
2 cups cooked gnocchi

DIRECTIONS

Warm oil on Sauté in your Instant Pot. In batches, sear chicken in the oil for 5 minutes until browned. Set aside in a bowl. In your pot, mix orange juice, water, sugar, chili sauce, garlic powder, vinegar, and soy sauce. Stir in chicken to coat. Seal the pressure lid, choose Pressure Cook on High, and set the timer to 7 minutes.

When ready, release the pressure quickly. Take ¼ cup liquid from the pot to a bowl. Stir in cornstarch to dissolve. Mix into sauce in the pot until the color is consistent. Press Sauté. Cook sauce for 5 minutes until thickened. Season with pepper and salt. Serve the chicken with gnocchi.

Hawaiian-Style Chicken Sliders with Salad

Servings: 12 | Ready in about: 2 hour

INGREDIENTS

Mango Slaw:
¼ cup apple cider vinegar
¼ cup olive oil
1 small pineapple, chopped
4 cups arugula
¼ cup chopped fresh cilantro
4 green onions, sliced

Hawaiian-Style Chicken:
1 cup brown sugar
½ cup chicken broth
½ cup soy sauce
½ cup honey
¼ cup orange juice
2 garlic cloves, minced

2 tbsp grated fresh ginger
1 tsp freshly ground black pepper
6 chicken breasts, halved
2 tbsp cornstarch
2 tbsp water
12 Hawaiian bread rolls

DIRECTIONS

In a bowl, mix oil and vinegar. Add pineapple, green onions, cilantro, and arugula and toss to coat. Refrigerate for 1 hour while the bowl is covered. In your Instant Pot, mix brown sugar, soy sauce, garlic, pepper, ginger, honey, chicken broth, and orange juice. Press Sauté. Allow the liquid to a simmer. Cook until the honey and brown sugar dissolves. Arrange chicken into the sauce and toss to coat. Seal the pressure lid, choose Pressure Cook.

Set the timer to 16 minutes. When ready, release the pressure quickly. Transfer chicken to a cutting board and shred it. In a small bowl, mix water and cornstarch. Stir into the sauce in the cooker. Set cooker to Sauté. Cook sauce for 2 to 3 minutes until it begins to thicken. Stir in the shredded chicken. Halve the loaf of Hawaiian rolls.

Set the halves, cut-side up, onto the air fry basket. Close the air fry lid. Select Bake set the temperature to 400°F, and set the time to 3 minutes. When ready, remove, transfer the shredded chicken to the bottom half of the rolls and apply a topping of salad. Replace the top half of the rolls and cut into individual sliders before serving.

Creamy Chicken and Quinoa Soup

Servings: 6 | Ready in about: 30 minutes

INGREDIENTS

2 tbsp butter
1 cup red onion, chopped
1 cup carrots, chopped
1 cup celery, chopped

4 chicken breasts, cubed
4 cups chicken broth
6 oz quinoa, rinsed
1 tbsp fresh parsley, chopped

Salt and black pepper to taste
4 oz mascarpone cheese, softened
1 cup milk
1 cup heavy cream

DIRECTIONS

Melt butter on Sauté in your Instant Pot. Add carrot, onion, and celery and cook for 5 minutes until tender. Add chicken broth to the pot. Mix in parsley, quinoa and chicken. Add pepper and salt for seasoning. Seal the pressure lid, choose Pressure Cook on High, and set the timer to 5 minutes. When ready, release the pressure quickly. Press Sauté. Add mascarpone cheese to the soup and stir well to melt completely. Mix in heavy cream and milk. Simmer the soup for 3 to 4 minutes until thickened and creamy.

Honey-Garlic Chicken & Okra

Servings: 4 | Ready in about: 25 minutes

INGREDIENTS

6 garlic cloves, grated
¼ cup tomato puree
½ cup soy sauce
⅓ cup honey
2 tbsp rice vinegar

1 tbsp olive oil
4 chicken breasts, sliced
1 cup rice, rinsed
½ tsp salt
2 cups water

2 cups frozen okra
1 tbsp cornstarch
1 tbsp water
2 tsp toasted sesame seeds
4 spring onions, thinly sliced

DIRECTIONS

In your Instant Pot, mix garlic, tomato puree, vinegar, soy sauce, ginger, honey, and oil. Toss in chicken to coat. In an ovenproof bowl, mix water, salt and rice. Set a trivet on top of chicken. Lower the bowl onto the trivet. Seal the pressure lid, choose Pressure Cook on High, and set the timer to 10 minutes. Release pressure naturally for 5 minutes, release the remaining pressure quickly. Use a fork to fluff the rice. Lay okra onto the rice.

Allow the okra steam in the residual heat for 3 minutes. Take the trivet and bowl from the pot. Set the chicken to a plate. Press Sauté. In a bowl, mix 1 tbsp of water and cornstarch until smooth. Stir into the sauce and cook until thickened. Divide the rice, chicken, and okra between bowls. Drizzle sauce over and top with spring onions and sesame seeds.

Asian-Style Chicken

Servings: 4 | Ready in about: 35 minutes

INGREDIENTS

- 1 lb chicken, cut in stripes
- 2 tomatoes, cubed
- 3 green peppers, cut in stripes
- 1 tbsp cumin powder
- 1 large onion
- 2 tbsp oil
- 1 tbsp mustard
- 1 pinch ginger
- 1 pinch fresh and chopped coriander

DIRECTIONS

Heat the oil in a deep pan. Add in the mustard, onion, ginger, cumin and green chili peppers. Sauté the mixture for 2-3 minutes. Then, add the tomatoes, coriander, and salt and keep stirring. Coat the chicken with oil, salt, and pepper and cook for 25 minutes on Air Fry mode at 380°F. Remove the chicken and pour the sauce over.

Crumbed Sage Chicken Scallopini

Servings: 4 | Ready in about: 12 minutes

INGREDIENTS

- 4 chicken breasts, skinless and boneless
- 3 oz breadcrumbs
- 2 tbsp grated Parmesan cheese
- 2 oz flour
- 2 eggs, beaten
- 1 tbsp fresh, chopped sage

DIRECTIONS

Place some plastic wrap underneath and on top of the chicken. Using a rolling pin beat the meat until it becomes fragile. In a bowl, combine Parmesan, sage, and breadcrumbs. Dip the chicken in the egg first, and then in the sage mixture. Spray with cooking oil and place the meat in your Instant Pot. Cook for 7 minutes on Air Fry at 390°F.

Chicken with Prunes

Servings: 6 | Ready in about: 55 minutes

INGREDIENTS

- 1 whole chicken, 3 lb
- ½ cup pitted prunes
- 3 minced cloves of garlic
- 2 tbsp capers
- 2 bay leaves
- 2 tbsp red wine vinegar
- 2 tbsp olive oil
- 1 tbsp dried oregano
- ¼ cup packed brown sugar
- 1 tbsp chopped fresh parsley
- Salt and black pepper to taste

DIRECTIONS

In a big and deep bowl, mix the prunes, olives, capers, garlic, olive oil, bay leaves, oregano, vinegar, salt, and pepper. Spread the mixture on the bottom of a baking tray, and place the chicken. Preheat your Instant Pot to 400°F. Sprinkle a little bit of brown sugar on top of the chicken, close the air fry lid and cook for 45-55 minutes on Air Fry mode. When ready, garnish with fresh parsley.

Creamy Chicken Pasta with Pesto Sauce

Servings: 8 | Ready in about: 30 minutes

INGREDIENTS

3½ cups water
4 chicken breast, cubed
8 oz macaroni pasta
1 tbsp butter
Salt and black pepper to taste
2 cups fresh collard greens, trimmed
1 cup cherry tomatoes, halved
½ cup basil pesto sauce
¼ cup cream cheese, softened
1 garlic clove, minced
¼ cup Asiago cheese, grated
Freshly chopped basil for garnish

DIRECTIONS

To your Instant Pot, add water, chicken, 2 tsp salt, butter, and macaroni, and stir well to mix and be submerged in water. Seal the pressure lid, choose Pressure Cook on High, and set the timer to 2 minutes. When ready, release the pressure quickly. Press Start, open the lid, get rid of ¼ cup water from the pot. Set to Sauté the pot.

Mix in collard greens, pesto sauce, garlic, remaining 1 tsp salt, cream cheese, tomatoes, and black pepper. Cook for 1 to 2 minutes as you stir, until sauce is creamy. Place the pasta into serving plates. Top with cheese and basil.

Thyme Chicken with Veggies

Servings: 4 | Ready in about: 40 minutes

INGREDIENTS

4 skin-on, bone-in chicken legs
2 tbsp olive oil
4 cloves garlic, minced
1 tsp fresh chopped thyme
½ cup dry white wine
1¼ cups chicken stock
1 cup carrots, thinly sliced
1 cup parsnip, thinly sliced
3 tomatoes, thinly sliced
1 tbsp honey
4 slices lemon
Fresh thyme, chopped for garnish

DIRECTIONS

Season the chicken with pepper and salt. Warm oil on Sauté in your Instant Pot. Arrange chicken legs into the hot oil. Cook for 3 to 5 minutes each side until browned. Place in a bowl and set aside. Cook thyme and garlic in the chicken fat for 1 minute until soft and lightly golden. Add wine into the pot to deglaze, scrape the pot's bottom to get rid of any brown bits of food. Simmer the wine for 2 to 3 minutes until slightly reduced in volume.

Add stock, carrots, parsnips, tomatoes, pepper and salt into the pot. Lay trivet onto veggies. Into the pot's steamer basket, arrange chicken legs. Set the steamer basket onto the trivet. Drizzle the chicken with honey then top with lemon slices. Seal the pressure lid, choose Pressure Cook, and set the timer to 12 minutes. Release pressure quickly. Place the chicken to a bowl. Drain the veggies and place them around the chicken. Garnish with thyme.

Cajun Shredded Chicken & Wild Rice

Servings: 6 | Ready in about: 45 minutes

INGREDIENTS

6 chicken thighs, skinless
1 tsp salt
½ tsp ground red pepper
½ tsp onion powder
½ tsp ground white pepper
1 tsp Cajun seasoning
1/8 tsp smoked paprika
2 tbsp olive oil
1 cup pumpkin, peeled and cubed
2 celery stalks, diced
2 onions, diced
2 garlic cloves, crushed
3 cups chicken broth, divided
1 ½ cups wild rice

DIRECTIONS

Season the chicken with salt, onion powder, Cajun seasoning, ground white pepper, ground red pepper, and smoked paprika. Warm oil on Sauté in your Instant Pot. Stir in celery and pumpkin and cook for 5 minutes. Set the vegetables on a plate. In batches, sear chicken in oil for 3 minutes each side until golden brown. Set on a plate.

In the pot, add 1/4 cup chicken stock to deglaze the pan, scrape away any browned bits from the bottom. Add garlic and onion and cook for 2 minutes until fragrant. Take back the celery and pumpkin to the pot. Add the wild rice and remaining chicken stock. Place the chicken over the rice mixture. Seal the pressure lid, choose Pressure Cook, and set the timer to 10 minutes. When ready, release the pressure quickly. Serve.

Chicken & Zucchini Pilaf

Servings: 4 | Ready in about: 40 minutes

INGREDIENTS

2 tsp olive oil
1 zucchini, chopped
1 cup leeks, chopped
2 garlic cloves, minced
1 tbsp chopped fresh rosemary
2 tsp chopped fresh thyme leaves
2 cups chicken stock
1 lb boneless and skinless chicken legs
1 cup rice, rinsed

DIRECTIONS

Set your Instant Pot to Sauté. Warm oil. Add in zucchini and cook for 5 minutes. Stir in thyme, leeks, rosemary, pepper, salt and garlic. Cook the mixture for 3-4 minutes. Add ½ cup chicken stock into the pot to deglaze. When liquid stops simmering, add in the remaining stock, rice, and chicken with more pepper and salt. Seal the pressure lid, choose Pressure Cook for 5 minutes. Once ready, do a quick release.

Lettuce Chicken Carnitas Wraps

Servings: 6 | Ready in about: 50 minutes

INGREDIENTS

2 tbsp canola oil
2 lb chicken thighs, boneless, skinless
1 cup pineapple juice
⅓ cup water
¼ cup soy sauce
2 tbsp maple syrup
1 tbsp rice vinegar
1 tsp chili-garlic sauce
3 tbsp cornstarch
Salt and black pepper to taste
12 large lettuce leaves
2 cups canned pinto beans, rinsed

DIRECTIONS

Warm oil on Sauté in your Instant Pot. In batches, sear chicken in the oil for 5 minutes until browned. Set aside in a bowl. Into your pot, mix chili-garlic sauce, pineapple juice, soy sauce, vinegar, maple syrup, and water. Stir in chicken to coat. Seal the pressure lid, choose Pressure Cook on High, and set the timer to 7 minutes.

Release pressure naturally for 10 minutes. Shred the chicken with two forks. Take ¼ cup liquid from the pot to a bowl. Stir in cornstarch to dissolve. Mix the cornstarch mixture with the mixture in the pot and return the chicken. Select Sauté and cook for 5 minutes until the sauce thickens. Add pepper and salt for seasoning. Transfer beans into lettuce leaves. Apply a topping of chicken carnitas and serve.

Hot Chicken Wings

Servings: 4 | Ready in about: 25 minutes

INGREDIENTS

8 chicken wings
1 tbsp ranch salad mix
1 tbsp garlic powder
1 tbsp onion powder
1 tbsp cayenne pepper
½ tsp paprika

DIRECTIONS

Combine the paprika, ranch salad mix, onion powder, garlic powder, and cayenne pepper in a bowl. Pour the seasoning all over the chicken and oil with cooking spray. Place in the air fry basket, close the air fry lid and cook for 15 minutes at 380°F. After half of the cooking time, shake the wings. Oil the chicken again with cooking spray and continue cooking until the wings are crispy. Serve hot.

Sriracha Chicken with Black Beans

Servings: 4 | Ready in about: 25 minutes

INGREDIENTS

½ cup soy sauce
½ cup chicken broth
3 tbsp honey
2 tbsp tomato paste
1 tbsp sriracha
1 (1 inch) piece fresh ginger, grated
3 garlic cloves, grated
4 boneless, skinless chicken drumsticks
1 tbsp cornstarch
1 tbsp water
2 tbsp toasted sesame seeds, divided
1 tbsp sesame oil
2 cups canned black beans
2 green onions, thinly sliced

DIRECTIONS

In your Instant Pot, mix the soy sauce, honey, ginger, tomato paste, chicken broth, sriracha, and garlic. Stir well until smooth. Toss in the chicken to coat. Seal the pressure lid, choose Pressure Cook on High, and set the timer to 3 minutes. Release the pressure immediately. Open the lid and press Sauté.

In a small bowl, mix water and cornstarch until no lumps remain. Stir into the sauce and cook for 5 minutes until thickened. Stir sesame oil and 1½ tbsp sesame seeds through the chicken mixture. Garnish with extra sesame seeds and green onions. Serve with black beans.

Chicken & Sweet Potato Corn Chowder

Servings: 8 | Ready in about: 40 minutes

INGREDIENTS

4 boneless, skinless chicken breast, diced
3 garlic cloves, minced
1 cup chicken stock
19 oz corn kernels, frozen
1 sweet potato, peeled and cubed
4 oz canned diced green chiles, drained
2 tsp chili powder
1 tsp ground cumin
2 cups cheddar cheese, shredded
2 cups creme fraiche
Salt and black pepper to taste
Cilantro leaves, chopped

DIRECTIONS

Mix chicken, corn, chili powder, cumin, chicken stock, sweet potato, green chiles, and garlic in your Instant Pot of the pot. Seal the pressure lid, choose Pressure Cook on High, and set the timer to 10 minutes.

When ready, release the pressure quickly. Set the chicken to a cutting board and use two forks to shred it. Return to pot and stir well into the liquid. Stir in cheese and creme fraiche. Season with pepper and salt. Cook for 2 to 3 minutes until cheese is melted. Place chowder into plates and top with cilantro.

Winter Chicken Thighs with Cabbage

Servings: 4 | Ready in about: 35 minutes

INGREDIENTS

1 tbsp lard
4 slices pancetta, diced
4 chicken thighs, boneless skinless
Salt and ground black pepper to taste
1 cup chicken broth
1 tbsp Dijon mustard
1 lb green cabbage, shredded
Fresh parsley, chopped

DIRECTIONS

Warm lard on Sauté in your Instant Pot. Fry pancetta for 5 minutes until crisp. Set aside. Season chicken with pepper and salt. Sear in the pot for 2 minutes each side until browned. In a bowl, mix mustard and chicken broth. To the pot, add pancetta and chicken broth mixture. Seal the pressure lid, choose Pressure Cook.

Set the timer to 6 minutes. When ready, release the pressure quickly. Open the lid, mix in green cabbage, seal again, and cook on High Pressure for 2 minutes. When ready, release the pressure quickly. Serve with parsley.

Saucy Chicken Breasts

Servings: 4 | Ready in about: 45 minutes

INGREDIENTS

4 chicken breasts, boneless and skinless
salt and ground black pepper to taste
2 tbsp olive oil
2 tbsp soy sauce
2 tbsp tomato paste
2 tbsp honey
2 tbsp minced garlic
½ cup chicken broth
1 tbsp cornstarch
1 tbsp water
½ cup chives, sliced

DIRECTIONS

Season the chicken with pepper and salt. Warm oil on Sauté in your Instant Pot. Add in chicken and cook for 5 minutes until lightly browned. In a bowl, mix garlic, soy sauce, honey, and tomato paste. Pour the mixture over the chicken. Stir in ½ cup broth. Seal the pressure lid, choose Pressure Cook, and set the timer to 12 minutes.

When ready, release the pressure quickly. Set the chicken to a bowl. Mix water and cornstarch to create a slurry. Briskly stir the mixture into the sauce that is remaining in the pan for 2 minutes until thickened. Serve the chicken with the sauce and chives.

Chicken with Tomatoes & Capers

Servings: 4 | Ready in about: 45 minutes

INGREDIENTS

4 chicken legs
Sea salt and black pepper to taste
2 tbsp olive oil
1 onion, diced
2 garlic cloves, minced
⅓ cup red wine
2 cups diced tomatoes
⅓ cup capers
¼ cup fresh basil
2 pickles, chopped

DIRECTIONS

Sprinkle pepper and salt over the chicken. Warm oil on Sauté in your Instant Pot. Add in onion and cook for 3 minutes until fragrant. Add in garlic and cook for 30 seconds until softened. Mix the chicken with vegetables and cook for 6 to 7 minutes until lightly browned. Add red wine to the pan to deglaze and stir in tomatoes.

Seal the pressure lid, choose Pressure Cook on High, and set the timer to 12 minutes. When ready, release the pressure quickly. To the chicken mixture, add basil, capers and pickles. Serve the chicken in plates covered with the tomato sauce mixture.

Chicken Burgers with Avocado

Servings: 8 | Ready in about: 15 minutes

INGREDIENTS

1 lb ground chicken
1 red onion, chopped
1 egg, beaten
4 buns, halved
1 small red potato, shredded
A pinch of ground cumin
A pinch of ground chili
Fresh cilantro, chopped
Salt and pepper to taste
1 Avocado, sliced
½ cup mayonnaise
1 tomato, sliced

DIRECTIONS

Mix the chicken, onion, egg, potato, cumin, chili, cilantro, salt, and pepper in a large bowl with your hands until you have an even burger mixture. Shape the mixture into 8 patties. Grease the air fry basket with cooking spray. Arrange the burgers onto the basket. Close the air fry lid and cook for 10 minutes, at 360°F. After 5 minutes, shake the patties. To assemble your burgers, spread mayonnaise on the bottom of each half of the buns, top with a chicken patty, then put over a tomato slice. Cover with the other half of the buns and arrange on a serving platter.

Shredded Chicken with Lentils & Rice

Servings: 4 | Ready in about: 45 minutes

INGREDIENTS

1 tsp olive oil
1 garlic clove, minced
1 small yellow onion, chopped
3 cups chicken broth, divided
4 boneless, skinless chicken thighs
1 cup white rice
½ cup dried lentils
Salt and ground black pepper to taste
Chopped fresh parsley for garnish

DIRECTIONS

Set your Instant Pot to Sauté. Warm oil. Add in onion and garlic and cook for 3 minutes until soft. Add in broth, rice, lentils, and chicken. Season with pepper and salt. Seal the pressure lid, choose Pressure Cook on High, and set the timer to 15 minutes. Once ready, do a quick release. Remove and shred the chicken in a large bowl. Set the lentils and rice into serving plates, top with shredded chicken and parsley and serve.

Crunchy Chicken Schnitzels

Servings: 4 | Ready in about: 25 minutes

INGREDIENTS

4 chicken breasts, boneless
1 cup flour
2 eggs, beaten
1 cup breadcrumbs
Salt and pepper to taste
2 tbsp fresh parsley, chopped
4 slices cold butter
4 slices lemon
Cooking spray

DIRECTIONS

Combine the breadcrumbs with the parsley in a dish and set aside. Season the chicken with salt and pepper. Coat in flour. Dip the coated chicken into the beaten egg followed by breadcrumbs. Spray the schnitzels with cooking spray. Put them into the air fry basket, close the air fry lid and cook for 10 minutes at 380°F. After 5 minutes, turn the schnitzels over. Arrange the schnitzels on a serving platter and place the butter and lemon slices over to serve.

Chicken Fajitas with Avocado

Servings: 4 | Ready in about: 30 minutes

INGREDIENTS

4 chicken breasts, boneless and skinless
1 taco seasoning
1 tbsp olive oil
1 (24 oz) can diced tomatoes
3 bell peppers, julienned
1 shallot, chopped
4 garlic cloves, minced
Juice of 1 lemon
salt and pepper to taste
4 flour tortillas
2 tbsp cilantro, chopped
1 avocado, sliced

DIRECTIONS

In a bowl, mix taco seasoning and chicken until evenly coated. Warm oil on Sauté in your Instant Pot. Sear chicken for 2 minutes per side until browned. To the chicken, add tomatoes, shallot, lemon juice, garlic, and bell peppers. Season with pepper and salt. Seal the pressure lid, choose Pressure Cook, and set the timer to 4 minutes. When ready, release the pressure quickly. Move the bell peppers and chicken to tortillas. Add avocado slices and serve.

Basil & Cheddar Stuffed Chicken

Servings: 4 | Ready in about: 25 minutes

INGREDIENTS

2 large chicken breasts, skinless
4 slices cheddar cheese
A handful of fresh basil leaves
4 cherry tomatoes, halved
Salt and pepper to taste
2 tbsp olive oil

DIRECTIONS

With a sharp knife, cut a slit into the side of each chicken breast. Put 2 slices of cheese, 3-4 basil leaves, and 4 cherry tomato halves into each slit. Use toothpicks to keep the chicken breasts closed. Season the meat with salt and pepper, and brush with some olive oil. Grease the air fry basket with the remaining olive oil.

Place the chicken breasts in the basket. Close the air fry lid and cook for 12 minutes at 390°F. After 6 minutes, turn the breasts over. Once ready, leave to sit the chicken breasts, then slice each one in half and serve with salad.

Tom Yum Wings

Servings: 2 | Ready in about: 4 hours 20 minutes

INGREDIENTS

8 chicken wings
1 tbsp water

2 tbsp potato starch
2 tbsp cornstarch

2 tbsp tom yum paste
½ tsp baking powder

DIRECTIONS

Combine the tom yum paste and water, in a small bowl. Place the wings in a large bowl, add the tom yum mixture and coat well. Cover the bowl and refrigerate for 4 hours. Combine the baking powder, cornstarch, and potato starch. Dip each wing in the starch mixture. Place on a lined baking dish in the pot and cook for 7 minutes on Air Fry at 370°F. Flip over and cook for 5 to 7 minutes more. Serve.

Cordon Bleu Chicken

Servings: 4 | Ready in about: 40 minutes

INGREDIENTS

4 skinless and boneless chicken breasts
4 slices ham
4 slices Swiss cheese

3 tbsp all-purpose flour
4 tbsp butter
1 tsp paprika

1 tsp chicken bouillon granules
½ cup dry white wine
1 cup heavy whipping cream

DIRECTIONS

Pound the chicken breasts and put a slice of ham and then a slice of swiss cheese on each of the breasts. Fold the edges over the filling and secure the sides with toothpicks. In a medium bowl, combine the paprika and the flour and coat the chicken pieces. Close the air fry lid and fry the chicken for 20 minutes on Air Fry mode at 380°F.

Meanwhile, in a large skillet over medium heat, melt the butter and add the bouillon and the wine. Reduce the heat to low. Add in the heavy cream and let simmer for 20-25 minutes. When the chicken is done, remove to a serving platter and drizzle with the sauce. Serve hot.

Korean-Style Barbecued Satay

Servings: 4 | Ready in about: 4h 15 minutes

INGREDIENTS

1 lb boneless,skinless chicken tenders
4 cloves garlic, chopped
4 scallions, chopped

2 tsp sesame seeds, toasted
1 tsp fresh ginger, grated
½ cup pineapple juice

½ cup soy sauce
⅓ cup sesame oil
1 pinch black pepper

DIRECTIONS

Skew each tender and trim any excess fat. Mix the other ingredients in one large bowl. Add the skewered chicken and place in the fridge for 4 to 24 hours. Preheat your Instant Pot to 370°F. Using a paper towel, pat the chicken dry. Fry for 10 minutes on Air Fry mode.

Herby Chicken with Asparagus Sauce

Servings: 4 | Ready in about: 1 hour

INGREDIENTS

1 (3 ½ lb) Young Whole Chicken
4 garlic cloves, minced
1 tsp olive oil
4 fresh thyme, minced
3 fresh rosemary, minced

2 lemons, zested and quartered
Salt and black pepper to taste
2 tbsp olive oil
8 oz asparagus, trimmed and chopped
1 onion, chopped

1 cup chicken stock
1 tbsp soy sauce
1 fresh thyme sprig
1 tbsp flour
Chopped parsley to garnish

DIRECTIONS

Rub all sides of the chicken with garlic, rosemary, black pepper, lemon zest, minced thyme, and salt. Into the chicken cavity, insert lemon wedges. Warm oil on Sauté in your Instant Pot. Add in onion and asparagus, and cook for 5 minutes until softened. Mix in chicken stock, 1 thyme sprig, black pepper, soy sauce, and salt.

Into the inner pot, set trivet over asparagus mixture. On top of the trivet, place your chicken with breast-side up. Seal the pressure lid, choose Pressure Cook on High, and set the timer to 20 minutes. Once ready, do a quick release. Remove the chicken to a serving platter. In the inner pot, sprinkle flour over asparagus mixture and blend the sauce with an immersion blender until desired consistency. Top the chicken with asparagus sauce and parsley.

Greek-Style Chicken with Potatoes

Servings: 4 | Ready in about: 40 minutes

INGREDIENTS

4 potatoes, peeled and quartered
4 cups water
2 lemons, zested and juiced
1 tbsp olive oil
2 tsp fresh oregano
Salt to taste

¼ tsp freshly ground black pepper
2 Serrano peppers, chopped
4 boneless skinless chicken drumsticks
3 tbsp finely chopped parsley
1 cup packed watercress
1 cucumber, thinly sliced

½ cup cherry tomatoes, quartered
¼ cup Kalamata olives, pitted
¼ cup hummus
¼ cup feta cheese, crumbled
Lemon wedges, for serving

DIRECTIONS

In the cooker, add water and potatoes. Set trivet over them. In a baking bowl, mix lemon juice, olive oil, black pepper, oregano, zest, salt, and red pepper flakes. Add chicken drumsticks in the marinade and stir to coat. Set the bowl with chicken on the trivet in the pot. Seal the lid, select Pressure and set the time to 15 minutes on High.

When ready, do a quick pressure release. Take out the bowl with chicken and the trivet from the pot. Drain potatoes and add parsley and salt. Split the potatoes among four serving plates and top with watercress, cucumber slices, hummus, cherry tomatoes, chicken, olives, and feta cheese. Garnished with a lemon wedge.

Honey-Glazed Chicken Kabobs

Servings: 4 | Ready in about: 20 minutes

INGREDIENTS

4 chicken breasts, skinless and cubed
4 tbsp honey

Juice from 1 Lime
½ tsp ground paprika

Salt and pepper to taste

DIRECTIONS

In a bowl, combine honey, soy sauce, lime juice, paprika, salt, and pepper. Add in chicken cubes and toss to coat. Load 8 small skewers with honey-glazed chicken. Lay the kabobs into the air fry basket, close the air fry lid and cook for 15 minutes at 360°F. After 8 minutes, turn the kabobs over. Drizzle the remaining honey sauce and serve.

Chicken Stroganoff with Fetucini

Servings: 4 | Ready in about: 35 minutes

INGREDIENTS

2 large boneless skinless chicken breasts
1½ tsp salt
2 tbsp butter
½ cup sliced onion
1 tbsp flour
½ cup dry white wine
2 cups chicken stock
8 oz fettucini
½ tsp Worcestershire sauce
1 cup sautéed mushrooms
¼ cup heavy cream
2 tbsp chopped fresh dill to garnish

DIRECTIONS

Season the chicken on both sides with salt and set aside. Choose Sauté. Melt the butter and sauté the onion until brown, about 3 minutes. Mix in the flour to make a roux, about 2 minutes and gradually pour in the dry white wine while stirring and scraping the bottom of the pot to release any browned bits.

Allow the white wine to simmer and to reduce by two-thirds. Pour in 1 ½ cups water, chicken stock, 1 tablespoon of salt, and fettucini. Mix and arrange the chicken on top of the fettucini. Lock the pressure lid to Seal. Choose Pressure Cook on High and the cooking time to 5 minutes. When done, perform a quick pressure release.

Transfer the chicken breasts to a cutting board to cool slightly, and then cut into bite-size chunks. Return the chicken to the pot and stir in the Worcestershire sauce and mushrooms. Add the heavy cream and cook until the mixture stops simmering. Ladle the stroganoff into bowls and garnish with dill.

Rosemary Lemon Chicken

Servings: 2 | Ready in about: 60 minutes

INGREDIENTS

2 chicken breasts
1 tsp minced ginger
2 rosemary sprigs
½ lemon, cut into wedges
1 tbsp soy sauce
½ tbsp olive oil
1 tbsp oyster sauce
3 tbsp brown sugar

DIRECTIONS

Place ginger, soy sauce, and olive oil in a bowl. Add the chicken and coat well. Cover the bowl and refrigerate for 30 minutes. Transfer the marinated chicken to the air fry basket. Close the air fry lid and cook for about 6 minutes on Air Fry at 390°F. Mix the oyster sauce, rosemary, and brown sugar in a bowl. Pour the sauce over the chicken. Arrange the lemon wedges in the dish. Return to the and cook for 13 more minutes on Air Fry mode.

Turkey Stuffed Potatoes

Servings: 4 | Ready in about: 30 minutes

INGREDIENTS

2 cups vegetable broth
1 tsp chili powder
1 tsp ground cumin
½ tsp onion powder
½ tsp garlic powder
1 lb turkey breasts
4 potatoes
2 tbsp fresh cilantro, chopped
1 Fresno chili pepper, chopped

DIRECTIONS

In your Instant Pot, combine chicken broth, cumin, garlic powder, onion powder, and chili powder. Toss in turkey to coat. Place a trivet over the turkey. Use a fork to pierce the potatoes and set them on the trivet. Seal the pressure lid, choose Pressure Cook on High, and set the timer to 20 minutes. When ready, release the pressure quickly.

Remove the trivet. Place the potatoes on a plate. Place turkey in a mixing bowl and use two forks to shred. Half each potato lengthwise. Stuff with shredded turkey. Top with cilantro, onion, and fresno pepper and serve.

Greek-Style Chicken

Servings: 6 | Ready in about: 45 minutes

INGREDIENTS

1 whole chicken (3 lb), cut in pieces
3 garlic cloves, minced
½ cup olive oil
½ cup white wine
1 tbsp fresh rosemary
1 tbsp chopped fresh oregano
1 tbsp fresh thyme
Juice from 1 lemon
Salt and black pepper, to taste

DIRECTIONS

In a large bowl, combine the garlic, rosemary, thyme, olive oil, lemon juice, oregano, salt, and pepper. Mix all ingredients very well and spread the mixture into the air fry basket. Stir in the chicken. Sprinkle with wine and cook for 45 minutes on Air Fry mode at 380°F.

Buttermilk Chicken Thighs

Servings: 6 | Ready in about: 4 hours 40 minutes

INGREDIENTS

1 ½ lb chicken thighs
1 tsp cayenne pepper
2 cups flour
1 tbsp paprika
1 tbsp baking powder
2 cups buttermilk

DIRECTIONS

Rinse and pat dry the chicken thighs. Place the chicken thighs in a bowl. Add cayenne pepper, 2 tsp salt, black pepper, and buttermilk, and stir to coat well. Refrigerate for 4 hours. In another bowl, mix the flour, paprika, 1 tsp salt, and baking powder. Dredge the chicken thighs, one at a time, in the flour, and then place on a lined dish. Close the air fry lid and cook for 18 minutes on Air Fry, flipping once halfway through.

Sticky Drumsticks

Servings: 4 | Ready in about: 50 minutes

INGREDIENTS

1 lb chickendrumsticks
2 tbsp honey
2 tsp dijon mustard

DIRECTIONS

Combine the honey, mustard, salt, and pepper in a large bowl. Add in the chicken and toss to coat. Cover and put in the fridge for 30 minutes. Preheat your Instant Pot to 380°F. Grease the air fry basket with cooking spray. Arrange the drumsticks on the basket. Cook for 20 minutes on Air Fry mode. After 10 minutes, shake the drumsticks.

Sweet Garlicky Chicken Wings

Servings: 4 | Ready in about: 20 minutes

INGREDIENTS

16 chicken wings
¼ cup butter
¼ cup honey
½ tsp salt
4 garlic cloves, minced
¾ cup potato starch

DIRECTIONS

Rinse and pat dry the wings, and place them in a bowl. Add the starch to the bowl, and mix to coat the chicken. Place the chicken in a baking dish that has been previously coated lightly with cooking oil. Close the air fry lid and cook for 5 minutes on Air Fry mode at 390°F. Whisk the rest of the ingredients in a bowl. Pour the sauce over the wings and cook for another 10 minutes.

Tuscany-Style Turkey Soup

Servings: 4 | Ready in about: 40 minutes

INGREDIENTS

- 1 lb hot turkey sausage
- 2 tbsp olive oil
- 2 tbsp melted butter
- 3 celery stalks, chopped
- 3 garlic cloves, chopped
- 1 red onion, chopped
- ½ cup dry white wine
- 4 cups chicken broth
- ½ tsp fennel seeds
- 1 (15-oz) can cannellini beans, rinsed
- 9 oz refrigerated tortellini
- 1 Parmesan cheese rind
- 2 cups chopped spinach
- 4 Italian bread slices
- ½ cup grated Parmesan cheese

DIRECTIONS

On the pot, choose Sauté. Heat olive oil and cook the sausage for 4 minutes until golden brown. Stir in the celery, garlic, and onion, season with salt and cook for 2 to 3 minutes, stirring occasionally. Pour in the wine and bring the mixture to a boil until the wine reduces by half. Scrape the bottom of the pot to let off any browned bits. Add the chicken stock, fennel seeds, tortellini, Parmesan rind, cannellini beans, and spinach.

Lock the pressure lid into place and to seal. Select Pressure. Adjust the pressure to High and the cooking time to 5 minutes. Brush the butter on the bread slices, and sprinkle with half of the cheese. Once the timer is over, perform a natural pressure release for 5 minutes. Grease a trivet with cooking spray and fix in the pot.

Lay the bread slices on the trivet. Close the air fry lid and choose Broil. Adjust the time to 5 minutes. When the bread has browned and crisp, transfer from the trivet to a cutting board and let cool for a couple of minutes. Cut the slices into cubes. Ladle the soup into bowls and sprinkle with the remaining cheese. Top with croutons.

Chicken Tenders with Broccoli & Rice

Servings: 3 | Ready in about: 60 minutes

INGREDIENTS

- 1 lb chicken tenderloins
- 1 package instant long grain rice
- 1 cup chopped broccoli
- 2 cups water
- 1 can condensed cream chicken soup
- 1 tbsp minced garlic

DIRECTIONS

Place the chicken quarters in your Instant Pot. Season with salt, pepper and a tbsp of oil and cook for 30 minutes on Roast at 390°F. In a bowl, mix rice, water, minced garlic, soup, and broccoli. Combine the mixture very well. Remove the chicken from the pot and place it on a platter to drain. Spread the rice mixture on the bottom of the dish and place the chicken on top of the rice. Close the air fry lid and cook for 30 minutes on Roast at 390°F.

Asian Turkey Lettuce Cups

Servings: 4 | Ready in about: 45 minutes

INGREDIENTS

- ¾ cup olive oil
- 4 cloves garlic, minced
- 3 tbsp maple syrup
- 2 tbsp pineapple juice
- 1 cup coconut milk
- 3 tbsp rice wine vinegar
- 3 tbsp soy sauce
- 1 tbsp Thai-style chili paste
- 1 lb turkey breasts, cut into strips
- 1 romaine lettuce, leaves separated
- ⅓ cup chopped peanuts
- ¼ cup chopped fresh cilantro leaves

DIRECTIONS

In your Instant Pot, mix peanut butter, garlic, rice wine vinegar, soy sauce, pineapple juice, honey, coconut milk, and chili paste until smooth. Add turkey strips and ensure they are submerged in the sauce. Seal the pressure lid, choose Pressure Cook on High, and set the timer to 12 minutes. When ready, release the pressure quickly. Place the turkey at the center of each lettuce leaf. Top with cilantro and chopped peanuts.

Spicy Buttered Turkey

Servings: 6 | Ready in about: 25 minutes

INGREDIENTS

6 turkey breasts, boneless and skinless
2 cups panko breadcrumbs
Salt and black pepper to taste
½ tsp cayenne pepper
1 stick butter, melted

DIRECTIONS

In a bowl, combine the panko breadcrumbs, pepper, cayenne pepper, and salt. Brush the butter over the turkey breast. Coat the turkey with the panko mixture. Arrange on a lined air fry basket. Close the air fry lid and cook for 15 minutes at 390°F on Air Fry, flipping the meat after 8 minutes.

Thyme Turkey Nuggets

Servings: 2 | Ready in about: 20 minutes

INGREDIENTS

8 oz turkey breast, boneless and skinless
1 egg, beaten
1 cup breadcrumbs
1 tbsp dried thyme
½ tsp dried parsley
Salt and pepper, to taste

DIRECTIONS

Mince the turkey in a food processor. Transfer to a bowl. Stir in the thyme and parsley, and season with salt and pepper. Take a nugget-sized piece of the turkey mixture and shape it into a ball, or another form. Dip it in the breadcrumbs, then egg, then in the breadcrumbs again. Place the nuggets onto a prepared baking dish. Close the air fry lid and cook for 10 minutes on Air Fry mode at 350°F.

Lemon Turkey Risotto

Servings: 4 | Ready in about: 40 minutes

INGREDIENTS

2 boneless turkey breasts, cut into strips
2 lemons, zested and juiced
1 tbsp dried oregano
2 garlic cloves, minced
½ tsp sea salt
1½ tbsp olive oil
1 onion, diced
2 cups chicken broth
1 cup Arborio rice, rinsed
Salt and black pepper to taste
¼ cup chopped fresh parsley, or to taste
8 lemon slices

DIRECTIONS

In a ziplock back, mix turkey, oregano, sea salt, garlic, juice and zest of two lemons. Marinate for 10 minutes. Warm oil on Sauté in your Instant Pot. Add onion and cook for 3 minutes until fragrant. Add rice and chicken broth and season with pepper and salt. Empty the ziplock having the chicken and marinade into the pot.

Seal the pressure lid, choose Pressure Cook on High, and set the timer to 12 minutes. When ready, release the pressure quickly. Divide the rice and turkey between 4 serving bowls. Garnish with lemon slices and parsley.

Turkey Meatballs with Rigatoni

Servings: 4 | Ready in about: 40 minutes

INGREDIENTS

2 tbsp canola oil
1 lb ground turkey
1 large egg
¼ cup bread crumbs
2 cloves garlic, minced
1 tsp dried oregano
3 cups tomato sauce
8 oz rigatoni
2 tbsp grated Grana Padano cheese

DIRECTIONS

In a bowl, combine ground turkey, bread crumbs, cumin, garlic, and egg. Season with oregano, salt, red pepper flakes, and pepper. Form the mixture into meatballs with well-oiled hands. Warm the oil on Sauté in your Instant Pot. Cook the meatballs for 3 to 4 minutes until browned on all sides. Remove to a plate.

Add rigatoni to the pot and cover with tomato sauce. Pour water into the pot enough to cover the pasta. Stir well. Throw in the meatballs. Seal the pressure lid, choose Pressure Cook on High, and set the timer to 10 minutes. When ready, release the pressure quickly. Serve topped with Grana Padano cheese.

Turkey and Brown Rice Salad with Peanuts

Servings: 4 | Ready in about: 60 minutes

INGREDIENTS

- 4 cups water
- 1 cup brown rice
- 2¼ tsp salt
- 1 lb turkey tenderloins
- 3 tsp peanut oil, divided
- 3 tbsp apple cider vinegar
- ⅛ tsp freshly ground black pepper
- ¼ tsp celery seeds
- A pinch of sugar
- ½ cup peanuts, toasted
- 3 celery stalks, thinly sliced
- 1 apple, cored and cubed

DIRECTIONS

Pour the water into the inner pot. Stir in the brown rice and 1 teaspoon of salt. Lock the pressure lid into the Seal position. Choose Pressure Cook on High and the cooking time to 10 minutes. Season the turkey on both sides with salt. Set aside. After cooking the brown rice, perform a natural pressure release for 10 minutes.

Spoon the rice into a bowl to cool completely. Put the turkey in the air fry basket and brush with 2 teaspoons of peanut oil. Fix in the basket. Close the air fry lid and choose Bake. Adjust the temperature to 375°F and the cooking time to 12 minutes. Pour the remaining peanut oil and the vinegar into a jar with a tight-fitting lid. Add the black pepper, celery seeds, salt, and sugar. Close the jar and shake until the ingredients properly combined.

When the turkey is ready, transfer to a plate to cool for several minutes. Cut it into bite-size chunks and add to the rice along with the peanuts, celery, and apple. Pour half the dressing over the salad and toss gently to coat, adding more dressing as desired. Proceed to serve the salad.

Creamy Turkey Enchilada Casserole

Servings: 6 | Ready in about: 70 minutes

INGREDIENTS

- 1 tbsp butter
- 1 yellow onion, diced
- 2 garlic cloves, minced
- 1 lb boneless, skinless turkey breasts
- 2 cups enchilada sauce
- ¼ tsp salt
- ¼ tsp freshly ground black pepper
- 1 (15-oz) can pinto beans, drained
- 8 tortillas, each cut into 8 pieces
- 1 (16-oz) bag frozen corn
- 2 cups shredded Monterey Jack cheese

DIRECTIONS

Choose Sauté on your Instant Pot. Melt the butter and cook the onion and garlic for 3 minutes, stirring occasionally. Put the turkey and enchilada sauce in the pot and season with salt and black pepper. Stir to combine. Seal the pressure lid, choose Pressure Cook on High, and set the time to 15 minutes.

When done cooking, perform a quick pressure release and carefully open the lid. Shred the turkey with two long forks while being careful not to burn your hands. Mix in the pinto beans, tortilla pieces, corn, and half of the cheese to the pot. Sprinkle the remaining cheese evenly on top of the casserole. Close the air fry lid. Choose Broil and set the time to 5 minutes. Press Start. When ready, allow the casserole to sit for 5 minutes before serving.

Spicy Chicken Wings

Servings: 2 | Ready in about: 25 minutes

INGREDIENTS

10 chicken wings
2 tbsp hot chili sauce
½ tbsp lime juice
½ tbsp honey
Salt and black pepper to taste

DIRECTIONS

Mix the lime juice, honey, and chili sauce. Toss the mixture over the chicken wings. Put the wings in the fryer's basket, close the air fry lid and cook for 25 minutes on Air Fry mode at 350°F. Shake the basket every 5 minutes.

Spicy Turkey Casserole

Servings: 5 | Ready in about: 45 minutes

INGREDIENTS

1 tbsp olive oil
½ sweet onion, diced
3 cloves garlic, minced
1 jalapeno pepper, minced
1 lb turkey breast, cubed
2 (14 oz) cans fire-roasted tomatoes
1 ½ cups water
1 cup salsa
2 bell peppers, cut into thick strips
2 tsp ancho chili powder
2 tsp chili powder
1 tsp ground cumin
Sea salt to taste
5 tbsp fresh oregano, chopped

DIRECTIONS

Warm the oil on Sauté in your Instant Pot. Add in garlic, onion and jalapeño and cook for 5 minutes until fragrant. Stir turkey into the pot and cook for 5-6 minutes until browned. Add in salsa, tomatoes, bell peppers, and water. Apply a seasoning of sea salt, ancho chili powder, cumin, and chili powder. Seal the pressure lid, choose Pressure Cook, and set the timer to 10 minutes. When ready, release the pressure quickly. Top with oregano and serve.

Greek Turkey Meatballs

Servings: 6 | Ready in about: 30 minutes

INGREDIENTS

1 onion, minced and divided
½ cup plain bread crumbs
⅓ cup feta cheese, crumbled
2 tsp salt, divided
½ tsp dried oregano
¼ tsp ground black pepper
1 lb ground turkey
1 egg, lightly beaten
1 tbsp olive oil
1 carrot, minced
½ celery stalk, minced
3 cups tomato puree

DIRECTIONS

In a mixing bowl, thoroughly combine half the onion, oregano, ground turkey, salt, bread crumbs, pepper, and egg and stir until everything is well incorporated. Heat oil on Sauté, and cook celery, remaining onion, and carrot for 5 minutes until soft. Pour in 2 cups water and tomato puree. Adjust the seasonings.

Roll the mixture into meatballs and drop into the sauce. Seal the pressure lid, choose Pressure Cook, and set the timer to 5 minutes. When done, release pressure naturally for 10 minutes. Serve topped with feta cheese.

RICE, GRAINS & PASTA

Indian-Style Beef with Rice

Servings: 5 | Ready in about: 40 minutes

INGREDIENTS

¼ cup yogurt
2 cloves garlic, smashed
1 tbsp olive oil
1 lime, juiced
Salt and black pepper to taste
2 lb beef stew meat, cubed
1 tbsp garam masala
1 tbsp fresh ginger, grated
1 ½ tsp smoked paprika
1 tsp ground cumin
¼ tsp cayenne pepper
3 tbsp butter
1 onion, chopped
1 (14-oz) can puréed tomatoes
½ cup beef broth
2 cups basmati rice, rinsed
½ cup heavy cream
½ bunch fresh cilantro, chopped

DIRECTIONS

In a bowl, mix garlic, lime juice, olive oil, pepper, salt, and yogurt. Stir in the beef to coat. In a different bowl, thoroughly mix paprika, garam masala, cumin, ginger, and cayenne pepper. Melt butter on Sauté and stir-fry the onion and garlic for 3 minutes until translucent. Sprinkle spice mixture over onion. Cook for about 30 seconds.

To the onion, add the beef-yogurt mixture. Cook for 3 to 4 minutes until the meat is slightly cooked. Mix in broth and puréed tomatoes. Set trivet over beef in the pot. In an oven-proof bowl, mix 2 cups water and rice. Set the bowl onto the trivet. Seal the pressure lid, press Pressure Cook, and set the timer to 10 minutes.

When ready, release pressure quickly. Remove the bowl with rice and trivet. Add pepper, salt and heavy cream into beef and stir. Fluff the rice and divide it into serving plates. Apply a topping of beef. Use cilantro to garnish.

Creamed Kale Parmesan Farro

Servings: 2 | Ready in about: 35 minutes

INGREDIENTS

1 tbsp butter
1 small onion, diced
1 cup pearl barley, rinsed and drained
2 garlic cloves, smashed
2 cups vegetable broth
½ cup grated Parmesan + for topping
1 cup kale, chopped
Juice of ½ lemon, juiced
Salt and black pepper to taste

DIRECTIONS

Warm butter on Sauté in your Instant Pot. Add in onion and cook for 3 minutes until soft. Stir in garlic and barley, and cook for 1-2 minutes until barley is toasted. Mix in broth. Seal the pressure lid and choose Pressure Cook.

Set the timer to 9 minutes. Release pressure naturally for 10 minutes. Add Parmesan cheese into barley mixture and stir until fully melted. Just before serving, add lemon juice and kale into barley mixture. Serve.

Simple Brown Rice

Servings: 6 | Ready in about: 30 minutes

INGREDIENTS

1 ½ cups brown rice
3 cups chicken broth
2 tsp lemon juice
2 tsp sesame olive oil
1 tbsp toasted sunflower seeds

DIRECTIONS

Add broth and brown rice to your Instant Pot. Seal the pressure lid, choose Pressure Cook on High, and set the timer to 15 minutes. When ready, release the pressure quickly. Do not open the lid for an additional 5 minutes. Use a fork to fluff rice. Add lemon juice, sunflower seeds and oil.

Veggie Quinoa Bowls with Pesto

Servings: 2 | Ready in about: 30 minutes

INGREDIENTS

1 cup quinoa, rinsed and drained
2 cups vegetable broth
Salt and ground black pepper to taste
1 potato, peeled, cubed
1 head broccoli, cut into small florets
1 bunch baby heirloom carrots, peeled
¼ cabbage, sliced
2 eggs
1 avocado, thinly sliced
¼ cup pesto sauce
Lemon wedges, for serving

DIRECTIONS

In your Instant Pot, mix broth, pepper, quinoa, and salt. Set trivet to the inner pot on top of quinoa and add a steamer basket on the trivet. Mix carrots, potato, eggs, and broccoli in the basket. Sprinkle with pepper and salt. Seal the pressure lid, choose Pressure Cook on High, and set the timer to 1 minute. Quick-release the pressure.

Take away the trivet and steamer basket from pot. Set the eggs in a bowl of ice water. Then peel and halve the eggs. Use a fork to fluff quinoa. Adjust the seasonings. In two bowls, equally divide avocado, quinoa, broccoli, eggs, carrots, potato, and a dollop of pesto. Serve alongside a lemon wedge.

Shrimp Risotto with Vegetables

Servings: 4 | Ready in about: 1 hour 15 minutes

INGREDIENTS

1 tbsp avocado oil
1 lb asparagus, roughly chopped
1 cup spinach, chopped
1½ cups mushrooms, sliced
1 cup rice, rinsed and drained
1¼ cups chicken broth
¾ cup coconut milk
1 tbsp coconut oil
16 shrimp, cleaned and deveined
Salt and ground black pepper to taste
¾ cup Parmesan cheese, shredded

DIRECTIONS

Warm the oil on Sauté in your Instant Pot. Add spinach, mushrooms and asparagus and cook for 10 minutes until cooked through. Add rice, coconut milk and broth to the pot as you stir. Seal the pressure lid, choose Pressure Cook on High, and set the timer to 40 minutes. Do a quick release, open the lid and put the rice on a serving plate.

To the pot, add coconut oil and press Sauté. Add shrimp and cook each side taking 4 minutes until cooked through and turns pink. Set the shrimp over rice and season with pepper and salt. Serve topped with Parmesan.

Red Lentil & Spinach Dhal

Servings: 6 | Ready in about: 35 minutes

INGREDIENTS

2 tbsp olive oil
1 red jalapeño, seeded and minced
1 cup spinach, chopped
4 cloves garlic, minced
1 tsp fresh ginger, peeled and grated
1 tbsp cumin seeds
1 tbsp coriander seeds
1 tsp ground turmeric
¼ tsp cayenne pepper
1½ cups red lentils
1 tomato, diced
¼ cup lemon juice
Salt to taste
Fresh Cilantro, chopped for garnish
Greek yogurt for garnish

DIRECTIONS

Heat oil on Sauté in your Instant Pot, add cayenne pepper, jalapeño pepper, ginger, turmeric, cumin, and garlic, and coriander and cook for 2-3 minutes until seeds become fragrant and begin to pop. Pour in 3 cups water, tomato, and lentils into pot and stir. Seal the pressure lid, choose Pressure Cook, and set the timer to 10 minutes.

Release pressure naturally for 10 minutes. Stir in spinach until wilted. Add lemon juice and season to taste. Divide between serving bowls. Garnish with yogurt and cilantro and serve.

Spicy Lentils with Chorizo

Servings: 10 | Ready in about: 50 minutes

INGREDIENTS

2 cups lentils, drained and rinsed
7 oz chorizo, sliced
1 onion, diced
2 garlic cloves, crushed
2 cups tomato sauce
2 cups vegetable broth
½ cup mustard
½ cup cider vinegar
3 tbsp Worcestershire sauce
2 tbsp maple syrup
2 tbsp liquid smoke
1 tbsp lime juice
2 cups brown sugar
1 tbsp salt
1 tbsp black pepper
1 tsp chili powder
1 tsp paprika
¼ tsp cayenne pepper

DIRECTIONS

Set to Sauté your Instant Pot. Add in chorizo and cook for 3 minutes as you stir until crisp. Add garlic and onion and cook for 2 more minutes until translucent. Mix tomato sauce, broth, cider vinegar, liquid smoke, Worcestershire sauce, lime juice, mustard, and maple syrup in a mixing bowl. Pour the mixture into the pot.

Add in pepper, chili powder, brown sugar, paprika, salt, and cayenne into the sauce as you stir to mix. Mix in lentils. Seal the pressure lid, choose Pressure Cook, and set the timer to 30 minutes. Release pressure quickly.

Baked Garbanzo Beans & Pancetta

Servings: 6 | Ready in about: 50 minutes

INGREDIENTS

3 strips pancetta, cut into strips
1 onion, diced
15 oz canned garbanzo beans
2 cups water
1 cup apple cider
2 garlic cloves, minced
½ cup ketchup
¼ cup sugar
1 tsp ground mustard powder
1 tsp salt
1 tsp ground black pepper
Fresh parsley to garnish

DIRECTIONS

Set your Instant Pot to Sauté. Cook pancetta for 5 minutes until crispy. Add onion and garlic, and cook for 3 minutes until soft. Mix in garbanzo beans, ketchup, sugar, salt, apple cider, mustard powder, water, and pepper. Seal the pressure lid, press Pressure Cook on High, and set the timer to 30 minutes. Once done, release pressure naturally for 10 minutes. Serve in bowls garnished with parsley.

Three-Bean Veggie Chili

Servings: 8 | Ready in about: 1 hour

INGREDIENTS

1 tbsp canola oil
1 onion, chopped
3 stalks of celery, chopped
1 green bell pepper, chopped
1 head broccoli, chopped into florets
2 tbsp minced garlic
2 tbsp chili powder
2 tsp ground cumin
4 cups vegetable broth
1 (28 oz) can tomatoes, crushed
½ cup pinto beans, soaked overnight
½ cup black beans, soaked overnight
½ cup cannellini beans, soaked overnight
1 bay leaf
Fresh parsley, chopped for garnish

DIRECTIONS

Warm oil on Sauté in your Instant Pot. Add onion and bell pepper, broccoli, and celery, and cook for about 8 minutes until softened. Mix in cumin, chili powder, and garlic and cook for another 1 minute. Add vegetable broth, tomatoes, black beans, salt, cannellini beans, pinto beans, and bay leaf to the pot.

Seal the pressure lid, choose Pressure Cook on High, and set the timer to 25 minutes. When ready, do a quick pressure release. Dispose of the bay leaf. Taste and adjust the seasonings. Sprinkle with fresh parsley and serve.

RICE, GRAINS & PASTA

Black Beans Tacos

Servings: 6 | Ready in about: 1 hour 30 minutes

INGREDIENTS

2 cups black beans, soaked overnight
1 cup shallots, chopped
4 cups water

1 tbsp dried oregano
1 tsp chili powder
6 soft Taco tortillas

1 avocado, sliced
Salt to taste
Fresh Cilantro for garnish

DIRECTIONS

Drain the beans and add to your Instant Pot. Mix in the onion, oregano and chili powder. Pour water. Seal the pressure lid, choose Pressure Cook on High, and set the timer to 60 minutes. Do a quick release, carefully open the lid and Allow cooling for a few minutes. Serve with taco tortillas, avocado slices and cilantro.

Parsley-Lime Bulgur Bowl

Servings: 4 | Ready in about: 30 minutes

INGREDIENTS

1 tbsp olive oil
1 small onion, chopped
2 cloves garlic, minced

1 cup bulgur wheat
2 ½ cups vegetable broth
1 tbsp lime juice, or more to taste

1 handful fresh parsley, roughly chopped
10 black olives to garnish
Salt and black pepper to taste

DIRECTIONS

Heat oil on Sauté in your Instant Pot, stir in garlic and onion and cook for 10 to 13 minutes until golden brown. Add in cilantro, bulgur, salt, 1 tbsp lime juice, and vegetable broth. Seal the pressure lid, choose Pressure Cook on High, and set the timer to 1 minute. Once ready, do a quick release. Use a fork to fluff bulgur. Add fresh parsley as you stir. Season with additional lime salt, juice, and pepper if desired. Serve in bowls topped with black olives.

Creamy Grana Padano Risotto

Servings: 6 | Ready in about: 25 minutes

INGREDIENTS

1 tbsp olive oil
1 white onion, chopped
1 tbsp butter

2 cups Carnaroli rice, rinsed
¼ cup dry white wine
4 cups chicken stock

Salt and white pepper to taste
2 tbsp Grana Padano cheese, grated
¼ tbsp Grana Padano cheese, flakes

DIRECTIONS

Warm oil on Sauté in your Instant Pot. Stir-fry onion for 3 minutes until soft and translucent. Add in butter and rice and cook for 2 minutes, stirring occasionally. Pour wine into the pot to deglaze, scrape away any browned bits of food from the bottom. Stir in stock, pepper, and salt. Seal the pressure lid, choose Pressure Cook on High. , and set the timer to 15 minutes. When ready, release the pressure quickly. Sprinkle with grated Parmesan cheese and stir well. Top with flaked cheese for garnish before serving.

Lemony Wild Rice Pilaf

Servings: 6 | Ready in about: 25 minutes

INGREDIENTS

4 cups vegetable broth
2 cups white wild rice, rinsed

1 tbsp butter
Zest and juice from 1 lemon

½ tsp salt
½ tsp ground black pepper

RICE, GRAINS & PASTA

DIRECTIONS

In your Instant Pot, mix rice, lemon zest, butter, and water. Seal the pressure lid, choose Pressure Cook on High, and set the timer to 3 minutes. When ready, release pressure naturally for 10 minutes. Sprinkle salt, lemon juice, and pepper over the pilaf and use a fork to gently fluff.

Spinach and Kidney Bean Stew

Servings: 4 | Ready in about: 45 minutes

INGREDIENTS

2 tbsp olive oil
1 onion, chopped
2 cloves garlic, minced
2 carrots, peeled and sliced
1 cup celery, chopped
4 cups vegetable broth
1 cup white kidney beans, soaked
1 tsp dried thyme
1 tsp dried rosemary
1 bay leaf
1 cup spinach, torn into pieces
Salt and black pepper to taste

DIRECTIONS

Set your Instant Pot to Sauté. Warm olive oil. Stir in garlic and onion and cook for 3 minutes until tender and fragrant. Mix in celery and carrots and cook for 2 to 3 minutes more until they start to soften. To the pot, add vegetable broth, bay leaf, thyme, rosemary, kidney beans, and salt. Seal the pressure lid, choose Pressure Cook.

Set the timer to 30 minutes. Quick release the pressure and add spinach to the beans as you stir and allow sit for 2 to 4 minutes until the spinach wilts. Add pepper and salt for seasoning.

Tri-Color Quinoa and Pinto Bean Bowl

Servings: 5 | Ready in about: 30 minutes

INGREDIENTS

1 tsp extra-virgin olive oil
1 green bell pepper, diced
1 onion, diced
1 tsp ground cumin
½ tsp salt
14 oz canned pinto beans, drained
1 cup organic Tri-Color Quinoa, rinsed
1 cup red salsa
1 cup vegetable broth

DIRECTIONS

Warm oil on Sauté in your Instant Pot. Add red onion and green bell pepper as you stir. Add salt and cumin for seasoning and cook for 7-8 minutes until fragrant. To the vegetable mixture, add quinoa, broth, salsa, and pinto beans. Seal the pressure lid, choose Pressure Cook on High, and set the timer to 12 minutes. When ready, do a quick pressure release. Use a fork to fluff quinoa and divide between serving bowls to serve.

Easy Vegan Sloppy Joes

Servings: 6 | Ready in about: 45 minutes

INGREDIENTS

2 cups water
1 cup pearl barley, rinsed
1 cup green onion, chopped
1 clove garlic, minced
2 cups tomato sauce
2 tbsp brown sugar
2 tbsp Worcestershire sauce
1 tsp Dijon mustard
1 tsp smoked paprika
1 tsp chili powder
6 brioche buns
Dill Pickles for garnish

DIRECTIONS

In your Instant Pot, mix Worcestershire sauce, water, onion, garlic, brown sugar, barley, tomato sauce, and spices. Seal the pressure lid, choose Pressure Cook on High, and set the timer to 25 minutes. When ready, release the pressure quickly. Press Sauté and cook until the mixture becomes thick. Transfer the sloppy joe mixture to the brioche buns and add a topping of dill pickles.

Rice Pilaf with Mushrooms

Servings: 6 | Ready in about: 35 minutes

INGREDIENTS

1 tbsp olive oil
2 cloves garlic, minced
1 yellow onion, finely chopped
2 cups button mushrooms, thinly sliced
4 cups vegetable stock
2 cups white rice
1 tsp salt
2 sprigs parsley, chopped

DIRECTIONS

Select Sauté in your Instant Pot. Add mushrooms, onion, and garlic, and stir-fry for 5 minutes until tender. Mix in rice, stock, and salt. Seal the pressure lid, choose Pressure Cook on High, and set the timer to 20 minutes. When ready, release pressure naturally for 10 minutes. Use a fork to fluff the rice and add parsley before serving.

Quinoa with Carrots and Onion

Servings: 6 | Ready in about: 15 minutes

INGREDIENTS

1 cup quinoa, rinsed
2 carrots, cut into sticks
1 large onion, sliced
2 tbsp olive oil
Salt to taste
Fresh cilantro, chopped for garnish

DIRECTIONS

Heat oil on Sauté in your Instant Pot. Add in onion and carrots and stir-fry for about 10 minutes until tender and crispy. Remove to a plate. Add 2 cups water, salt and quinoa to the steel pot of the pot. Seal the pressure lid, choose Pressure Cook on High, and set the timer to 1 minute. Once ready, do a quick release. Fluff the cooked quinoa with a fork. Transfer to a serving plate and top with the carrots and onion. Serve scattered with cilantro.

Cherry Tomato-Basil Linguine

Servings: 4 | Ready in about: 22 minutes

INGREDIENTS

2 tbsp olive oil
1 small onion, diced
2 garlic cloves, minced
1 cup cherry tomatoes, halved
1 ½ cups vegetable stock
¼ cup julienned basil leaves
1 tsp salt
½ tsp ground black pepper
¼ tsp red chili flakes
1 lb Linguine noodles, halved
Fresh basil leaves for garnish
½ cup Parmigiano-Reggiano, grated

DIRECTIONS

Warm oil on Sauté in your Instant Pot. Add onion and cook for 2 minutes until soft. Mix in garlic and tomatoes and sauté for 4 minutes. Pour in vegetable stock, salt, basil, red chili flakes, and pepper. Add linguine to the tomato mixture until covered. Seal the pressure lid, choose Pressure Cook on High, and set the timer to 5 minutes.

When ready, naturally release the pressure for 5 minutes. Stir the mixture to ensure it is broken down. Divide into plates. Top with basil and Parmigiano-Reggiano cheese and serve.

Chorizo Mac and Cheese

Servings: 6 | Ready in about: 30 minutes

INGREDIENTS

1 lb macaroni
3 oz chorizo, chopped
1 tbsp garlic powder
2 tbsp minced garlic
2 cups milk
2 cups Cheddar cheese, shredded

DIRECTIONS

Put chorizo in your Instant Pot, select Sauté and stir-fry until crisp, about 5 minutes. Set aside. Wipe the pot with kitchen paper. Add in 3 cups water, macaroni, and salt to taste. Seal lid and cook on for 5 minutes High Pressure. When ready, release the pressure quickly. Stir in cheese and milk until the cheese melts. Divide the mac and cheese between serving bowls. Top with chorizo and serve.

Indian Yellow Lentils

Servings: 6 | Ready in about: 30 minutes

INGREDIENTS

1 tbsp ghee
2 tsp cumin seeds
1 onion, chopped
4 garlic cloves, minced
1-inch piece of ginger, peeled, minced
Sea salt salt
1 tomato, chopped
2 cups split yellow lentils, soaked
2 tbsp garam masala
½ tsp ground turmeric
½ tsp cayenne pepper
1 tbsp fresh cilantro, finely chopped

DIRECTIONS

Warm ghee on Sauté in your Instant Pot. Add cumin seeds and cook for 10 seconds until they begin to pop. Stir in onion and cook for 2 to 3 minutes until softened. Mix in ginger and garlic and cook for 1 minute as you stir.

Sprinkle with salt. Mix in tomato and cook for 3 to 5 minutes until the mixture breaks down. Stir in turmeric, lentils, garam masala, and cayenne and cover with water. Seal the pressure lid, choose Pressure Cook on High, and set the timer to 8 minutes. When ready, release pressure quickly. Serve in bowls sprinkled with fresh cilantro.

South American Black Bean Chili

Servings: 8 | Ready in about: 1 hour 10 minutes

INGREDIENTS

1 tsp olive oil
1 onion, chopped
3 cloves garlic, minced
6 cups vegetable broth
2 cups black beans, soaked
1 jalapeño pepper, deseeded and diced
1 tsp dried oregano
1 tsp dried chili flakes
Salt to taste
Cotija Cheese, crumbled for garnish
Fresh cilantro for garnish

DIRECTIONS

Warm oil on Sauté in your Instant Pot. Add in garlic and onion and cook for 3 to 4 minutes until fragrant. Add beans, vegetable broth, oregano, chili flakes, salt and jalapeño pepper. Seal the pressure lid, choose Pressure Cook on High, and set the timer to 35 minutes. When ready, quick-release pressure. Divide between serving plates. Apply a topping of cilantro and cotija cheese to serve.

Pomodoro Sauce with Rigatoni and Kale

Servings: 6 | Ready in about: 15 minutes

INGREDIENTS

1 lb rigatoni pasta
15 oz canned tomato sauce
3 garlic cloves, minced
1 tsp chili flakes
2 tsp salt
2 tbsp extra-virgin olive oil
1 handful fresh basil, minced
1 cup kale, chopped
¼ cup Parmesan cheese

DIRECTIONS

In your Instant Pot, mix tomato sauce, salt, pasta, chili flakes, and garlic powder. Cover with water. Seal lid and cook for 5 minutes on Low Pressure. When ready, release the pressure quickly. Stir in kale until wilted. Plate the pasta and top with the parmesan and basil. Drizzle olive oil over the pasta.

Spicy Pinto Bean and Corn Stew

Servings: 6 | Ready in about: 1 hour 5 minutes

INGREDIENTS

2 tbsp olive oil
1 onion, chopped
1 red bell pepper, chopped
1 tbsp dried oregano

1 tbsp ground cumin
1 tsp red pepper flakes
3 cups vegetable stock
2 cups dried pinto beans, soaked

14 oz canned tomatoes, chopped
1 tbsp white wine vinegar
½ cup fresh chives, chopped
¼ cup fresh corn kernels

DIRECTIONS

Set your Instant Pot to Sauté. Stir in oil, bell pepper, pepper flakes, oregano, onion, and cumin. Cook for 3 minutes until soft. Mix in pinto beans, vegetable stock, and tomatoes. Seal the pressure lid, choose Pressure Cook on High, and set the timer to 30 minutes. Release pressure naturally for 20 minutes. Add in salt and vinegar. Divide in serving plates and top with corn and fresh chives.

Simple Jasmine Rice

Servings: 4 | Ready in about: 25 minutes

INGREDIENTS

2 cups jasmine rice

3 ½ cups of water

Salt and black pepper to taste

DIRECTIONS

Stir rice and water together in your Instant Pot. Season with salt to taste. Seal the pressure lid, press Pressure Cook on High, and set the timer to 15 minutes. When ready, release pressure naturally for 10 minutes. Use a fork to fluff rice. Season with black pepper before serving.

Chili-Garlic Rice Noodles with Tofu

Servings: 6 | Ready in about: 20 minutes

INGREDIENTS

½ cup soy sauce
2 tbsp brown sugar
2 tbsp rice vinegar

1 tbsp sweet chili sauce
1 tbsp sesame oil
1 tsp fresh minced garlic

20 oz extra firm tofu, pressed and cubed
8 oz rice noodles
¼ cup chopped fresh chives, for garnish

DIRECTIONS

Heat the oil on Sauté in your Instant Pot and fry the tofu for 5 minutes until golden brown. Set aside. To the pot, add 2 cups water, garlic, olive oil, vinegar, brown sugar, soy sauce, and chili sauce and mix well until smooth. Stir in rice noodles. Seal the pressure lid, choose Pressure Cook on High, and set the timer to 3 minutes. When ready, release the pressure quickly. Split the noodles between bowls. Top with tofu and fresh chives before serving.

Chicken Ragù Bolognese

Servings: 8 | Ready in about: 50 minutes

INGREDIENTS

2 tbsp olive oil
6 oz bacon, cubed
1 onion, minced
1 carrot, minced
1 celery stalk, minced

2 garlic cloves, crushed
¼ cup tomato paste
¼ tsp crushed red pepper flakes
1 ½ lb ground chicken
½ cup white wine

1 cup milk
1 cup chicken broth
Salt to taste
1 lb spaghetti

DIRECTIONS

Warm oil on Sauté in your Instant Pot. Add in bacon and fry for 5 minutes until crispy. Add celery, carrot, garlic and onion and cook for 5 minutes until fragrant. Mix in red pepper flakes and tomato paste and cook for 2 minutes. Break chicken into small pieces and place in the pot. Cook for 10 minutes as you stir until browned. Pour in wine and simmer for 2 minutes. Add in chicken broth and milk.

Seal the pressure lid, choose Pressure Cook on High, and set the timer to 15 minutes. When ready, release the pressure quickly. Add in the spaghetti and stir. Seal the pressure lid again, choose Pressure Cook on High, and set the timer to another 5 minutes. When ready, release the pressure quickly. Check the pasta for doneness. If necessary press Sauté and cook for an additional 2 minutes. Adjust the seasoning and serve right away.

Chicken and Chickpea Stew

Servings: 6 | Ready in about: 40 minutes

INGREDIENTS

- 1 lb boneless, skinless chicken legs
- 2 tsp ground cumin
- ½ tsp cayenne pepper
- 2 tbsp olive oil
- 1 onion, minced
- 2 jalapeño peppers, minced
- 3 garlic cloves, crushed
- 2 tsp freshly grated ginger
- ¼ cup chicken stock
- 1 (24 oz) can crushed tomatoes
- 2 (14 oz) cans chickpeas, drained
- Salt to taste
- ⅔ cup coconut milk
- ¼ cup fresh parsley, chopped
- 2 cups hot cooked basmati rice

DIRECTIONS

Season the chicken with salt, cayenne pepper, and cumin. Set your Instant Pot to Sauté. Warm oil. Add in jalapeño peppers and onion and cook for 5 minutes until soft. Mix in ginger and garlic and cook for 3 minutes until tender. Add ¼ cup chicken stock into the pot to ensure the pan is deglazed, from the pan's bottom scrape any browned bits of food. Mix the onion mixture with chickpeas, tomatoes, and salt. Stir in the chicken to coat in sauce.

Seal the pressure lid, choose Pressure Cook, and set the timer to 20 minutes. When ready, release the pressure quickly. Remove the chicken from the cooker and slice into chunks. Into the remaining sauce, mix in coconut milk. Simmer for 5 minutes on Sauté. Split rice into 6 bowls. Top with chicken, sauce, and cilantro for garnish.

Turkey Fajita Tortiglioni

Servings: 6 | Ready in about: 35 minutes

INGREDIENTS

- 2 tsp chili powder
- 1 tsp cumin
- 1 tsp onion powder
- 1 tsp garlic powder
- ½ tsp thyme
- 1 ½ lb turkey breast, cut into strips
- 1 tbsp olive oil
- 1 medium red onion, cut into wedges
- 4 garlic cloves, minced
- 3 cups chicken broth
- 1 cup salsa
- 16 oz tortiglioni
- 1 red bell pepper, sliced diagonally
- 1 yellow bell pepper, sliced diagonally
- 1 green bell pepper, sliced diagonally
- 1 cup shredded Gouda cheese
- ½ cup sour cream
- ½ cup chopped parsley

DIRECTIONS

In a bowl, mix chili powder, cumin, garlic powder, onion powder, salt, and oregano. Reserve 1 tsp seasoning. Coat turkey with the remaining seasoning. Warm the oil on Sauté in your Instant Pot. Add in turkey strips and cook for 4 to 5 minutes until browned. Place the turkey in a bowl. Cook the onion and garlic lightly for 1 minute until soft.

In the pot, mix salsa and chicken broth and scrape the bottom of any brown bits. Into the broth mixture, stir in tortiglioni pasta and cover with bell peppers and turkey. Seal the pressure lid, choose Pressure Cook for 5 minutes.

When ready, do a quick pressure release. Open the lid and sprinkle with gouda cheese and reserved seasoning and stir well. Divide into plates and top with sour cream. Add parsley for garnishing and serve.

Rigatoni with Sausage and Spinach

Servings: 4 | Ready in about: 45 minutes

INGREDIENTS

- 1 tbsp butter
- ½ cup diced red bell pepper
- 1 onion, chopped
- 3 cups vegetable broth
- ¼ cup tomato purée
- 4 sausage links, sliced
- 2 tsp chili powder
- Salt and ground black pepper to taste
- 12 oz rigatoni pasta
- 1 cup baby spinach
- ½ cup Parmesan cheese

DIRECTIONS

Warm the butter on Sauté in your Instant Pot. Add red bell pepper, onion, and sausage, and cook for 5 minutes.

Mix in vegetable broth, chili powder, tomato paste, salt, and pepper to combine. Stir in rigatoni pasta.

Seal the pressure lid, choose Pressure Cook on High, and set the timer to 12 minutes. When ready, naturally release pressure for 20 minutes. Stir in spinach and let simmer until wilted. Top with Parmesan cheese and serve.

Black-Eyed Peas with Kale

Servings: 6 | Ready in about: 30 minutes

INGREDIENTS

- 1 tsp olive oil
- 1 onion, thinly sliced
- 2 garlic cloves, minced
- 1 cup fire-roasted red peppers, diced
- ½ tsp ground allspice
- ½ tsp red pepper, crushed
- Salt to taste
- 1 ½ cups black-eyed peas, soaked
- 1 ½ cups vegetable broth
- 1 bay leaf
- 1 (15 oz) can fire roasted tomatoes
- 2 cups chopped kale

DIRECTIONS

Warm oil on Sauté in your Instant Pot. Add onion and cook for 5 minutes until fragrant. Add garlic and fire roasted red peppers and cook for 1 more minute until softened. To the vegetable mixture, add a seasoning of salt, crushed red pepper, and allspice. Add vegetable broth, bay leaf, and black-eyed peas to the pot.

Seal the pressure lid, choose Pressure Cook on High, and set the timer to 5 minutes. When ready, do a quick pressure release. Remove the bay leaf and discard. Mix the peas with kale and tomatoes. Close the air fry lid and cook for 2 minutes on Bake at 380 F. Adjust the seasoning and serve.

Shrimp Lo Mein

Servings: 2 | Ready in about: 20 minutes

INGREDIENTS

- 1 tbsp sesame oil
- 1 lb shrimp, peeled and deveined
- ½ cup diced onion
- 2 cloves garlic, minced
- 1 cup carrots, cut into strips
- 1 cup green beans, washed
- 2 cups vegetable stock
- 3 tbsp soy sauce
- 2 tbsp rice wine vinegar
- 10 oz lo mein egg noodles
- ½ tsp toasted sesame seeds
- Sea salt and ground black pepper to taste

DIRECTIONS

Warm oil on Sauté in your Instant Pot. Stir-fry the shrimp for 5 minutes. Remove to a plate and set aside. Add in garlic and onion and cook for 3 minutes until fragrant. Mix in soy sauce, carrots, vegetable stock, green beans, and rice wine vinegar. Add noodles into the mixture and ensure they are covered. Season with pepper and salt.

Seal the pressure lid, choose Pressure Cook on High, and set the timer to 5 minutes. When ready, release the pressure quickly. Plate the lo mein, add the reserved shrimp, sprinkle with sesame seeds, and serve.

Cheese and Spinach Stuffed Shells

Servings: 6 | Ready in about: 1 hour

INGREDIENTS

2 cups onion, chopped
1 cup carrot, chopped
3 garlic cloves, minced
3 ½ tbsp olive oil,
1 (28 oz) canned tomatoes, crushed
12 oz jumbo shell pasta
1 tbsp olive oil
2 cups ricotta cheese, crumbled
1 ½ cup feta cheese, crumbled
2 cups spinach, chopped
¾ cup grated Pecorino Romano cheese
2 tbsp chopped fresh chives
1 tbsp chopped fresh dill
Salt and ground black pepper to taste
1 cup shredded cheddar cheese

DIRECTIONS

Warm olive oil on Sauté in your Instant Pot. Add in onion, carrot, and garlic, and cook for 5 minutes until tender. Stir in tomatoes and cook for another 10 minutes. Remove to a bowl and set aside. Wipe the pot with a damp cloth, add pasta and cover with enough water. Seal the pressure lid, choose Pressure Cook on High, and set the timer to 5 minutes. Do a quick pressure and drain the pasta. Lightly grease olive oil to a baking sheet.

In a bowl, combine feta and ricotta cheeses. Add in spinach, Pecorino Romano, dill, and chives and stir. Adjust the seasonings. Fill the shells with the mixture. Spread 4 cups tomato sauce on the baking sheet. Place the stuffed shells over with seam-sides down and sprinkle cheddar cheese atop. Use aluminum foil to the cover the baking dish.

Pour 1 cup of water in the pot and insert the trivet. Lower the baking dish onto the trivet. Seal the pressure lid, choose Pressure Cook on High, and set the timer to 15 minutes. Once ready, do a quick release. Take away the foil. Place the stuffed shells to serving plates and top with tomato sauce before serving.

Chipotle Mac and Cheese

Servings: 6 | Ready in about: 15 minutes

INGREDIENTS

12 oz macaroni
1 tsp salt
1 tbsp chipotle chili powder
½ tsp ground black pepper
4 tbsp butter
1½ cup milk
4 cups sharp Cheddar cheese, grated
2 cups Pecorino Romano cheese, grated
Salt and black pepper to taste

DIRECTIONS

To your Instant Pot, add salt, 4 cups cold water and macaroni. Seal the pressure lid, choose Pressure Cook on High, and set the timer to 4 minutes. When ready, release the pressure quickly. Add butter to the pasta and stir until melts. Stir in milk, chipotle chili powder, and black pepper. Pour in Pecorino Romano and Cheddar cheeses and stir until well melted. Add pepper and salt to season. Serve.

Pasta Caprese Ricotta-Basil Fusilli

Servings: 3 | Ready in about: 15 minutes

INGREDIENTS

1 tbsp olive oil
1 onion, thinly sliced
6 garlic cloves, minced
1 tsp red pepper flakes
2 ½ cups dried fusilli
1 (15 oz) can tomato sauce
1 cup tomatoes, halved
1 cup water
¼ cup basil leaves
1 tsp salt
1 cup Ricotta cheese, crumbled
2 tbsp chopped fresh basil

DIRECTIONS

Warm the oil on Sauté in your Instant Pot. Add in red pepper flakes, garlic, and onion and cook for 3 minutes. Mix in fusilli, tomatoes, water, tomato sauce, and salt. Seal the pressure lid, choose Pressure Cook, and set the timer to 4 minutes. When ready, release the pressure quickly. Top with the ricotta and chopped basil to serve.

Beef-Stuffed Pasta Shells

Servings: 4 | Ready in about: 35 minutes

INGREDIENTS

2 tbsp olive oil
1 lb ground beef
16 oz pasta shells
2 cups water
15 oz tomato sauce
15-oz can black beans, drained
15-oz canned corn, drained
10 oz red enchilada sauce
4 oz diced green chiles
1 cup shredded mozzarella cheese
Salt and ground black pepper to taste
Finely chopped parsley for garnish

DIRECTIONS

Heat oil on Sauté in your Instant Pot. Add ground beef and cook for 7 minutes until it starts to brown. Mix in pasta, tomato sauce, enchilada sauce, black beans, water, corn, and green chiles and stir to coat well.

Seal the pressure lid, choose Pressure Cook on High, and set the timer to 10 minutes. When ready, do a quick pressure release. Into the pasta mixture, mix in mozzarella cheese until melted. Garnish with parsley to serve.

Pork Spaghetti with Spinach and Tomatoes

Servings: 4 | Ready in about: 35 minutes

INGREDIENTS

2 tbsp olive oil
½ cup onion, chopped
1 garlic clove, minced
1 lb pork sausage meat
2 cups water
1 (14 oz) can diced tomatoes, drained
½ cup sun-dried tomatoes
1 tbsp dried oregano
1 tsp Italian seasoning
1 fresh jalapeño chile, minced
1 tsp salt
8 oz dried spaghetti, halved
1 cup spinach

DIRECTIONS

Warm oil on Sauté in your Instant Pot. Add in onion and garlic and cook for 2 minutes until softened. Stir in sausage meat and cook for 5 minutes. Stir in jalapeño, water, sun-dried tomatoes, Italian seasoning, oregano, diced tomatoes, and salt. Mix spaghetti and press to submerge into the sauce.

Seal the pressure lid, choose Pressure Cook on High, and set the timer to 9 minutes. When ready, release the pressure quickly. Stir in spinach, close lid again, and simmer on Keep Warm for 5 minutes until spinach is wilted.

Baked Rigatoni with Beef Tomato Sauce

Servings: 4 | Ready in about: 75 minutes

INGREDIENTS

1 tbsp butter
2 lb ground beef
2 (24-oz) cans tomato sauce
1 cup dry red wine
16-oz dry rigatoni
½ tsp garlic powder
1 cup cottage cheese
1 cup shredded mozzarella cheese
½ cup chopped fresh parsley

DIRECTIONS

Choose Sauté your Instant Pot. Melt the butter, add the beef and cook for 5 minutes, or until browned and cooked well. Stir in the tomato sauce, 1 cup water, wine, and rigatoni. Season with the garlic powder and salt. Put the pressure lid together and lock in the Seal position. Choose Pressure Cook and set the time to 2 minutes.

When the timer is done, perform a natural pressure release for 10 minutes, then a quick pressure release and carefully open the lid. Stir in the cottage cheese and evenly sprinkle the top of the pasta with the mozzarella cheese. Close the air fry lid. Choose Broil, and set the time to 3 minutes.. Cook for 3 minutes, or until the cheese has melted, slightly browned, and bubbly. Garnish with the parsley and serve immediately.

BEEF, PORK & LAMB

Ground Beef Stuffed Empanadas

Servings: 2 | Ready in about: 60 minutes

INGREDIENTS

1 tbsp olive oil
1 garlic clove, minced
½ white onion, chopped
¼ lb ground beef
6 green olives, pitted and chopped
¼ tsp cumin powder
¼ tsp paprika
⅛ tsp cinnamon powder
2 small tomatoes, chopped
8 square gyoza wrappers
1 egg, beaten

DIRECTIONS

Choose Sauté on your Instant Pot. Put the oil, garlic, onion, and beef in the preheated pot and cook for 5 minutes, stirring occasionally, until the fragrant and the beef is no longer pink. Stir in the olives, cumin, paprika, and cinnamon and cook for an additional 3 minutes. Add the tomatoes and cook for 1 more minute. Spoon the beef mixture into a plate and allow cooling for a few minutes.

Meanwhile, put the air fry basket in the pot. Close the air fry lid, choose Air Fry, set the temperature to 400°F, and the time to 5 minutes. Lay the gyoza wrappers on a flat surface. Place 1 to 2 tablespoons of the beef mixture in the middle of each wrapper. Brush the edges of the wrapper with egg and fold in half to form a triangle.

Pinch the edges together to seal. Place 4 empanadas in a single layer in the preheated basket. Close the air fry lid. Choose Air Fry, set the temperature to 400°F, and set the time to 7 minutes. Once the timer is done, remove the empanadas from the basket and transfer to a plate. Repeat with the remaining empanadas.

Winter Pot Roast with Biscuits

Servings: 6 | Ready in about: 75 minutes

INGREDIENTS

2 tbsp olive oil
1 (3-lb) chuck roast
Salt and black pepper to taste
⅔ cup dry red wine
⅔ cup beef broth
1 tsp dried oregano leaves
1 bay leaf
1 small red onion, peeled and quartered
1 lb small butternut squash, diced
2 carrots, cut into 1-inch pieces
¾ cup frozen pearl onions
6 refrigerated biscuits

DIRECTIONS

On the pot, choose Sauté. Heat the olive oil until shimmering. Season the beef on both sides with salt and add to the pot. Cook undisturbed for 3 minutes or until deeply browned. Flip the roast over and brown the other side for 3 minutes. Transfer the beef to a wire rack. Pour the oil out of the pot and add in the wine. Scrape the bottom of the pot to let off any browned bits. Bring to a boil and cook for 2 minutes or until the wine has reduced by half.

Mix in the beef broth, oregano, bay leaf, black pepper, and red onion. Stir to combine and add the beef with its juices. Seal the pressure lid and choose Pressure Cook on High and the cooking time to 35 minutes. After cooking, perform a quick pressure release. Carefully open the pressure lid. Add the butternut squash, carrots, and pearl onions to the pot. Seal the pressure lid and choose Pressure Cook on High and the time to 2 minutes.

After cooking, perform a quick pressure release, and open the lid. Transfer the beef to a cutting board and cover with aluminum foil. Put a trivet in the upper position of the pot and cover it with a circular piece of aluminum foil. Put the biscuits on the trivet and put a trivet in the pot. Close the air fry lid and choose Bake. Adjust the temperature to 300°F and the cooking time to 15 minutes. After 8 minutes, open the lid and flip the biscuits over.

After baking, remove the trivet and biscuits. Allow the biscuits to cool for a few minutes. While the biscuits cook, remove the foil from the beef and cut it against the grain into slices. Remove and discard the bay leaf and transfer the beef to a serving platter. Spoon the vegetables and the sauce over the beef. Serve with the biscuits.

Smoky Horseradish Spare Ribs

Servings: 4 | Ready in about: 55 minutes

INGREDIENTS

1 spare rack ribs

1 tsp salt

1 cup smoky horseradish sauce

DIRECTIONS

Season all sides of ribs with salt and cut into 3 pieces. Cut a trivet into 3 pieces. Pour 1 cup of water into your Instant Pot. Fix in a trivet and put the ribs on top, bone-side down. Seal the pressure lid, choose Pressure Cook on High and the time to 18 minutes. After cooking, perform a quick pressure release and carefully open the lid.

Take out the trivet with ribs and pour out the water from the pot. Set a trivet and ribs in the pot. Close the air fry lid and choose Air Fry. Adjust the temperature to 400°F and the cooking time to 20 minutes.

After 10 minutes, open the lid and turn the ribs. Lightly baste the bony side of the ribs with the smoky horseradish sauce and close the lid to cook further. After 4 minutes, open the lid and turn the ribs again. Baste the meat side with the remaining sauce and close the lid to cook until the ribs are done.

Steak with Chips

Servings: 4 | Ready in about: 50 minutes

INGREDIENTS

4 potatoes, cut into wedges

1 tsp sweet paprika

1 tbsp olive oil

1 tsp salt, divided

1 tsp ground black pepper

4 rib-eye steaks

DIRECTIONS

Put the air fry basket in your Instant Pot. Close the air fry lid. Choose Air Fry, set the temperature to 390°F, and set the time to 5 minutes. Meanwhile, rub all over with olive oil. Put the potatoes in the preheated air fry basket and season with ½ teaspoon of salt and ½ teaspoon of black pepper and sweet paprika.

Close the air fry lid. Choose Air Fry, set the temperature to 400°F, and set the time to 35 minutes. Season the steak on both sides with the remaining salt and black pepper. When done cooking, remove potatoes to a plate. Grease the air fry basket with cooking spray and put the steaks in the basket.

Close the air fry lid. Choose Air Fry, set the temperature to 400°F, and set the time to 8 minutes. When ready, check the steaks for your preferred doneness and cook for a few more minutes if needed. Take out the steaks from the basket and rest for 5 minutes. Serve the steaks with the potato wedges and the steak sauce.

Thai Roasted Beef

Servings: 2 | Ready in about: 4 hours 20 minutes

INGREDIENTS

1 lb ground beef

2 tbsp soy sauce

Thumb-sized piece of ginger, chopped

3 chilies, deseeded and chopped

4 garlic cloves, chopped

1 tsp brown sugar

Juice of 1 lime

2 tbsp mirin

2 tbsp cilantro, chopped

2 tbsp basil, chopped

2 tbsp oil

2 tbsp fish sauce

DIRECTIONS

Place all ingredients, except beef, salt, and pepper, in a blender. Pulse until smooth. Season the beef with salt and pepper. Place the meat and Thai mixture in a zipper bag. Shake well to combine and let marinate in the fridge for about 4 hours. Place the beef in the air fry basket and cook for about 12 minutes, or a little more for well done, on Air Fry mode at 350°F. Let sit for 5 minutes before serving.

Greek Beef Gyros

Servings: 4 | Ready in about: 55 minutes

INGREDIENTS

1 lb beef sirloin, cut into thin strips
1 onion, thinly sliced
⅓ cup beef broth
2 tbsp fresh lemon juice
2 tbsp olive oil
2 tsp dry oregano
1 clove garlic, minced
Salt and black pepper to taste
4 slices pita bread
1 cup Greek yogurt
2 tbsp fresh dill, chopped

DIRECTIONS

In your Instant Pot, mix beef, beef broth, oregano, garlic, lemon juice, pepper, onion, olive oil, and salt. Seal the pressure lid, choose Pressure Cook on High, and set the timer to 30 minutes. Release pressure naturally for 15 minutes. Divide the beef mixture between the pita bread slices, top with yogurt and dill, and roll up to serve.

Sweet Gingery Beef & Broccoli

Servings: 4 | Ready in about: 70 minutes

INGREDIENTS

1 tbsp olive oil
2 lb skirt steak, cut into strips
4 garlic cloves, minced
½ cup coconut aminos
⅔ cup dark brown sugar
½ tsp ginger puree
2 tbsp cornstarch
1 head broccoli, trimmed into florets
3 scallions, thinly sliced

DIRECTIONS

Choose Sauté on your Instant Pot. Pour the oil and beef into the pot and brown the beef strips on both sides, about 5 minutes in total. Remove the beef from the pot and set aside. Add the garlic to the oil and sauté for 1 minute or until fragrant. Stir in the coconut aminos, ½ cup of water, brown sugar, and ginger to the pot. Mix evenly and add the beef. Seal the pressure lid, choose Pressure Cook on High, and set the time to 10 minutes.

In a small bowl, whisk combine the cornstarch and 3 tbsp water. When done cooking, perform a quick pressure release. Choose Sauté. Pour in the cornstarch mixture and stir continuously until the sauce becomes syrupy. Add the broccoli, stir to coat in the sauce, and cook for another 5 minutes. Top with scallions and serve.

Beef & Broccoli Sauce

Servings: 4 | Ready in about: 35 minutes

INGREDIENTS

2 lb chuck roast, boneless and cut into thin strips
4 cloves garlic, minced
7 cups broccoli florets
1 tbsp olive oil
1 cup beef broth
1 tbsp cornstarch
¾ cup soy sauce

DIRECTIONS

Open the lid of your Instant Pot and select Sauté. Add the olive oil, and once heated, add the beef and minced garlic. Cook the meat until brown. Stir in soy sauce and beef broth. Seal the lid and select Pressure Cook on High for 10 minutes. Once the timer has ended, do a quick pressure release and remove the meat and set aside.

Fetch out a quarter of the liquid into a bowl, add the cornstarch, and mix it until it is well dissolved. Pour the mixture into the pot and place a trivet. Place the broccoli florets on it and seal the lid. Select Steam for 5 minutes.

When ready, do a quick pressure release and open the lid. Remove the trivet, stir the sauce, add the meat and close the air fry lid. Cook for 5 minutes on Broil mode. The sauce should be thick enough when you finish cooking. Dish the beef broccoli sauce into a serving bowl and serve with a side of cooked pasta.

Honey Short Ribs with Rosemary Potatoes

Servings: 4 | Ready in about: 105 minutes

INGREDIENTS

4 bone-in beef short ribs, silver skin
Salt and black pepper to taste
2 tbsp olive oil
1 onion, chopped
2 tbsp honey
½ cup beef broth
2 tbsp minced fresh rosemary
3 garlic cloves, minced
2 potatoes, cut into 1-inch pieces

DIRECTIONS

Choose Sauté on your Instant Pot. Season the short ribs on all sides with ½ teaspoon of salt and ½ teaspoon of pepper. Heat 1 tablespoon of olive oil and brown the ribs on all sides, about 10 minutes total. Stir in the onion, honey, broth, 1 tablespoon of rosemary, and garlic. Seal the pressure lid, choose Pressure Cook on High, and set the time to 40 minutes.. In a large bowl, toss the potatoes with the remaining oil, rosemary, salt, and black pepper.

When the ribs are ready, perform a quick pressure release and carefully open the lid. Fix a trivet in the higher position of the pot, which is over the ribs. Put the potatoes on the trivet. Close the air fry lid. Choose Bake set the temperature to 350°F, and set the time to 15 minutes.

Once the potatoes are tender and roasted, use tongs to pick the potatoes and the short ribs into a plate. Set aside. Choose Sauté and set to High. Simmer the sauce for 5 minutes and spoon the sauce into a bowl. Allow sitting for 2 minutes and scoop off the fat that forms on top. Serve the ribs with the potatoes and sauce.

Sticky BBQ Baby Back Ribs

Servings: 4 | Ready in about: 35 minutes

INGREDIENTS

1 ½ tbsp smoked paprika
3 tbsp brown sugar
2 tsp garlic powder
3 lb rack baby back ribs, cut into quarters
1 cup beer
1 cup barbecue sauce

DIRECTIONS

In a bowl, mix the paprika, brown sugar, garlic, salt, and black pepper. Season all sides of the ribs with the rub. Pour the beer into your Instant Pot, put the ribs in the air fry basket, and place the basket in the pot. Seal the pressure lid, choose Pressure Cook on High, and set the time to 10 minutes.

When done cooking, perform a quick pressure release, and carefully the open the lid. Close the air fry lid. Choose Air Fry, set the temperature to 400°F, and the time to 15 minutes. After 10 minutes, open the lid, and brush the ribs with the barbecue sauce. Close the lid to cook further for 5 minutes.

Beef Congee (Chinese Rice Porridge)

Servings: 6 | Ready in about: 1 hour

INGREDIENTS

1 cup jasmine rice
2 cloves garlic, minced
1 (1 inch) piece fresh ginger, minced
6 cups beef stock
1 cup kale, roughly chopped
1 cups water
2 lb ground beef
Salt and black pepper to taste
Fresh cilantro, chopped

DIRECTIONS

Run cold water and rinse rice. Add garlic, rice, and ginger into your Instant Pot. Pour in water and stock and spread the beef on top of rice. Seal the pressure lid, choose Pressure Cook on High, and set the timer to 30 minutes. Once ready, release pressure naturally for 10 minutes. Stir in kale to obtain the desired consistency. Add pepper and salt for seasoning. Divide into serving plates and top with cilantro.

Pineapple Appetizer Ribs

Servings: 4 | Ready in about: 30 minutes

INGREDIENTS

2 lb cut spareribs
7 oz salad dressing

5 oz canned pineapple juice
2 cups water

Salt and black pepper to taste

DIRECTIONS

Sprinkle the ribs with salt and pepper and place them in a saucepan. Pour water and cook the ribs for around 12 minutes on high heat. Drain the ribs and arrange them in your Instant Pot. Sprinkle with garlic salt. Close the air fry lid and cook for 15 minutes at 390°F on Air Fry mode. Prepare the sauce by combining the salad dressing and the pineapple juice. Serve the ribs with this delicious dressing sauce!

Beef Carnitas

Servings: 4 | Ready in about: 55 minutes

INGREDIENTS

2 ½ lb bone-in country ribs
¼ cup orange juice

2 tbsp beef stock
1 tbsp lime juice

1 small onion, cut into 8 wedges
3 garlic cloves, smashed and peeled

DIRECTIONS

Season the ribs with salt on all sides. In your Instant Pot, combine the orange juice, stock, and lime juice. Drop in the onion and garlic. Stir. Put the ribs in your Instant Pot. Seal the pressure lid, choose Pressure Cook on High and the cooking time to 25 minutes. After cooking, do a natural pressure release for 12 minutes.

Transfer the ribs to a plate to cool slightly. Remove and discard the bones. Run the juice in the pot through a fat separator and set aside for a few minutes. Pour the sauce back into the pot and reserve the fat. Oil a trivet with cooking spray and lay the ribs in a single layer on the trivet. Baste with the reserved fat. Put the trivet in the pot.

Close the air fry lid and choose Air Fry. Adjust the temperature to 375°F for 6 minutes. After crisping, put the beef back in the sauce and shred the meat. Stir the beef into the sauce. Serve the carnitas with flatbread or on rice.

Classic Carbonnade Flamande

Servings: 4 | Ready in about: 70 minutes

INGREDIENTS

2 lb brisket, cut into 2 or 3 pieces
1 tbsp olive oil
1 large onion, sliced

8 fluid oz stout
¼ tsp dried rosemary leaves
¼ cup beef broth

½ tsp Dijon-style mustard
½ tsp brown sugar to taste
2 tbsp chopped fresh chervil

DIRECTIONS

Season the brisket with salt. On the pot, choose Sauté. Heat the olive oil in your Instant Pot until shimmering and sear the brisket. Cook, without turning, for 4 minutes or until browned. Use tongs to turn the beef and move to the side. Add the onion on the other side. Cook, stirring, for 1 to 2 minutes or until slightly softened.

Pour in the stout, scraping off any browned bits from the bottom of the pot. Simmer and cook until the stout has reduced by about half. Stir in the rosemary and broth. Seal the pressure lid, choose Pressure Cook on High and the cooking time to 35 minutes. After cooking, perform a natural pressure release for 10 minutes.

Remove the beef onto a cutting board. Scoop off any excess fat on the sauce and stir in the mustard and brown sugar. Choose Sauté. Simmer the sauce and cook until reduced to a thin gravy. Taste and adjust the seasoning. Slice the beef and return to the sauce to reheat. Serve over mashed potatoes or noodles and garnish with chervil.

Peanut Sauce Beef Satay

Servings: 4 | Ready in about: 60 minutes

INGREDIENTS

1 lb flank steak
½ tsp salt

For the Cucumber Relish
½ cucumber
½ cup rice vinegar

For the Sauce
1 tbsp coconut oil
1 tbsp onion, minced
1 tsp garlic, minced

1 tbsp lime juice
1½ tsp red curry paste

¼ cup water
2 tbsp sugar

1 cup coconut milk
2 tsp red curry paste
1 tsp brown sugar

1 tbsp coconut aminos
1 tbsp coconut oil

1 tsp salt
1 serrano chile, cut into thin rounds

⅓ cup water
½ cup peanut butter
1 tbsp lime juice

DIRECTIONS

Season the steak with salt. Put in a resealable plastic bag. In a small bowl, whisk the lime juice, curry paste, coconut aminos, and coconut oil. Pour the marinade over the steak, seal the bag, and massage the bag to coat the meat. Let sit for 20 minutes. Cut the cucumber into ¼-inch slices, then into quarters. In a bowl, whisk the vinegar, water, sugar, and salt until the sugar and salt dissolve. Add the cucumber pieces. Refrigerate until needed.

To make the sauce, on the pot, choose Sauté. Heat the coconut oil until shimmering and sauté the onion and garlic in your Instant Pot. Cook for 1 to 2 minutes or until fragrant. Stir in the coconut milk, curry paste, and brown sugar. Seal the pressure lid, choose Pressure Cook on High and the cooking time to 1 minute.

After cooking, perform a quick pressure release. Pour in the water and mix. Remove the meat from the marinade, holding the meat above the bag for a while to drain the excess marinade, put on the trivet, and put the trivet with the steak in the sauce. Close the air fry lid, choose Broil, adjust the cooking time to 14 minutes, and press Start to begin cooking. After about 7 minutes, open the lid and turn the steak. Close the lid and begin broiling.

Transfer the steak to a cutting board and allow resting for a few minutes. While the steak cools, mix the peanut butter and lime juice into the sauce. Taste and adjust the seasoning. Cut the steak into thin slices and serve with the peanut sauce and cucumber relish.

Cheeseburgers in Hoagies

Servings: 4 | Ready in about: 65 minutes

INGREDIENTS

1 tbsp olive oil
1 (14 oz) can French onion soup
1 lb chuck beef roast
1 onion, sliced

2 tbsp Worcestershire sauce
2 Cups beef broth
Salt and black pepper to taste
1 tsp garlic powder

3 slices Provolone cheese
3 hoagies, halved
3 tsp mayonnaise

DIRECTIONS

Season the beef with garlic powder, salt, and pepper. On your Instant Pot, select Sauté. Heat the olive oil and brown the beef on both sides for about 5 minutes. Remove the meat onto a plate. To the pot, add the onions and cook until soft. Then, pour the beef broth and stir while scraping the bottom of every stuck bit. Add the onion soup, Worcestershire sauce, and beef. Seal the lid and select Pressure Cook on High for 20 minutes.

Once the timer has stopped, do a natural pressure release for 10-15 minutes, and then a quick pressure release to let out any remaining steam. Use two forks to shred the meat. Close the air fry lid and cook on Bake for 10 minutes at 350°F. When ready, open the lid and strain the juice of the pot through a sieve into a bowl. Assemble the burgers by slathering mayo on halved hoagies, spoon the shredded meat over and top each hoagie with cheese.

Beef & Cabbage Stew

Servings: 4 | Ready in about: 30 minutes

INGREDIENTS

1 cup rice
1 large head cabbage, cut in chunks
1 lb ground beef
Salt and black pepper to taste
½ cup chopped onion
4 cloves garlic, minced
2 tbsp butter
1 bay leaf
1 cup diced tomatoes
1 ½ cup beef broth
¼ cup Plain vinegar
2 tbsp Worcestershire sauce
1 tbsp paprika powder
1 tbsp dried oregano
Chopped parsley to garnish

DIRECTIONS

Set your Instant Pot on Sauté. Melt the butter and add the beef. Brown it for about 6 minutes and add in the onions, garlic, and bay leaf. Stir and cook for 2 more minutes. Stir in the oregano, paprika, salt, pepper, rice, cabbage, vinegar, broth, and Worcestershire sauce. Cook for 3 minutes, stirring occassionally.

Add the tomatoes but don't stir. Seal the lid and select Pressure Cook mode on High for 5 minutes. Once the timer is done, let the pot sit closed for 5 minutes and then do a quick pressure. Open the lid. Stir the sauce, remove the bay leaf, and adjust the seasoning with salt. Dish the cabbage sauce in serving bowls and serve with bread rolls.

Tasty Baby Porcupine Meatballs

Servings: 4 | Ready in about: 30 minutes

INGREDIENTS

1 cup rice
1 lb of ground beef
1 onion, chopped
1 green bell pepper, finely chopped
1 tsp celery salt
2 tbsp Worcestershire sauce
1 garlic clove, minced
2 cups of tomato juice
1 tsp oregano

DIRECTIONS

Combine the rice, ground beef, onion, celery, salt, green peppers, and garlic. Shape into balls of 1 inch each. Arrange the balls on the air fry basket of your Instant Pot. Close the air fry lid and cook for 15 minutes at 390°F.

After 8 minutes, shape the balls. Heat the tomato juice, cloves, oregano, and Worcestershire sauce in a saucepan over medium heat. Pour in the meatballs, bring to a boil, and simmer for 10 minutes, stirring often.

Pot Roast with Broccoli

Servings: 4 | Ready in about: 35 minutes

INGREDIENTS

2 lb beef chuck roast
3 tbsp olive oil, divided into 2
Salt to taste
1 cup beef broth
1 packet onion soup mix
1 cup chopped broccoli
2 red bell peppers, seeded and quartered
1 yellow onion, quartered

DIRECTIONS

Season the chuck roast with salt and set aside. Select Sauté on your Instant Pot. Add the olive oil, and once heated, add the chuck roast. Sear for 5 minutes on each side. Then, pour in the beef broth. In a zipper bag, add broccoli, onions, peppers, the remaining olive oil, and onion soup. Close the bag and shake the mixture to coat the vegetables well. Use tongs to remove the vegetables into the pot and stir with a spoon.

Seal the lid and select Pressure Cook on High for 18 minutes. Once the timer has stopped, do a quick pressure release, and open the pressure lid. Make cuts on the meat inside the pot and close the air fry lid. Cook on Air Fry for 10 minutes at 380°F until nice and crispy. Serve with the vegetables and a drizzle of the sauce in the pot.

Beef & Green Bell Pepper Pot

Servings: 4 | Ready in about: 55 minutes

INGREDIENTS

- 2 lb beef chuck roast, cut in 4 pieces
- 1 tbsp onion powder
- 1 tbsp garlic powder
- 1 tbsp Italian Seasoning
- 1 cup beef broth
- 1 medium white onion, sliced
- 1 green bell pepper, seeded and sliced
- 1 red bell pepper, seeded and sliced
- 2 tbsp olive oil

DIRECTIONS

Rub the beef with pepper, salt, garlic powder, Italian seasoning, and onion powder. Select Sauté on your Instant Pot. Heat 1 tbsp oil, add the beef pieces and sear them on both sides until brown, for about 5 minutes. Use a pair of tongs to remove them onto a plate after. Pour the beef broth and fish sauce into the pot to deglaze the bottom while you use a spoon to scrape any stuck beef bit at the bottom. Add the meat back to the pot.

Seal the lid and select Pressure Cook on High for 30 minutes. Once the timer has stopped, do a quick pressure release, and open the pot. Use two forks to shred the beef inside the pot. Close the air fry lid and select Broil mode for 10 minutes. When ready, set aside the meat and discard the liquid. Wipe clean the pot.

Select Sauté, heat the remaining oil, add the beef with onions and peppers. Sauté them for 3 minutes and season with salt and pepper. Turn off the pot and dish the stir-fried beef into serving plates.

Beef Soup with Tortillas

Servings: 8 | Ready in about: 30 minutes

INGREDIENTS

- 2 tbsp olive oil
- 6 green bell pepper, diced
- 2 medium yellow onion, chopped
- 3 lb ground beef, grass-fed
- Salt and black pepper to taste
- 3 tbsp chili powder
- 2 tbsp cumin powder
- 2 tsp paprika
- 1 tsp garlic powder
- 1 tsp cinnamon
- 1 tsp onion powder
- 6 cups chopped tomatoes
- ½ cup chopped green chilies
- 3 cups bone broth
- 3 cups milk

Topping:
Chopped Jalapenos, cilantro and green onions, sliced Avocados, lime juice

DIRECTIONS

Select Sauté on your Instant Pot. Pour in the oil and add the yellow onion and green peppers. Sauté until they are soft for about 5 minutes. Include the ground beef, stir the ingredients, and let the beef cook for about 8 minutes until it browns. Add the chili powder, cumin powder, black pepper, paprika, cinnamon, garlic powder, onion powder, and green chilies. Give them a good stir. Top with tomatoes, milk, and bone broth.

Seal the lid and select Pressure Cook on High for 20 minutes. Once the timer has ended, do a quick pressure release. Adjust the taste with salt and pepper. Dish the taco soup into serving bowls and add the toppings. Serve warm with a side of tortillas.

Beef and Bell Pepper with Onion Sauce

Servings: 6 | Ready in about: 62 minutes

INGREDIENTS

- 2 lb round steak pieces, 6 to 8 pieces
- ½ green bell pepper, finely chopped
- ½ red bell pepper, finely chopped
- ½ yellow bell pepper, finely chopped
- 1 yellow onion, finely chopped
- 2 cloves garlic, minced
- Salt and black pepper to taste
- ¼ cup flour
- 2 tbsp olive oil

DIRECTIONS

Wrap the steaks in plastic wrap, place on a cutting board, and use a rolling pin to pound flat of about 2-inch thickness. Remove the plastic wrap and season with salt and pepper. Mix the chopped peppers, onion, and garlic in a bowl. Spoon the bell pepper mixture onto the flattened steaks and roll them to have the peppers inside.

Use some toothpicks to secure the beef rolls and dredge the steaks in all-purpose flour while shaking off any excess flour. Place them on a plate. Select Sauté on your Instant Pot and heat the oil. Add the beef rolls and brown them for about 6 minutes. Pour ½ cup water over the meat, seal the lid and select Pressure Cook for 20 minutes.

Once the timer has stopped, do a natural pressure release for 10 minutes. Close the air fry lid and cook for 10 minutes on Broil mode. When ready, remove the meat to a plate and spoon the sauce from the pot over. Serve the stuffed meat rolls with a side of steamed veggies.

Beef & Pepperoncini Peppers

Servings: 4 | Ready in about: 55 minutes

INGREDIENTS

14 oz jar pepperoncini peppers, with liquid
2 lb beef roast, cut into cubes
1 pack brown gravy mix
1 pack Italian salad dressing mix

DIRECTIONS

Place the beef, pepperoncini peppers, brown gravy mix, Italian salad dressing mix, and ½ cup water in your Instant Pot. Seal the lid and select Pressure Cook on High for 35 minutes. Once the timer has stopped, do a quick pressure release, and open the pot. Close the air fry lid and cook on Bake mode for 15 to 20 minutes at 380°F, until nice and tender. Shred the beef and serve the beef sauce on plates with a side of a veggie mash.

Short Ribs with Egg Noodles

Servings: 4 | Ready in about: 65 minutes

INGREDIENTS

4 lb bone-in short ribs
Salt and black pepper to taste
Low-sodium beef broth
6 oz egg noodles
2 tbsp prepared horseradish
6 tbsp Dijon mustard
1 garlic clove, minced
3 tbsp melted unsalted butter
1 ½ cups panko bread crumbs

DIRECTIONS

Season the short ribs on all sides with 1½ teaspoons of salt. Pour 1 cup of broth into in your Instant Pot. Put a trivet in the lower position in your Instant Pot, and place the short ribs on top. Seal the pressure lid, choose Pressure Cook on High and the time to 25 minutes. After cooking, perform a natural pressure release for 5 minutes, then a quick pressure release, and carefully open the lid. Remove the trivet and short ribs.

Pour the cooking liquid into a measuring cup to get 2 cups. If lesser than 2 cups, add more broth and season with salt and pepper. Add the egg noodles and the remaining salt. Stir and submerge the noodles as much as possible. Seal the pressure lid, choose Pressure Cook on High and the cooking time to 4 minutes.

In a bowl, combine the horseradish, Dijon mustard, garlic, and black pepper. Brush the sauce on all sides of the short ribs and reserve any extra sauce. In another bowl, mix the butter and breadcrumbs. Coat the ribs with the crumbs. Put the ribs back on the trivet. After cooking, do a quick pressure release. Stir the noodles, which may not be quite done but will continue cooking. Return the trivet and beef to the pot in the upper position.

Close the air fry lid and choose Bake. Adjust the temperature to 400°F and the cooking time to 15 minutes. After 8 minutes, open the lid and turn the ribs over. Close the lid and continue cooking. Serve the beef and noodles, with the extra sauce on the side.

Asian Beef Curry

Servings: 4 | Ready in about: 40 minutes

INGREDIENTS

1 ½ lb beef brisket, cut in cubes
1 tbsp olive oil
2 cloves garlic, minced
¼-inch ginger, peeled and sliced
2 bay leaves

2 star anises
1 large carrot, chopped
1 medium onion, chopped
2 tbsp red curry paste
1 cup milk

1 Potato, peeled and chopped
1 tbsp sugar
2 tsp oyster sauce
2 tsp flour
3 tbsp water

DIRECTIONS

Select Sauté on your Instant Pot. Heat oil, add garlic, ginger, and red curry paste. Stir-fry them for 1 minute. Stir in onion and beef. Cook for 4 minutes. Add the carrots, bay leaves, potato, star anises, sugar, and water. Stir. Seal the lid and select Pressure Cook on High for 25 minutes. Once the timer goes off, do a quick pressure release.

In a bowl, add the flour and 4 tablespoons of milk. Mix well with a spoon and pour it into your Instant Pot along with the oyster sauce and remaining milk. Stir it gently not to break the potato. Close the air fry lid and cook on Broil mode for about 3 minutes, until the sauce thickens and meat is tender. After, turn off the pot. Spoon the sauce into soup bowls and serve with a side of rice.

Beef & Cheese Stuffed Mushrooms

Servings: 3 | Ready in about: 10 minutes

INGREDIENTS

6 white mushrooms, stems removed
2 cups cooked leftover beef, cubed

½ cup vegetable broth
2 oz cream cheese, softened

1 cup shredded Cheddar cheese
1 tsp olive oil

DIRECTIONS

In a bowl, add the beef, cream cheese, and cheddar cheese. Use a spoon to mix them. Spoon the beef mixture into the mushrooms and place the mushrooms in the inner pot of your Instant Pot. Drizzle them with olive oil, and add the broth. Seal the lid and select Pressure Cook on High for 3 minutes.

Once the timer is off, do a quick pressure release and open the pressure lid, discard the liquid, and remove the mushrooms. Place a trivet and lay the mushrooms on it. Close the air fry lid and cook for 2 to 3 minutes on Air Fry mode at 350°F. Remove the stuffed mushrooms onto a plate and serve hot.

Beef Stew with Beer

Servings: 4 | Ready in about: 60 minutes

INGREDIENTS

2 lb beef stewed meat, cut into bite-size pieces
Salt and black pepper to taste
¼ cup flour
3 tbsp butter

2 tbsp Worcestershire sauce
2 cloves garlic, minced
1 packet dry onion soup mix

2 cups beef broth
1 medium bottle beer
1 tbsp tomato paste

DIRECTIONS

In a zipper bag, add beef, salt, all-purpose flour, and pepper. Close the bag up and shake it to coat the meat well with the mixture. Select Sauté on your Instant Pot. Melt the butter, and brown the beef on both sides for 5 minutes. Pour the broth to deglaze the bottom of the pot. Stir in tomato paste, beer, Worcestershire sauce, and the onion soup mix. Seal the lid and select Pressure Cook on High for 25 minutes.

Once the timer is done, do a natural pressure release for 10 minutes, and then a quick pressure release to let out any remaining steam. Open the pressure lid and close the air fry lid. Cook on Broil mode for 10 minutes. Spoon the beef stew into serving bowls and serve over a bed of vegetable mash with steamed greens.

Meatballs with Spaghetti Sauce

Servings: 6 | Ready in about: 20 minutes

INGREDIENTS

- 2 lb ground beef
- 1 cup breadcrumbs
- 1 onion, finely chopped
- 2 cloves garlic, minced
- Salt and pepper, to taste
- 1 tsp dried oregano
- 3 tbsp milk
- 1 cup water
- 1 cup grated Parmesan cheese
- 2 eggs, cracked into a bowl
- 4 cups spaghetti sauce
- 1 tbsp olive oil

DIRECTIONS

In a bowl, add beef, onion, breadcrumbs, parmesan, eggs, garlic, milk, salt, oregano, and pepper. Mix well with hands and shape bite-size balls. Open your Instant Pot and add the spaghetti sauce, water, and meatballs.

Close the lid, secure the pressure valve, and select Steam mode on High pressure for 6 minutes. Once the timer is done, do a natural pressure release for 5 minutes, then do a quick pressure release to let out any extra steam, and open the lid. Dish the meatball sauce over cooked pasta and serve.

Spiced Beef Chili

Servings: 4 | Ready in about: 40 minutes

INGREDIENTS

- 2 lb ground beef
- 2 tbsp olive oil
- 1 large red bell pepper, chopped
- 1 large yellow bell pepper, chopped
- 1 white onion, chopped
- 2 cups chopped tomatoes
- 2 cups beef broth
- 2 carrots, cut into little bits
- 2 tsp onion powder
- 2 tsp garlic powder
- 5 tsp chili powder
- 2 tbsp Worcestershire sauce
- 2 tsp paprika
- ½ tsp cumin powder
- 2 tbsp chopped parsley

DIRECTIONS

Select Sauté on your Instant Pot and add the olive oil and ground beef. Cook the meat until brown, stirring occasionally, for about 8 minutes. Top with the remaining ingredients and mix well. Seal the lid, and cook on Pressure Cook on High for 15 minutes. Once the timer has ended, do a quick pressure release, and open the lid. Stir the stew and close the air fry lid. Cook on Broil mode for 10 minutes. Dish into serving bowls. Serve.

Spiced Beef Shapes

Servings: 12 | Ready in about: 40 minutes

INGREDIENTS

- 1 ½ lb ground beef
- ½ cup minced onion
- 2 tbsp chopped mint leaves
- 3 garlic cloves, minced
- 2 tsp paprika
- 2 tsp coriander seeds
- ½ tsp cayenne pepper
- 1 tsp salt
- 1 tbsp chopped parsley
- 2 tsp cumin
- ½ tsp ground ginger
- 24 skewers, soaked in water

DIRECTIONS

Combine all ingredients in a large bowl. Make sure to mix well with your hands until the herbs and spices are evenly distributed and the mixture is well incorporated. Shape the beef mixture into 12 shapes around 2 skewers. Close the air fry lid and cook for 12 - 15 minutes on Air Fry mode at 330°F, or until preferred doneness. Serve.

Beef & Garbanzo Bean Chili

Servings: 10 | Ready in about: 45 minutes

INGREDIENTS

1 lb garbanzo beans, soaked overnight
1 tbsp olive oil
2 onions, finely chopped
2 ½ lb ground beef
1 small jalapeño with seeds, minced
6 garlic cloves, minced
¼ cup chili powder
2 tbsp ground cumin
2 tsp salt
1 tsp smoked paprika
1 tsp dried oregano
1 tsp garlic powder
¼ tsp cayenne pepper
2 ½ cups beef broth
1 (6 oz) can tomato puree

DIRECTIONS

Add the garbanzo beans to your Instant Pot and pour in cold water to cover 1 inch. Seal the pressure lid, choose Pressure Cook on High, and set the timer to 20 minutes. When ready, release the pressure quickly. Drain beans and rinse with cold water. Set aside. Wipe clean the pot and set it to Sauté. Warm olive oil, add in onion and cook for 3 minutes until soft. Add jalapeño, ground beef, and minced garlic and stir-fry for 5 minutes.

Stir in chili powder, kosher salt, garlic powder, paprika, cumin, oregano, and cayenne pepper, and cook until soft, about 30 seconds. Pour beef broth, garbanzo beans, and tomato paste into the pot. Seal the pressure lid, choose Pressure Cook on High, and set the timer to 20 minutes. When ready, release pressure naturally for about 10 minutes. Open the lid, press Sauté, and cook as you stir until desired consistency is attained. Serve.

Cheddar Cheeseburgers

Servings: 4 | Ready in about: 20 minutes

INGREDIENTS

1 lb ground beef
1 (1 oz) packet dry onion soup mix
1 cup water
4 burger buns
4 tomato slices
4 Cheddar cheese slices
4 small leaves lettuce
Mayonnaise, Mustard, Ketchup for garnish

DIRECTIONS

In a bowl, add beef and onion mix, and mix well with hands. Shape in 4 patties and wrap each in foil paper. Pour the water into the inner steel insert of your Instant Pot, and fit in the steamer rack. Place the wrapped patties on the trivet. Seal the lid and cook for 10 minutes on Pressure Cook. Once ready, do a quick pressure release.

Use a set of tongs to remove the wrapped beef onto a flat surface and carefully unwrap the patties. In each half of the buns, put a lettuce leaf, then a beef patty, a slice of cheese, and a slice of tomato. Top it with the other halves of buns. Serve with some ketchup, mayonnaise, and mustard.

Beef & Vegetable Stew

Servings: 4 | Ready in about: 70 minutes

INGREDIENTS

2 lb brisket, cut into 2-inch pieces
4 cups beef broth
1 tbsp Dijon mustard
1 tbsp olive oil
1 lb small potato, quartered
¼ lb carrots, cut into 2-inch pieces
1 large red onion, quartered
3 cloves garlic, minced
1 bay leaf
2 fresh thyme sprigs
2 tbsp cornstarch
3 tbsp chopped cilantro to garnish

DIRECTIONS

Pour broth, cornstarch, mustard, ½ teaspoon salt, and ½ teaspoon pepper in a bowl. Whisk them and set aside. Season the beef with salt and pepper. On your Instant Pot, select Sauté. Add the olive oil, and once heated, add the beef strips. Flip halfway through to brown evenly. That should take 7 to 10 minutes.

Add potato, carrots, onion, garlic, thyme, mustard mixture, and bay leaf. Stir once more. Seal the lid and select Pressure Cook for 35 minutes. Once the timer has ended, do a quick pressure release. Remove the bay leaf. Close the air fry lid and cook for 10 minutes on Broil mode. Serve the soup with a bread of your choice.

Beef Roast with Peanut Satay Sauce

Servings: 4 | Ready in about: 40 minutes

INGREDIENTS

1 lb beef roast, cut into cubes
Salt and black pepper to taste
½ cup coconut milk, light
½ cup Peanut Satay sauce
2 cups diced carrots

DIRECTIONS

Place the beef into your Instant Pot. In a bowl, mix in coconut milk, salt, pepper, and satay sauce. Pour over the beef. Add the carrots too. Seal the lid and select Pressure Cook on High for 15 minutes. Once the timer has ended, do a natural pressure release for 10 minutes. Give it a stir and close the air fry lid. Cook for 10 minutes on Bake mode at 400°F. Use a spoon to dish the meat into a serving plate, and serve with a side of steamed greens.

Chipotle Beef Brisket

Servings: 4 | Ready in about: 1 hour 10 minutes

INGREDIENTS

2 tsp smoked paprika
½ tsp dried oregano
1 tbsp Worcestershire sauce
½ tsp ground cumin
½ tsp garlic powder
1 tsp chipotle powder
¼ tsp cayenne pepper
2 lb beef brisket
2 tbsp olive oil
1 cup beef broth
¼ cup red wine
A handful of parsley, chopped

DIRECTIONS

In a bowl, combine oregano, cumin, cayenne pepper, garlic powder, paprika, Worcestershire sauce and chipotle powder. Rub the seasoning mixture on the beef to coat. Warm olive oil on Sauté in your Instant Pot. Add in beef and cook for 3 to 4 minutes on each side until browned completely. Pour in beef broth and red wine.

Seal the pressure lid, choose Pressure Cook on High, and set the timer to 50 minutes. Release the Pressure naturally for 10 minutes. Place the beef on a cutting board and Allow cooling for 10 minutes before slicing. Arrange the beef slices on a serving platter, pour the cooking sauce over and scatter with parsley to serve.

Brisket Chili con Carne

Servings: 6 | Ready in about: 1 hour 25 minutes

INGREDIENTS

1 tbsp ground black pepper
2 tsp salt
1 tsp sweet paprika
1 tsp cayenne pepper
1 tsp chili powder
½ tsp garlic salt
½ tsp onion powder
1 (4 lb) beef brisket
1 cup beef broth
2 bay leaves
2 tbsp Worcestershire sauce
14 oz canned black beans, drained

DIRECTIONS

In a bowl, combine pepper, paprika, chili powder, cayenne pepper, salt, onion powder and garlic salt. Rub onto brisket pieces to coat. Add the brisket to your Instant Pot. Cover with Worcestershire sauce and water. Seal the pressure lid, choose Pressure Cook, and set the timer to 50 minutes. Release pressure naturally for 10 minutes. Transfer the brisket to a cutting board. Drain any liquid present in the using a fine-mesh strainer. Get rid of any solids and fat. Slice brisket, arrange the slices onto a platter, add the black beans on the side, and spoon the cooking liquid over.

Meatloaf with Cheesy Mashed Potatoes

Servings: 6 | Ready in about: 45 minutes

INGREDIENTS

Meatloaf:
1 ½ lb ground beef
1 onion, diced
1 egg
1 potato, grated
¼ cup tomato puree
1 tsp garlic powder
1 tsp salt
1 tsp ground black pepper

Mashed Potatoes:
4 potatoes, chopped
2 cups water
½ cup milk
2 tbsp butter
Salt and black pepper to taste
1 cup ricotta cheese

DIRECTIONS

In a bowl, combine ground beef, eggs, 1 tsp pepper, garlic powder, potato, onion, tomato puree, and 1 tsp salt to obtain a consistent texture. Shape the mixture into a meatloaf and place onto an aluminum foil. Arrange potatoes onto your Instant Pot and pour water over them. Place a trivet onto potatoes and set the foil sheet with meatloaf onto the trivet. Seal the pressure lid, choose Pressure Cook on High, and set the timer to 22 minutes.

When ready, release the pressure quickly. Place the meatloaf on a cutting board to cool before slicing. Drain the liquid out of the pot. Mash potatoes in the pot with pepper, milk, ricotta cheese, salt, and butter until smooth and all the liquid is absorbed. Plate the potatoes and lean a meatloaf slice to one side of the potato pile before serving.

Beef & Pumpkin Stew

Servings: 6 | Ready in about: 35 minutes

INGREDIENTS

2 tbsp canola oil
2 lb stew beef, cut into 1-inch chunks
1 cup red wine
1 onion, chopped
1 tsp garlic powder
1 tsp salt
3 whole cloves
1 bay leaf
3 carrots, sliced
½ butternut pumpkin, sliced
2 tbsp cornstarch
3 tbsp water

DIRECTIONS

Warm oil on Sauté in your Instant Pot. Add beef and brown for 5 minutes on each side. Deglaze the pot with wine, scrape the bottom to get rid of any browned beef bits. Add in onion, salt, bay leaf, cloves, and garlic powder. Seal the pressure lid, choose Pressure Cook on High, and set the timer to 15 minutes.

When ready, release the pressure quickly. Add in pumpkin and carrots without stirring. Seal the pressure lid again, choose Pressure Cook on High, and set the timer to 5 minutes. When ready, release the pressure quickly.

In a bowl, mix water and cornstarch until cornstarch dissolves completely. Mix into the stew. Allow the stew to simmer while uncovered on Keep Warm for 5 minutes until you attain the desired thickness.

Beef & Cherry Tagine

Servings: 4 | Ready in about: 1 hour 20 minutes

INGREDIENTS

2 tbsp olive oil
1 onion, chopped
1 ½ lb stewing beef, trimmed
1 tsp ground cinnamon
½ tsp paprika
½ tsp turmeric
½ tsp salt
¼ tsp ground ginger
¼ tsp ground allspice
1-star anise
1 cup water
1 tbsp honey
1 cup dried cherries, halved
¼ cup toasted almonds, slivered

DIRECTIONS

Set your Instant Pot to Sauté. Warm olive oil. Add in onions and cook for 3 minutes until fragrant. Mix in beef and cook for 2 minutes each side until browned. Stir in anise, cinnamon, turmeric, allspice, salt, paprika, and ginger. Cook for 2 minutes until aromatic. Add in honey and water. Seal the lid, choose Pressure Cook for 50 minutes.

Meanwhile, in a bowl, soak dried cherries in hot water until softened. Once ready, release pressure naturally for 15 minutes. Drain cherries and stir into the tagine. Top with toasted almonds before serving.

Beef Pho with Swiss Chard

Servings: 6 | Ready in about: 1 hour 10 minutes

INGREDIENTS

- 2 tbsp coconut oil
- 1 yellow onion, quartered
- ¼ cup minced fresh ginger
- 2 tsp coriander seeds
- 2 tsp ground cinnamon
- 2 tsp ground cloves
- 9 cups water
- 2 lb Beef Neck Bones
- 2 ½ tsp kosher salt
- 8 oz rice noodles
- 3 tbsp sugar
- 2 tbsp fish sauce
- 10 oz sirloin steak
- A handful of fresh cilantro, chopped
- 2 scallions, chopped
- 2 jalapeño peppers, sliced
- 2 cups Swiss chard, chopped
- Freshly ground black pepper to taste

DIRECTIONS

Melt the oil on Sauté in your Instant Pot. Add ginger and onions and cook for 4 minutes until the onions are softened. Stir in cloves, cinnamon and coriander seeds and cook for 1 minute until soft. Add in water, salt, beef meat and bones. Seal the pressure lid, choose Pressure Cook for 30 minutes. Release pressure quickly.

Transfer the meat to a large bowl. Cover with it enough water and soak for 10 minutes. Drain the water and slice the beef. In hot water, soak rice noodles for 8 minutes until softened and pliable. Drain and rinse with cold water. Drain liquid from cooker into a separate pot through a fine-mesh strainer. Get rid of any solids.

Add fish sauce and sugar to the broth. Transfer into the pot and simmer on Sauté. Place the noodles in four separate soup bowls. Top with steak slices, scallions, swiss chard, sliced jalapeño pepper, cilantro, red onion, and pepper. Spoon the broth over each bowl to serve.

Caribbean Ropa Vieja

Servings: 6 | Ready in about: 1 hour 10 minutes

INGREDIENTS

- Salt and black pepper to taste
- 2 lb beef skirt steak
- 3 ½ cups beef stock
- 2 bay leaves
- ¼ cup olive oil
- 1 red onion, halved and thinly sliced
- 1 green bell pepper, thinly sliced
- 1 red bell pepper, thinly sliced
- ¼ cup minced garlic
- 1 tsp dried oregano
- 1 tsp ground cumin
- 1 cup tomato sauce
- 1 cup dry red wine
- 1 tbsp vinegar
- ¼ cup cheddar cheese, shredded

DIRECTIONS

Season the skirt steak with pepper and salt. Add water to your Instant Pot. Mix in bay leaves and flank steak. Seal the pressure lid, choose Pressure Cook on High, and set the timer to 35 minutes. When ready, release the pressure quickly. Remove skirt steak to a cutting board and allow to sit for about 5 minutes. When cooled, shred the beef using two forks. Drain the pressure cooker, and reserve the bay leaves and 1 cup liquid.

Warm the oil on Sauté. Add onion, red bell pepper, cumin, garlic, green bell pepper, and oregano and continue cooking for 5 minutes until vegetables are softened. Stir in reserved liquid, tomato sauce, bay leaves and red wine. Return shredded beef to the pot with vinegar. Season with pepper and salt. Seal the pressure lid, choose Pressure Cook on High, and set the timer to 15 minutes. Release pressure naturally for 10 minutes. Serve with cheese.

Short Ribs with Mushrooms & Asparagus Sauce

Servings: 6 | Ready in about: 1 hour 15 minutes

INGREDIENTS

3 ½ lb boneless beef short ribs, cut into pieces
Salt and black pepper to taste
3 tbsp olive oil
1 onion, diced
1 cup dry red wine
1 tbsp tomato puree
2 carrots, peeled and chopped
2 garlic cloves, minced
5 sprigs parsley, chopped
2 sprigs rosemary, chopped
3 sprigs oregano, chopped
4 cups beef stock
10 oz mushrooms, quartered
1 cup asparagus, trimmed and chopped
1 tbsp cornstarch

DIRECTIONS

Apply a seasoning of black pepper and salt to the ribs. Warm oil on Sauté in your Instant Pot. In batches, add the short ribs to the oil and cook for 3 to 5 minutes each side until browned. Set aside on a bowl. Add onions to the hot oil and cook for 3 to 5 minutes until soft. Add tomato puree and red wine into the pot to deglaze, scrape the bottom to get rid of any browned beef bits. Cook for 2 minutes until wine reduces slightly.

Return the ribs to pot and top with carrots, oregano, rosemary, and garlic. Add in beef broth. Seal the pressure lid, choose Pressure Cook on High, and set the timer to 35 minutes. Release pressure naturally for 10 minutes. Transfer ribs to a plate. Strain and get rid of herbs and vegetables, and return cooking broth to the pot. Add mushrooms and asparagus to the broth. Press Sauté and cook for 2 to 4 minutes until vegetables are soft.

In a bowl, mix ¼ cup cold water and cornstarch until cornstarch dissolves completely. Add the cornstarch mixture into the broth as you stir for 1 to 3 minutes until the broth thickens slightly. Season the sauce with black pepper and salt. Pour the sauce over ribs, add chopped parsley for garnish before serving.

Meatballs with Marinara Sauce

Servings: 6 | Ready in about: 35 minutes

INGREDIENTS

1½ lb ground beef
⅓ cup warm water
¾ cup grated Parmigiano-Reggiano
½ cup bread crumbs
1 egg
2 tbsp fresh parsley
¼ tsp garlic powder
¼ tsp dried oregano
Salt and black pepper to taste
½ cup capers
1 tsp olive oil
3 cups marinara sauce

DIRECTIONS

In a large bowl, mix ground beef, garlic powder, pepper, oregano, bread crumbs, egg, and salt. Shape into meatballs. Warm the oil on Sauté in your Instant Pot. Add meatballs to the oil and brown for 2-3 minutes and all sides. Pour water and marinara sauce over the meatballs. Seal the pressure lid, choose Pressure Cook, and set the timer to 10 minutes. When ready, release the pressure quickly. Top with capers and Parmigiano-Reggiano cheese.

Beef Stew with Veggies

Servings: 6 | Ready in about: 1 hour 15 minutes

INGREDIENTS

¼ cup flour
2 tsp salt, divided
1 tsp paprika
1 tsp ground black pepper
2 lb beef chuck, cubed
2 tbsp olive oil
2 tbsp butter
1 onion, diced
3 garlic cloves, minced
1 cup dry red wine
2 cups beef stock
1 tbsp dried Italian seasoning
2 tsp Worcestershire sauce
4 cups potatoes, diced
2 celery stalks, chopped
3 cups carrots, chopped
3 tomatoes, chopped
2 bell pepper, thinly sliced
Salt and black pepper to taste
A handful of fresh parsley, chopped

DIRECTIONS

In a bowl, mix black pepper, beef, flour, paprika, and 1 tsp salt. Toss the ingredients and ensure the beef is coated. Warm butter and oil on Sauté. Add in beef and cook for 8- 10 minutes until browned. Set aside on a plate. To the same fat, add garlic, onion, and celery, bell peppers, and cook for 4-5 minutes until tender.

Deglaze with wine, scrape the bottom to get rid of any browned beef bits. Pour in remaining salt, beef stock, Worcestershire sauce, and Italian seasoning. Return beef to the pot. Add carrots, tomatoes, and potatoes. Seal the pressure lid, choose Pressure Cook on High, and set the timer to 35 minutes. Release pressure naturally for 10 minutes. Taste and adjust the seasonings as necessary. Serve on plates and scatter over the parsley.

Beef & Bacon Chili

Servings: 6 | Ready in about: 1 hour

INGREDIENTS

2 lb stewing beef, trimmed
Salt and black pepper to taste
4 oz smoked bacon, cut into strips
2 tsp olive oil, divided
1 onion, diced

2 bell peppers, diced
3 garlic cloves, minced
1 tbsp ground cumin
1 tsp chili powder
½ tsp cayenne pepper

1 chipotle in adobo sauce, chopped
2 cups beef broth
29 oz canned whole tomatoes
15 oz canned kidney beans, drained

DIRECTIONS

Set Sauté on your Instant Pot and fry the bacon until crispy, about 5 minutes. Set aside. Rub the beef with ½ tsp black pepper and 1 tsp salt. In the bacon fat, brown beef for 5-6 minutes. Transfer to a plate.

Warm the oil. Add in garlic, peppers and onion and cook for 3 to 4 minutes until soft. Stir in cumin, cayenne pepper, the extra pepper and salt, chopped chipotle, and chili powder and cook for 30 seconds until soft. Return beef and bacon to the pot with vegetables and spices. Add in tomatoes and broth.

Seal the pressure lid, choose Pressure Cook on High, and set the timer to 45 minutes. When ready, release the pressure quickly. Stir in beans. Let simmer on Keep Warm for 10 minutes until flavors combine.

Braised Short Ribs with Creamy Sauce

Servings: 6 | Ready in about: 1 hour 55 minutes

INGREDIENTS

3 lb beef short ribs
Salt and black pepper to taste
2 tbsp olive oil
1 onion, chopped
1 large carrot, chopped

1 celery stalk, chopped
3 garlic cloves, chopped
2 cups beef broth
1 (14.5 oz) can diced tomatoes
½ cup dry red wine

¼ cup red wine vinegar
2 bay leaves
¼ tsp red pepper flakes
2 tbsp chopped parsley
1/2 cup cheese cream

DIRECTIONS

Season your short ribs with 1 tsp black pepper and salt. Warm olive oil on Sauté in your Instant Pot. Add in short ribs and sear for 3 minutes each side until browned. Set aside on a bowl. Drain everything only to be left with 1 tbsp of the remaining fat from the pot. Set on Sauté, and stir-fry garlic, carrot, onion, and celery in the hot fat for 4 to 6 minutes until fragrant. Stir in broth, wine, red pepper flakes, vinegar, tomatoes, bay leaves, pepper, and salt.

Turn the pot to Sauté on Low and bring the mixture to a boil. With the bone-side up, lay short ribs into the braising liquid. Seal the pressure lid, choose Pressure Cook on High, and set the timer to 40 minutes.

When ready, release the pressure quickly. Set the short ribs on a plate. Get rid of bay leaves. Using an immersion blender, blitz the liquid for 1 minute. Add cream cheese, pepper and salt and blend until smooth. Arrange the ribs onto a serving plate, pour the sauce over and top with parsley.

Italian-Style Pot Roast

Servings: 5 | Ready in about: 1 hour 30 minutes

INGREDIENTS

2 ½ lb beef brisket, trimmed
2 tbsp olive oil
1 onion, chopped
3 garlic cloves, minced

1 cup beef broth
¾ cup dry red wine
2 fresh thyme sprigs
2 fresh rosemary sprigs

4 oz pancetta, chopped
6 carrots, chopped
1 bay leaf
A handful of parsley, chopped

DIRECTIONS

Warm olive oil on Sauté in your Instant Pot. Fry the pancetta for 4-5 minutes until crispy. Set aside. Season the beef with pepper and salt and add it to the pot and brown for 5 to 7 minutes for each. Remove and set aside on a plate. In the same oil, fry garlic and onion for 3 minutes until softened. Pour in red wine and beef broth to deglaze the bottom, scrape the bottom of the pot to get rid of any browned bits of food.

Return the beef and pancetta to the pot and add rosemary sprigs and thyme. Seal the pressure lid, choose Pressure Cook on High, and set the timer to 50 minutes. When ready, release the pressure quickly. Add carrots and bay leaf to the pot. Seal the pressure lid again, choose Pressure Cook on High, and set the timer to 4 minutes.

When ready, release the pressure quickly. Get rid of the thyme, bay leaf and rosemary sprigs. Place beef on a serving plate and sprinkle with parsley to serve.

Stewed Beef with Portobello Mushrooms

Servings: 5 | Ready in about: 40 minutes

INGREDIENTS

1 lb boneless chuck steak, cut into chunks
¼ cup flour
1 tsp salt
1 tsp ground black pepper

1 cup pancetta, chopped
½ cup red burgundy wine
1¼ cup beef broth
1 carrot, diced

2 cups Portobello mushrooms, quartered
4 shallots, sliced
3 garlic cloves, crushed
A handful of parsley, chopped

DIRECTIONS

Toss beef with black pepper, salt, and flour in a large bowl to coat. Set Sauté on your Instant Pot. Cook pancetta for 5 minutes until brown and crispy. Pour in approximately half the beef and cook for 5 minutes each side until browned all over. Transfer the pancetta and beef to a plate. Sear remaining beef and transfer to the plate.

Add in beef broth and wine to deglaze the pan, scrape the pan's bottom to get rid of any browned bits of food. Return beef and pancetta to cooker. Stir in garlic, carrot, shallots, and mushrooms. Seal the pressure lid, choose Pressure Cook, and set the timer to 30 minutes. When ready, release the pressure quickly. Garnish with parsley.

BBQ Sticky Baby Back Ribs with

Servings: 6 | Ready in about: 40 minutes

INGREDIENTS

2 tbsp olive oil
1 rack baby back ribs, cut into bones
Salt and black pepper to taste

1 tbsp mustard powder
1 tbsp smoked paprika
1 tbsp dried oregano

1/3 cup ketchup
1 cup barbecue sauce
½ cup apple cider

DIRECTIONS

In a bowl, thoroughly combine salt, mustard powder, smoked paprika, oregano, and black pepper. Rub the mixture over the ribs. Warm oil on Sauté in your Instant Pot. Add in the ribs and sear for 1 to 2 minutes for each side until browned. Pour apple cider and barbecue sauce into your Instant Pot. Turn the ribs to coat.

Seal the pressure lid, choose Pressure Cook for 30 minutes. When ready, release the pressure quickly. Place the air fry basket in the pot. Close the air fry lid, choose Air Fry, set the temperature to 390°F, and the time to 5 minutes.

Place the ribs with the sauce in the air fry basket. Close the air fry lid. Preheat the unit by selecting Air Fry, setting the temperature to 390°F, and setting the time to 7 minutes. When ready, the ribs should be sticky with a dark brown color. Transfer the ribs to a serving plate. Baste with the sauce to serve.

Swedish Meatballs with Mashed Cauliflower

Servings: 6 | Ready in about: 1 hour

INGREDIENTS

- ¾ lb ground beef
- ¾ lb ground pork
- 1 large egg, beaten
- ½ onion, minced
- ¼ cup bread crumbs
- 1 tbsp water
- Salt and black pepper to taste
- 4 tbsp butter, divided
- 2 cups beef stock
- 3 tbsp flour
- ½ tsp red wine vinegar
- 1 ¾ cup heavy cream, divided
- 1 head cauliflower, cut into florets
- ¼ cup sour cream
- ¼ cup fresh chopped parsley

DIRECTIONS

In a mixing bowl, mix ground beef, onion, salt, bread crumbs, ground pork, egg, water, and pepper. Shape meatballs. Warm 2 tbsp of butter on Sauté in your Instant Pot. Add meatballs and cook until browned, about 5-6 minutes. Set aside. Pour beef stock in the pot to deglaze, scrape the pan to get rid of browned bits of food.

Stir vinegar and flour with the liquid in your Instant Pot until smooth. Bring to a boil. Stir ¾ cup heavy cream into the liquid. Arrange meatballs into the gravy. Place trivet onto meatballs. Arrange cauliflower florets onto the trivet. Seal the pressure lid, choose Pressure Cook on High, and set the timer to 8 minutes.

When ready, release the pressure quickly. Set the cauliflower in a mixing bowl. Add in the remaining 1 cup heavy cream, pepper, sour cream, salt, and 2 tbsp butter and use a potato masher to mash the mixture until smooth. Spoon the mashed cauliflower onto serving bowls. Top with gravy and meatballs. Add parsley for garnishing.

Beer-Braised Short Ribs with Mushrooms

Servings: 4 | Ready in about: 1 hour

INGREDIENTS

- 2 lb beef short ribs
- 1 tsp smoked paprika
- ½ tsp dried oregano
- ½ tsp cayenne pepper
- 1 tbsp olive oil
- 1 small onion, sliced
- 4 garlic cloves, smashed
- 1 cup beer
- ⅓ cup beef broth
- 1 cup crimini mushrooms, sliced
- 1 tbsp soy sauce
- 1 bell pepper, diced

DIRECTIONS

In a small bowl, combine pepper, paprika, cayenne pepper, salt, and oregano. Rub the seasoning mixture on all sides of the short ribs. Warm oil on Sauté in your Instant Pot. Add mushrooms and cook until browned, about 6-8 minutes. Set aside.

Add short ribs to the pot, and cook for 3 minutes for each side until browned. Set aside on a plate. Throw in garlic and onion to the oil and stir-fry for 2 minutes until fragrant.

Add in beer to deglaze, scrape the pot's bottom to get rid of any browned bits of food. Bring to a simmer and cook for 2 minutes until reduced slightly. Stir in soy sauce, bell pepper and beef broth. Dip short ribs into the liquid in a single layer. Seal the pressure lid, choose Pressure Cook on High, and set the timer to 40 minutes. Release pressure naturally for about 10 minutes. Divide the ribs with the sauce into bowls and top with fried mushrooms.

Classic Beef Bourguignon

Servings: 4 | Ready in about: 45 minutes

INGREDIENTS

2 lb stewing beef, cut into large chunks
Salt and pepper, to taste
2 ½ tbsp olive oil
¼ tsp red wine vinegar
¼ cup pearl onion

3 tsp tomato paste
½ lb mushrooms, sliced
2 carrots, peeled and chopped
1 onion, sliced
2 cloves garlic, crushed

1 cup red wine
2 cups beef broth
1 bunch thyme
½ cup cognac
2 tbsp flour

DIRECTIONS

Select Sauté on your Instant Pot. Season the beef with salt, pepper, and a light sprinkle of flour. Heat the oil and brown the meat on all sides. Pour in the cognac and stir to deglaze the bottom. Add in thyme, red wine, broth, paste, garlic, mushrooms, onion, and pearl onions. Seal the lid and select Pressure Cook for 25 minutes. Once the timer is off, do a quick pressure release. Close the air fry lid and cook for 10 minutes on Broil at 390 F. When ready, remove the thyme, adjust the taste with salt and pepper, and add the vinegar. Stir the sauce and serve hot.

Beef & Turnip Chili

Servings: 6 | Ready in about: 30 minutes

INGREDIENTS

1 tbsp olive oil
1 yellow onion, chopped
4 garlic cloves, minced
2 tbsp tomato puree
1 tbsp chili powder

2 tsp ground cumin
1 tsp dried oregano
½ tsp ground turmeric
1 pinch cayenne pepper
1 lb ground beef meat

1 (28 oz) can whole tomatoes
2 cups beef stock
1 lb turnips, peeled and cubed
2 tomatoes, chopped
1 bell pepper, chopped

DIRECTIONS

Warm oil on Sauté in your Instant Pot. Add in onion and garlic and cook for 3 minutes until softened. Stir in chili powder, turmeric, cumin, tomato puree, oregano, and cayenne pepper for 2 to 3 minutes until very soft. Add beef and cook for 5 minutes until browned. Mix in tomatoes, turnips, bell pepper, and beef stock. Seal the pressure lid, choose Pressure Cook on High, and set the timer to 15 minutes. When ready, release the pressure quickly. Serve.

Mississippi Pot Roast with Potatoes

Servings: 6 | Ready in about: 1 hour 40 minutes

INGREDIENTS

1 tbsp canola oil
2 lb chuck roast
2 tsp salt
½ tsp black pepper
¼ cup butter

1 onion, finely chopped
1 tsp onion powder
1 tsp garlic powder
½ tsp dried thyme
½ tsp dried parsley

6 cups beef broth
½ cup pepperoncini juice
10 pepperoncini
5 potatoes, peeled and sliced
2 bay leaves

DIRECTIONS

Warm oil on Sauté in your Instant Pot. Season chuck roast with pepper and salt, then sear in the hot oil for 2 to 4 minutes for each side until browned. Set aside. Melt butter and cook the onion for 3 minutes until fragrant. Sprinkle with dried parsley, onion powder, dried thyme, and garlic powder and stir for 30 seconds.

Into the pot, stir bay leaves, beef broth, pepperoncini juice, and pepperoncini. Nestle chuck roast down into the liquid. Seal the pressure lid, choose Pressure Cook on High, and set the timer to 60 minutes. Release pressure naturally for about 10 minutes. Set the chuck roast to a cutting board and use two forks to shred. Serve immediately.

Traditional Beef Stroganoff

Servings: 6 | Ready in about: 1 hour 15 minutes

INGREDIENTS

¼ cup flour
Salt and black pepper to taste
2 lb beef stew meat
2 tbsp olive oil
1 onion, chopped
2 garlic cloves, minced
1 cup beef broth
3 cups fresh mushrooms, chopped
8 oz sour cream
1 tbsp chopped fresh parsley
1 cup long-grain rice, cooked

DIRECTIONS

In a large bowl, combine salt, pepper and flour. Add beef and massage to coat beef in flour mixture. Warm oil on Sauté in your Instant Pot. Brown the beef for 4 to 5 minutes. Add garlic and onion and cook for 3 minutes until fragrant. Add beef broth to the pot. Seal the pressure lid, choose Pressure Cook on High, and set the timer to 35 minutes. When ready, release the pressure quickly. Stir mushrooms and sour cream into the beef mixture.

Seal the pressure lid again, choose Pressure Cook on High, and set the timer to 2 minutes. When ready, release the pressure quickly. Season the stroganoff with pepper and salt. Scoop over cooked rice before serving.

Peppercorn Meatloaf

Servings: 8 | Ready in about: 35 minutes

INGREDIENTS

4 lb ground beef
1 tbsp basil
1 tbsp oregano
1 tbsp parsley
1 onion, diced
1 tbsp Worcestershire sauce
3 tbsp ketchup
½ tsp salt
1 tsp ground peppercorns
10 whole peppercorns, for garnishing
1 cup breadcrumbs

DIRECTIONS

Place the beef in a large bowl. Add all of the ingredients except the whole peppercorns and the breadcrumbs. Mix with your hand until well combined. Stir in the breadcrumbs. Put the meatloaf on a lined baking dish. Insert in your Instant Pot, close the air fry lid and cook for 25 minutes on Air Fry mode at 350°F. Garnish the meatloaf with the whole peppercorns and let cool slightly before serving.

Italian Beef Sandwiches with Pesto

Servings: 4 | Ready in about: 1 hour

INGREDIENTS

1 ½ lb beef steak, cut into strips
Salt and black pepper to taste
1 tbsp olive oil
¼ cup dry red wine
1 cup beef broth
1 tbsp oregano
1 tsp onion powder
1 tsp garlic powder
4 hoagie rolls, halved
8 slices mozzarella cheese
½ cup sliced pepperoncini peppers
4 tbsp pesto

DIRECTIONS

Sprinkle pepper and salt to season the beef cubes and bring to room temperature. Warm oil on Sauté in your Instant Pot. Add in the beef and sear for 2 to 3 minutes for each side until browned. Add wine into the pot to deglaze, scrape the bottom to get rid of any browned beef bits. Stir garlic powder, beef broth, onion powder, and oregano into the pot. Seal the pressure lid, choose Pressure Cook on High, and set the timer to 25 minutes.

Release pressure naturally for 10 minutes. Spread each bread half with pesto, put beef on top, place pepperoncini slices over, add mozzarella cheese slices and cover with the second half of bread to serve.

BEEF, PORK & LAMB

Ranch Flavored Pork Roast with Gravy

Servings: 4 | Ready in about: 25 minutes

INGREDIENTS

2 lb pork roast, cut into 2-inch slabs
1 tbsp Italian Seasoning
1 tbsp Ranch Dressing
1 tsp red wine vinegar
2 cloves garlic, minced

Salt and pepper, to taste
1 small onion, chopped
1 tbsp olive oil
2 tsp onion powder
½ tsp paprika

2 cups vegetable broth
2 tbsp cornstarch
2 tbsp water
Chopped parsley to garnish

DIRECTIONS

Season the pork roast with salt and pepper, and set aside. In a bowl, add Italian seasoning, ranch dressing, red wine vinegar, garlic, onion powder, and paprika. Open in your Instant Pot, select Sauté, and heat the oil. Sauté the onion, until translucent. Pour the gravy mixture and broth over and add the pork. Seal the lid and select Pressure Cook on High for 15 minutes. Once the timer has ended, do a quick pressure release, and open the pot.

Remove the pork roast with a slotted spoon onto a serving plate. Mix the cornstarch with the water in a small bowl and add it to the sauce. Select Sauté. Stir and cook the sauce for 4 minutes until thickens. Once the gravy is ready, turn off the pot and spoon the sauce over the pork. Garnish with parsley and serve with a turnip mash.

Hot Pork Carnitas Lettuce Cups

Servings: 6 | Ready in about: 30 minutes + overnight refrigerated

INGREDIENTS

3 lb pork shoulder
2 tbsp olive oil
1 head lettuce, leaves removed
2 Limes, cut in wedges
2 carrots, grated

1 ½ cup water
1 onion, chopped
½ tsp Cayenne pepper
½ tsp coriander powder
1 tsp cumin powder

1 tsp garlic powder
1 tsp white pepper
2 tsp dried oregano
1 tsp red pepper flakes
Salt to taste

DIRECTIONS

In a bowl, add onion, cayenne, coriander, garlic, cumin, white pepper, dried oregano, red pepper flakes, and salt. Mix them well with a spoon. Drizzle over the pork and rub to coat. Then, wrap the meat in plastic wrap and refrigerate overnight. On the next day, open your Instant Pot lid, and select Sauté. Pour 2 tablespoons of olive oil in the pot and while heating, take the pork out from the fridge, remove the wraps and place it in your Instant Pot.

Brown it on both sides for 6 minutes and then pour the water. Seal the lid and select Pressure Cook on High for 15 minutes. Once the timer has stopped, do a quick pressure release. Use two forks to shred the pork, inside the pot. Close the air fry lid, and select Bake mode. Set for 10 minutes at 350°F.

When ready, turn off the heat and begin assembling. Arrange double layers of lettuce leaves on a flat surface, make a bed of grated carrots in them, and spoon the pulled pork on them. Serve with lime wedges for freshness.

Tomatillo & Sweet Potato pork Chili

Servings: 6 | Ready in about: 70 minutes

INGREDIENTS

1 ½ lb pork roast, cut into 1-inch cubes
1 lb tomatillos, husks removed
2 tbsp olive oil, divided into 2
1 bulb garlic, tail sliced off, peeled
2 green chilies

3 cups chicken broth
1 green bell pepper, roughly chopped
Salt and pepper, to taste
½ tsp cumin powder
1 tsp dried oregano

1 bay leaf
1 bunch cilantro, chopped
2 sweet potatoes, peeled and cut into ½-inch cubes

BEEF, PORK & LAMB

DIRECTIONS

Put the garlic bulb in a baking dish. Drizzle a bit of 1 portion of olive oil over the garlic bulb. Place the green bell peppers, onion, green chilies, and tomatillos on the dish in a single layer. Close the air fry lid and cook for 15 minutes at 400°F on Air Fry. Set aside to cool. Place the garlic in a blender. Add green bell pepper, tomatillos, onions, and green chilies. Pulse for a few minutes not to be smooth but slightly chunky.

Now, open the lid of your Instant Pot, and select Sauté. Pour in the remaining olive oil and while is heating, season the pork cubes with salt and pepper. Then, brown the pork, for about 5 minutes. Stir in oregano, cumin, bay leaf, pour in the blended green sauce, potatoes, and add the chicken broth. Stir well. Seal the lid and select Pressure Cook on High for 25 minutes. Once the timer has ended, let the pot sit closed for 10 minutes.

After, do a natural pressure release for 5 minutes, and then a quick pressure release to let the remaining steam out. Open the pot. Remove and discard the bay leaf, add half of the cilantro, adjust with salt and pepper, and stir. Close the air fry lid to give it nice and tender taste. Cook on Broil mode for 10 minutes. Dish the chili into serving bowls and garnish it with the remaining chopped cilantro. Serve topped with a side of chips or crusted bread.

Sweet-Garlic Pork Tenderloin

Servings: 4 | Ready in about: 30 minutes

INGREDIENTS

2 lb pork tenderloin
2 tbsp olive oil
¼ cup honey
½ cup chicken broth
Salt and black pepper to taste
1 clove garlic, minced
1 tsp sage powder
1 tbsp Dijon mustard
¼ cup Balsamic vinegar
1 tbsp Worcestershire sauce
½ tbsp cornstarch
4 tbsp water

DIRECTIONS

Season the pork with salt and pepper. Select Sauté in your Instant Pot. Heat the oil and brown the pork on both sides for about 4 minutes in total. Remove the pork to a plate and set aside. Add in honey, chicken broth, balsamic vinegar, garlic, Worcestershire sauce, mustard, and sage. Stir the ingredients and return the pork to the pot. Seal the lid and select Pressure Cook on High for 15 minutes. Once the timer has ended, do a quick pressure release.

Remove the pork to a plate and wrap it in aluminum foil. Mix the cornstarch with water and pour it into the pot. Select Sauté mode, stir the mixture and cook until it thickens. Then, turn the pot off after the desired thickness is achieved. Unwrap the pork and use a knife to slice it with 3 to 4-inch thickness. Arrange the slices on a serving platter and spoon the sauce all over it. Serve with a syrupy sautéed Brussels sprouts and red onion chunks.

Pork Tenderloin with Garlic and Ginger

Servings: 4 | Ready in about: 23 minutes

INGREDIENTS

2 lb pork tenderloin
½ cup soy sauce
¼ cup sugar
3 tbsp grated ginger
2 cloves garlic, minced
2 tbsp sesame oil
2 tsp cornstarch
Chopped scallions to garnish
Sesame seeds to garnish

DIRECTIONS

In your Instant Pot, add soy sauce, sugar, half cup of water, ginger, garlic, and sesame oil. Use a spoon to stir them. Add in the pork. Seal the lid and select Pressure Cook on High for 12 minutes. Once the timer has ended, do a quick pressure release, and open the pot. Remove the pork and set aside.

In a bowl, mix the cornstarch with 2 tbsp water until smooth and pour it into the pot. Bring back the pork. Close the air fry lid and press Broil. Cook for 5 minutes until the sauce has thickened. Stir the sauce, every 1-2 minutes to avoid burning. Once the sauce is ready, serve the pork with a side endive salad. Spoon the sauce all over it.

Mediterranean Tender Pork Roast

Servings: 6 | Ready in about: 60 minutes

INGREDIENTS

3 lb pork roast, cut into 3-inch pieces
1 tsp Cavender's Greek seasoning
1 tsp onion powder
1 cup beef broth
½ cup Kalamata olives, pitted
¼ cup fresh lemon juice

DIRECTIONS

Put the pork chunks in the inner pot of your Instant Pot. In a bowl, add greek seasoning, onion powder, beef broth, lemon juice, olives, and salt to taste. Mix using a spoon and pour the sauce over the pork. Seal the lid and select Pressure Cook on High for 35 minutes. Once the timer is off, do a natural pressure release for 10 minutes.

Open the pot. Use two forks to shred the roast inside to pot and close the air fry lid. Cook on Broil mode for 10 minutes, until nice and tender. Serve with a green salad, potatoes or rice.

Pork Sandwiches with Slaw

Servings: 8 | Ready in about: 20 minutes

INGREDIENTS

2 lb chuck roast
¼ cup sugar
1 tsp Spanish paprika
1 tsp garlic powder
1 white onion, sliced
2 cups beef broth
Salt to taste
2 tbsp apple cider vinegar

Assembling:
4 Buns, halved
1 cup white Cheddar cheese, grated
4 tbsp mayonnaise
1 cup red cabbage, shredded
1 cup white cabbage, shredded

DIRECTIONS

Place the pork roast on a clean flat surface and sprinkle with paprika, garlic powder, sugar, and salt. Use your hands to rub the seasoning on the meat. Open your Instant Pot, add beef broth, onions, pork, and apple cider vinegar. Seal the lid and select Pressure Cook on High for 12 minutes. Once ended, do a quick pressure release.

Remove the roast to a cutting board, and use two forks to shred them. Return to the pot, close the air fry lid, and cook for 3 minutes on Air Fry at 300°F. In the buns, spread the mayo, add the shredded pork, some cooked onions from the pot, and shredded red and white cabbage. Top with the cheese.

Cuban-Style Pork

Servings: 8 | Ready in about: 2 hour 30 minutes

INGREDIENTS

½ cup orange juice
¼ cup lime juice
¼ cup canola oil
¼ cup chopped fresh cilantro
1 tsp red pepper flakes
8 cloves garlic, minced
1 tbsp ground cumin
1 tbsp fresh oregano
3 lb pork shoulder

DIRECTIONS

In a bowl, mix orange juice, olive oil, cumin, salt, pepper, oregano, lime juice, and garlic. Add into a large plastic bag alongside the pork. Seal and massage the bag to ensure the marinade covers the pork completely. Place in the refrigerator for an hour to overnight. In your Instant Pot, set the removed pork from bag.

Add the marinade on top. Seal the pressure lid, choose Pressure Cook on High, and set the timer to 50 minutes. Release pressure naturally for 15 minutes. Transfer the pork to a cutting board. Use a fork to break into smaller pieces. Skim and get rid of the fat from liquid in the cooker. Serve the liquid with pork and sprinkle with cilantro.

BBQ Pork Ribs

Servings: 2 | Ready in about: 45 minutes

INGREDIENTS

½ lb rack baby back ribs
Salt and pepper to season
¼ cup beef broth
½ cup Barbecue sauce
3 tbsp apple cider vinegar

DIRECTIONS

Select Sauté on your Instant Pot. Heat the oil. Season the ribs with salt and pepper. Cook them to brown, for 1 to 2 minutes per side. Pour the barbecue sauce, broth, and apple cider vinegar over the ribs and use tongs to flip so they are well coated. Close the lid and pressure valve and set to Pressure Cook on High for 30 minutes.

Once the timer goes off, do a natural pressure release for 12 minutes. Close the air fry lid and set to Air Fry mode for 5 minutes at 350°F. Make sure the sauce is thick enough. Use a knife to slice the ribs and over the sauce all over it. Serve the ribs with a generous side of steamed but crunchy green beans.

Garlicky Braised Pork Neck Bones

Servings: 6 | Ready in about: 40 minutes

INGREDIENTS

3 lb pork neck bones
4 tbsp olive oil
Salt and black pepper to taste
2 cloves garlic, smashed
1 tbsp tomato paste
1 tsp dried thyme
1 white onion, sliced
½ cup red wine
1 cup beef broth

DIRECTIONS

Open your Instant Pot and select Sauté. Warm the olive oil. Season the pork neck bones with salt and pepper. After, place them in the oil to brown on all sides. Work in batches. Each batch should cook in about 5 minutes. Remove them onto a plate. Add the onion and season with salt to taste. Stir and cook the onions until soft for 5 minutes. Add garlic, thyme, pepper, and tomato paste. Cook for 2 minutes, constantly.

Pour in the red wine to deglaze the bottom. Add the pork neck bones back to the pot and pour the beef broth over it. Seal the lid and select Pressure Cook for 10 minutes. Once the timer has ended, do a quick pressure release. Close the air fry lid and cook on Broil mode for 5 minutes, until nice and tender. Dish the pork neck into a serving bowl and serve with the red wine sauce spooned over and a right amount of broccoli mash.

Sweet & Sour Pork

Servings: 4 | Ready in about: 40 minutes

INGREDIENTS

1 lb pork loin, cut into chunks
2 tbsp white wine
15 oz canned peaches
¼ cup beef stock
2 tbsp sweet chili sauce
2 tbsp honey
2 tbsp soy sauce
2 tbsp cornstarch
¼ cup water

DIRECTIONS

Into your Instant Pot, mix soy sauce, beef stock, white wine, juice from the canned peaches, and sweet chili sauce. Stir in pork to coat. Seal the pressure lid, choose Pressure Cook on High, and set the timer to 5 minutes. Release pressure naturally for 10 minutes. Remove the pork to a serving plate. Chop the peaches into small pieces.

In a bowl, mix water and cornstarch until cornstarch dissolves completely. Stir the mixture into your Instant Pot. Press Sauté and cook for 5 more minutes until you obtain the desired thick consistency. Add in the chopped peaches and stir well. Serve the pork topped with peach sauce and enjoy.

Crispy Pork Fajitas

Servings: 5 | Ready in about: 1 hour 30 minutes

INGREDIENTS

- 1 tbsp ground cumin
- 2 tsp dried oregano
- 1 tsp paprika
- 1 tsp onion powder
- 1 tsp salt
- 1 tsp ground black pepper
- 1/2 tsp ground cinnamon
- 3 lb boneless pork shoulder
- ¾ cup vegetable broth
- ¼ cup pineapple juice
- 1 lime, juiced
- 4 cloves garlic, crushed
- 2 bay leaves
- 5 corn tortillas, warmed
- ½ cup queso Cotija, crumbled

DIRECTIONS

In a bowl, combine cumin, paprika, pepper, onion powder, oregano, salt, and cinnamon. Toss in pork to coat. Place the pork in your Instant Pot and allow settling for 15 to 30 minutes. Add in chicken broth, garlic, lime juice, bay leaves, and pineapple juice. Seal the pressure lid, choose Pressure Cook, and set the timer to 50 minutes. When ready, release pressure naturally for 15 minutes, then release the remaining pressure quickly.

Transfer the pork to a rimmed baking sheet and use two forks to shred the meat. Reserve the juices in a bowl. Place the Cook & air fry basket into the inner pot. Close the air fry lid and choose Air Fry. Adjust the temperature to 380°F and the time to 4 minutes to preheat. Add the baking sheet to the air fry basket. Close the air fry lid.

Select Air Fry. Adjust the temperature to 375°F and the cook time to 10 minutes. After 5 minutes, open the lid and toss the meat. Continue cooking until the pork is done. Skim and get rid of fat from the liquid remaining. Dispose of the bay leaves. Over the pork, pour the liquid and serve alongside warm corn tortillas and queso fresco.

Garlick & Ginger Pork with Coconut Sauce

Servings: 6 | Ready in about: 45 minutes

INGREDIENTS

- 3 lb shoulder roast
- 1 tbsp olive oil
- Salt and black pepper to season
- 2 cups coconut milk
- 1 tsp Coriander powder
- 1 tsp cumin powder
- 3 tbsp grated ginger
- 3 tsp minced garlic
- ½ cup beef broth
- 1 onion, peeled and quartered
- Parsley leaves (unchopped), to garnish

DIRECTIONS

In a bowl, add coriander, salt, pepper, and cumin. Use a spoon to mix them. Season the pork with the spice mixture. Rub the spice onto meat, with hands. Open the lid of your Instant Pot, add olive oil, pork, onions, ginger, garlic, broth and coconut milk. Seal the lid and select Pressure Cook on High for 30 minutes.

Once the timer has stopped, do a quick pressure release. Give it a good stir and close the air fry lid. Cook for 10 minutes on Broil mode, until you perfect texture and creaminess. Dish the meat with the sauce into a serving bowl, garnish it with the parsley and serve with a side of bread or cooked shrimp.

Pork Chops with Broccoli and Gravy

Servings: 6 | Ready in about: 45 minutes

INGREDIENTS

Pork Chops:
- 1 tsp garlic powder
- 1 tsp onion powder

Gravy:
- 3 tbsp flour

- 1 tsp red pepper flakes
- 6 boneless pork chops
- 1 broccoli head, broken into florets

- ½ cup heavy cream

- 1 cup chicken stock
- ¼ cup butter, melted
- ¼ cup milk

- Salt and black pepper to taste

DIRECTIONS

Combine salt, garlic powder, red pepper flakes, onion powder, and black pepper. Rub the mixture to the pork chops. Place stock and broccoli into the pot. Lay the pork chops on top. Seal the pressure lid, choose Pressure Cook on High, and set the timer to 15 minutes. When ready, release the pressure quickly.

Transfer the pork chops and broccoli to a plate. Press Sauté and simmer the liquid remaining in the pot. Mix cream and flour. Pour into the simmering liquid and cook for 5 to 7 minutes until thickened and bubbly. Season with pepper and salt. Top the chops with gravy before, drizzle melted butter over broccoli and serve.

Pork Chops with Squash Purée

Servings: 4 | Ready in about: 45 minutes

INGREDIENTS

2 tbsp olive oil
2 sprigs thyme, chopped
2 sprigs rosemary, chopped
4 pork chops
1 cup mushrooms, chopped
4 cloves garlic, minced
1 cup chicken broth
1 tbsp soy sauce
1 lb butternut squash, cubed
1 tbsp olive oil
1 tsp cornstarch

DIRECTIONS

Set to Sauté your Instant Pot and heat 1 tbsp of olive oil. Add in the pork chops and sear for 1 minute for each side until lightly browned. Add in garlic and mushrooms and cook for 5-6 minutes until tender. Stir in rosemary and thyme for 1 minute. Pour in soy sauce and broth. Transfer pork chops to a wire trivet and place it into the pressure cooker. Over the chops, place a cake pan. Add butternut squash in the pot and drizzle with 1 tbsp olive oil.

Seal the pressure lid, choose Pressure Cook on High, and set the timer to 10 minutes. When ready, release the pressure quickly. Remove the pan and trivet from the pot. Stir cornstarch into the mushroom mixture.

Cook for 2 minutes until the sauce thickens. Transfer the mushroom sauce to an immersion blender and blend until you attain the desired consistency. Scoop sauce into a cup with a pour spout. Smash the squash into a purée. Set pork chops on a plate and ladle squash puree next to them. Top the pork chops with gravy.

Pork Tenderloin with Sweet Pepper Sauce

Servings: 4 | Ready in about: 35 minutes

INGREDIENTS

1 ¼ pork tenderloin, cut into 2 pieces
Salt and black pepper to taste
2 tbsp olive oil
½ cup dry white wine
1 lb russet potatoes, quartered
¼ cup chicken stock
1 thyme sprig
2 medium garlic cloves, finely minced
1 roasted red bell pepper, cut into strips
6 pickled pimientos, quartered
2 tsp pickling liquid from the peppers
2 tbsp unsalted butter

DIRECTIONS

Season the pork pieces with salt and black pepper on all sides. On your Instant Pot, choose Sauté. Pour in the oil into the pot and heat until shimmering. Add the pork, sear for 4-5 minutes until browned on all sides. Remove the pork to a plate. Pour in the wine into the pot and scrape off any browned bits at the bottom.

Let the wine cook until reduced by one-third. Stir in the potatoes, chicken stock, thyme, and garlic. Return the pork to the pot. Seal the pressure lid, choose Pressure Cook on High and the cook time to 20 minutes. After cooking, perform a natural pressure release for 10 minutes. Carefully open the pressure lid.

Remove the pork and allow resting while you finish the sauce. Remove and discard the thyme. Choose Sauté. Cook the potatoes for 2 to 4 minutes or until tender. Stir in the roasted pepper, pimiento, and the pickling liquid. Taste and adjust the seasoning. Right before serving, turn off the heat and stir in the butter. Slice the tenderloin and lay the pieces on a platter. Ladle the peppers and potatoes around the pork and spoon the sauce over.

The Crispiest Roast Pork

Servings: 4 | Ready in about: 50 minutes

INGREDIENTS

4 pork tenderloins
1 tsp five spice seasoning
½ tsp white pepper
¾ tsp garlic powder
1 tsp salt
Cooking spray

DIRECTIONS

Place the pork, white pepper, garlic powder, five seasoning, and salt into a bowl and toss to coat. Leave to marinate at room temperature for 30 minutes. Place the pork into the air fry basket, greased with cooking spray, close the air fry lid and cook for 20 minutes at 360°F. After 10 minutes, turn the tenderloins. Serve hot.

Pork Carnitas Wraps

Servings: 12 | Ready in about: 1 hour 15 minutes

INGREDIENTS

2 tsp grapeseed oil
1 (4 to 5 lb) boneless pork shoulder
1 onion, sliced
2 garlic cloves, minced
2 oranges, juiced
2 limes, juiced
2 tbsp sweet smoked paprika
1 tbsp dried oregano
1 tbsp salt
2 jalapeños, sliced
1 avocado, sliced
Fresh cilantro leaves, chopped
2 tsp ground black pepper
12 corn tortillas, warmed

DIRECTIONS

Warm oil on Sauté in your Instant Pot. Add in pork and cook for 5 minutes until golden. Transfer the pork to a plate. Add garlic and onions to the inner pot and cook for 2 to 3 minutes until soft. Add lime and orange juices into the pot to deglaze, scrape the bottom to get rid of any browned bits of food. Stir in pepper, paprika, salt and oregano. Return the pork to pot. Stir to coat in seasoning and liquid. Seal the pressure lid, choose Pressure Cook.

Set the timer to 35 minutes. When ready, release the pressure quickly. Press Sauté. When the liquid starts to simmer, use two forks to shred the pork. Cook for 10 more minutes until liquid is reduced by half. Serve in warmed tortillas topped with jalapeños, avocado slices and cilantro.

Savory Pork Loin with Celery Sauce

Servings: 4 | Ready in about: 35 minutes

INGREDIENTS

2 lb pork loin roast
Salt and pepper, to taste
3 cloves garlic, minced
1 medium onion, diced
2 tbsp butter
3 stalks celery, chopped
3 carrots, chopped
1 cup vegetable broth
2 tbsp Worcestershire sauce
½ tbsp sugar
1 tsp yellow mustard
2 tsp dried basil
2 tsp dried thyme
1 tbsp cornstarch
¼ cup water

DIRECTIONS

Select Sauté on your Instant Pot, and heat oil. Season the pork with salt and pepper. Sear the pork to golden brown on both sides, about 4 minutes. Then, add the garlic and onions, and cook them until soft, for about 4 minutes. Top with the celery, carrots, broth, Worcestershire sauce, mustard, thyme, basil, and sugar. Seal the lid and select Pressure Cook on High for 15 minutes. Once the timer is off, do a quick pressure release.

Next, add the cornstarch to the water in a bowl, and mix with a spoon, until nice and smooth. Add it to the pot, close the air fry lid, and cook on Broil mode, for 3 - 5 minutes, until the sauce becomes a slurry with a bit of thickness, and the pork is nice and tender. Adjust the seasoning, and ladle to a serving platter. Serve.

Pulled Pork Tacos

Servings: 5 | Ready in about: 1 hour 25 minutes

INGREDIENTS

- 3 tbsp sugar
- 3 tsp taco seasoning
- 1 tsp ground black pepper
- 2 lb pork shoulder, cut into chunks
- 1 cup beer
- 1 cup vegetable broth
- ¼ cup plus 2 tbsp lemon juice
- ¼ cup mayonnaise
- 2 tbsp honey
- 2 tsp mustard
- 3 cups shredded cabbage
- 5 taco tortillas

DIRECTIONS

In a bowl, combine sugar, taco seasoning, and black pepper. Rub the mixture onto pork pieces to coat well. Allow to settling for 30 minutes. Into the pot, add 1/4 cup lemon juice, broth, pork and beer. Seal the pressure lid, choose Pressure Cook on High, and set the timer to 50 minutes.

Meanwhile in a large bowl, mix mayonnaise, mustard, 2 tbsp lemon juice, cabbage and honey until well coated. Release pressure naturally for 15 minutes before doing a quick release. Transfer the pork to a cutting board and Allow cooling before using two forks to shred. Skim and get rid of fat from liquid in the pressure cooker. Return pork to the pot and mix with the liquid. Top the pork with slaw on taco tortillas before serving.

Spicy Pork Roast with Peanut Sauce

Servings: 6 | Ready in about: 30 minutes

INGREDIENTS

- 3 lb pork roast
- 1 cup Hot water
- 1 large red bell pepper, seeded and sliced
- Salt and black pepper to taste
- 1 large white onion, sliced
- ½ cup soy sauce
- 1 tbsp plain vinegar
- ½ cup peanut butter
- 1 tbsp lime juice
- 1 tbsp garlic powder
- 1 tsp ginger puree
- 2 chilies, deseeded, chopped
- Chopped Peanuts to garnish
- Chopped green onions to garnish
- Lime Wedges to garnish

DIRECTIONS

Add the soy sauce, vinegar, peanut butter, lime juice, garlic powder, chilies, and ginger puree, to a bowl. Whisk together and even. Add a few pinches of salt and pepper, and mix it. Open your Instant Pot, and place the pork in. Pour the hot water and peanut butter mixture over it. Seal the lid and select Pressure Cook for 15 minutes.

Once the timer has stopped, do a quick pressure release. Use two forks to shred it, inside the pot, and close the air fry lid. Cook on Broil mode for 4 - 5 minutes, until the sauce thickens. On a bed of cooked rice, spoon the meat with some sauce and garnish it with the chopped peanuts, green onions, and the lemon wedges.

Pork Chops with Plum Sauce

Servings: 4 | Ready in about: 20 minutes

INGREDIENTS

- 4 pork chops
- 1 tsp cumin seeds
- Salt and black pepper to taste
- 2 cups firm plums, pitted and sliced
- 1 tbsp vegetable oil
- ¾ cup vegetable stock

DIRECTIONS

Sprinkle salt, cumin, and pepper on the pork chops. Set your Instant Pot to Sauté. Warm oil. Add the chops and cook for 3 to 5 minutes until browned and set aside on a bowl. Arrange plum slices on the bottom of the pot. Place the pork chops on top of the plumes. Add any juice from the plate over the pork and apply stock around the edges.

Seal lid and cook on High pressure for 8 minutes. When ready, do a quick pressure release. Transfer the pork chops to a serving plate and spoon over the plum sauce before serving.

BEEF, PORK & LAMB

Baby Back Ribs with BBQ Sauce

Servings: 4 | Ready in about: 45 minutes

INGREDIENTS

2 lb baby back pork ribs
4 cups orange juice
Juice from 1 lemon
For BBQ sauce:

2 tbsp honey
½ cup ketchup
Juice from ½ lemon
1 tbsp Worcestershire sauce

1 tsp mustard
2 tsp paprika
½ tsp cayenne pepper
Salt to taste

DIRECTIONS

Mix all the BBQ sauce ingredients in a bowl until well incorporated. Set aside. Place ribs in your Instant Pot. Add in lemon juice and orange juice. Seal the pressure lid, choose Pressure Cook on High, and set the timer to 20 minutes. Release pressure naturally for 15 minutes. Preheat oven to 400° F. Line the sheet pan with aluminum foil.

Transfer the ribs to a baking dish. Do away with the cooking liquid. Onto both sides of ribs, brush barbecue sauce. Place in the pot, close the air fry lid, and select Bake at 390 F. Cook for 10 minutes until browned and caramelized. Set the ribs aside and cut into individual bones to serve.

Red Pork & Chickpea Stew

Servings: 6 | Ready in about: 40 minutes

INGREDIENTS

1 tbsp olive oil
1 (3 lb) boneless pork shoulder, cubed
1 white onion, chopped
15 oz canned chickpeas, drained

½ cup sweet paprika
2 tsp salt
1 tbsp chilli powder
1 bay leaf

2 red bell peppers, chopped
6 cloves garlic, minced
1 tbsp cornstarch

DIRECTIONS

Set on Sauté. Add pork and oil and allow cooking for 5 minutes until browned. Add in the onion, paprika, bay leaf, salt, 1 ½ cups water, chickpeas, and chili powder. Seal the pressure lid, choose Pressure Cook for 8 minutes.

Do a quick release. Discard bay leaf. Remove 1 cup of cooking liquid from the pot. Add to a blender alongside garlic, 1 tbsp water, cornstarch, and red bell peppers. Blend well until smooth. Pour in the pot and mix well.

Jamaican Pulled Pork with Mango Sauce

Servings: 6 | Ready in about: 1 hour 15 minutes

INGREDIENTS

1 ½ tsp onion powder
1 tsp sea salt
1 tsp dried thyme
1 tsp ground black pepper

1 tsp cayenne pepper
1 tsp ground allspice
½ tsp ground nutmeg
½ tsp ground cinnamon

3 lb pork shoulder
1 mango, cut into chunks
1 tbsp olive oil
2 tbsp fresh cilantro, finely minced

DIRECTIONS

In a bowl, combine onion powder, thyme, allspice, cinnamon, sugar, pepper, sea salt, cayenne, and nutmeg. Coat the pork shoulder with olive oil. Season with seasoning mixture. Warm oil on Sauté in your Instant Pot. Add in the pork and cook for 5 minutes until browned completely. To the pot, add ½ cup water and mango chunks.

Seal the pressure lid, choose Pressure Cook on High, and set the timer to 45 minutes. Release pressure naturally for 15 minutes, then release the remaining pressure quickly. Transfer the pork to a cutting board and allow cooling. To make the sauce, pour the cooking liquid in a food processor and pulse until smooth. Use two forks to shred the pork and arrange on a serving platter. Serve the pulled pork topped with mango salsa and fresh cilantro.

Chunky Pork Meatloaf with Mashed Potatoes

Servings: 4 | Ready in about: 55 minutes

INGREDIENTS

1 tbsp olive oil
1 cup chopped white onion
2 garlic cloves, minced
12 oz pork meatloaf
2 tsp salt
½ tsp black pepper

3 tbsp chopped fresh cilantro
¼ tsp dried rosemary
12 individual saltine crackers, crushed
1¾ cups full cream milk, divided
2 large eggs
1 tsp yellow mustard

1 tsp Worcestershire sauce
½ cup heavy cream
2 lb potatoes, cut into large chunks
3 tbsp unsalted butter
¼ cup barbecue sauce

DIRECTIONS

Select Sauté in your Instant Pot. Heat the olive oil until shimmering and sauté the onion and garlic in the oil. Cook for about 2 minutes until the onion softens. Transfer the onion and garlic to a plate and set aside. In a bowl, crumble the meatloaf mix into small pieces. Sprinkle with 1 teaspoon of salt, the pepper, cilantro, and thyme. Add the sautéed onion and garlic. Sprinkle the crushed saltine crackers over the meat and seasonings.

In a small bowl, beat ¼ cup of milk, the eggs, mustard, and Worcestershire sauce. Pour the mixture on the layered cracker crumbs and gently mix the ingredients in the bowl with your hands. Shape the meat mixture into an 8-inch round. Cover a trivet with aluminum foil and carefully lift the meatloaf on the trivet.

Pour the remaining 1½ cups of milk and the heavy cream into the inner pot. Add the potatoes, butter, and remaining salt. Place a trivet with meatloaf over the potatoes in the upper position in the pot. Seal the pressure lid, choose Pressure Cook on High and the cook time to 25 minutes.

After cooking, perform a quick pressure release, and carefully open the pressure lid. Brush the meatloaf with the barbecue sauce. Close the air fry lid, choose Broil and adjust the cook time to 7 minutes. Press Start to begin grilling. When the top has browned, remove the trivet, and transfer the meatloaf to a serving platter. Mash the potatoes in the pot. Slice the meatloaf and serve with the mashed potatoes.

Italian Sausage with Potato Mash & Gravy

Servings: 4 | Ready in about: 40 minutes

INGREDIENTS

2 lb potatoes, peeled and halved
4 Italian sausages
1 cup water + 2 tbsp water
⅓ cup green onion, sliced

Salt and pepper, to taste
4 tbsp milk
¼ cup + 2 tbsp 2 tbsp butter
1 tbsp cornstarch

3 tbsp balsamic vinegar
1 onion, sliced thinly
1 cup + 2 tbsp beef broth

DIRECTIONS

Put the potatoes in in your Instant Pot and pour in 1 cup water. Seal the lid and select Steam for 15 minutes. Do a quick pressure release and remove the potatoes to a bowl. Add in a quarter cup butter and use a masher to mash them until the butter is well mixed. Slowly add the milk and mix it using a spoon. Add the green onions, season with pepper and salt and fold it in with the spoon. Set aside.

Pour out the liquid in your Instant Pot, and use paper towels to wipe inside the pot dry. Select Sauté and melt two tablespoons of butter. Brown the sausages on each side for 3 minutes. Remove to the potato mash and cover with aluminium foil to keep warm. Set aside. Back into the pot, add the two tablespoons of the beef broth to deglaze the bottom of the pot while stirring and scraping the bottom with a spoon. Add the remaining butter and onions. Sauté the onions until translucent, then pour in the balsamic vinegar. Stir for another minute.

In a bowl, mix the cornstarch with water and pour into the pot. Add the remaining beef broth. Allow the sauce to thicken and adjust the seasoning. Turn off the heat once a slurry is formed. Dish the mashed potatoes and sausages in serving plates. Spoon the gravy over it and serve immediately with steamed green beans.

Ragu with Pork & Rigatoni

Servings: 6 | Ready in about: 70 minutes

INGREDIENTS

4 oz sweet and hot Italian sausage, casings removed

1 lb boneless pork shoulder
1 tsp salt
2 tbsp olive oil
1 medium onion, chopped
2 garlic cloves, minced or pressed

1 medium carrot, peeled and chopped
1 celery stalk, diced
½ cup dry red wine
⅛ tsp red pepper flakes
1 (28-oz) can crushed tomatoes

2 tbsp tomato paste
2 tsp dried Italian herb mix
1 cup water, divided
12 oz rigatoni
½ cup grated Parmesan + for serving

DIRECTIONS

Season the pork shoulder with ½ teaspoon of salt. On your Instant Pot, choose Sauté. Heat in the olive oil until shimmering and add the pork. Sear on one side for 4 minutes or until browned. Then, add the sausage, the onion, garlic, carrot, and celery. Sauté for 2 minutes or until the vegetables just start softening.

Stir in the wine, use a wooden spoon to scrape the bottom of any browned bits. Cook for 2 to 3 minutes until the wine has reduced by half. Add the red prepper flakes, tomatoes, tomato paste, remaining salt, and the dried herbs. Stir to combine. Seal the pressure lid. Choose Pressure Cook on High, and the cook time to 20 minutes.

After cooking, perform a natural pressure release for 10 minutes, then a quick pressure release. Carefully open the lid. Mix the sauce and shred the pork with two forks and break the sausage apart. Add the water and the rigatoni. Seal the pressure lid again and choose Pressure Cook on High and the cook time to 4 minutes.

After cooking, perform a quick pressure release, and carefully open the lid. Sprinkle the cheese over the sauce and pasta. Close the air fry lid and choose Broil. Adjust the time to 7 minutes. Press Start to broil the cheese. After cooking, open the lid. The cheese should be brown and crispy. Cool slightly and serve.

Ranch Pork with Mushroom Sauce

Servings: 4 | Ready in about: 22 minutes

INGREDIENTS

4 pork loin chops
1 (15 oz) can mushroom soup cream

1 oz Ranch Dressing and Seasoning mix
½ cup chicken broth

Chopped parsley to garnish

DIRECTIONS

Add pork, mushroom soup cream, ranch dressing and seasoning mix, and chicken broth inside your Instant Pot. Seal the lid and select Pressure Cook on High for 10 minutes. Once the timer has ended, do a natural pressure release for 10 minutes, then a quick pressure release to let the remaining steam out. Close the air fry lid and cook for 5 minutes on Broil mode, until tender. Serve with well-seasoned sautéed cremini mushrooms, and the sauce.

Apple & Onion Topped Pork Chops

Servings: 3 | Ready in about: 25 minutes

INGREDIENTS

Topping:
1 small onion, sliced
2 tbsp olive oil

1 tbsp apple cider vinegar
2 tsp thyme

¼ tsp brown sugar
1 cup sliced apples

Meat:
¼ tsp smoked paprika
1 tbsp olive oil

3 pork chops
1 tbsp apple cider vinegar

Salt and pepper, to taste

DIRECTIONS

Place all topping ingredients in a baking dish and then in your Instant Pot. Cook for 4 minutes on Air Fry. Place the pork chops in a bowl. Add olive oil, vinegar, paprika, and season with salt and pepper. Stir to coat them well. Remove the topping from the dish. Add the pork chops in the dish, close the air fry lid and cook for 10 minutes on Air Fry mode at 350°F. Place the topping on top, return to the pot and cook for 5 more minutes.

Pork Chops with Cremini Mushroom Sauce

Servings: 4 | Ready in about: 35 minutes

INGREDIENTS

4 pork chops
1 tbsp olive oil
3 cloves garlic, minced
Salt and pepper, to taste

1 tsp garlic powder
1 (10 oz) can mushroom soup
8 oz Cremini mushrooms, sliced
1 small onion, chopped

1 cup beef broth
1 sprig fresh thyme
Chopped parsley to garnish

DIRECTIONS

Select Sauté on your Instant Pot. Add oil, mushrooms, garlic, and onion. Sauté them, stirring occasionally until nice and translucent, for 3 minutes. Season the pork chops with salt, garlic powder, and pepper, and add them to the pot followed by the thyme and broth. Seal the lid and select Pressure Cook on High for 10 minutes.

Once the timer has ended, do a natural pressure release for about 10 minutes. Close the air fry lid and cook on Broil mode for 5 minutes. When ready, add the mushroom soup. Stir it until the mixture thickens a little bit. Dish the pork and gravy into a serving bowl and garnish with parsley. Serve.

Honey Barbecue Pork Ribs

Servings: 2 | Ready in about: 4 h 35 minutes

INGREDIENTS

1 lb pork ribs
½ tsp five spice powder
1 tsp salt

3 garlic cloves, chopped
1 tsp black pepper
1 tsp sesame oil

1 tbsp honey, plus more for brushing
4 tbsp barbecue sauce
1 tsp soy sauce

DIRECTIONS

Chop the ribs into smaller pieces and place in a large bowl. In a separate bowl, whisk together all of the other ingredients. Add to the bowl with the pork, and mix until the pork is thoroughly coated. Cover the bowl, place it in the fridge, and let it marinade for about 4 hours. Place the ribs in the basket of your Instant Pot. Close the air fry lid and cook for 15 minutes on Air Fry at 350°F. Brush the ribs with some honey and cook for 15 minutes.

Philippine-Style Pork Chops

Servings: 6 | Ready in about: 20 minutes + marinating time

INGREDIENTS

2 lb pork chops
2 bay leaves

2 tbsp soy sauce
5 garlic cloves, coarsely chopped

1 tbsp peppercorns
1 tbsp peanut oil

DIRECTIONS

Combine the bay leaves, soy sauce, garlic, salt, peppercorns, and oil in a bowl. Rub the mixture onto meat. Wrap the pork with a plastic foil and refrigerate for 2 hours. Place the pork in your Instant Pot, close the air fry lid and cook for 20 minutes on Air Fry at 390°F, flipping the chops, and cook for another 10 minutes. Discard bay leaves.

Char Siew Pork Ribs

Servings: 6 | Ready in about: 4 hours 55 minutes

INGREDIENTS

2 lb pork ribs
2 tbsp char siew sauce
2 tbsp minced ginger

2 tbsp hoisin sauce
2 tbsp sesame oil
1 tbsp honey

4 garlic cloves, minced
1 tbsp soy sauce

DIRECTIONS

Whisk together all marinade ingredients, in a small bowl. Coat the ribs well with the mixture. Place in a container with a lid, and refrigerate for 4 hours. Place the ribs in the basket but do not throw away the liquid from the container. Close the air fry lid and cook for 40 minutes on Air Fry at 350°F. Stir in the liquid, increase the temperature to 350°F, and cook for 10 minutes.

Juicy Barbecue Pork Chops

Servings: 4 | Ready in about: 100 minutes

INGREDIENTS

3 tbsp brown sugar
1 tbsp salt
1 ½ tbsp smoked paprika

2 tsp garlic powder
1 tbsp freshly ground black pepper
4 bone-in pork chops

1 tbsp olive oil
1½ cups chicken broth
4 tbsp barbecue sauce

DIRECTIONS

Choose Sauté on your Instant Pot. In a small bowl, mix the brown sugar, salt, paprika, garlic powder, and black pepper. Season both sides of the pork with the rub. Heat the oil in the preheated pot and sear the pork chops, one at a time, on both sides, about 5 minutes per chop. Set aside. Pour the chicken broth into the pot.

With a wooden spoon, scrape the bottom of the pot of any browned bits. Place the air fry basket in the upper position of the pot. Put the pork chops in the basket and brush with 2 tablespoons of barbecue sauce. Seal the pressure lid, choose Pressure Cook and set to High. Set the time to 5 minutes, then cooking. When the timer is done, perform a natural pressure release for 10 minutes, then a quick pressure release, and carefully open the lid.

Apply the remaining barbecue sauce on both sides of the pork and close the air fry lid. Choose Broil and set the time to 3 minutes. When ready, check for your desired crispiness and remove the pork from the basket.

Bolognese-Style Pizza

Servings: 4 | Ready in about: 70 minutes

INGREDIENTS

4 pizza crusts
½ cup canned crushed tomatoes

1 yellow bell pepper, sliced
½ lb ground pork, cooked and crumbled

1 cup shredded mozzarella cheese
1 tsp red chili flakes, divided

DIRECTIONS

Place a trivet in your Instant Pot. Close the air fry lid, choose Air Fry, set the temperature to 400°F, and the time to 5 minutes. Grease one side of a pizza crust with cooking spray and lay on the preheated rack, oiled side up. Close the air fry lid. Choose Air Fry, set the temperature to 400°F, and set the time to 4 minutes. baking.

Remove the crust from the trivet and flip. Top the crust with 2 tablespoons of crushed tomatoes, a quarter of bell pepper, 2 ounces of ground pork, ¼ cup of mozzarella cheese, and ¼ tablespoon of red chili flakes. Close the air fry lid. Choose Broil and set the time to 3 minutes. Choose Start to continue baking. When done baking and crispy, remove the pizza from the trivet. Repeat with the remaining pizza crusts and ingredients. Serve.

Teriyaki Pork Noodles

Servings: 4 | Ready in about: 60 minutes

INGREDIENTS

8 oz egg noodles
1 lb green beans, trimmed
1 tbsp olive oil
Salt and black pepper to taste
1 pork tenderloin, trimmed and cut into 1-inch pieces
1 cup teriyaki sauce
Cooking spray
Sesame seeds, for garnish

DIRECTIONS

Pour the egg noodles and cover with enough water in your Instant Pot. Seal the pressure lid, choose Pressure Cook on High, and set the time to 2 minutes. In a large bowl, toss the green beans with the olive oil, salt, and black pepper. In another bowl, toss the pork with the teriyaki sauce. When the egg noodles are ready, perform a quick pressure release, and carefully open the lid. Fix a trivet in the pot, which will be over the egg noodles.

Grease a trivet with cooking spray and place the pork on the trivet. Also, lay the green beans around the pork. Close the air fry lid. Choose Broil and set the time to 12 minutes. When done cooking, check for your desired crispiness. Serve the pork and green beans over the drained egg noodles and garnish with sesame seeds.

Italian Sausage with Garlic Mash

Servings: 6 | Ready in about: 30 minutes

INGREDIENTS

1 ½ cups water
6 Italian sausages
1 tbsp olive oil
2 garlic cloves, smashed
4 large potatoes, cut into chunks
⅓ cup butter, melted
¼ cup milk, at room temperature
Salt and ground black pepper to taste
1 tbsp chopped chives

DIRECTIONS

Select Sauté on your Instant Pot and heat olive oil. Cook for 8-10 minutes, turning periodically until browned. Set aside. Wipe the pot with paper towels. Add in water and set a trivet over. Place potatoes on the trivet. Seal the pressure lid, choose Pressure Cook, and set the timer to 12 minutes. When ready, release the pressure quickly.

Remove the trivet from the pot. Drain water from the pot. Return potatoes to pot. Add in salt, butter, pepper, garlic, and milk and use a hand masher to mash until no large lumps remain. Using an immersion blender, blend potatoes on Low for 1 minute until fluffy and light. Avoid over-blending to ensure the potatoes do not become gluey! Transfer the mash to a serving plate, top with sausages and scatter chopped chives over to serve.

Potato & Ground Pork Chili

Servings: 6 | Ready in about: 55 minutes

INGREDIENTS

1 tbsp olive oil
1 small onion, diced
2 garlic cloves, minced
1 lb ground pork
2 bell peppers, chopped
6 potatoes, peeled and sliced
1cup carrots, chopped
1 cups corn kernels, roasted
1 cups tomato puree
1 cups diced tomatoes
1 cup chicken broth
1 tbsp ground cumin
1 tbsp chili powder
Salt and black pepper to taste

DIRECTIONS

Warm the olive on Sauté and stir-fry onions and garlic until soft, for about 3 minutes. Stir in pork and cook until thoroughly browned, about 5-6 minutes. Add the remaining ingredients, and stir to combine. Seal the pressure lid, choose Pressure Cook on High, and set the timer to 25 minutes. Once ready, do a quick release. Set to Sauté. Cook uncovered for 15 more minutes. Serve warm.

Vietnamese Pork Soup

Servings: 4 | Ready in about: 40 minutes

INGREDIENTS

- 2 tbsp olive oil
- 2 yellow onions, halved
- 1 piece fresh ginger, halved lengthwise
- 2 tsp fennel seeds
- 1 tsp red pepper flakes
- ½ tsp coriander seeds
- 10 black peppercorns
- 2-star anise
- 8 cups water
- 1 lb pork tenderloin, cut into thin strips
- 2 tsp salt
- 8 oz rice noodles
- 1 lime, cut into wedges
- A handful of fresh cilantro leaves

DIRECTIONS

Set your Instant Pot to Sauté. Warm oil. Add ginger and onions and cook for 4 minutes. Add in red pepper flakes, fennel seeds, star anise, peppercorns, and coriander seeds. Cook for 1 minute as you stir. Add water, salt and pork into your Instant Pot. Seal the pressure lid, choose Pressure Cook on High, and set the timer to 60 minutes.

Release the pressure naturally for 10 minutes. Soak rice noodles in hot water for 8 minutes until softened and pliable. Stop the cooking process by draining and rinsing with cold water. Separate the noodles into soup bowls. Remove the pork from the cooker and ladle among bowls. Strain the broth to get rid of solids. Pour it over the pork and noodles. Season with red pepper flakes. Garnish with lime wedges and cilantro leaves.

Sweet Potato Gratin with Peas & Prosciutto

Servings: 4 | Ready in about: 30 minutes

INGREDIENTS

- 1 ½ lb sweet potatoes, quartered
- ½ tsp salt or to taste
- ⅛ tsp freshly ground black pepper
- ½ cup heavy cream, or more to taste
- 1 cup shredded Provolone cheese
- 10 oz prosciutto, cooked and diced
- ¾ cup frozen peas, thawed
- ½ cup grated Pecorino Romano
- 3 tbsp chopped fresh chives

DIRECTIONS

Pour 1 cup of water into the inner pot and put a trivet in your Instant Pot. Place the sweet potatoes on the trivet. Seal the pressure lid, choose Pressure Cook on High and the cook time to 4 minutes. After cooking, perform a quick pressure release, and carefully open the lid. Remove the trivet. Empty the water out of the pot.

Put the potatoes back in the pot and season with the salt and pepper. Use a large fork to break the potatoes into pieces about ½ inch on a side. Mix in the heavy cream, Provolone cheese, and prosciutto. Gently stir in the peas. Sprinkle the mixture with the Pecorino Romano. Close the air fry lid and choose Bake. Adjust the temperature to 400°F and the cook time to 10 minutes. When the top of the gratin has browned, sprinkle with chives and serve.

Chorizo Stuffed Yellow Bell Peppers

Servings: 4 | Ready in about: 40 minutes

INGREDIENTS

- 4 large yellow bell peppers
- 2 tsp olive oil
- ¾ lb chorizo
- 1 small onion, diced
- ⅔ cup diced fresh tomatoes
- 1 ½ cups cooked rice
- 1 cup shredded Mexican blend cheese
- Salt and black pepper to taste

DIRECTIONS

Cut about ¼ inch off the top of each pepper. Cut through the ribs inside the peppers and pull out the core and remove as much of the ribs as possible. On your Instant Pot, choose Sauté. Heat the oil until shimmering and cook in the chorizo while breaking the meat with a spatula. Cook until just starting to brown, about 2 minutes. Add the onion and sauté until the vegetables soften and the chorizo has now browned, about 3 minutes.

Turn the pot off and scoop the chorizo and vegetables into a medium bowl. Add the tomatoes, rice, and ½ cup of cheese to the bowl. Mix to combine well. Spoon the filling mixture into the bell peppers to the brim. Clean the inner pot with a paper towel and return the pot to the base. Pour 1 cup of water into your Instant Pot and fix in a trivet. Put the peppers on the trivet and cover the tops loosely with a piece of foil.

Seal the pressure lid and choose Pressure Cook and the time to 12 minutes. After cooking, perform a quick pressure release and carefully open the lid. Remove the foil from the top of the peppers and sprinkle the remaining ½ cup of cheese on the peppers. Close the air fry lid, choose Broil, adjust the time to 5 minutes, and press Start to broil the cheese. After 4 minutes, open the lid and check the peppers. The cheese should have melted and browned a bit. If not, close the lid and continue cooking. Let the peppers cool for several minutes before serving.

Sausage with Noodles and Braised Cabbage

Servings: 4 | Ready in about: 35 minutes

INGREDIENTS

3 oz serrano ham, diced
1 small onion, sliced
⅓ cup dry white wine

1 cup chicken stock
1 tsp salt
¼ tsp black pepper

5 oz wide egg noodles
4 cups shredded green cabbage
1½ lb smoked sausage, cut into 4 pieces

DIRECTIONS

On your Instant Pot, choose Sauté. Put the ham in the pot and cook for 6 minutes until crisp. Using a slotted spoon, transfer the ham to a paper towel-lined plate to drain, leaving the fat in the pot. Sauté the onion to the pot for about 2 minutes or until the onion starts to soften. Pour in the wine and simmer until the wine reduces slightly while scraping the bottom of the pot with a wooden spoon to let off any browned bits.

Pour in the chicken stock, salt, black pepper, and noodles. Stir, while pushing the noodles as much as possible into the sauce. Put the cabbage on top of the noodles and the sausages on the cabbage. Lock the pressure lid into place and seal. Choose Pressure Cook on High and the cook time to 3 minutes.

When the cooking time is over, do a quick pressure release, and carefully open the lid. Stir the noodles and cabbage and adjust the taste with seasoning. Grease a trivet with cooking spray and fix in the pot. Transfer the sausages to the trivet. Choose Bake. Adjust the temperature to 390°F and the cook time to 8 minutes.

After 4 minutes, open the lid and check the sausages. When browned, turn the sausages, close the lid, and cook to brown the other side. Ladle the cabbage and noodles into a bowl and top with the bacon. Serve with the sausages.

Italian Sausage & Cannellini Stew

Servings: 6 | Ready in about: 45 minutes

INGREDIENTS

1 tbsp olive oil
1 lb Italian sausages, halved
1 celery stalk, chopped
1 carrot, chopped

1 onion, chopped
1 sprig fresh sage
1 sprig fresh rosemary
1 bay leaf

1 cup Cannellini Beans, soaked
2 cups vegetable stock
3 cups fresh spinach
1 tsp salt

DIRECTIONS

Warm oil on Sauté in your Instant Pot. Add in sausage pieces and sear for 5 minutes until browned. Set aside on a plate. To the pot, add celery, onion, bay leaf, sage, carrot, and rosemary. Cook for 3 minutes to soften slightly.Stir in vegetable stock and beans. Arrange seared sausage pieces on top of the beans.

Seal the pressure lid, choose Pressure Cook on High, and set the timer to 10 minutes. Release pressure naturally for 20 minutes. Once ready, do a quick release. Get rid of bay leaf, rosemary and sage. Mix in spinach and serve.

Calzones with Sausage and Mozzarella

Servings: 4 | Ready in about: 35 minutes

INGREDIENTS

2 tbsp olive oil
1 green bell pepper, seeded and chopped
2 or 3 Italian sausages
1 lb frozen bread dough
¼ cup tomato sauce
1 cup shredded mozzarella cheese

DIRECTIONS

On your Instant Pot, choose Sauté. Heat 1 tbsp of olive oil and sauté the bell pepper for 1 minute or until just starting to soften. Remove the pepper into a plate and set aside. Brown the sausages for 2 to 3 minutes on one side. Turn the sausages and brown the other side. Add ¾ cup of water to the inner pot. Seal the pressure lid. Choose Pressure Cook for 4 minutes. After cooking, perform a quick pressure release and carefully open the pressure lid.

Remove the sausages from the pot onto a cutting board and cool for several minutes. Discard the water in the pot. When the sausages have cooled, slice into ¼-inch rounds. Cut 4 pieces of parchment paper and divide the dough into 4 equal pieces. One at a time and on a piece of parchment, use your hands to press each dough into a circle.

Make the calzones. One after the other, spread 1 tablespoon of tomato sauce over half a dough circle, leaving a ½-inch clear border. Arrange the sausage rounds in a single layer and sprinkle a quarter of the green peppers over the top. Top with a quarter cup of cheese. Use the parchment to pull the other side of the dough over the filling and pinch the edges together to seal. Repeat the process with another dough.

Cut the parchment around each calzone, so it is about ½ inch larger than the calzone. Brush the calzones with some of the remaining olive oil. With a large spatula, transfer the two calzones to the trivet set it in the pot. Close the air fry lid and choose Bake. Adjust the temperature to 400°F and the cook time to 12 minutes.

After 6 minutes, check the calzones, which will be a dark golden brown. Remove the trivet and turn the calzones over. Remove the parchment paper and brush the tops with a little olive oil. Return the trivet to the pot. Close the lid and continue cooking for the last 6 minutes. While the first two calzones bake, assemble the remaining two. When the first set of calzones are done, transfer to a wire rack to cool and bake the second batch.

Beer-Braised Hot Dogs with Peppers

Servings: 6 | Ready in about: 15 minutes

INGREDIENTS

1 tbsp olive oil
6 sausages pork sausage links
1 green bell pepper, sliced into strips
1 red bell pepper, sliced into strips
1 yellow bell pepper, sliced into strips
2 spring onions, sliced
1 ½ cups beer
6 hot dog rolls

DIRECTIONS

Warm oil on Sauté in your Instant Pot. Add in sausage links and sear for 5 minutes until browned. Set aside on a plate. Into the pot, pile peppers. Lay the sausages on top. Add beer into the pot. Seal the pressure lid, choose Pressure Cook on High, and set the timer to 5 minutes. When ready, release the pressure quickly. Serve sausages in buns topped with onions and peppers.

Sweet Carrots with Crumbled Bacon

Servings: 8 | Ready in about: 30 minutes

INGREDIENTS

3 slices bacon, crumbled
4 lb carrots, peeled and sliced
½ cup fresh orange juice
¼ cup olive oil
3 tbsp honey
1 tsp salt
2 tsp cornstarch
1 tbsp cold water

DIRECTIONS

Fry the bacon in your Instant Pot on Sauté until crisp, 5 minutes; set aside. In a bowl, mix salt, olive oil, orange juice, and maple syrup. Add the mixture and carrots to the pot and mix well to coat. Seal the pressure lid, choose Pressure Cook on High, and set the timer to 6 minutes. When ready, release the pressure quickly.

Transfer carrots to a serving dish. Press Sauté. In a bowl, mix cold water and cornstarch until cornstarch dissolves completely. Add to the liquid remaining in the pressure cooker. Simmer sauce as you stir for 2 minutes to obtain a thick and smooth consistency. Ladle sauce over the carrots and scatter over the crumbled bacon.

Holiday Honey-Glazed Ham

Servings: 10 | Ready in about: 30 minutes

INGREDIENTS

- ½ cup apple cider
- ¼ cup honey
- 1 tbsp Dijon mustard
- ¼ cup brown sugar
- 2 tbsp orange juice
- 2 tbsp pineapple juice (optional)
- ½ tsp ground cinnamon
- ¼ tsp grated nutmeg
- 1 pinch ground cloves
- 1 (5 lb) ham, bone-in

DIRECTIONS

Set on Sauté in your Instant Pot. Mix in apple cider, mustard, pineapple juice, cloves, cinnamon, brown sugar, honey, orange juice, and nutmeg. Cook until sauce becomes warm and the sugar and spices are completely dissolved. Lay ham into the sauce. Seal the pressure lid, choose Pressure Cook, and set the timer to 10 minutes.

When ready, release the pressure quickly. Line aluminum foil to a baking sheet. Transfer the ham to the prepared baking sheet. On Sauté, cook the remaining liquid for 4 to 6 minutes until you have a thick and syrupy glaze. Brush the glaze onto ham. Set the glazed ham in the pot, close the air fry lid, and press Bake.

Cook for 3 to 5 minutes at 400 F until the glaze is caramelized. Place the ham on a cutting board and slice. Transfer to a serving bowl and drizzle glaze over the ham.

Sausage with Celeriac & Potato Mash

Servings: 4 | Ready in about: 45 minutes

INGREDIENTS

- 1 tbsp olive oil
- 4 pork sausages
- 1 onion
- 2 cups vegetable broth
- ½ cup water
- 4 potatoes, peeled and diced
- 1 cup celeriac, chopped
- 2 tbsp butter
- ¼ cup milk
- Salt and black pepper to taste
- 1 tbsp heavy cream
- 1 tsp Dijon mustard
- ½ tsp dry mustard powder
- Fresh flat-leaf parsley, chopped

DIRECTIONS

Warm oil on Sauté in your Instant Pot. Add in sausages and cook for 1 to 2 minutes for each side until browned. Set the sausages to a plate. To the same pot, add onion and cook for 3 minutes until fragrant. Add sausages on top of onions and pour water and broth over them. Place a trivet over onions and sausages. Put potatoes and celeriac in the steamer basket and transfer it to the trivet. Seal the pressure lid, choose Pressure Cook for 11 minutes.

When ready, release the pressure quickly. Transfer potatoes and celeriac to a bowl and set sausages on a plate and cover them with aluminum foil. Using a potato masher, mash potatoes and celeriac together with black pepper, milk, salt and butter until mash becomes creamy and fluffy. Adjust the seasonings. Set the pot to Sauté.

Add the onion mixture and bring to a boil. Cook for 5 to 10 minutes until the mixture is reduced and thickened. Into the gravy, stir in dry mustard, salt, pepper, mustard and cream. Place the mash in 4 bowls in equal parts, top with a sausage or two, and gravy. Add parsley for garnishing.

Tasty Ham with Collard Greens

Servings: 4 | Ready in about: 10 minutes

INGREDIENTS

20 oz collard greens, washed and cut
2 cubes of chicken bouillon
4 cups water
½ cup diced sweet onion
2 ½ cups diced ham

DIRECTIONS

Place the ham at the bottom of the inner pot. Add collard greens and onion. Add chicken cubes to the water and dissolve it. Pour the mixture into your Instant Pot. Close the lid, secure the pressure valve, to seal properly.

Select Steam mode on High pressure for 5 minutes. Once the timer has ended, do a quick pressure release, and open the lid. Spoon the vegetables and the ham with sauce into a serving bowl. Serve.

Winter Minestrone with Pancetta

Servings: 6 | Ready in about: 40 minutes

INGREDIENTS

2 tbsp olive oil
2 oz pancetta, chopped
1 onion, diced
1 parsnip, peeled and chopped
2 carrots, peeled and sliced into rounds
2 celery stalks,
2 garlic cloves, minced
1 tbsp dried basil
1 tbsp dried thyme
1 tbsp dried oregano
6 cups chicken broth
2 cups green beans, chopped
1 (15 oz) can diced tomatoes
1 (15 oz) can chickpeas, rinsed
1 ½ cups small shaped pasta
Salt and ground black pepper to taste
½ cup grated Parmesan cheese

DIRECTIONS

Warm oil on Sauté in your Instant Pot. Add onion, carrots, garlic, pancetta, celery, and parsnip, and cook for 5 minutes until they become soft. Stir in basil, oregano, green beans, broth, tomatoes, pepper, salt, thyme, vegetable broth, chickpeas, and pasta. Seal the pressure lid, choose Pressure Cook on High, and set the timer to 6 minutes.

Release pressure naturally for 10 minutes then release the remaining pressure quickly. Ladle the soup into bowls and serve garnished with grated Parmesan cheese.

Holiday Apricot-Lemon Ham

Servings: 12 | Ready in about: 1 hour

INGREDIENTS

¼ cup water
5 lb smoked ham
¾ cup apricot jam
½ cup brown sugar
Juice from 1 Lime
2 tsp mustard
½ tsp ground cardamom
¼ tsp ground nutmeg
Black pepper to taste

DIRECTIONS

Into your Instant Pot, add water and ham to the steel pot of a pressure cooker. In a bowl, combine jam, lemon juice, cardamom, pepper, nutmeg, mustard, and brown sugar. Pour the mixture over the ham. Seal the pressure lid, choose Pressure Cook on High, and set the timer to 10 minutes.

When ready, release the pressure quickly. Transfer the ham to a cutting board. Allow to sit for 10 minutes. Press Sauté. Simmer the liquid and cook for 4 to 6 minutes until thickened into a sauce. Slice ham and place onto a serving bowl. Drizzle with sauce before serving.

Crunchy Cashew Lamb Rack

Servings: 4 | Ready in about: 30 minutes

INGREDIENTS

3 oz chopped cashews
1 tbsp chopped rosemary
1 ½ lb rack of lamb
1 garlic clove, minced
1 tbsp breadcrumbs
1 egg, beaten
1 tbsp olive oil
Salt and pepper, to taste

DIRECTIONS

Combine the olive oil with the garlic and brush this mixture onto the lamb. Combine the rosemary, cashews, and breadcrumbs, in a small bowl. Brush the egg over the lambs, and then coat it with the cashew mixture.

Place the lamb in your Instant Pot, close the air fry lid and cook for 25 minutes on Air Fry at 390°F. Then increase to 390°F, and cook for 5 more minutes. Cover with a foil and let sit for a couple of minutes before serving.

Herbed Lamb Chops

Servings: 4 | Ready in about: 30 minutes

INGREDIENTS

4 lamb chops
1 garlic clove, peeled
1 tbsp plus
2 tsp olive oil
½ tbsp oregano
½ tbsp thyme

DIRECTIONS

Coat the garlic clove with 1 tsp of olive oil and cook in your Instant Pot for 10 minutes on Air Fry. Mix the herbs and seasonings with the remaining olive oil. Using a towel, squeeze the hot roasted garlic clove into the herb mixture and stir to combine. Coat the lamb chops with the mixture well, and place in the pot. Close the air fry lid and cook for about 8 to 12 minutes on Air Fry mode at 390°F, until crispy on the outside.

Lamb Chops & Creamy Potato Mash

Servings: 8 | Ready in about: 40 minutes

INGREDIENTS

8 lamb cutlets
Salt to taste
3 sprigs rosemary leaves, chopped
3 tbsp butter, softened
1 tbsp olive oil
1 tbsp tomato puree
1 green onion, chopped
1 cup beef stock
5 potatoes, peeled and chopped
⅓ cup milk
4 cilantro leaves, for garnish

DIRECTIONS

Rub rosemary leaves and salt to the lamb chops. Warm oil and 2 tbsp of butter on Sauté in your Instant Pot. Add in the lamb chops and cook for 1 minute for each side until browned. Set aside on a plate. In the pot, mix tomato puree and green onion. Cook for 2-3 minutes. Add beef stock into the pot to deglaze, scrape the bottom to get rid of any browned bits of food. Return lamb cutlets alongside any accumulated juices to the pot.

Set a trivet on lamb cutlets. Place steamer basket on the trivet. Arrange potatoes in the steamer basket. Seal the pressure lid, choose Pressure Cook, and set the timer to 4 minutes. When ready, release the pressure quickly.

Remove the trivet and steamer basket from pot. In a high speed blender, add potatoes, milk, salt, and remaining tbsp butter. Blend well until you obtain a smooth consistency. Divide the potato mash between serving dishes. Lay lamb chops on the mash. Drizzle with cooking liquid obtained from pressure cooker. Apply cilantro for garnish.

DESSERTS & BEVERAGES

Wheat Flour Cinnamon Balls

Servings: 4 | Ready in about: 20 minutes

INGREDIENTS

⅓ cup whole-wheat flour
⅓ cup all-purpose flour
½ tsp baking powder

3 tbsp sugar, divided
¼ tsp ground cinnamon, plus ½ tbsp
¼ tsp sea salt

2 tbsp cold butter, cut into small pieces
¼ cup plus 1½ tbsp whole milk
Cooking spray

DIRECTIONS

Mix the whole-wheat flour, all-purpose flour, baking powder, 1 tablespoon of sugar, ¼ teaspoon of cinnamon, and the salt in a medium bowl. Add the butter and use a pastry cutter to cut into the butter to be broken into little pieces until resembling cornmeal. Pour in the milk and mix until the dough forms into a ball.

Knead the dough on a flat surface until a smooth both is achieved. Divide the dough into 8 pieces and roll each piece into a ball. Put the balls in the air fry basket with space in between each ball and oil the balls with cooking spray. Close the air fry lid. Choose Air Fry, set the temperature to 350°F, and cook for 10 minutes. In a bowl, combine the remaining sugar and cinnamon. When done baking, toss the balls in the cinnamon and sugar mixture.

White Filling Coconut and Oat Cookies

Servings: 4 | Ready in about: 30 minutes

INGREDIENTS

5 ½ oz flour
1 tsp vanilla extract

3 oz sugar
½ cup oats

1 small egg, beaten
¼ cup coconut flakes

Filling
1 oz white chocolate, melted
2 oz butter

4 oz powdered sugar
1 tsp vanilla extract

DIRECTIONS

Beat all cookie ingredients, with an electric mixer, except the flour. When smooth, fold in the flour. Drop spoonfuls of the batter onto a prepared cookie sheet. Close the air fry lid and cook in your Instant Pot at 350°F for about 18 minutes on Air Fry mode. Let cool. Prepare the filling by beating all ingredients together. Spread the mixture on half of the cookies. Top with the other halves to make cookie sandwiches.

Apple Vanilla Hand Pies

Servings: 8 | Ready in about: 40 minutes

INGREDIENTS

1 (2-crust) package refrigerated pie crusts, at room temperature
2 apples, peeled, cored, and diced
3 tbsp sugar

1 lemon, juiced
¼ tsp salt

1 tsp vanilla extract
1 tsp corn-starch

DIRECTIONS

In a bowl, combine the apples, sugar, lemon juice, salt, and vanilla. Allow the mixture to stand for 10 minutes, then drain, and reserve 1 tablespoon of the liquid. In a small bowl, whisk the corn-starch into the reserved liquid and then, mix with the apple mixture. Put the piecrusts on a lightly floured surface and cut into 8 (4-inch- diameter) circles. Spoon a tablespoon of apple mixture in the center of the circle, with ½ an inch's border around the dough.

Brush the edges with water and fold the dough over the filling. Press the edges with a fork to seal. Cut 3 small slits on top of each pie and oil with cooking spray. Arrange the pies in a single layer in the air fry basket. Close the air fry lid. Choose Air Fry, set the temperature to 350°F, and set the time to 12 minutes. Once done baking, remove, and place the pies on a wire rack to cool. Repeat with the remaining hand pies.

Raspberry Crumble

Servings: 6 | Ready in about: 40 minutes

INGREDIENTS

1 (16-oz) package frozen raspberries
2 tbsp arrowroot starch
1 tsp freshly squeezed lemon juice
5 tbsp sugar, divided
½ cup all-purpose flour
⅔ cup brown sugar
½ cup rolled oats
⅓ cup cold butter, cut into pieces
1 tsp cinnamon powder

DIRECTIONS

Place the raspberries in the baking pan. In a small mixing bowl, combine the arrowroot starch, 1 tablespoon of water, lemon juice, and 3 tablespoons of sugar. Pour the mixture all over the raspberries. Put a trivet in the lower position of the pot. Cover the pan with foil and pour 1 cup water into your Instant Pot. Put the pan on the trivet. Put the pressure lid together, and lock in the Seal position. Choose Pressure Cook for 10 minutes.

In a bowl, mix the flour, brown sugar, oats, butter, cinnamon, and remaining sugar until crumble forms. When done pressure-cooking, do a quick release and carefully open the lid. Remove the foil and stir the fruit mixture. After, spread the crumble evenly on the berries. Close the air fry lid, choose Air Fry, set the temperature to 400°F, and the time to 10 minutes. Cook until the top has browned and the fruit is bubbling. Serve.

Almond Banana Dessert

Servings: 1 | Ready in about about: 8 minutes

INGREDIENTS

1 Banana, sliced
1 tbsp Coconut oil
2 tbsp Almond Butter
½ tsp Cinnamon

DIRECTIONS

Melt oil on Sauté in your Instant Pot. Add banana slices and fry them for a couple of minutes, or until golden on both sides. Top the fried bananas with almond butter and sprinkle with cinnamon.

Dark Chocolate Brownies

Servings: 6 | Ready in about: 40 minutes

INGREDIENTS

1 cup water
2 eggs
⅓ cup granulated sugar
¼ cup olive oil
⅓ cup flour
⅓ cup cocoa powder
⅓ cup dark chocolate chips
⅓ cup chopped Walnuts
1 tbsp milk
½ tsp baking powder
1 tbsp vanilla extract
A pinch salt

DIRECTIONS

To your Instant Pot, add water and set in a trivet. In a bowl, beat eggs and sugar to mix until smooth. Stir in olive oil, cocoa powder, milk, salt baking powder, chocolate chips, flour, walnuts, vanilla, and sea salt.

Transfer the batter to a greased springform pan and place the pan on the trivet. Close the air fry lid and select Bake. Adjust the temperature to 250°F and the cook time to 20 minutes. When the time is up, open the lid. Allow the brownie to cool for 10 minutes before cutting. Use powdered sugar to dust the brownies before serving lightly.

Raspberry Cream Tart

Servings: 4 | Ready in about: 55 minutes+ Chilling time

INGREDIENTS

1 refrigerated piecrust, for the raspberries
2 ½ cups fresh raspberries, divided
1 tbsp arrowroot starch

2 tbsp water
¼ cup sugar
¼ tsp grated lemon zest

1 tsp lemon juice
Pinch salt

For The Filling

1 tsp vanilla extract
8 oz cream cheese, at room temperature

½ cup confectioners' sugar
¼ cup heavy cream

DIRECTIONS

Roll out the pie crust and fit into a tart pan. Do not stretch the dough to prevent shrinking when cooking. Use a fork to prick all over the bottom of the dough. Place a trivet in your Instant Pot in the lower position of the pot and put the tart pan on top. Close the air fry lid, choose Bake. Adjust the temperature to 250°F, and the cook time to 15 minutes. When done baking, open the lid and check the crust. It should be lightly brown around the edges.

Close the air fry lid again. Adjust the temperature to 375°F and the cook time to 4 minutes. Press Start to begin baking. After 3 minutes, check the crust, which should be a deep golden brown color by now. If not, cook for the remaining 1 minute. Remove the trivet and set the crust aside to cool.

Fetch out 1 cup of berries into the inner pot. In a small bowl, whisk the arrowroot starch and water until smoothly mixed. Pour the slurry on the raspberries along with the sugar, lemon zest, lemon juice, and salt. Mix to distribute the slurry among the raspberries. Seal the pressure lid, choose Pressure Cook and the cook time to 2 minutes.

Once done cooking, perform a quick pressure release and carefully open the lid. The raspberries will have softened. Add the remaining 1 ½ cups of raspberries, stirring to coat with the cooked mixture. Then, allow cooling.

In a bowl and with a hand mixer, whisk the vanilla extract and cream cheese until evenly combined and smooth. Mix in the confectioners' sugar and whisk again until the sugar has fully incorporated and the mixture is light and smooth. With clean whisks and in another bowl, beat the heavy cream until soft peaks form.

Fold the heavy cream into the vanilla mixture until both are evenly combined. To assemble, spoon the cream filling into the piecrust and scatter the remaining raspberries on the cream. Chill for 30 minutes before cutting.

Vanilla Hot Lava Cake

Servings: 8 | Ready in about: 40 minutes

INGREDIENTS

1 cup butter
4 tbsp milk
4 tsp vanilla extract

1 ½ cups chocolate chips
1 ½ cups sugar
Powdered sugar to garnish

7 tbsp flour
5 eggs
1 cup water

DIRECTIONS

Grease the cake pan with cooking spray. Open your Instant Pot, fit in a trivet and pour in the water. In a heatproof bowl, add the butter and chocolate and melt them in the microwave for about 2 minutes. Remove it from the microwave. Add sugar and stir it well. Add the eggs, milk, and vanilla extract and stir again. Finally, add the flour and stir it until even and smooth. Pour the batter into the greased cake pan and use the spatula to level it.

Place the pan on the trivet in the pot, close the lid, secure the pressure valve, and select Pressure on High for 15 minutes. Once the timer has gone off, do a natural pressure release for 10 minutes. Place the pan on a flat surface. Put a plate over the pan and flip the cake over into the plate. Pour the powdered sugar in a fine sieve and sift it over the cake. Use a knife to cut the cake into 8 slices and serve immediately (while warm).

Mixed Berry Cobbler

Servings: 4 | Ready in about: 40 minutes

INGREDIENTS

2 bags frozen mixed berries

3 tbsp arrowroot starch

1 cup sugar

For the topping

1 cup self-rising flour

5 tbsp powdered sugar, divided

1 tbsp melted unsalted butter

¼ tsp cinnamon powder

⅔ cup crème fraiche

1 tbsp whipping cream

DIRECTIONS

Pour the blackberries into your Instant Pot along with the arrowroot starch and sugar. Mix to combine. Seal the pressure lid, choose Pressure Cook and the time to 3 minutes. After cooking, perform a quick pressure release. In a small bowl, whisk the flour, cinnamon powder, and 3 tablespoons of sugar. In a separate small bowl, whisk the crème fraiche with the melted butter. Pour the cream mixture on the dry ingredients and combine evenly.

Spoon 2 to 3 tablespoons of dough on top over the peaches and spread out slightly on top. Brush the topping with the whipping cream and sprinkle with the remaining sugar. Close the air fry lid and choose Bake. Adjust the temperature to 325°F and the cook time to 12 minutes. Check after 8 minutes. When ready, the topping should be cooked through and lightly browned. Allow cooling before slicing. Serve warm.

White Chocolate Chip Cookies

Servings: 8 | Ready in about: 30 minutes

INGREDIENTS

6 oz self-rising flour

2 oz white chocolate chips

1 ½ tbsp milk

3 oz brown sugar

1 tbsp honey

4 oz butter

DIRECTIONS

Beat the butter and sugar until fluffy. Then, beat in the honey, milk, and flour. Gently fold in the chocolate chips. Drop spoonfuls of the mixture onto a prepared cookie sheet. Close the air fry lid and cook for 18 minutes on Air Fry mode at 350°F. Once the timer beeps, make sure the cookies are just set.

Tasty Créme Brulee

Servings: 4 | Ready in about: 30 minutes + 6 hours of cooling

INGREDIENTS

3 cups heavy whipping cream

7 large egg yolks

2 cups water

6 tbsp sugar

2 tbsp vanilla extract

DIRECTIONS

In a mixing bowl, add the yolks, vanilla, whipping cream, and half of the swerve sugar. Use a whisk to mix them until they are well combined. Pour the mixture into the ramekins and cover them with aluminium foil. Open your Instant Pot, fit in a trivet, and pour in the water. Place 3 ramekins on the trivet and place the remaining ramekins to sit on the edges of the ramekins below. Seal the lid and select Pressure Cook on High for 8 minutes.

Once the timer has stopped, do a natural pressure release for 10 minutes, then a quick pressure release to let out the remaining pressure. With a napkin in hand, remove the ramekins onto a flat surface and then into a refrigerator to chill for at least 6 hours. After refrigeration, remove the ramekins and remove the aluminium foil.

Equally, sprinkle the remaining sugar on it and return to the pot. Close the crisping lid, select Bake mode, set the timer to 4 minutes on 380°F. Serve the crème brulee chilled with whipped cream.

New York Cheesecake

Servings: 12 | Ready in about: 1 hour

INGREDIENTS

For the Crust:
1 cup graham crackers crumbs
2 tbsp butter, melted
1 tsp sugar

For the Filling:
2 cups cream cheese, softened
1 tsp vanilla extract
1 pinch salt
½ cup sugar
Zest from 1 orange
2 eggs, at room temperature

DIRECTIONS

Fold a 20-inch piece of aluminum foil in half lengthwise twice and set on the pressure cooker. Spray a parchment paper with cooking spray and line to the base of a 7-inch springform pan. In a bowl, combine melted butter, salt, sugar and graham crackers crumbs. Press into the bottom and about ⅓ up the sides of the pan.

Transfer the pan to the freezer as you prepare the filling. In a separate bowl, beat sugar, cream cheese, salt, orange zest, and vanilla until smooth. Beat eggs into the filling, one at a time. Stir until combined. Add the filling over the chilled crust in the pan. To your Instant Pot, add 1 cup water and set a trivet into the pot. Carefully center the springform pan on the prepared foil sling. Lower pan into the inner pot using sling and place on steam trivet.

Close the air fry lid and select Bake. Adjust the temperature to 250°F and the cook time to 40 minutes. Let cool the cheesecake before transferring to a refrigerator for 2 hours or overnight. Use a paring knife to run along the edges between the pan and cheesecake to remove the cheesecake and set to the plate.

Simple Vanilla Cheesecake

Servings: 6 | Ready in about: 60 minutes

INGREDIENTS

1 ½ cups finely crushed graham crackers
16 oz cream cheese, at room temperature
1 tbsp all-purpose flour
2 tbsp sugar
½ cup brown sugar
1½ tsp vanilla extract
4 tbsp unsalted butter, melted
¼ cup sour cream
2 eggs

DIRECTIONS

Grease a spring form pan with cooking spray, then line the pan with parchment paper, grease with cooking spray again, and line with aluminium foil. This is to ensure that there are no air gaps in the pan. In a mixing bowl, mix the graham cracker crumbs, sugar, and butter. Spoon the mixture into the pan and press firmly into with a spoon.

In a deep bowl and with a hand mixer, beat the beat the cream cheese and brown sugar until well-mixed. Whisk in the sour cream to be smooth and stir in the flour, vanilla, and salt. Crack the eggs in and beat but not to be overly smooth. Pour the mixture into the pan over the crumbs. Pour 1 cup water into your Instant Pot.

Put the spring form pan on the trivet and put the trivet in the pot. Seal the pressure lid, choose Pressure Cook on High, and set the time to 35 minutes. Once done baking, perform a natural pressure release for 10 minutes, then a quick pressure release to let out any remaining pressure. Carefully open the lid. Remove the pan from the trivet and allow the cheesecake to cool for 1 hour. Cover the cheesecake with foil and chill in the refrigerator.

Chocolate and Banana Squares

Servings: 6 | Ready in about about: 25 minutes

INGREDIENTS

½ cup Butter
3 Bananas
2 tbsp Cocoa Powder

DIRECTIONS

Place bananas and butter in a bowl and mash finely with a fork. Add the cocoa powder and stir until well combined. Pour the banana and almond batter into a greased baking dish. Pour 1 cup water in the pot and lower a trivet. Place the baking dish on top of the trivet and seal the pressure lid. Select Pressure, set the timer to 15 minutes at High pressure. When it goes off, do a quick release. Let cool for a few minutes before cutting into squares

Holiday Cranberry Cheesecake

Servings: 8 | Ready in about: 1 hour

INGREDIENTS

1 cup coarsely crumbled cookies
2 tbsp butter, melted
1 cup mascarpone cheese, softened
½ cup sugar
2 tbsp sour cream
½ tsp vanilla extract
2 eggs, room temperature
1/3 cup dried cranberries
1 cup water

DIRECTIONS

Fold a 20-inch piece of aluminum foil in half lengthwise twice and set on the pressure cooker. In a bowl, combine melted butter and crushed cookies. Press firmly to the bottom and about 1/3 of the way up the sides of a 7-inch springform pan. Freeze the crust while the filling is being prepared.

In a separate bowl, beat together mascarpone cheese and sugar to obtain a smooth consistency. Stir in vanilla extract and sour cream. Beat one egg and add into the cheese mixture to combine well. Do the same with the second egg. Stir cranberries into the filling. Transfer the filling into the crust. Into your Instant Pot, add water and set a trivet at the bottom. Center the springform pan onto the prepared foil sling. Lower the pan onto the trivet.

Fold foil strips out of the way of the lid. Close the air fry lid and select Bake. Adjust the temperature to 250°F and the cook time to 40 minutes. When the time is up, open the lid and let to cool the cheesecake. When, transfer the cheesecake to a refrigerator for 2 hours or overnight. Use a paring knife to run along the edges between the pan and cheesecake to remove the cheesecake and set to the plate.

Strawberry & Lemon Ricotta Cheesecake

Servings: 6 | Ready in about: 35 minutes

INGREDIENTS

10 oz cream cheese
¼ cup sugar
½ cup Ricotta cheese
One lemon, zested and juiced
2 eggs, cracked into a bowl
1 tsp lemon extract
3 tbsp sour cream
1 ½ cups water
10 strawberries, halved to decorate

DIRECTIONS

In the electric mixer, add the cream cheese, quarter cup of sugar, ricotta cheese, lemon zest, lemon juice, and lemon extract. Turn on the mixer and mix the ingredients until a smooth consistency is formed. Reduce the speed of the mixer and add the eggs. Fold it in at low speed until it is fully incorporated.

Make sure not to fold the eggs in high speed to prevent a cracker crust. Grease the spring form pan with cooking spray and use a spatula to spoon the mixture into the pan. Level the top with the spatula and cover it with foil. Open your Instant Pot, fit in a trivet, and pour in the water. Place the cake pan on the trivet. Seal the lid and select Pressure Cook on High for 15 minutes. Mix the sour cream and one tablespoon of sugar. Set aside.

Once the timer has gone off, do a natural pressure release for 10 minutes, then a quick pressure release to let out any extra steam, and open the lid. Remove the trivet with pan, place the spring form pan on a flat surface, and open it. Use a spatula to spread the sour cream mixture on the warm cake. Refrigerate the cake for 8 hours. Top with strawberries. Slice it into 6 pieces and serve while firming.

DESSERTS & BEVERAGES

Berry Vanilla Pudding

Servings: 4 | Ready in about: 35 minutes + 6h for refrigeration

INGREDIENTS

1 cup heavy cream
4 egg yolks
4 tbsp water + 1 ½ cups water
½ cup milk
1 tsp vanilla extract
½ cup sugar
4 raspberries
4 blueberries

DIRECTIONS

Turn on your Instant Pot and select Sauté. Add four tablespoons for water and the sugar. Stir it constantly until it dissolves. Press Stop. Add milk, heavy cream, and vanilla. Stir it with a whisk until evenly combined. Crack the eggs into a bowl and add a tablespoon of the cream mixture. Whisk it and then very slowly add the remaining cream mixture while whisking. Fit a trivet at the bottom of the pot, and pour one and a half cup of water in it.

Pour the mixture into four ramekins and place them on the trivet. Close the lid of the pot, secure the pressure valve, and select Pressure Cook on High for 4 minutes. Once done, do a quick pressure release. With a napkin in hand, remove the ramekins onto a flat surface. Let cool for about 15 minutes and then refrigerate them for 6 hours. Garnish with the raspberries and blueberries. Enjoy immediately or refrigerate.

Chocolate Vanilla Swirl Cheesecake

Servings: 8 | Ready in about: 60 minutes + Chilling time

INGREDIENTS

4 oz chocolate wafer cookies, crushed into crumbs
2 tbsp unsalted butter, melted
16 oz cream cheese, at room temperature
½ cup sugar
2 tbsp heavy cream
2 tsp vanilla extract
2 tbsp sour cream
2 large eggs
3 oz sweet chocolate chips, melted

DIRECTIONS

In a bowl, mix the cookie crumbs and butter. Spoon the crumbs into a spring form pan and press all around with a spoon. Place a trivet in your Instant Pot and put the spring form pan on top. Close the air fry lid and choose Air Fry. Adjust the temperature to 350°F and the time to 6 minutes. Bake until fragrant. Remove the pan and let cool.

In a medium bowl and using a hand mixer, beat the cream cheese until smooth. Add the sugar and beat until smooth. Pour in the heavy cream, vanilla extract, and sour cream. Whisk again and crack the eggs into the bowl one after the other while whisking. Spoon ½ cup of the cream mixture into a bowl and mix in chocolate chips.

Pour the remaining cream mixture into the spring form pan, drop spoonfuls of the chocolate mixture with even distance on the filling and run the tip of a skewer through each chocolate drop to marbleize the top of the filling. Cover the filling with aluminium foil. Pour 1 cup of water into the inner pot. Fix in a trivet the pot and put the spring form pan on top. Seal the pressure lid, choose Pressure Cook on High and the cook time to 25 minutes.

After cooking, do a natural pressure release for 10 minutes, and then a quick pressure release to let out any remaining pressure. Carefully open the lid and remove the cheesecake from the pot. Take off the foil. Let the cheesecake rest for 15 to 20 minutes and then refrigerate the cooled cake for 3 to 4 hours to chill through.

Air Fried Doughnuts

Servings: 4 | Ready in about: 25 minutes

INGREDIENTS

8 oz self-rising flour
1 tsp baking powder
½ cup milk
2 ½ tbsp butter
1 egg
2 oz brown sugar

DESSERTS & BEVERAGES

DIRECTIONS

Beat the butter with the sugar, until smooth. Beat in eggs, and milk. In a bowl, combine the flour with the baking powder. Gently fold the flour into the butter mixture. Form donut shapes and cut off the center with cookie cutters. Arrange on a lined baking sheet and cook in your Instant Pot for 15 minutes on Air Fry mode at 350°F. Serve with whipped cream.

Classic Caramel-Walnut Brownies

Servings: 4 | Ready in about: 60 minutes+ cooling time

INGREDIENTS

8 oz white chocolate
8 tbsp unsalted butter
1 cup sugar
2 tsp almond extract
A pinch of salt
2 large eggs, at room temperature
¾ cup all-purpose flour
½ cup caramel sauce
½ cup toasted walnuts

DIRECTIONS

Put the white chocolate and butter in a small bowl and pour 1 cup of water into the inner pot. Place a trivet in the lower position of the pot and put the bowl on top. Close the air fry lid. Choose Bake. Adjust the temperature to 375°F and the cook time to 10 minutes to melt the white chocolate and butter. Check after 5 minutes and stir. As soon as the chocolate has melted, remove the bowl from the pot.

Use a small spatula to transfer the chocolate mixture into a medium and stir in the almond extract, sugar, and salt. One after another, crack each egg into the bowl and whisk after each addition. Mix in the flour until smooth, about 1 minute. Grease a round cake pan with cooking spray or line the pan with parchment paper. Pour the batter into the prepared pan and place on the trivet.

Close the air fry lid and choose Bake. Adjust the temperature to 250°F and the time to 25 minutes. Once the time is up, open the lid and check the brownies. The top should be just set. Blot out the butter that may pool to the top using a paper towel. Close the air fry lid again and adjust the temperature to 300°F for 15 minutes.

Once the time is up, open the lid and check the brownies. A toothpick inserted into the center should come out with crumbs sticking to it but no raw batter. Drizzle the caramel sauce on top of the brownies and scatter with the walnuts. Close the air fry lid again and adjust the temperature to 325°F for 8 minutes. When the nuts are brown and the caramel is bubbling, take out the brownies, and allow cooling for at least 30 minutes and cut into squares.

Cinnamon Apple Crisp

Servings: 5 | Ready in about: 30 minutes

INGREDIENTS

Topping:
½ cup oat flour
½ cup old-fashioned rolled oats
½ cup granulated sugar
¼ cup olive oil

Filling:
5 apples, peeled, cored, and halved
2 tbsp arrowroot powder
½ cup water
1 tsp ground cinnamon
¼ tsp ground nutmeg
½ tsp vanilla paste

DIRECTIONS

In a bowl, combine sugar, oat flour, rolled oats, and olive oil to form coarse crumbs. Ladle the apples into your Instant Pot. Mix water with arrowroot powder in a bowl. Stir in salt, nutmeg, cinnamon, and vanilla and toss in the apples to coat. Apply oat topping to the apples. Seal the pressure lid, choose Pressure Cook on High, and set the timer to 10 minutes. Release pressure naturally for 5 minutes, then release the remaining pressure quickly.

Blueberry Muffins

Servings: 10 | Ready in about: 30 minutes

INGREDIENTS

1 ½ cup flour
½ tsp salt
½ cup sugar

¼ cup vegetable oil
2 tsp vanilla extract
1 cup blueberries

1 egg
2 tsp baking powder
Yogurt, as needed

DIRECTIONS

Combine all the flour, salt and baking powder in a bowl. In a bowl, place the oil, vanilla extract, and egg. Fill the rest of the bowl with yogurt. Whisk the mixture until fully incorporated. Combine the wet and dry ingredients. Gently fold in the blueberries. Divide the mixture between 10 muffin cups. Close the air fry lid and cook for 10 minutes on Air Fry mode at 350°F, until nice and crispy.

Molten Lava Cake

Servings: 4 | Ready in about: 20 minutes

INGREDIENTS

3 ½ oz butter, melted
3 ½ tbsp sugar

1 ½ tbsp self-rising flour
3 ½ oz dark chocolate, melted

2 eggs

DIRECTIONS

Grease 4 ramekins with butter. Beat the eggs and sugar until frothy. Stir in the butter and chocolate. Gently fold in the flour. Divide the mixture between the ramekins and bake in your Instant Pot for 10 minutes on Air Fry mode at 390°F. Let cool for 2 minutes before turning the lava cakes upside down onto serving plates.

Cheat Apple Pie

Servings: 9 | Ready in about: 30 minutes

INGREDIENTS

4 apples, diced
2 oz butter, melted
2 oz sugar

1 oz brown sugar
2 tsp cinnamon
1 egg, beaten

3 large puff pastry sheets
¼ tsp salt

DIRECTIONS

Whisk the white sugar, brown sugar, cinnamon, salt, and butter together. Place the apples in a baking dish and coat them with the mixture. Slide the dish into your Instant Pot and cook for 10 minutes on Roast at 350°F.

Meanwhile, roll out the pastry on a floured flat surface, and cut each sheet into 6 equal pieces. Divide the apple filling between the parts. Brush the edges of the pastry squares with the egg. Fold and seal the edges with a fork.Place on a lined baking sheet and cook in the fryer at 350°F for 8 minutes on Roast. Flip over, increase the temperature to 390°F, and cook for 2 more minutes.

Lemon Cheesecake with Strawberries

Servings: 8 | Ready in about: 3 hour

INGREDIENTS

Crust:

4 oz graham crackers

1 tsp ground cinnamon

3 tbsp butter, melted

DESSERTS & BEVERAGES

Filling:

1 lb mascarpone cheese, softened
¾ cup sugar
¼ cup sour cream, at room temperature
2 eggs, at room temperature
1 tsp vanilla extract
1 tsp lemon zest
1 tbsp lemon juice
1 pinch salt
1 cup strawberries, halved

DIRECTIONS

In a food processor, beat cinnamon and graham crackers to attain a texture almost same as sand. Mix in melted butter. Press the crumbs into the bottom of a 7-inch springform pan in an even layer. In a stand mixer, beat sugar, mascarpone cheese, and sour cream for 3 minutes to combine well and have a fluffy and smooth mixture.

Scrape the bowl's sides and add eggs, lemon zest, salt, lemon juice, and vanilla extract. Carry on to beat the mixture until you obtain a consistent color and all ingredients are completely combined. Pour filling over crust. Into the inner pot of your Instant Pot, add 1 cup water and set in a trivet. Insert the springform pan on the trivet.

Close the air fry lid and select Bake. Adjust the temperature to 250°F and the cook time to 40 minutes. Remove cheesecake and let cool for 1 hour. Transfer to a serving plate and garnish with strawberry halves on top. Use a paring knife to run along the edges between the pan and cheesecake to remove the cheesecake and set to the plate.

Pumpkin Cake

Servings: 8 | Ready in about: 1 hour 30 minutes

INGREDIENTS

3 eggs
⅔ cup sugar
1 cup flour
½ cup half-and-half
¼ cup olive oil
1 tsp baking powder
1 tsp vanilla extract
1 tsp ground cinnamon
½ tsp ground nutmeg
1 cup shredded pumpkin + for topping
½ cup chopped walnuts
2 cups water

Frosting:

4 oz cream cheese, room temperature
8 tbsp butter
½ cup confectioners sugar
½ tsp vanilla extract
⅛ tsp salt

DIRECTIONS

In a bowl, beat eggs and sugar to get a smooth mixture. Mix in oil, flour, vanilla extract, cinnamon, half-and-half, baking powder, and nutmeg. Stir well to obtain a fluffy batter. Fold walnuts and pumpkin through the batter. Add batter into a 6-inch cake pan and cover with aluminum foil. Into your Instant Pot, add water and set a trivet.

Lay cake pan gently onto the trivet. Close the air fry lid and select Bake. Adjust the temperature to 250°F and the cook time to 40 minutes. Beat cream cheese, confectioners' sugar, salt, vanilla extract, and butter in a mixing bowl until smooth. Place in the refrigerator until needed for use. Remove cake from the pan and transfer to the cooking wire rack to cool. Over the cake, spread frosting and apply a topping of shredded carrots, as desired.

Homemade Apple Cider

Servings: 6 | Ready in about: 45 minutes

INGREDIENTS

6 green apples, cored and chopped
3 cups water
¼ cup orange juice
2 cinnamon sticks

DIRECTIONS

In a blender, add orange juice, apples, and water and blend until smooth. Use a fine-mesh strainer to strain and press using a spoon. Get rid of the pulp. In the cooker, mix the strained apple puree, and cinnamon sticks. Seal the pressure lid, choose Pressure Cook on High, and set the timer to 10 minutes. Release the pressure naturally for 15 minutes, then quick release the remaining pressure. Strain again and do away with the solids.

No Flour Lime Muffins

Servings: 6 | Ready in about: 30 minutes

INGREDIENTS

2 eggs plus 1 yolk
Juice and zest of 2 limes

1 cup yogurt
¼ cup superfine sugar

8 oz cream cheese
1 tsp vanilla extract

DIRECTIONS

With a spatula, gently combine the yogurt and cheese. In another bowl, beat together the rest of the ingredients. Gently fold the lime with the cheese mixture. Divide the batter between 6 lined muffin tins. Close the air fry lid and cook in your Instant Pot for 10 minutes on Air Fry mode at 330°F.

The Most Chocolaty Fudge

Servings: 8 | Ready in about: 55 minutes

INGREDIENTS

1 cup sugar
7 oz flour, sifted
1 tbsp honey

¼ cup milk
1 tsp vanilla extract
1 oz cocoa powder

2 eggs
4 oz butter
1 orange, juice and zest

Icing:
1 oz butter, melted
4 oz powdered sugar

1 tbsp brown sugar
1 tbsp milk

2 tsp honey

DIRECTIONS

In a bowl, mix the dry ingredients for the fudge. Mix the wet ingredients separately. Combine the two mixtures gently. Transfer the batter to a prepared The air fry basket. Close the air fry lid and cook for about 35 minutes on Roast mode at 350°F. Once the timer beeps, check to ensure the cake is cooked. For the Topping: whisk together all of the icing ingredients. When the cake is cooled, coat it with the icing. Let set before slicing the fudge.

Air Fried Snickerdoodle Poppers

Servings: 6 | Ready in about: 30 minutes

INGREDIENTS

1 can of Pillsbury Grands Flaky Layers Biscuits
1 box instant vanilla Jell-O

1 ½ cups cinnamon sugar

Melted butter, for brushing

DIRECTIONS

Unroll the flaky biscuits and cut them into fourths. Roll each ¼ into a ball. Arrange the balls on a lined baking sheet, and cook in your Instant Pot for 7 minutes, or until golden, on Air Fry mode at 350°F. Prepare the Jell-O following the package's instructions. Using an injector, inject some of the vanilla pudding into each ball. Brush the balls with melted butter and then coat them with cinnamon sugar.

Valencian Horchata

Servings: 6 | Ready in about: 20 minutes

INGREDIENTS

2 cups water
1 cup chufa seed, overnight soak

¼ stick cinnamon
Zest from 1 lemon

2 tbsp sugar
4 cups cold water

DESSERTS & BEVERAGES

DIRECTIONS

In your Instant Pot, combine cinnamon, chufa seed and 4 cups water. Seal the pressure lid, choose Pressure Cook on High, and set the timer to 1 minute. Release pressure naturally for 10 minutes, then release the remaining pressure quickly. In a blender, add chufa seed mixture, lemon zest and sugar. Blend well to form a paste.

Add 2 cups cold water into a large container. Strain the blended chufa mixture into the water. Mix well and place in the refrigerator until ready for serving. Add cinnamon stick for garnishing.

Pineapple Cake

Servings: 4 | Ready in about: 50 minutes

INGREDIENTS

2 oz dark chocolate, grated
8 oz self-rising flour
4 oz butter

7 oz pineapple chunks
½ cup pineapple juice
1 egg

2 tbsp milk
½ cup sugar

DIRECTIONS

Preheat your Instant Pot to 390°F. Place the butter and flour into a bowl and rub the mixture with your fingers until crumbed. Stir in the pineapple, sugar, chocolate, and juice. Beat the eggs and milk separately, and then add them to the batter. Transfer the batter to a previously prepared (greased or lined) cake pan, and cook for 40 minutes on Roast mode. Let cool for at least 10 minutes before serving.

Cinnamon Mulled Red Wine

Servings: 6 | Ready in about: 30 minutes

INGREDIENTS

3 cups red wine
2 tangerines, sliced
¼ cup honey

6 whole cloves
6 whole black peppercorns
2 cardamom pods

8 cinnamon sticks
1 tsp fresh ginger, sliced
6 tangerine wedges

DIRECTIONS

In the pot, combine red wine, honey, cardamom pods, 2 cinnamon sticks, cloves, tangerines slices, ginger, and peppercorns. Seal the pressure lid, choose Pressure Cook on High, and set the timer to 5 minutes. Release pressure naturally for 20 minutes. Using a fine mesh strainer, strain your wine. Discard spices. Divide the warm wine into glasses and add tangerine wedges and a cinnamon stick for garnishing before serving.

Moon Milk

Servings: 2 | Ready in about: 10 minutes

INGREDIENTS

1 cup milk
1 tsp coconut oil
1/2 tsp cinnamon, plus more for garnish
1/2 tsp ground turmeric

¼ cup hemp hearts
1/2 tsp maca powder
1/8 tsp ground cardamom
1 pinch ground nutmeg

1 pinch ground ginger
1 pinch freshly ground black pepper
1 tsp honey

DIRECTIONS

To your Instant Pot, add milk. Press Sauté and heat the milk for 4 minutes until the point of starting to bubble. Stir in coconut oil, turmeric, nutmeg, pepper, ginger, hemp hearts, maca powder, cinnamon, and cardamom. Press Cancel and allow mixture to cool for about a minute. Whisk in honey. Transfer the mixture into a mug to serve.

Raspberry Cheesecake

Servings: 6 | Ready in about about: 30 minutes

INGREDIENTS

- 1 ½ cups Graham Cracker Crust
- 1 cup Raspberries
- 3 cups Cream Cheese
- 1 tbsp fresh Orange Juice
- 3 Eggs
- ½ stick Butter, melted
- ¾ cup Sugar
- 1 tsp Vanilla Paste
- 1 tsp finely grated Orange Zest

DIRECTIONS

Insert a trivet into your Instant Pot and add 1 ½ cups of water. Grease a spring form. Mix in graham cracker crust with sugar and butter in a bowl. Press the mixture to form a crust at the bottom. Blend the raspberries and cream cheese with an electric mixer. Crack in the eggs and keep mixing until well combined.

Mix in the remaining ingredients, and give it a good stir. Pour this mixture into the pan, and cover the pan with aluminium foil. Lay the spring form on the tray. Select Pressure Cook and set the time to 20 minutes at High pressure. Once the cooking is complete, do a quick pressure release. Refrigerate the cheesecake for at least 2 hours.

Chocolate Soufflé

Servings: 2 | Ready in about: 25 minutes

INGREDIENTS

- 2 eggs, whites and yolks separated
- ¼ cup butter, melted
- 2 tbsp flour
- 3 tbsp sugar
- 3 oz chocolate, melted
- ½ tsp vanilla extract

DIRECTIONS

Beat the yolks along with the sugar and vanilla extract. Stir in butter, chocolate, and flour. Whisk the whites until a stiff peak forms. Working in batches, gently combine the egg whites with the chocolate mixture. Divide the batter between two greased ramekins. Close the air fry lid and cook for 14 minutes on Roast at 330°F.

Lemon & Blueberries Compote

Servings: 4 | Ready in about about: 10 minutes + chilling time

INGREDIENTS

- 2 cups Blueberries
- 2 tbsp Cornstarch
- ¾ cups Coconut Sugar
- Juice of ½ Lemon
- ½ cup Water + 2 tbsp

DIRECTIONS

Place blueberries, lemon juice, 1/2 cup water, and coconut sugar in your cooker. Seal the pressure lid, choose Steam and set the timer to 3 minutes at High pressure. Once done, do a quick pressure. Combine the cornstarch and water in a bowl. Stir in the mixture into the blueberries and cook until the mixture thickens on Sauté in your Instant Pot. Transfer the compote to a bowl and let cool completely before refrigerating for 2 hours.

Almond Milk

Servings: 4 | Ready in about: 20 minutes

INGREDIENTS

- 1 cup raw almonds, soaked overnight, rinsed and peeled
- 1 cup cold water
- 2 dried apricots, chopped
- 2 tbsp honey
- 1 vanilla bean
- 4 cups water

DIRECTIONS

In your Instant Pot, mix a cup of cold water with almonds and apricots. Seal the pressure lid, choose Pressure Cook on High, and set the timer to 1 minute. When ready, release the pressure quickly. Open the lid. The almonds should be soft and plump, and the water should be brown and murky. Use a strainer to drain almonds.

Rinse with cold water for 1 minute. To a high-speed blender, add the rinsed almonds, vanilla bean, honey, and 4 cups water. Blend for 2 minutes until well combined and frothy. Line a cheesecloth to the strainer.

Place the strainer over a bowl and strain the milk. Use a wooden spoon to press milk through the cheesecloth and get rid of solids. Place almond milk in an airtight container and refrigerate.

Tiramisu Cheesecake

Servings: 12 | Ready in about: 1 hour + chilling time | Serves: 12

INGREDIENTS

- 1 tbsp Kahlua Liquor
- 1 ½ cups Ladyfingers, crushed
- 1 tbsp Granulated Espresso
- 1 tbsp Butter, melted
- 16 oz Cream Cheese, softened
- 8 oz Mascarpone Cheese, softened
- 2 Eggs
- 2 tbsp Powdered Sugar
- ½ cup White Sugar
- 1 tbsp Cocoa Powder
- 1 tsp Vanilla Extract

DIRECTIONS

In a bowl, beat the cream cheese, mascarpone, and white sugar. Gradually beat in the eggs, powdered sugar, and vanilla. Combine the Kahlua Liquor, Ladyfingers, Espresso, and melted butter f in another bowl. Spray a springform pan with cooking spray. Press the ladyfinger crust at the bottom. Pour the filling over.

Cover the pan with a paper towel and then close it with aluminum foil. Pour 1 cup of water in your Instant Pot and lower a trivet. Place the pan inside and seal the pressure lid. Select Pressure Cook and set time to 35 minutes. Do a quick pressure release. Allow to cool completely before refrigerating the cheesecake for 4 hours.

Coconut Pear Delight

Servings: 2 | Ready in about about: 15 minutes

INGREDIENTS

- ¼ cup Flour
- 1 cup Coconut Milk
- 2 Large Pears, peeled and diced
- ¼ cup Shredded Coconut, unsweetened

DIRECTIONS

Combine all ingredients in your Instant Pot. Seal the pressure lid, select Pressureand set the timer to 5 minutes at High pressure. When ready, do a quick pressure release. Divide the mixture between two bowls.

Pear Wedges

Servings: 3 | Ready in about about: 15 minutes

INGREDIENTS

- 2 Pears, peeled and cut into wedges
- 3 tbsp Almond Butter
- 2 tbsp Olive Oil

DIRECTIONS

Pour 1 cup of water in the pot. Place the pear wedges in a steamer basket and then lower the basket at the bottom. Seal the pressure lid, and cook for 2 minutes on High pressure. When the timer goes off, do a quick pressure release. Remove the basket, discard the water and wipe clean the cooker. Press the Sauté and heat the oil. Add the pears and cook until browned. Top them with almond butter, to serve.

Delicious Pecan Stuffed Apples

Servings: 6 | Ready in about about: 20 minutes

INGREDIENTS

3 ½ lb Apples, cored
½ cup dried Apricots, chopped
¼ cup Sugar
¼ cup Pecans, chopped
¼ cup Graham Cracker Crumbs
¼ tsp Cardamom
½ tsp grated Nutmeg
½ tsp ground Cinnamon
1 ¼ cups Red Wine

DIRECTIONS

Lay the apples at the bottom of your Instant Pot and pour in the red wine. Combine the other ingredients, except the crumbs. Seal the pressure lid, and cook on Pressure Cook for 15 minutes. Once ready, do a quick pressure release. Top with graham cracker crumbs and serve!

Tasty Coconut Cake

Servings: 4 | Ready in about about: 55 minutes

INGREDIENTS

3 Eggs, Yolks and Whites separated
¾ cup Coconut Flour
½ tsp Coconut Extract
1 ½ cups warm Coconut Milk
½ cup Coconut Sugar
2 tbsp Coconut Oil, melted

DIRECTIONS

In a bowl, beat in the egg yolks along with the coconut sugar. In a separate bowl, beat the whites until soft form peaks. Stir in coconut extract and coconut oil. Fold in the coconut flour. Line a baking dish and pour the batter inside. Cover with aluminum foil. Pour 1 cup water in your Instant Pot and add a trivet. Lower the dish onto the trivet. Seal the pressure lid, choose Pressure Cook, and set the time to 35 minutes. Do a quick pressure release.

Brown Sugar & Butter Bars

Servings: 6 | Ready in about about: 55 minutes

INGREDIENTS

1 cup Flour
1 ½ cups Water
1 Egg
½ cup Peanut Butter, softened
½ cup Butter, softened
1 cup Oats
½ cup Sugar
½ tsp Baking Soda
½ cup Brown Sugar

DIRECTIONS

Grease a springform pan and line it with parchment paper. Set aside. Beat together the eggs, peanut butter, butter, white sugar, and brown sugar. Fold in the oats, flour, and baking soda. Press the batter into the pan. Cover the pan with a paper towel and with a piece of foil. Pour the water into the pot and add a trivet.

Lower the springform pan onto the trivet. Seal the pressure lid, choose Pressure Cook, and set the time to 35 minutes. When ready, do a quick release. Wait for 15 minutes before inverting onto a plate and cutting into bars.

Cherry Pie

Servings: 6 | Ready in about about: 45 minutes

INGREDIENTS

1 9-inch double Pie Crust
2 cups Water
½ tsp Vanilla Extract
4 cups Cherries, pitted
¼ tsp Almond Extract
4 tbsp Quick Tapioca
1 cup Sugar
A pinch of Salt

DIRECTIONS

Pour water your Instant Pot and add a trivet. Combine the cherries with tapioca, sugar, extracts, and salt in a bowl. Place one pie crust at the bottom of a lined springform pan. Spread the cherries mixture and top with the other crust. Lower the pan onto the trivet. Seal the pressure lid, choose Pressure Cook on High, and set the time to 18 minutes. Once ready, do a quick pressure release. Let cool the pie on a cooling rack. Slice to serve.

Milk Dumplings in Sweet Sauce

Servings: 20 | Ready in about about: 30 minutes

INGREDIENTS

6 cups Water
2 ½ cups Sugar
3 tbsp Lime Juice
6 cups Milk
1 tsp ground Cardamom

DIRECTIONS

Bring to a boil the milk on Sauté your Instant Pot and stir in the lime juice. The solids should start to separate. Pour milk through a cheesecloth-lined colander. Drain as much liquid as you can. Place the paneer on a smooth surface. Form a ball and divide into 20 equal pieces.

Pour water in the Foofi and bring to a boil on Sauté in the pot. Add in sugar and cardamom and cook until dissolved. Shape the dumplings into balls, and place them in the syrup. Seal the pressure lid and choose Pressure Cook on High, and set the time to 5 minutes. Once done, do a quick pressure release. Let cool and serve.

Poached Peaches

Servings: | Ready in about about: 15 minutes | Serves: 4 | Per serving: Calories 140. Carbs 15g. Fat 1g. Protein 1g

INGREDIENTS

½ cup Black Currants
4 Peaches, peeled, pits removed
1 cup Freshly Squeezed Orange Juice
1 Cinnamon Stick

DIRECTIONS

Place black currants and orange juice in a blender. Blend until the mixture becomes smooth. Pour the mixture in your Instant Pot, and add the cinnamon stick. Add the peaches to the steamer basket and then insert the basket into the pot. Seal the pressure lid, select Pressure, and set to 5 minutes at High pressure. When done, do a quick pressure release. Serve the peaches drizzled with sauce, to enjoy!

Savory Peaches with Chocolate Biscuits

Servings: 4 | Ready in about about: 20 minutes

INGREDIENTS

4 small Peaches, halved lengthwise and pitted
8 dried Dates, chopped
4 tbsp Walnuts, chopped
1 cup Coarsely Crumbled Cookies
1 tsp Cinnamon Powder
¼ tsp grated nutmeg
¼ tsp ground Cloves

DIRECTIONS

Pour 1 cup water into your Instant Pot and add a trivet. Arrange the peaches on a greased baking dish cut-side-up. To prepare the filling, mix all of the remaining ingredients. Stuff the peaches with the mixture. Cover with aluminium foil and lower it onto the trivet. Seal the lid, choose Pressure Cook on High, and set the time to 15 minutes. Do a quick pressure release. Let cool completely and serve.

Almond and Apple Delight

Servings: 4 | Ready in about about: 14 minutes

INGREDIENTS

3 Apples, peeled and diced
½ cup Almonds, chopped or slivered
½ cup Milk
¼ tsp Cinnamon

DIRECTIONS

Place all ingredients in your Instant Pot. Stir well to combine and seal the pressure lid. Cook on Pressure for 4 minutes at High. Release the pressure quickly. Divide the mixture among 4 serving bowls.

Gingery Chocolate Pudding

Servings: 4 | Ready in about about: 20 minutes

INGREDIENTS

Zest and Juice from ½ Lime
2 oz chocolate, coarsely chopped
¼ cup Sugar
2 tbsp Butter, softened
3 Eggs, separated into whites and yolks
¼ cup Cornstarch
1 cup Almond Milk
A pinch of Salt
½ tsp Ginger, caramelized
1 ½ cups of Water

DIRECTIONS

Combine together the sugar, cornstarch, salt, and softened butter in a bowl. Mix in lime juice and grated lime zest. Add in the egg yolks, ginger, almond milk, and whisk to mix well.

Mix in egg whites. Pour this mixture into custard cups and cover with aluminium foil. Add 1 ½ cups of water to your Instant Pot. Place a trivet into the pot, and lower the cups onto the trivet.

Seal the pressure lid, choose Pressure Cook on High, and set the time to 25 minutes. Once the cooking is complete, do a quick pressure release. Carefully open the pressure lid, and stir in the chocolate. Serve chilled.

Fruity Sauce

Servings: 2 | Ready in about about: 15 minutes

INGREDIENTS

1 cup Pineapple Chunks
1 cup Berry Mix
2 Apples, peeled and diced
¼ cup Almonds, chopped
¼ cup Fresh Orange Juice
1 tbsp Olive Oil

DIRECTIONS

Pour ½ cup of water, orange juice, and fruits in your Instant Pot. Give it a good stir and seal the pressure lid. Press Pressure Cook and set the timer to 5 minutes at High. When it goes off, release the pressure quickly. Blend the mixture with a hand blender and immediately stir in the coconut oil. Serve sprinkled with chopped almonds.

Orange Banana Bread

Servings: 12 | Ready in about about: 45 minutes

INGREDIENTS

3 ripe Bananas, mashed
1 ¼ cups Sugar
1 cup Milk
2 cups all-purpose Flour
1 tsp Baking Soda
1 tsp Baking Powder
1 tbsp Orange Juice
1 stick Butter, room temperature
A pinch of Salt
¼ tsp Cinnamon
½ tsp Pure Vanilla Extract

DESSERTS & BEVERAGES

DIRECTIONS

In a bowl, mix flour, baking powder, baking soda, sugar, vanilla, and salt. Add in the bananas, cinnamon, and orange juice. Slowly stir in the butter and milk. Stir until everything is well combined. Pour the batter into a round pan. Place a trivet in your Instant Pot and fill with 2 cups of water. Place the pan on the trivet. Seal the pressure lid, select Pressure Cook and and set the time to 40 minutes at High. Do a quick pressure release.

Vanilla Chocolate Spread

Servings: 16 | Ready in about about: 25 minutes

INGREDIENTS

1 ¼ lb Hazelnuts, halved
½ cup Cocoa Powder
½ cups icing Sugar, sifted

1 tsp Vanilla Extract
¼ tsp Cardamom, grated
¼ tsp Cinnamon powder

½ tsp grated Nutmeg
10 oz Water

DIRECTIONS

Place the hazelnut in a blender and blend until you obtain a paste. Place in the cooker along with the remaining ingredients. Seal the pressure lid on your Instant Pot, choose Pressure Cook on High, and set the time to 15 minutes. Once the cooking is over, allow for a natural pressure release, for 10 minutes.

Apricots with Honey Sauce

Servings: 4 | Ready in about about: 15 minutes

INGREDIENTS

8 Apricots, pitted and halved
2 cups Blueberries
¼ cup Honey

1 ½ tbsp Cornstarch
½ Vanilla Bean, sliced lengthwise
¼ tsp ground Cardamom

½ Cinnamon stick
1 ¼ cups Water

DIRECTIONS

Add all ingredients, except for the honey and the cornstarch to your Instant Pot. Seal the pressure lid, choose Pressure Cook on High, and set the time to s 8 minutes. Do a quick pressure release and open the pressure lid.

Remove the apricots with a slotted spoon. Choose Sauté, add the honey and cornstarch, then let simmer until the sauce thickens, about 5 minutes. Split up the apricots among plates and top with the blueberry sauce to serve.

Coconut Milk Crème Caramel

Servings: 4 | Ready in about about: 20 minutes

INGREDIENTS

2 Eggs
7 oz Condensed Coconut Milk

½ cup Coconut Milk
1 ½ cups Water

½ tsp Vanilla
4 tbsp Caramel Syrup

DIRECTIONS

Divide the caramel syrup between 4 small ramekins. Pour water in your Instant Pot and add a trivet. In a bowl, beat the rest of the ingredients. Divide them between the ramekins.Cover them with aluminum foil and lower onto the trivet. Seal the pressure lid, and choose Pressure Cook on High, and set the time to 15 minutes. Once cooking is completed, do a quick pressure release. Let cool completely. To unmold the flan, insert a spatula along the ramekin' sides and flip onto a dish.

Chocolate Fondue

Servings: 12 | Ready in about about: 5 minutes

INGREDIENTS

10 oz Milk Chocolate, melted
2 tsp Coconut Liqueur

8 oz Heavy Whipping Cream
¼ tsp Cinnamon Powder

1 ½ cups Lukewarm Water
A pinch of Salt

DIRECTIONS

Add all the ingredients, except for the liqueur in a heatproof bowl. Transfer this recipient to the metal trivet. Pour 1 ½ cups of water into Heatproof Bowl, and place the trivet inside. Seal the pressure lid, choose Pressure Cook on High, and set the time to 5 minutes. Once the cooking is complete, do a quick pressure release. Pull out the container with tongs. Mix in the coconut liqueur and serve right now with fresh fruits. Enjoy!

Homemade Egg Custard

Servings: 4 | Ready in about about: 20 minutes

INGREDIENTS

1 Egg plus 2 Egg yolks
½ cup Sugar

½ cups Milk
2 cups Heavy Cream

½ tsp pure rum extract
2 cups Water

DIRECTIONS

Beat the egg and the egg yolks in a bowl. Gently add pure rum extract. Mix in the milk and heavy cream. Give it a good, and add the sugar. Pour this mixture into 4 ramekins. Add 2 cups of water in your Instant Pot, insert a trivet, and lay the ramekins on the trivet. Choose Pressure Cook on High, and set the time to 10 minutes. Do a quick pressure release. Wait a bit before removing from ramekins.

Cinnamon Butternut Squash Pie

Servings: 4 | Ready in about about: 30 minutes

INGREDIENTS

1 lb Butternut Squash, diced
1 Egg
¼ cup Honey

½ cup Milk
½ tsp Cinnamon
½ tbsp Cornstarch

1 cup Water
A pinch of Sea Salt

DIRECTIONS

Pour the water inside your Instant Pot and add a trivet. Lower the butternut squash onto the trivet. Seal the pressure lid, and cook on Pressure for 4 minutes at High pressure. Whisk all remaining ingredients in a bowl. Do a quick pressure. Drain the squash and add it to the milk mixture. Pour the batter into a greased baking dish. Place in the cooker, and seal the pressure lid. Choose Pressure Cook on High, and set the time to 10 minutes. Do a quick pressure release. Transfer pie to wire rack to cool.

RECIPE INDEX

Acorn Squash Soup with Coconut Milk, 34
Air Fried Doughnuts, 184
Air Fried Pin Wheels, 43
Air Fried Snickerdoodle Poppers, 188
Alaskan Cod with Fennel & Beans, 78
Almond and Apple Delight, 194
Almond Banana Dessert, 179
Almond Milk, 190
Aloo Gobi with Cilantro, 57
Apple & Onion Topped Pork Chops, 168
Apple Vanilla Hand Pies, 178
Apricots with Honey Sauce, 195
Artichoke with Garlic Mayo, 63
Asian Beef Curry, 146
Asian-Style Chicken, 111
Asian-Style Tofu Soup, 56
Asian Turkey Lettuce Cups, 121
Asparagus with Feta, 60
Asparagus Wrapped in Prosciutto with Dip, 38
Autumn Succotash with Basil-Crusted Fish, 72
Avocado Rolls, 64
Baby Back Ribs with BBQ Sauce, 166
Bacon & Cheese Dip, 39
Baked Garbanzo Beans & Pancetta, 127
Baked Rigatoni with Beef Tomato Sauce, 136
Barbecue Chicken Sandwiches, 14
Basic Applesauce with Cinnamon, 31
Basil & Cheddar Stuffed Chicken, 116
BBQ Chicken Drumettes, 104
BBQ Chicken Drumsticks, 37
BBQ Chicken & Kale Quesadillas, 91
BBQ Pork Ribs, 161
BBQ Sticky Baby Back Ribs with , 154
Beef and Bell Pepper with Onion Sauce, 144
Beef & Bacon Chili, 153
Beef & Broccoli Sauce, 139
Beef & Cabbage Stew, 143
Beef Carnitas, 141
Beef & Cheese Stuffed Mushrooms, 146
Beef & Cherry Tagine, 150
Beef Congee (Chinese Rice Porridge), 140
Beef & Garbanzo Bean Chili , 148
Beef & Green Bell Pepper Pot, 144
Beef Neck Bone Stock, 30
Beef & Pepperoncini Peppers, 145
Beef Pho with Swiss Chard, 151
Beef & Pumpkin Stew, 150
Beef Roast with Peanut Satay Sauce, 149
Beef Soup with Tortillas, 144

Beef Stew with Beer, 146
Beef Stew with Veggies, 152
Beef-Stuffed Pasta Shells, 136
Beef & Turnip Chili, 156
Beef & Vegetable Stew, 148
Beer-Braised Hot Dogs with Peppers , 174
Beer-Braised Short Ribs with Mushrooms, 155
Berry Vanilla Pudding, 184
Black Beans Tacos, 128
Black-Eyed Peas with Kale, 134
Black Refried Beans & Chicken Fajitas, 88
Blueberry Muffins, 186
Bok Choy & Zoodle Soup, 46
Bolognese-Style Pizza, 170
Braised Short Ribs with Creamy Sauce, 153
Brazilian Cheese Balls, 35
Brisket Chili con Carne, 149
Broccoli & Potato Soup, 27
Brown Sugar & Butter Bars, 192
Buffalo Chicken Meatballs with Ranch Dip, 38
Buffalo Chicken & Navy Bean Chili , 105
Buttered Leafy Greens, 56
Buttermilk Chicken Thighs, 120
Butternut Squash Cake Oatmeal, 14
Butternut Squash Curry, 34
Cajun Baked Turnips, 51
Cajun Chicken with Rice & Peas, 108
Cajun Roasted Chicken with Potato Mash, 96
Cajun Salmon with Creamy Grits, 73
Cajun Salmon with Lemon, 76
Cajun Shredded Chicken & Wild Rice, 112
Calzones with Sausage and Mozzarella, 174
Caribbean Ropa Vieja, 151
Carrot & Lentil Chili, 60
Cauliflower and Cheddar Tater Tots, 42
Cauliflower Cheese Soup, 29
Chai Latte Steel-Cut Oatmeal, 16
Char Siew Pork Ribs, 170
Cheat Apple Pie, 186
Cheat Hawaiian Pizza, 24
Cheddar Cheeseburgers, 148
Cheese and Spinach Stuffed Shells , 135
Cheese & Bacon Grits, 17
Cheese bombs wrapped in Bacon, 37
Cheeseburgers in Hoagies, 142
Cheesy Buffalo Chicken, 96
Cheesy Prosciutto Egg Bake, 11

Cheesy Smashed Sweet Potatoes, 37
Cheesy Stuffed Mushrooms, 54
Cherry Pie, 192
Cherry Tomato-Basil Linguine, 130
Chicken and Cheese Bake, 42
Chicken and Chickpea Stew, 133
Chicken Broth, 30
Chicken Burgers with Avocado, 115
Chicken Cacciatore, 103
Chicken Caesar Salad with Salted Croutons, 100
Chicken Cassoulet with Frijoles, 89
Chicken Chickpea Chili, 105
Chicken Chili with Cannellini Beans, 96
Chicken Fajitas with Avocado, 116
Chicken & Farro Soup, 29
Chicken Florentine, 89
Chicken & Green Bean Coconut Curry, 97
Chicken in Pineapple Gravy, 109
Chicken in Tikka Masala Sauce, 106
Chicken Meatballs in Tomato Sauce, 108
Chicken Meatballs Primavera, 95
Chicken Noodle Soup, 24
Chicken Noodle Soup with Crispy Bacon, 100
Chicken Potato Pot Pie, 90
Chicken Ragù Bolognese, 132
Chicken Shawarma Wrap, 94
Chicken Stroganoff with Fetucini, 119
Chicken & Sweet Potato Corn Chowder , 114
Chicken Tenders with Broccoli & Rice, 121
Chicken & Veggie Tacos with Guacamole, 101
Chicken with BBQ Sauce, 106
Chicken with Beans & Bacon, 102
Chicken with Cilantro Rice, 88
Chicken with Crunchy Coconut Dumplings, 86
Chicken with Prunes, 111
Chicken with Tomatoes & Capers, 115
Chicken with Tomato Salsa, 93
Chicken & Zucchini Pilaf, 113
Chili-Garlic Rice Noodles with Tofu, 132
Chipotle Beef Brisket , 149
Chipotle Chili, 55
Chipotle Mac and Cheese, 135
Chipotle Vegetarian Chili, 67
Chocolate and Banana Squares, 182
Chocolate Fondue, 196
Chocolate Soufflé, 190
Chocolate Vanilla Swirl Cheesecake, 184
Chorizo Mac and Cheese, 130

Chorizo & Shrimp Boil, 80
Chorizo Stuffed Yellow Bell Peppers, 172
Chunky Pork Meatloaf with Mashed Potatoes, 167
Cinnamon Apple Crisp, 185
Cinnamon Butternut Squash Pie, 196
Cinnamon Mulled Red Wine, 189
Cinnamon Pumpkin Oatmeal, 19
Classic Beef Bourguignon, 156
Classic Caramel-Walnut Brownies, 185
Classic Carbonnade Flamande, 141
Classic French Onion Soup, 26
Coconut Milk Crème Caramel, 195
Coconut Pear Delight, 191
Cod Cornflakes Nuggets, 77
Colorful Vegetable Medley, 68
Coq au Vin, 98
Cordon Bleu Chicken, 117
Crab Cakes, 84
Crabmeat with Broccoli Risotto, 80
Creamed Kale Parmesan Farro, 125
Cream of Cauliflower & Butternut Squash, 50
Cream of Mushroom & Spinach Soup, 28
Cream of Pumpkin Chipotle Soup, 26
Creamy Cauliflower & Asparagus Farfalle, 52
Creamy Chicken and Quinoa Soup, 110
Creamy Chicken Pasta with Pesto Sauce, 112
Creamy Crab Soup, 83
Creamy Grana Padano Risotto, 128
Creamy Mashed Potatoes with Spinach, 58
Creamy Quinoa & Mushroom Pilaf, 33
Creamy Tomato & parsley Dip, 39
Creamy Turkey Enchilada Casserole, 123
Creamy Zucchini Muffins, 20
Crème de la Broc, 52
Crispy Cheesy Straws, 42
Crispy Chicken Thighs with Carrot Roast, 86
Crispy Cod on Lentils, 70
Crispy Nachos, 67
Crispy Pancetta Hash with Baked Eggs, 11
Crispy Pork Fajitas, 162
Crispy Rosemary Potato Fries, 41
Crumbed Sage Chicken Scallopini, 111
Crunchy Cashew Lamb Rack, 177
Crunchy Chicken Schnitzels, 116
Crustless Mediterranean Quiche, 21
Cuban-Style Pork, 160
Cumin Baby Carrots, 44
Curry Egg Salad, 22
Dark Chocolate Brownies, 179
Delicious Coconut Shrimp, 85
Delicious Pecan Stuffed Apples, 192
Easy Green Squash Gruyere, 54

Easy Spanish Rice, 49
Easy Vegan Sloppy Joes, 129
Egg Crumpet Sandwich, 15
Eggplant Chips with Honey, 43
Eggplant Lasagna, 55
Egg Rolls, 22
Fall Celeriac Pumpkin Soup, 59
Farfalle Tuna Casserole with Cheese, 71
Feta & Poached Egg Tomato Topper, 17
Fire-Roasted Tomato and Chorizo Soup, 34
Fish Finger Sandwich, 76
Flavorful Vegetable Stock, 33
French Dip Sandwiches, 13
Fried Beef Dumplings, 38
Fruity Sauce, 194
Garganelli with Swiss Cheese and Mushrooms, 46
Garlic and Rosemary Mushrooms, 44
Garlic Herb Roasted Chicken, 87
Garlick & Ginger Pork with Coconut Sauce, 162
Garlicky Braised Pork Neck Bones, 161
Garlicky Chicken on Green Bed, 23
Garlic Veggie Mash with Parmesan, 62
Gingery Chocolate Pudding, 194
Greek Beef Gyros, 139
Greek-Style Chicken, 120
Greek-Style Chicken with Potatoes, 118
Greek Turkey Meatballs, 124
Green Beans with Feta & Nuts, 60
Green Cream Soup, 56
Green Lasagna Soup, 67
Green Minestrone, 58
Green Vegan Dip, 40
Grilled Tofu Sandwich, 68
Ground Beef Stuffed Empanadas, 137
Haddock with Sanfaina, 74
Ham and Cheese Sandwich, 17
Ham & Mozzarella Eggplant Boats, 23
Hawaiian-Style Chicken Sliders with Salad, 110
Hearty Winter Vegetable Soup, 28
Herbed Chicken & Biscuit Chili, 90
Herbed Homemade Ghee, 15
Herbed Lamb Chops, 177
Herb Salmon with Barley & Haricot Verts, 70
Herby Chicken Breasts, 90
Herby Chicken with Asparagus Sauce, 118
Herby Fish Skewers, 45
Herby-Garlic Potatoes, 58
Herby Millet with Cherry Tomatoes, 66
Holiday Apricot-Lemon Ham, 176
Holiday Cranberry Cheesecake, 183
Holiday Egg Brulee, 39
Holiday Honey-Glazed Ham, 175
Homemade Apple Cider, 187

Homemade Chicken Soup, 26
Homemade Egg Custard, 196
Homemade Spinach Hummus, 41
Homemade Vegetables Soup, 23
Honey Barbecue Pork Ribs, 169
Honey-Garlic Chicken, 103
Honey-Garlic Chicken & Okra, 110
Honey-Glazed Acorn Squash, 62
Honey-Glazed Chicken Kabobs, 118
Honey Short Ribs with Rosemary Potatoes, 140
Hot Buttery Chicken Meatballs, 36
Hot Chicken Wings, 36
Hot Chicken Wings, 113
Hot Crispy Chicken with Potatoes, 95
Hot Pork Carnitas Lettuce Cups, 158
Indian Butter Chicken, 106
Indian-Style Beef with Rice, 125
Indian Vegan Curry, 57
Indian Yellow Lentils, 131
Italian Beef Sandwiches with Pesto, 157
Italian Chicken with Herby Dumplings, 92
Italian Sausage & Cannellini Stew, 173
Italian Sausage Patties, 24
Italian Sausage with Garlic Mash, 171
Italian Sausage with Potato Mash & Gravy, 167
Italian-Style Flounder, 75
Italian-Style Pot Roast, 154
Jamaican Pulled Pork with Mango Sauce, 166
Juicy Barbecue Pork Chops, 170
Juicy Orange Chicken, 109
Kale-Artichoke Bites, 36
Kale-Egg Frittata, 12
Korean-Style Barbecued Satay, 117
Lamb Chops & Creamy Potato Mash, 177
Leek and Potato Soup with Sour Cream, 31
Lemon and Paprika Chicken Thighs, 92
Lemon & Blueberries Compote, 190
Lemon Cheesecake with Strawberries, 186
Lemon Chicken Tenders with Broccoli, 86
Lemon Cod Goujons & Rosemary Chips, 70
Lemon Turkey Risotto, 122
Lemony Wild Rice Pilaf, 128
Lettuce Chicken Carnitas Wraps, 113
Mackerel en Papillote with Vegetables, 73
Maple Giant Pancake, 15
Mashed Broccoli with Cream Cheese, 54
Mashed Parsnips & Cauliflower, 62
Meatballs with Marinara Sauce, 152
Meatballs with Spaghetti Sauce, 147
Meatloaf with Cheesy Mashed Potatoes, 150

Mediterranean Stuffed Chicken Breasts, 97
Mediterranean-Style Steamed Cod, 74
Mediterranean Tender Pork Roast, 160
Melt-in-the-Middle Meatballs, 43
Mexican Chicken & Wild Rice Bowls, 93
Mexican Green Chili Chicken, 99
Mexican-Style Chicken Soup, 29
Milk Dumplings in Sweet Sauce, 193
Minestrone Soup, 27
Mississippi Pot Roast with Potatoes, 156
Mixed Berry Cobbler, 181
Molten Lava Cake, 186
Monk Fish with Greens, 75
Moon Milk, 189
Morning Burrito Bowls, 68
Mushroom Brown Rice Pilaf, 58
Mushroom Risotto with Swiss Chard, 48
Mushroom & Shrimp Egg Wrappers, 79
Mussel Chowder with Oyster Crackers, 83
New York Cheesecake, 182
New York Steak and Minty Cheese, 42
No Flour Lime Muffins, 188
Nutty & Zesty Brussels Sprouts with Raisins, 44
Onion and Cheese Omelet, 19
Orange Banana Bread, 194
Orange Pepper and Artichoke Frittata, 16
Paella Señorito, 84
Paneer Cheese Balls, 68
Paneer Cutlet, 69
Paprika Buttered Chicken, 104
Paprika & Garlic Salmon, 76
Paprika Shirred Eggs, 19
Parmesan Cabbage Side Dish, 44
Parmesan Tilapia, 76
Parsley-Lime Bulgur Bowl, 128
Parsley Mashed Cauliflower, 61
Parsley Oyster Stew, 84
Pasta Caprese Ricotta-Basil Fusilli, 135
Pasta with Roasted Veggies, 64
Peanut Sauce Beef Satay, 142
Pear Wedges, 191
Penne all'Arrabbiata with Seafood & Chorizo, 85
Peppercorn Meatloaf, 157
 Perfect Chicken Wings Broth, 30
Pesto Chicken with Roasted Pepper Sauce, 100
Pesto Minestrone with Cheesy Bread, 53
Pesto Quinoa Bowls with Veggies, 60
Pesto Stuffed Chicken with Green Beans , 107
Philippine-Style Pork Chops, 169
Pickle and Potato Salad with Feta, 25
Pilau Rice with Veggies, 53
Pineapple Appetizer Ribs, 141
Pineapple Cake, 189
Pine nuts and Steamed Asparagus, 48
Pistachio Crusted Salmon, 74
Plum Breakfast Clafoutis, 16
Poached Peaches, 193
Poblano & Tomato Stuffed Squash, 66
Pomodoro Sauce with Rigatoni and Kale, 131
Pork Carnitas Wraps, 164
Pork Chops with Broccoli and Gravy, 162
Pork Chops with Cremini Mushroom Sauce, 169
Pork Chops with Plum Sauce, 165
Pork Chops with Squash Purée, 163
Pork Sandwiches with Slaw, 160
Pork Spaghetti with Spinach and Tomatoes, 136
Pork Tenderloin with Garlic and Ginger, 159
Pork Tenderloin with Sweet Pepper Sauce, 163
Potato Chowder with Peppery Prawns, 82
Potato Filled Bread Rolls, 65
Potato & Ground Pork Chili , 171
Pot Roast with Broccoli, 143
Prawn Toast, 82
Prosciutto, Mozzarella & Egg in a Cup, 18
Pulled Chicken & Peach Salsa, 107
Pulled Pork Tacos, 165
Pumpkin Cake , 187
Punjabi Palak Paneer, 57
Quick Chicken Fried Rice, 88
Quick Chicken Noodle Soup, 25
Quick Crispy Cheese Lings, 69
Quick Crispy Kale Chips, 63
Quick & Easy Fried Salmon, 78
Quick Soft-Boiled Eggs, 19
Quinoa & Veggie Stuffed Peppers, 65
Quinoa with Carrots and Onion, 130
Ragu Bolognese, 31
Ragu with Pork & Rigatoni, 168
Ramen Spicy Soup with Collard Greens, 30
Ranch Flavored Pork Roast with Gravy, 158
Ranch Pork with Mushroom Sauce, 168
Raspberry and Vanilla Pancake, 20
Raspberry Cheesecake, 190
Raspberry-Cranberry Chia Oatmeal, 12
Raspberry Cream Tart, 180
Raspberry Crumble, 179
Red Beans & Rice, 63
Red Lentil Soup with Tortilla Topping, 32
Red Lentil & Spinach Dhal , 126
Red Pork & Chickpea Stew, 166
Rice & Olives Stuffed Mushrooms, 47
Rice Pilaf with Mushrooms , 130
Rice Stuffed Zucchini Boats, 46
Rigatoni with Sausage and Spinach , 134
Roasted Squash & Rice with Crispy Tofu, 50
Roasted Vegetable Salad, 66
Rosemary Lemon Chicken, 119
Rosemary Sweet Potato Medallions, 69
Sage Chicken Thighs, 104
Salmon with Dill Chutney, 72
Salsa Verde Chicken, 107
Saucy Chicken Breasts, 115
Saucy Shredded Chicken, 92
Sausage and Bacon Cheesecake, 18
Sausage & Shrimp Paella, 78
Sausage with Celeriac & Potato Mash , 175
Sausage with Noodles and Braised Cabbage, 173
Sausage Wrapped Scotch Eggs, 13
Savory Custards with Ham & Cheese, 14
Savory Peaches with Chocolate Biscuits, 193
Savory Pork Loin with Celery Sauce, 164
Scottish Seafood Curry, 81
Scrumptious Honey-Mustard Hot Dogs, 40
Seafood Gumbo, 82
Seared Scallops with Butter-Caper Sauce, 85
Shakshuka with Goat Cheese, 11
Short Ribs with Egg Noodles, 145
Short Ribs with Mushrooms & Asparagus Sauce, 152
Shredded Chicken with Lentils & Rice, 116
Shrimp Lo Mein, 134
Shrimp Risotto with Vegetables, 126
Simple Air Fried Ravioli, 66
Simple Brown Rice, 125
Simple Jasmine Rice, 132
Simple Vanilla Cheesecake, 182
Smoked Salmon Pilaf with Walnuts, 79
Smoky Horseradish Spare Ribs, 138
South American Black Bean Chili , 131
Spaghetti with Arugula & Scallops, 81
Spiced Beef Chili, 147
Spiced Beef Shapes, 147
Spicy Acorn Squash Soup, 28
Spicy Beef Broth, 33
Spicy Borscht Soup, 32
Spicy Buttered Turkey, 122
Spicy Cauliflower Rice with Peas, 62
Spicy Chicken Wings, 124
Spicy Chicken Wings with Lemon, 108
Spicy Deviled Eggs, 13
Spicy Lentils with Chorizo, 127
Spicy Pepper & Sweet Potato Skewers, 64
Spicy Pinto Bean and Corn Stew, 132
Spicy Pork Roast with Peanut Sauce, 165
Spicy Salsa Chicken with Feta , 102
Spicy Tangy Salmon with Wild Rice, 77
Spicy Turkey Casserole, 124

RECIPE INDEX

Spinach and Kidney Bean Stew, 129
Spinach & Butternut Squash Stew, 49
Spinach & Mushroom Chicken Stew, 102
Spinach Pesto Spaghetti Squash, 52
Squash Parmesan & Linguine, 48
Sriracha Chicken with Black Beans, 114
Steak with Chips, 138
Steamed Artichokes with Lemon Aioli, 61
Steamed Sea Bass with Turnips, 75
Stewed Beef with Portobello Mushrooms, 154
Sticky BBQ Baby Back Ribs, 140
Sticky Drumsticks, 120
Sticky Noodles with Tofu & Peanuts, 49
Sticky Orange Chicken, 103
Strawberry Bread French Toast, 12
Strawberry & Lemon Ricotta Cheesecake, 183
Swedish Meatballs with Mashed Cauliflower, 155
Sweet Bread Pudding with Raisins, 21
Sweet Carrots with Crumbled Bacon, 174
Sweet Garlicky Chicken Wings, 120
Sweet-Garlic Pork Tenderloin, 159
Sweet Gingery Beef & Broccoli, 139
Sweet-Heat Pickled Cucumbers, 41
Sweet Paprika Hard-Boiled Eggs, 35
Sweet Potato & Egg Salad , 24
Sweet Potato Gratin with Peas & Prosciutto, 172
Sweet Sesame Chicken Wings, 87
Sweet & Sour Pork, 161
Swiss Cheese & Mushroom Tarts, 47
Tahini Sweet Potato Mash, 59
Tandoori Chicken Thighs, 94
Tandoori Chicken with Cilantro Sauce, 101
Tangy Cheesy Arancini, 35
Tangy Risotto & Roasted Bell Peppers, 50
Tasty Baby Porcupine Meatballs, 143
Tasty Coconut Cake, 192
Tasty Créme Brulee, 181
Tasty Ham with Collard Greens, 176
Teriyaki Chicken Wings, 40
Teriyaki Pork Noodles, 171
Thai Roasted Beef, 138
Thai Vegetable Stew, 61
The Crispiest Roast Pork, 164
The Most Chocolaty Fudge, 188
Three-Bean Veggie Chili, 127
Three Meat Cheesy Omelet, 20
Thyme Chicken with Veggies, 112
Thyme Turkey Nuggets, 122
Tiramisu Cheesecake, 191
Toasted Herb and Garlic Bagel, 20
Tomatillo & Sweet Potato pork Chili, 158
Tomato & Mozzarella Bruschetta, 45
Tomato Soup with Cheese Croutons, 22
Tom Yum Wings, 117
Traditional Beef Stroganoff, 157
Traditional Chicken Cordon Bleu, 98
Traditional Mahi Mahi, 72
Tri-Color Quinoa and Pinto Bean Bowl, 129
Tuna Patties, 77
Tuna Salad with Asparagus & Potatoes, 71
Turkey and Brown Rice Salad with Peanuts, 123
Turkey Fajita Tortiglioni, 133
Turkey Meatballs with Rigatoni, 122
Turkey Scotch Eggs, 45
Turkey Stuffed Potatoes, 119
Tuscany-Style Turkey Soup, 121
Two-Bean Zucchini Soup, 32
Valencian Horchata, 188
Vanilla Chocolate Spread, 195
Vanilla Hot Lava Cake, 180
Vegan Carrot Gazpacho, 55
Vegetable Soup, 27
Vegetable Tortilla Pizza, 65
Vegetarian Black Bean Soup, 32
Vegetarian Minestrone Soup, 59
Veggie Quinoa Bowls with Pesto, 126
Veggie Salmon Balls, 18
Veggie Skewers, 64
Very Berry Breakfast Puffs, 21
Vietnamese Pork Soup, 172
Warm Bacon & Potato Salad, 25
Wheat Flour Cinnamon Balls, 178
White Chocolate Chip Cookies, 181
White Filling Coconut and Oat Cookies, 178
White Wine Black Mussels , 80
White Wine Chicken, 99
White Wine Mussels, 84
Whole Chicken with Lemon & Onion Stuffing, 105
Wine Chicken with Mushrooms & Brussel Sprouts, 91
Winter Chicken Thighs with Cabbage, 114
Winter Minestrone with Pancetta, 176
Winter Pot Roast with Biscuits, 137
Wrapped Asparagus in Bacon, 40
Za'atar Chicken with Lemony Couscous, 109
Zucchini & Quinoa Stuffed Red Peppers, 51

Made in the USA
Coppell, TX
06 December 2020